Principles of Insurance Production Volume I

Principles of Insurance Production Volume I

PETER R. KENSICKI, D.B.A., CPCU, CLU, FLMI

Vice President
Insurance Institute of America

ROBERT S. SMITH, J.D., CPCU

Florida Association of Insurance Agents

THOMAS S. MARSHALL, CPCU, CLU

President
Marshall General Agency, Inc.

SEEMAN WARANCH, CPCU

President
INSCO Group

DARWIN B. CLOSE, Ph.D., CPCU, CLU

Professor of Insurance
Bowling Green State University

Second Edition • 1986

INSURANCE INSTITUTE OF AMERICA

720 Providence Road, Malvern, Pennsylvania 19355-0770

First Printing • July 1986

Library of Congress Catalog Number 86-80640
International Standard Book Number 0-89462-027-4

Printed in the United States of America

The Accredited Adviser in Insurance designation (AAI) is the result of a joint effort of the Insurance Institute of America, Inc. and the Independent Insurance Agents of America, Inc.

Foreword

Over the years, the American Institute for Property and Liability Underwriters and the Insurance Institute of America have responded to the educational needs of the property-liability insurance industry by developing new programs.

The American Institute maintains and administers the program leading to the Chartered Property Casualty Underwriter (CPCU) professional designation.

The Insurance Institute of America offers programs leading to the Certificate in General Insurance, the Associate in Claims (AIC) designation, the Associate in Management (AIM) designation, the Associate in Risk Management (ARM) designation, the Associate in Underwriting (AU) designation, the Associate in Loss Control Management (ALCM) designation, the Accredited Adviser in Insurance (AAI) designation, the Associate in Premium Auditing (APA) designation, the Associate in Research and Planning (ARP) designation, and the Associate in Insurance Accounting and Finance (AIAF) designation as well as the Introduction to Property and Liability Insurance (INTRO) course and the Supervisory Management (SM) courses.

Throughout the development of this series of texts it has been—and will continue to be—necessary to draw on the knowledge and skills of Institute staff members. These individuals will receive no royalties on texts sold, and their writing responsibilities are seen as an integral part of their professional duties. We have proceeded in this way to avoid any possibility of conflicts of interests.

We invite and welcome any and all criticisms of our publications. It is only with such comments that we can hope to provide high quality texts, materials, and programs. Comments should be directed to the Curriculum Department of the Institutes.

Edwin S. Overman, Ph.D., CPCU
President

Preface

Educational activities in the property and liability insurance business have traditionally been directed toward the technical side—coverages and rating details. In relatively recent years, technical aspects of the specialties within the business have been spotlighted by the Insurance Institute of America's designation programs in Claims, Risk Management, Management, Underwriting, Loss Control, Premium Auditing, Research and Planning, and Insurance Accounting and Finance. This book is the first academic work concentrating on the distribution of the insurance product to the final consumer. This book, and the two that follow it, is for the producer of insurance.

The word "producer" is used because each of the four types of insurance distribution systems employs some group of people to sell the product. In the independent distribution system, "producer" means agent or broker. For exclusive agency systems, the word agent is again descriptive. Direct writers of insurance use company employees who may be called agents, special representatives, account specialists, and so on. Mail order insurance companies distribute their products through people who draft letters and answer WATS telephone lines and carry no titles that the general public would find descriptive of salespersons. Therefore, the umbrella term "producer" is used in this program to describe those with sales responsibilities to their companies and the public.

Insurance must be sold. Underwriting, loss control, adjusting, and other functions are vital to a well run insurance business. But if the insurance product were not sold, few of the insurance personnel performing these functions would be employed. The insurance product has three dimensions: coverage, price, and service. Therefore, selling insurance requires a "technical" knowledge of insurance coverages. In many cases, coverage dictates price; but producers must be aware of price differentials among their competitors and insurance companies. Finally, the amount of pre- and post-sale service available to the client rounds out the insurance product.

Knowledge of the insurance product is not enough for the

sophisticated, successful insurance producer. Equally essential is an understanding of insurance markets or groups of potential insureds. How would a producer's sales approach to a new car dealer differ from the approach to a used car dealer? How do automobile dealers differ from a homeowners prospect? Can the personal auto policy be sold the same way ocean marine cargo insurance is sold? Not only the technical insurance policy differences but also differing sales approaches to different types of buyers (markets) must be learned.

The final ingredient for a successful producer is selling skills. Each producer must know how to ask questions of prospects, handle objections, close, and so forth. A knowledge of insurance products, insurance markets, and selling skills is essential to success in insurance sales.

This first book in the Accredited Adviser in Insurance (AAI) Program, and the second book (*Multiple-Lines Insurance Production*), address two of these three sales essentials: technical knowledge and market knowledge. It is our belief that selling skills cannot be taught solely through a textbook. Producers should take a selling skills course elsewhere to round out their education.

The AAI Program consists of three courses and examinations, each based on a single textbook. Each text is original and written for the AAI Program. In this text, essential background material is presented along with common personal lines insurance products, including life insurance. Beginning with Chapter 8, commercial lines insurance products are analyzed. AAI 82 continues and concludes the study of commercial lines insurance. AAI 83 and its text (*Agency Operations and Sales Management*) pull together two different topics. The producer must understand his or her office environment in order to sell efficiently. Further, sales management, the ability to determine which markets to sell to, is highlighted.

Each course in the AAI Program leads to a national examination. Candidates who successfully complete all three examinations will receive the Insurance Institute of America Accredited Adviser in Insurance designation. The designation carries with it the responsibility to continue the education process begun with the AAI Program. A continuing education requirement must be met by all AAIs to retain the designation.

Texts for the AAI Program are written assuming no insurance background on the part of candidates. Yet the material is at such a level that the veteran producer will gain much from his or her study. New to these texts is a series of "Checkpoints" contained within each chapter. Checkpoints are questions placed at a logical stopping point in the studying process. They ask specific content questions about the material, but also indicate that an appropriate place to stop studying has been reached if time is short. Educational objectives, key terms and concepts, review questions, and discussion questions are contained in the Course Guide for AAI 81.

The experiences of many successful producers have been blended into the text. Hundreds of producers from around the country contributed their successes and failures to the program. Wherever possible, these cases are used to illustrate the appropriate points. To that end, candidates and readers of all texts in this series are encouraged to send their "mini case histories" or selling successes and failures to the Institute's Director of Producer Education for inclusion in succeeding editions of the texts. If the AAI Program is to be practical, these experiences are vital. Because so many contributed to the final product, it is not possible to list every contributor by name. The authors gratefully thank all who contributed their time, energy, and efforts to the making of this text.

Three producers looked at each chapter of the first edition and offered critical reviews: Ronald T. Anderson, J.D., CPCU, CLU; Stephen Horn II, CPCU, ARM, AAI; and Kenneth W. Morrison, L.L.B., CIC. The Independent Insurance Agents of America, Inc., provided reviews by some of its members. During the summer of 1980, Bernard L. Webb, FCAS, CPCU, Professor of Actuarial Science and Insurance, Georgia State University, worked on the AAI Program as the Robert E. Early Visiting Scholar. Professor Webb's special knowledge of the insurance business contributed to all aspects of this text and the accompanying Course Guide.

Reviewers for this second edition of the text include: Ralph J. Monaco, CPCU, AAI; David G. Shirlaw, CPCU, AAI; Cynthia R. Ziegler, AAI; Dean E. Brooks, CPCU, CLU; Christopher J. Amrhein, AAI; Raymond R. Ried, Jr., CPCU, ARM; John E. Becker II, CPCU; David VanDelinder, CPCU; DeWitt E. Altpeter, J.D., AIC, AAI; and Jeanne M. Heisler, CPCU, CLU, CIC, CPIW.

The authors wish to offer their thanks to those members of the Institute staff who have been deeply involved in this project. They sometimes transformed rough manuscripts into a book.

For the second edition, each author was responsible for certain chapters. In addition to editing the entire text, Peter Kensicki was exclusively responsible for Chapters 1, 2, 5, and 7. Bob Smith was the principal author of Chapters 4 and 9 in this edition and other chapters in the first edition. Tom Marshall wrote the material in Chapters 10 and 11. Seeman Waranch wrote the material in Chapters 12 and 13. Darwin Close wrote Chapter 3 in the first edition. Many of the chapters were enhanced by contributing authors who are listed elsewhere.

The authors accept full responsibility for all errors and omissions. Readers detecting errors or wishing to add to the content of future editions are again encouraged to send their contributions and criticisms to the Institute.

Peter R. Kensicki
Robert S. Smith
Thomas S. Marshall
Seeman Waranch
Darwin B. Close

Contributing Authors

The Insurance Institute of America and the authors acknowledge, with deep appreciation, the help of the following contributing authors:

George B. Flanigan, Ph.D., CPCU
Associate Professor
Department of Business Administration
University of North Carolina—Greensboro

Joseph E. Johnson, D.B.A., CPCU
Head, Department of Business Administration
University of North Carolina—Greensboro

James J. Ross, AAI
Director of Communications
Independent Insurance Agents of New Jersey
Highland Park, NJ

Christopher J. Amrhein, AAI
Florida Association of Insurance Agents
Tallahassee, FL

Table of Contents

CHAPTER 1

The Insurance Business: An Overview

INTRODUCTION

In most businesses, "nothing happens until something is sold." This statement is as true for the insurance business as it is for other businesses. The Accredited Adviser in Insurance (AAI) program is primarily about selling—agents and brokers selling insurance protection to individuals and organizations.

Modern sales techniques are frequently based on what is sometimes called the "sales trilogy"—the three fundamental elements necessary to the sale of any product: (1) product knowledge; (2) market knowledge (that is, knowing where to sell the product); and (3) selling skills. The AAI program will explore all three of these fundamental elements as they apply to the insurance business.

The AAI program is made up of three courses—AAI 81 Principles of Insurance Production, AAI 82 Multiple Lines Insurance Production, and AAI 83 Agency Operations and Sales Management. This first course of the program, AAI 81, will provide an introductory overview of the insurance business, examine the selling process (the selling skills element of the "sales trilogy"), present a foundation of legal principles, and begin an examination of insurance coverages (the product knowledge element of the "sales trilogy.") AAI 82 will continue this examination of insurance coverages as a vital element in insurance sales. Case histories will be introduced which demonstrate the relationship between product knowledge and successful sales. AAI 83, the last course of the program, will describe the operations of a producer's office—operations that provide the necessary support for the sales staff and contribute to client satisfaction—and will also examine marketing management techniques (the "market knowledge" element of the sales trilogy).

Primarily, the AAI program is designed to be an educational tool that producers can use to increase their product knowledge, their marketing knowledge, and their selling skills and, through this increased knowledge, improve their service to clients and increase their sales. Before these studies can profitably begin, however, it is necessary to gain an overview of the insurance business. This chapter will concentrate on basic insurance definitions and concepts, the place of the insurance business in our economy, the benefits society derives from the insurance business, and an analysis of insurance organizations and insurance marketing systems.

DEFINITIONS AND PRINCIPLES OF INSURANCE

Introduction

The insurance business is misunderstood by many insureds. The producer, one who sells insurance and related services, is ideally situated to explain the insurance business to the consumer. The producer is the front line educator for the insurance business. To be successful as an educator, the producer must have a grasp of insurance theory and principles.

The principles of insurance can also help producers learn the business faster and become productive more quickly—that is, a knowledge of principles can eliminate the frustration of learning through trial and error. If a producer learns the principles of risk management, the long "in the trenches" learning time can be decreased and the producer can apply these principles to provide insurance coverage for clients.

Basic insurance definitions and principles are also necessary so that a common language is developed and exchanges of information can be more efficient. The term "producer" is an example.

Definitions

Producer *A producer sells insurance and related services.* The producer may be an "agent"—the authorized representative of an insurance company; or a "broker"—the authorized representative of an insured. For the sake of simplicity, the producer's employer or office will be called "the agency" throughout this text. In this sense, the "independent agent" in Pierre, South Dakota, the sales representative of Liberty Mutual in Chicago, the Nationwide agent in Belpre, Ohio, and the broker in New York all work out of "an agency."

Insurers and Insurance Markets It is a common practice to use the terms insurers and insurance markets interchangeably. For producers, "marketing" frequently means placing business with an insurer. In the AAI program, *marketing will mean finding, selling, and servicing insureds.* Markets are homogeneous groups of insureds or potential insureds (people with money to buy a producer's products). One important part of marketing is obtaining acceptance of a submission of an account by an underwriter or insurer. When placing business with an insurer is discussed, it will be clearly identified. In all other cases, "markets" will refer to those groups of potential buyers or actual insureds, not insurance companies.

Risk and Related Terms The word risk has a variety of meanings in the insurance business. Risk has been used to mean "insured," "exposure," "relative probability of the outcome of an event," and other things. For the AAI program, *risk will mean the chance of financial loss.* Humanity faces a series of "risks" daily—the risk that an investment will increase or decrease in value, that food will or will not be poisoned, that furnaces will or will not explode, and so on. Insurance protects against the chance of financial loss accidentally brought about by a specific cause or causes.

Loss means a reduction in value of an asset and the financial consequences of a reduction in value of an asset. Loss has a double barreled meaning as there are both *direct* and *indirect* losses. An example of a direct loss is the burning of a home. Because of the fire, what was a valuable asset is now relatively worthless. But some losses occur as the indirect result of a direct loss. If the family who lived in the house destroyed by fire had to incur the expense of temporarily living in a motel while the house was repaired, that would be an indirect loss.

Types of Risk Chances of financial loss can be subcategorized. Basically, risks are classed in two ways: all risks are either *fundamental* or *particular* and either *pure* or *speculative.*

Fundamental or Particular Risk. *A fundamental risk is a risk to which everyone in a society or at least a large number of people, are exposed to loss in a single occurrence. A particular risk is a risk to which relatively few members of a society are exposed to loss in a single occurrence.* For instance, the threat of recession and subsequent unemployment can be said to be a fundamental risk. Everyone working for a living or deriving a living from some working person may be subject to a financial loss. On the other hand, if a group of investors contribute to a project to develop a commercial process to convert wood chips into fuel oil, and the project fails (or succeeds) because of poor (or good) management, it is only this particular group of investors that is hurt or benefited, and the risk to these investors would be called a particular risk. Many times making a distinction can be difficult.

Is disability a fundamental or particular risk? Disability is a risk that each member of society faces and would therefore seem to be fundamental. But the timing of disability may make it a particular risk. The disability of a key scientist during the developmental phase of the wood chip conversion project mentioned above could be a particular risk for the investors.

Producers have an interest in the distinction between fundamental and particular risks. Particular risks lend themselves more readily to treatment by insurance. No producer has the opportunity to sell an "unemployment insurance" plan or a Social Security plan. Producers *do* have the opportunity to sell homeowners policies and life insurance.

Pure and Speculative Risk. *Pure risk is a chance of financial loss which does not simultaneously offer a chance of financial gain. A speculative risk offers not only the chance of financial loss but also the opportunity for gain.*

Pure risks are generally insurable and hence important to the producer. If an individual owns a new Mercedes-Benz, he or she is going to suffer a loss if the car is involved in an accident. The same individual's financial position will not be changed, however, if no accident occurs. Pure risks have sometimes been described as loss or no loss situations.

On the other hand, if an individual decides to place a $100 bet on a horse with a payoff of two to one, that person *may* lose $100 or *may* win $200. Two elements are important with speculative risks: first, there is the chance of a gain; and, second, individuals usually *create* a speculative risk. Individuals do not usually create pure risks, and there is no opportunity for financial gain. Gambling is the classic example of a speculative risk, but business ventures (the wood chip processing example) are also speculative risks.

Generally, risks that are particular and pure are insurable risks.

Loss Frequency and Loss Severity *Loss frequency is the number of times loss occurs over a specific period of time. Loss severity is the amount of loss usually expressed in financial terms.* Loss frequency is usually stated in terms of a fraction or a decimal (or a decimal converted to a percentage). These terms can be explained through consideration of the flip of a coin—a speculative risk.

Assume that John bets George $500 on the toss of a coin—if the coin lands heads up, John wins; if the coin lands tails up, George wins. If the coin is "fair," that is, has two sides, a head and a tail, each with

WALT DISNEY
HOME VIDEO

NO POSTAGE
NECESSARY
IF MAILED
IN THE
UNITED STATES

BUSINESS REPLY MAIL

FIRST-CLASS MAIL PERMIT NO. 151 BURBANK, CA

POSTAGE WILL BE PAID BY ADDRESSEE

WALT DISNEY HOME VIDEO
PO BOX 7089
BURBANK CA 91510-9958

A Walt Disney MASTERPIECE

THE LION KING

Please tell us about yourself. Even if you have sent in one of these cards in the past, we at Walt Disney Home Video want to hear from you again! Your feedback will aid us in improving the quality of future video releases. Please mail this today. We will pay the postage.

PLEASE PRINT NEATLY IN BLACK INK USING UPPERCASE LETTERS ONLY.

FIRST NAME: BARBARA
LAST NAME: GODISH
PHONE: 814-255-1991
STREET NUMBER: 804
STREET NAME: SUNNEHANNA DR
APT. NO.:
CITY: JOHNSTOWN
STATE: PA
ZIP: 15905

THANK YOU!

If you have questions, please write to:
Buena Vista Home Video, Consumer Relations
P.O. Box 908, Lakewood, CA 90714-0908

1. Did you receive this videocassette as a gift?
   1. [ ] Yes–(SKIP TO QU. 6)
   2. [x] No–(CONTINUE)

2. How did you first discover this videocassette was available for purchase?
   1. [x] Advertising–TV, newspaper, magazine, radio
   2. [ ] Ad in another video–brochure, preview
   3. [ ] Friends/Family/Someone told me about it
   4. [ ] Read a magazine article/review
   5. [ ] Saw it in the store/Browsing in store
   6. [ ] Through the mail/mail catalog
   7. [ ] Other: ____

3. What is the one main reason you purchased this videocassette?
   1. [x] A child asked for it
   2. [ ] Someone else asked for it
   3. [ ] Makes a great gift
   4. [ ] Own other Disney videos and wanted more
   5. [ ] It is a Disney Classic
   6. [ ] Good for the whole family
   7. [ ] Saw it in the store
   8. [ ] I like the movie
   9. [ ] Price/Good value
   10. [ ] Other reasons: ____

4. What was the name of the store where this video was bought? Walmart

5. What price did you pay for this video, before receiving any rebate? 15

6. Primarily, for whom was this videocassette purchased?

Males: 1. [ ] 2 yrs. or younger 2. [x] 3-5 yrs. 3. [ ] 6-8 yrs. 4. [ ] 9-12 yrs. 5. [ ] 13-17 yrs. 6. [ ] 18-24 yrs. 7. [ ] 25-34 yrs. 8. [ ] 35-44 yrs. 9. [ ] 45-54 yrs. 10. [ ] 55+ yrs.

Females: 1. [x] 2 yrs. or younger 2. [ ] 3-5 yrs. 3. [ ] 6-8 yrs. 4. [ ] 9-12 yrs. 5. [ ] 13-17 yrs. 6. [ ] 18-24 yrs. 7. [ ] 25-34 yrs. 8. [ ] 35-44 yrs. 9. [ ] 45-54 yrs. 10. [ ] 55+ yrs.

1. [ ] Whole Family

7. Did you send away for either of the $5 rebates?

	Yes	No, But Plan To Send For It	No. Not Interested
$5 Pillsbury Rebate	1. [ ]	2. [ ]	3. [ ]
$5 Mattel Lion King Toys Rebate	1. [ ]	2. [ ]	3. [ ]

8. How many of the following prerecorded videocassettes do you OWN and, of these, how many did you PURCHASE in the past 12 months? (INCLUDING THIS VIDEO)

	# OWNED	# BOUGHT IN PAST 12 MOS.
TOTAL VIDEOS, ANY TYPE:	20	3
Total Disney Videocassettes, any type:	6	2

9. Which of the following DISNEY videocassettes do you already own? (CHECK ALL THAT YOU OWN)
   1. [x] 101 Dalmatians
   2. [x] Aladdin
   3. [x] Beauty and the Beast
   4. [ ] Fantasia
   5. [x] The Fox and the Hound
   6. [x] The Jungle Book
   7. [ ] Peter Pan
   8. [ ] Pinocchio
   9. [ ] The Return of Jafar
   10. [ ] Snow White

10. Are you: 1. [ ] Male 2. [x] Female

11. Your age: 1. [ ] 12 yrs. or younger 2. [ ] 13-17 yrs. 3. [ ] 18-24 yrs. 4. [x] 25-34 yrs. 5. [ ] 35-44 yrs. 6. [ ] 45-54 yrs. 7. [ ] 55-64 yrs. 8. [ ] 65+ yrs.

12a. How many children 17 yrs. or younger live in your household? # of children 2 or [ ] No Children

12b. What are the ages of the children in your household? (CHECK ALL THAT APPLY)

Boys: [ ] Under 6 mos. [ ] 6-11 mos. [ ] 1 yr. [ ] 2 yrs. [ ] 3 yrs. [x] 4 yrs. [ ] 5 yrs. [ ] 6 yrs. [ ] 7 yrs. [ ] 8 yrs. [ ] 9 yrs. [ ] 10 yrs. [ ] 11 yrs. [ ] 12 yrs. [ ] 13-17 yrs.

Girls: [ ] Under 6 mos. [ ] 6-11 mos. [x] 1 yr. [ ] 2 yrs. [ ] 3 yrs. [ ] 4 yrs. [ ] 5 yrs. [ ] 6 yrs. [ ] 7 yrs. [ ] 8 yrs. [ ] 9 yrs. [ ] 10 yrs. [ ] 11 yrs. [ ] 12 yrs. [ ] 13-17 yrs.

13. What is your annual household income?
   1. [ ] Below $20,000
   2. [ ] $20,000-$29,999
   3. [ ] $30,000-$39,999
   4. [ ] $40,000-$49,999
   5. [x] $50,000-$74,999
   6. [ ] $75,000-$99,999
   7. [ ] $100,000-$149,999
   8. [ ] $150,000+

Walt Disney Home Video distributed by Buena Vista Home Video, Burbank, CA 91521.
Printed in U.S.A.

P-4441

an equal probability of occurrence, the chance of loss for both John and George is 1/2 or 0.50 or 50 percent. Theoretically, if a coin is flipped an infinite number of times, it will come up heads half of the times and tails half of the times. The frequency will be, in this case, 0.50 times the number of flips. The severity, or amount of the loss, in this case, is $500 per loss.

The frequency and severity of losses may lead producers to provide additional services for clients. If, for example, a producer is selling insurance to a bakery with a fleet of 500 trucks, the producer may recommend that those potential losses that have a high frequency and a low severity (such as collision) might be best treated through the risk management tool of retention. If physical damage to the delivery trucks historically involved fifty trucks a year (plus or minus five trucks) and average a $600 loss per accident, it may be best for the company to pay those losses out of current income rather than to "trade dollars" with an insurer. On the other hand, a tornado that could wipe out the entire fleet of trucks in a few minutes (a low frequency, high severity condition) could properly be an exposure to treat with insurance. In this case, the producer may obtain an order for insurance by saving the bakery a significant amount of money through recommending retention.

As a general statement, the exposures best suited for insurance treatment are those with a low frequency and high severity.

The Law of Large Numbers The law of large numbers is closely related to degree of risk and forms one basis for insurance company operations. The law of large numbers also has significance for a producer and the agency. Without becoming involved in the mathematics, the law of large numbers basically says the greater the number of similar units exposed to a similar loss, the more accurate the loss predictions based on that data will be.

For instance, John promises George $500 if George draws a spade from an honest fifty-two card deck. In return, George must pay John $125 in order to draw a card. George faces a loss frequency of 39/52, 3/4, 0.75, or 75 percent. On one draw, George's degree of risk is relatively high. But if George were to view this as an opportunity over the course of a year, drawing two cards a day, his losses should be very near zero at the end of the year.

In life insurance, statistics are readily available as to the probability of death of individuals of a certain age. If females age twenty-four have a probability of death of 0.056, and one female age twenty-four is insured, it is ridiculous to say that 0.056 of this female will die in her twenty-fourth year. Either the insured female dies or does not die. The actual death rate will be either 1.00 or 0.00. But if an insurance company had 100,000 females aged twenty-four, then they could be reasonably sure that 5,600 females would die at age twenty-four.

Carrying the example on, exactly 5,600 females dying at age twenty-four would not likely happen, but the range would be relatively close, say between 5,200 and 6,000. Suppose there is another life insurance company with 1,000,000 females age twenty-four insured. They expect 56,000 deaths from the group, but the range turns out to be between 55,000 and 57,000. Even though the range for the second group is 2,000 deaths (57,000 − 55,000) the range is a smaller percentage of the expected number of deaths than in the first case. Two thousand is 3.57 percent of the 56,000 expected deaths, whereas 800 deaths, in the first example, is 14.3 percent of the 5,600 expected deaths.

For producers who have so-called "contingency" commission contracts with insurers, the more business given to a particular insurer in a particular "line" or type of insurance, the more predictable the "contingent" commissions should become. One assumption here is that the business given to an insurer is "homogeneous" or made up of similar insureds.

Perils and Hazards The construction of an insurance policy includes an important section that describes or lists the causes of loss for which the insurer will pay if losses occur. *A peril is a cause of loss.* In the standard fire policy, the perils, or causes of loss for which coverage applies, are fire, lightning, and loss by removal. In some inland marine policies, the description or list of events might read, "We insure against all risks of direct physical loss of or damage to the property covered except. . . ." This latter provision is called an "all-risks" form but could just as easily be called an "all-perils" form. The standard fire policy is an example of a named or limited perils form.

A hazard is anything that increases the frequency or severity of a loss. A loss reduction technique, like an automatic sprinkler system, is not a hazard for the fire peril. Presumably the sprinkler system *decreases* the severity of loss from a fire, but a hazard *increases* either the frequency or severity of loss, or both. An example of a hazard in life insurance would be becoming a race car driver. The probability of an *early* death increases with that occupation. The severity remains the same. The severity of some illnesses increases without periodic medical examinations, but the probability of incurring a particular disease would not increase. A final example, storing 500 gallons of gasoline in the basement of a home, would increase both the frequency and severity of loss.

There are three types of hazards: physical, moral, and morale.

Physical Hazards. A physical hazard is something that can be seen, felt, or touched, and that increases the probability or severity of a loss due to a peril. A physical hazard is a tangible characteristic of the property, persons, or operations insured. A building in a flood plain, storage of excessive amounts of combustibles, or keeping oily rags near a furnace, are all physical hazards. Insurance coverage may be suspended if hazards controlled by the insured change, with the insured's knowledge, in a way that increases the probability of loss.

Producers who take the time to visually inspect and become familiar with their clients' property and operations may be able to spot physical hazards and suggest corrective action. In some cases, insurers will request that their loss control representatives or engineers look at a prospect's operations. In some cases, insurance will not be available unless insureds take corrective action. In other cases, a building or activity that has been "engineered" may be acceptable though the general class is not. For instance, a properly protected restaurant may be accepted by an insurance company though the general class of restaurants is a generally unacceptable line.

When a producer submits an application for insurance, pictures of the prospect's facility and a concise verbal description of the operations will help the underwriter make a decision. The more information the producer can pass on to the underwriter about the physical hazards and action being taken to correct them, the more likely it is that the application will be accepted.

Moral Hazards. Moral hazards are subjective characteristics of the insured that tend to increase the probability or severity of loss. Moral hazards are more difficult to detect than physical hazards. In some cases, reputation may play a significant role.

The insurance contract is one of "utmost good faith." The insured has certain responsibilities within the insurance contract. If those responsibilities are met, payment may be made at time of loss. Certain other requirements help protect the insurer from the moral hazard—in forms where the insured must report insured values periodically, provisions are included for timely and accurate reports. If either or both are not made, loss payments are adjusted downward. But pre-underwriting on the part of the producer will help eliminate most of the problems.

If a prospect has a "reputation" for less than honest dealings, or has gone bankrupt repeatedly, or has had a series of questionable fires, or has associates who are known felons, or any of a hundred activities that cast a shadow on the insured's integrity, it is probably a good idea to not solicit the account. The insurance business must exist in a climate of honesty.

Morale Hazards. Morale hazards may be difficult to detect and to treat for producers and insurers. On the other hand, morale hazards may be observable—such as poor housekeeping standards. Morale hazards stem from an attitude of the insured. With physical hazards, a physical inspection can uncover potential defects in the exposure. With moral hazards, retail credit inspections may uncover previous undesirable activities or habits. But the unseen psychological attitudes of insureds or prospects may be difficult to detect.

Insureds who have the attitude "who cares, it is insured" are insureds with a morale hazard. If a producer spots an obvious housekeeping physical hazard (oil on a concrete factory floor) and brings the hazard to the attention of management, the reaction can give a clue to management's attitude. If no action is taken, the morale hazard as well as the physical hazard may be present. Insureds with the morale hazard will eventually tend to have more losses. The losses may severely affect the producer's profitability, relations with underwriters and companies, and the producer's own pocketbook.

Indemnity, the Heart of Insurance Indemnity has many potential meanings. The intent of insurance, and the definition of *indemnity* for the AAI program, *is to place the insured in the financial position held immediately prior to a loss.* Indemnity is an imperfect concept in an imperfect world. With so many clauses and parts of an insurance contract affecting the loss payment, true indemnity is probably rare. The risk management process and the selling process used by a producer should attempt to achieve true indemnity. But insureds are basically reluctant to purchase "the best combination available." Premiums may be expensive. The attempt should be made by the producer to upgrade coverages and loss control activities in order to provide the maximum protection for the available premium.

There are a host of policy provisions that seek to control loss payment so that the insured is not "overpaid." In many cases, producers will be able to explain why certain provisions are in insurance contracts by referring to the principle of indemnity. In property insurance, for instance, it is common to find a loss payable clause or a mortgage clause. These are used when a mortgage or other lien exists on property. One function of the clause is to allocate a loss payment among those with an interest in the property. If a fully insured building suffers a total loss from an insured peril, payments would go to both the insured and the mortgagee (or lienholder). Assume the building was worth and was insured for $100,000 and a mortgage was outstanding for $50,000. Equity (and the principle of indemnity) would require that the mortgagee and the insured split the $100,000 payment. This mortgage clause is one example of the indemnity principle at work.

Insurable Interest *Insurable interest is the financial interest an entity has in the continued existence of the subject of insurance.* There are a multitude of court cases relative to what constitutes insurable interest. A few generalizations may be made.

Insurable Interest in Life Insurance. The general rule is that an insurable interest in the life of the insured must exist at the time the policy is issued. There is no requirement for an insurable interest to exist at the time of death. Thus, two people in a partnership may insure each other's life while the partnership exists. If the partnership is dissolved, no further insurance may be purchased by either partner on the life of the other partner, assuming there is no relationship other than the business between the former partners, which establishes an insurable interest. The contracts purchased while the partnership existed remain valid if premiums are paid. At the death of a former partner, the policy will be paid.

People have an unlimited insurable interest in their own lives. Spouses, children, and parents, grandchildren and grandparents, and others have insurable interests in the lives of close relations. A business relationship may also create an insurable interest. A corporation has an insurable interest in executives and key personnel. A creditor has an insurable interest in the life of a debtor. The nature and extent of the insurable interest is a question of fact that the life insurance underwriter will want to establish prior to issuing a policy.

Insurable Interest in Property-Liability Insurance. The general rule is that *an insurable interest must exist at the time of loss.* A homeowner has an insurable interest in the home and its contents. A corporation has an insurable interest in its plant and equipment. A lessor and, perhaps, the lessee, have insurable interests in leased equipment. When an insurable interest exists, some attempt should be made by the producer to treat that interest.

A lessor may require the lessee to be responsible for damage to a rented building. In that case, the lessee has an insurable interest in the building. If, on the other hand, the lessee is "held harmless" for building damage, the insurable interest rests with the owner.

A previous owner may not assign his or her insurance contract to a new owner without the insurer's consent. The insurance contract is a personal contract. Underwriters want to know of any potential moral or morale hazards that may be present with a new owner. But anyone with an insurable interest may insure an object to the extent of that insurable interest. Again, the nature and extent of an insurable interest is a subject of fact for every situation.

Requisites of an Ideally Insurable Exposure If there exists an insurable interest on a particular and pure risk, the exposure is usually insurable. Theoretically there are five requirements that must be met for an exposure to be commercially insurable:

1. Many persons exposed independently to the loss.
2. The exposures will not be too heterogeneous (dissimilar).
3. The losses will be definite as to cause, time, place, and amount.
4. The expected loss for each insured during the policy period will be calculable.
5. The loss will be accidental from the viewpoint of the insured.[1]

Independence. The probability of an occurrence or loss for each insured is not related to others. For an exposure to be commercially insurable, many persons must independently purchase insurance. The function of insurance is to reduce risk. By combining *independent* exposures in *large* numbers, insurers allow the "law of large numbers" to work. Without the law of large numbers and the combination of many similar insureds, insurers could not reduce risk. The more insureds, the more accurate the statistical data the insurer uses to predict losses.

Similarity of Exposures. Another way to state item two is, "exposures will be homogeneous or similar." Just a large number of insureds independent of each other is not enough. By definition, the exposures must be similar if the law of large numbers is to work.

Definiteness. For statistics to be accurate, losses must be definite. A large portion of each property-liability policy is devoted to loss adjustment procedures. To make loss procedures work, definiteness is important. Definiteness carries over into the next requirement, calculability.

Calculability. Expected loss amounts must be of a frequency and in an amount to allow calculation of equitable rates. During the Three Mile Island nuclear accident, the losses were definite as to time, place and, roughly, amount. Yet how can the catastrophic nature of a nuclear facility exploding be calculated? Long-term effects of radiation are still a mystery to the medical profession. The financial consequences of these long-term radiation effects almost defy calculation.

Accidental. Accidental means that the loss is a random event so that the law of large numbers may operate. Accidental also means that losses are neither *intended* from the activities of the insured nor *expected* by the insured from forces outside of the insured's control. For instance, a producer was called early one morning and asked to add an additional location to an existing insurance package. The location was beachfront property, and a strong hurricane was due to hit the coast at 6 P.M. on that date. Allowing the property to be covered at that time is "selecting against the insurer." The fact that the hurricane happens to hit the insured's beachfront property and causes damage is an accident. It is beyond his control. However, if the insured is allowed to purchase insurance to cover such a loss after the insured becomes aware of the expected loss, the loss would not be accidental from the standpoint of the insurance coverage.

Insurability With an understanding of the five requirements for an insurable exposure, it is easier to see why certain exposures are not commercially insurable. Certain exposures are considered too few in number to combine (military personnel's lives in wartime), or not similar (foreign credit exposures), or not definite in time, place, or amount (wear and tear), or catastrophic (war, nuclear) or, finally, not accidental from the insured's point of view (building in a flood plain) for insurers to handle commercially. If an exposure of an insured is commercially uninsurable, it is good public relations to explain why in terms of the requisites of an insurable exposure rather than just saying the coverage is not available. A properly phrased answer builds confidence and respect for the producer in the eyes of a client or prospect.

Some of the examples used above *are* insured commercially. Suffice it to say that some restrictions exist on those types of exposures that render them insurable. Without the restrictions, they would not be commercially insurable.

Risk Management and Insurance The risk management process will be treated in depth in AAI 82, *Multiple-Lines Insurance Production.* A definition is appropriate here.

Risk Management. Risk management *is a process designed to systematically manage the pure risks of an individual or organization.* It can also be defined as a series of steps encompassing what risk managers do:

1. Identify and analyze the loss exposures faced by their business or family
2. Formulate alternatives for dealing with loss exposures.
3. Select the apparent best technique or combination of techniques to treat the exposure.
4. Implement the decisions made
5. Monitor these decisions

Insurance is one important risk management technique which should be considered while performing step two of the risk management process.

A risk manager may, in addition to or in lieu of insurance, avoid, control, transfer, or retain the risk.

Avoidance means the risk has been eliminated. A way to avoid the risks of skydiving is not to skydive. Controlling the risk means to take some action to reduce hazards or exposure to perils. Adding an alarm system to a jewelry store is an example of control for the burglary and robbery perils. The earlier example of the lessor requiring the lessee to be responsible for building damage is an example of a noninsurance risk transfer. Finally, the bakery that pays its truck physical damage losses out of current income is one example of risk retention.

Insurance. There are almost as many definitions of *insurance* as there are authors. A risk manager would define insurance as "a *technique* that makes it possible to transfer the financial consequences of potential accidental losses from the insured firm, family, or individual to an insurer."[2] As a mechanism, insurance is a *social device* under which two or more persons make or promise to make contributions to a fund from which the insurer promises to make certain cash payments or renders certain services to those contributors who suffer losses that are accidental from their point of view. From a pure theory standpoint, Pfeffer called insurance, "... a device for the *reduction* of uncertainty of one party, called the insured, through the transfer of particular risks to another party, called the insurer, who offers a restoration, at least in part, of economic losses suffered by the insured."[3] States have legislated individual definitions of insurance.

These definitions are not exhaustive, but they serve to point out that there are a variety of definitions of insurance that are acceptable. What is important in any definition is a recognition of the following four elements:

1. at least two and almost universally more than two people contribute to a fund or pool;
2. the insurer administers the pool and invests it as a financial intermediary—reducing overall premium charges to insureds;
3. accidental losses are paid from this pool to those who helped form the pool; and
4. the relationship between the contributors and the pool is contractual.

Checkpoints

1. Define "risk," list the types of risk, and give an example of each type.
2. Describe the types of risk that are generally considered insurable.

3. Based on your answer to 2, explain why insurance is not gambling.
4. Define:
   a. chance of financial loss
   b. degree of risk
   c. peril
   d. physical hazard
   e. moral hazard
   f. morale hazard
   g. indemnity
5. Explain the difference between life and property-liability insurance with regard to when an insurable interest must exist.
6. List the requisites of an ideal commercially insurable exposure.

THE NATURE AND CONTRIBUTIONS OF THE INSURANCE BUSINESS

The Dual Nature of Insurers

Contributions to the economy and society at large made by the insurance business arise from the dual nature of insurers. The primary role of insurers is to provide protection against financial losses. But insurers also operate as financial intermediaries—that is, they collect small sums of money from large numbers of people and put this pool of capital to use through investments and loans.

Economic Benefits of Insurance The insurance business provides six measurable benefits to society that exceed the cost of producing those benefits:

1. Indemnification for losses
2. Reduction of the uncertainty in society
3. A more equitable assessment of the cost of uncertainty
4. A source of long-term funds
5. A reduction of losses
6. Promotion of business competition

Indemnification directly helps those who suffer financial losses by restoring them to the financial position they held prior to the loss. But others also benefit. Employees may keep jobs that would otherwise be lost. The tax base of the community remains stable and perhaps grows with reconstruction. Suppliers and purchasers retain their customers.

Reduction of the uncertainty for society is not the same as loss reduction. Whether or not one is insured may not alter loss frequencies and severities, but knowing that, if a loss occurs, the financial consequences of the loss will be minimized reduces uncertainty. From an insurer's standpoint, the more entities insured, the more predictable losses become, decreasing the uncertainty of insurers. Insurance also provides a degree of social stability, a better price structure for products and services, and increases competition, helping to hold down prices throughout society.

Because businesses "know" the cost of insurance protection, they can plan for premium payments and spread premiums throughout their price structures. Businesses can treat insurance costs as a cost of doing business. This is more equitable to the consumer who bears the ultimate costs than if businesses tried to constantly rely on the price of their products to cover all potential losses.

As financial intermediaries, insurers make long-term funds available to businesses and governments. Insurance activities also provide long-term funds. Credit can be extended over a longer period of time because of the financial guarantees made available through insurance. To amplify, home mortgages and auto loans are more readily made because of the availability of insurance to repay the loans in the event of loss. Sureties are more apt to write bonds for contractors that not only have a strong balance sheet but also have substantial amounts of life insurance on key personnel. Similarly, banks are more likely to loan money to organizations if their key personnel are insured in favor of the company.

Loss control activities help to prevent losses or to reduce the impact of losses on property and persons. Arson programs sponsored by insurers have helped reduce "for profit" losses in many cities. Defensive driving courses have reduced collision losses. Construction and engineering techniques reduce accident frequency and severity. These benefits directly accrue to society and individuals.

All of these benefits, together, help to promote competition in business. The job of people in business is to make their assets profitable. Knowing that those assets will be replaced if destroyed makes them more willing to engage in business. Generally, the greater the number of people who provide goods or services, the lower the price of goods or services to the ultimate consumer.

Economic Costs of Insurance The benefits to society produced by the insurance business outweigh their costs. But the costs *are* considerable. First, many human and material resources are expended to operate the insurance business. If these resources were not used in the insurance business, they could be used in other businesses (perhaps at a reduced cost because of reduced demand). Second, *moral* hazard losses are true costs of the insurance business. These losses occur *because* of insurance. Arson for profit is one example of a moral hazard loss. *Morale* hazard losses are also true costs of insurance to society. The manufacturer who "keeps a sloppy house" by storing flammables carelessly is an example of a morale hazard. While it is true that this manufacturer *might* suffer a loss without insurance, it is at least possible that insurance increased the manufacturer's carelessness.

Insurers are aware of these costs to society and take direct action to reduce them. Package policies (discussed in a later chapter) reduce the amount of time, paper work, and human effort used. Careful underwriting attempts to uncover moral and morale hazards. Policy design and loss adjustment in conjunction with underwriting also attempt to minimize the effects of moral and morale hazards. The insurance business has extensive educational efforts aimed at the consumer. These efforts include attempts to show consumers how their attitudes toward losses affect premiums. Programs like National Fire Prevention Week, Lock-Your-Car campaigns, and so on, help reduce losses. Many insurers and trade associations now direct educational advertisements to the general public to show how large court judgments affect their premiums. (See Exhibit 1-1.)

The Insurance Business and the Economy Insurers are a vital segment of the economy. Not only do insurers provide protection of property and income, but insurers are also financial intermediaries.[4] Basically, a financial intermediary is any entity that obtains money from one source and redirects it to another. Banks, savings and loan associations, and insurance companies basically collect small sums of money from their clients, pool the money, and lend larger sums to or invest larger sums in other entities. Not all financial intermediaries operate in this manner. Consumer and sales finance companies typically obtain large sums of money in the commercial paper market and lend it in smaller sums to individuals and businesses. Investment bankers who, in that capacity, exclusively supply funds to entities by selling large blocks of securities, obtain both small and large sums of money for corporations and governmental bodies who need those funds.

It is important to understand the role of insurers as financial intermediaries. Many consumers feel that it is justifiable to overvalue a claim because, "Insurance companies have all the money. I'm just getting my share." It is a major failure of the insurance business that consumers do not understand why insurers "have all the money." Indeed, if insurers, banks, savings and loans, savings banks, and pension funds did not pool money for use by other segments of the business community, the economy would slow down significantly. Insurers provide a service to society when they are efficient collectors and distributors of capital.

The need for efficient collectors and distributors of capital implies

Exhibit 1-1
Educational Advertisement*

One of these men drives himself to work, drives himself home and drives up his cost of living.

He doesn't see it that way. He's been driving himself to the office every day for several years now. He actually enjoys the ride.

Problem is, with today's energy crisis, the man on the right is wasting both fuel and money. Gas prices alone make the trip expensive. And his auto insurance premium is higher than it has to be.

The man on the left has decided to conserve and save. When the gasoline shortage began, he and some neighbors started carpooling to work. So together they consume less gas. That cuts expenses right there. What's more, because each of them drives fewer miles, they save money on their auto insurance as well.

As a major group of property and casualty insurance companies, we're doing our best to help you keep your insurance rates affordable. That's why most auto insurers are offering discounts to those individuals who reduce the total number of miles or times they drive to work.

For example, people who normally drive 30 miles to and from work every day can save up to 22% on car insurance premiums just by carpooling. All they have to do is drive to work two days a week instead of five.

People who switch to public transportation to get to work save even more on their premiums—up to 31% in some states. Their car becomes classified "for pleasure use only," a less expensive category.

Here's what we're doing to control costs:

■ Offering premium discounts to those who reduce the total number of miles they drive each week to work. Discounts will vary by company, by state and by the type of coverage you have.
■ Cracking down on insurance fraud practices through the Insurance Crime Prevention Institute and the National Automobile Theft Bureau.
■ Working through the Insurance Institute for Highway Safety to make cars and roads safer.
■ Investigating injury and repair claims more thoroughly.

Here's what you can do:

■ Cut down on your driving by carpooling or by using public transportation.
■ Use your auto seat belt and shoulder harness.
■ Talk to your insurance agent or company about ways to lower the cost of your auto insurance coverage.
■ Lock your car. Don't invite trouble.

Affordable insurance is our business...and yours.

This message is presented by the **American Insurance Association,** 85 John Street, New York, New York 10038.

*Reprinted with permission of the American Insurance Association.

that there is a demand for capital to be used in business pursuits and that capital is scarce. Both implications are accurate. There would be no need for a study of economics without scarcity. There would be little need for money without scarcity. There would be little justification for an insurance business without scarcity. The scarcity of products and services determines, the price of those products and services. The desirability of those products and services is expressed in terms of money. For example, gold is a scarce commodity compared to sand. Therefore, gold commands a higher price than sand. Cherry hardwood is relatively scarce compared to pine, and therefore carries a higher price. The scarcity and desirability of a commodity or service determines in aggregate, how much the commodity or service will cost.

Economic Questions Any economic system must answer three questions:

1. What products should be produced and in what quantity?
2. How will these products be produced?
3. For whom will the products be produced?

The questions concerning what products to produce and in what numbers are generally answered, in a private enterprise economy, by people going into a business to provide desired goods or services. These entrepreneurs anticipate the acceptance of the goods they produce. If successful, they receive rewards. In more centralized economies, such as under a socialist system, what products are produced, and in what numbers is established by a central planning authority based on a bureaucratic perception of what is needed.

The "how" and "for whom" questions are answered by an allocation system developed by the economy. Under a totally free enterprise system, the marketplace decides who gets what and how it is produced. Under a *private* enterprise system, the solution is the same but with the addition of some governmental control. (Hawaii, for example, has determined that everyone within the state should have automobile insurance. For those individuals who are on welfare and cannot afford the premium, the premium is included in their welfare benefits package.) Under a socialistic system, a central planning authority would usually make allocation decisions. The key difference between private enterprise and a socialistic system is that, under private enterprise, money acts as the rationing or allocation device. Under socialism, the central planning authority rations.

The fact that the insurance business exists under *all* economic systems establishes the importance of the business. It also establishes that the insurance business can efficiently satisfy asset protection needs under various economic systems.

The Insurance Business *Is* Different

Some knowledgeable people in the insurance business feel that the idea that insurance is different provides a universal excuse for the business to ignore business practices of other, noninsurance businesses and to avoid "explaining" the insurance business to the public. Traditionally, they say, the business has taken a "we are different, we are too technical for you (the consumer) to understand, so trust us" stance. Consequently, when major problems arise—the rate classification controversy for automobiles, or excessive losses and rapidly rising premiums in lines like professional or products liability—the business receives a relatively poor reception from the public. This attitude frequently places the burden of "educating" the public squarely on the shoulders of producers. Sales presentations and the actions taken jointly by producers and insurers at the time of a loss can go a long way toward improving the public image of the insurance business.

But the idea that the insurance business is different also states a fundamental truth—the insurance business *is* different from other, noninsurance businesses. (There are also major differences between the life and the property-liability insurance businesses.) But, these differences should not be an excuse for the producer or the business as a whole not to explain the nature and purpose of the business to consumers. A simplified example will illustrate these differences.

A business, Crowley Manufacturing, Inc., needs a company car for its president and is also renewing its commercial insurance. The price of the car is $8,000 and the insurance premiums total $8,000. An order is placed through Crowley's fleet department for the car to be delivered in sixty days. At the same time, Crowley's manager renews the insurance policy which will expire in sixty days. The auto manufacturer goes through the following accounting transactions that match its production of the car. Raw material is ordered, creating an asset, inventory of raw material, and an offsetting liability of trade accounts payable. The raw material is gradually processed into an actual automobile, reducing raw material inventory and increasing finished goods inventory and wages payable. The auto manufacturer sells the car to the dealer, FOB shipping point, and reduces its finished goods inventory by the value of the car as carried on the books, registers a "sale" for the sales price to the dealer, and increases accounts receivable for the amount of the sale. Within some period after billing, the accounts payable are reduced as all manufacturing expenses are paid. An income statement can be drawn at this point to show the exact amount of profit or loss to the manufacturer. The whole process would take 90 to 120 days for the auto company to know its exact financial status from the production and sale of the car.

The insurance transaction is different. The insurer receives the application from the producer and begins processing the account. The insurer is willing to accept the business from Crowley Manufacturing, Inc., and tells the producer to issue a binder (temporary coverage document) in the event a policy is not physically issued at renewal. The insurer establishes no accounting entries at this point. On the renewal date, the insurer establishes the following accounts. Written premium for $8,000, a commission payable account (dependent on the level of commissions to be paid), and an "unearned premium" liability for the entire $8,000. Another asset account is also established, perhaps called "accounts current," for the premium less commissions due from the producer. Typically, the insurer will give the producer thirty to sixty days to pay this account. At renewal, the producer bills Crowley Manufacturing. Crowley pays both the dealer and the producer promptly. The producer, using excellent financial management techniques, waits the entire allowable period before paying the account current. At that point, the insurer reduces the accounts current and increases cash. Technically, the unearned premium reserve (liability) is reduced daily by a proportionate amount reflecting each "day's protection." Only at the end of the policy year does the unearned premium reserve reach zero and all of the premium become "sales" or earned premium.

Some major differences in the accounting cycles of the insurance company and the manufacturing firm exist thus far: at the end of 120 days from order, the manufacturer knows its profit, but the insurer has not the slightest notion of its profit.

To slightly but realistically complicate the example, assume that three things happen to Crowley Manufacturing two weeks before the policy year ends. First, the president's car is in a minor collision (covered by the policy) to the extent of $850. Second, an employee is injured on the job to the extent that he will be off the job for two months. Third, a visitor to Crowley's plant trips over a tool negligently left on the sidewalk by an employee, injuring the visitor to the same extent as the injured employee in the second example. The visitor, however, does not immediately report the accident to Crowley Manufacturing.

At the end of the policy period, the insurer has three additional expenses (or, actually, liabilities if all losses are not paid by the end of the year). The first liability is for the physical damage to the president's car. The loss was reported, adjusted, but not yet paid in cash as the bill from the body shop is not yet in. The second liability is for the workers' compensation loss to the employee. This liability has been reported to the insurer, but the adjuster has not yet had a chance to evaluate the loss. The third liability is for the injury to the visitor. Not only has the insurer not had a chance for its adjuster to evaluate the loss, the loss has not yet even been reported to the company! But it is a valid loss that must eventually be paid and charged to Crowley Manufacturing's premium.

At the end of the year, then, the auto manufacturer is completely "free" of any accounting transactions. It knows how much profit has been made. The insurer has fully earned its premium, but still does not know its profit. Estimations are necessary. A liability account called "reported, adjusted, not paid" is established for the collision loss and directly charged to losses paid. A reasonable estimate of the amount to be paid under the workers' compensation coverage can be established because of accurate historical statistics available from workers' compensation losses. This liability is called "reported, but not adjusted." It is an estimate, but reasonably accurate. Finally, the insurer knows that some losses have occurred that have not been reported. It does not know which of its policyholders is affected, but does recognize that "something has occurred to someone." A final liability account, the IBNR (incurred but not reported), is established for this loss. This is the least accurate liability. From these accounts, the insurer strikes the balance sheet and income statement indicating its *estimate* of its profit and financial position. But because of the potential for a lawsuit and a long time span between the actual accident to payment to the injured visitor, it may be years before the insurer has a "true" profit or loss picture for the year.

Differences between insurers and noninsurers are real. The product-accounting cycle for the property-liability company appears to be one year (or the length of the policy) but actually can be much longer due to incurred but not reported losses and subsequent liabilities. The cycle for the manufacturer is significantly shorter.

There are also nonaccounting differences. From an operations standpoint, a manufacturer can gain what economists call "economies of scale" up to certain levels of production. Insurers and producers are not subject to such economies, within certain limits. The insurance business is "labor intensive," that is, people play a vital role in the business—people to sell, underwrite, type, adjust, and administer. Equipment plays a relatively minor part—computers, cars, and office equipment—when compared to the vast plants and assembly line equipment used by the manufacturer. To generate "more" business, the manufacturer must add large sums to its plant and equipment before hiring production employees. To write "more" business, insurers and producers need to fill the unused portion of their employees' time, if any, or add personnel.

The final major difference is that the insurance business, particularly from the producer's standpoint, is truly entrepreneurial. Capital requirements for entry into the business are relatively small when compared to manufacturing or other service businesses. Certainly it takes less capital to become an insurance producer than to enter the oil or automobile industries. Insurance sales is also one of the relatively few occupations where the limit on income is determined by the desire and effectiveness of the individual. Many producers actually earn more than insurance company presidents. It is hard to imagine the presidents of General Motors, Exxon, or Proctor and Gamble encouraging any of their employees or associates to do the same.

But these differences should not act as an excuse for the insurance business or blind the insurance business to the fundamental similarities. Businesses operate to make a profit (an excess of revenue over expenses). Profit enables businesses to grow and prosper—to devote resources to product development, to improvement of working conditions, to sell more products, thus minimizing price increases. Profit also enables businesses to pay taxes—taxes which governments at various levels use to improve the quality of life for all of its citizens, especially those who are unable to work and generate their own profit, surplus, or savings. Without profit, business and government cease to function.

Like other businesses, the insurance organization must be efficient if it is to make a profit. Any organization that has expenses in excess of revenue must eventually go out of business.

Like other businesses, insurance organizations are competitive. Not only must all businesses compete for market shares within their own business, but they also compete with other businesses for the consumer's dollar. Insurance producers, for example, not only compete with other producers but also with auto dealers, department stores, and so on, for the disposable income of consumers. Like the sales representatives of other businesses and industries, producers must educate consumers on wise spending—not only informing clients of the wisest use of their insurance dollars, but also, in some cases, convincing them to give up other consumer items to adequately protect the assets they have accumulated.

A final similarity between the insurance business and other businesses (and there are many other similarities) is that its product must be sold. Producers play a vital role in the insurance business and are in a position of respect that requires integrity, professionalism, and efficiency.

Checkpoints

1. List the two major functions of the insurance business.

2. Define financial intermediary.
3. List the benefits of the insurance business to society.
4. List the costs of the insurance business to society.
5. List three questions any economic system must answer concerning its scarce resources.
6. State one major similarity and one major difference between the insurance business and other industries.

THE ORGANIZATION OF THE INSURANCE BUSINESS

Insurer Organizations

The organizational forms of insurance companies vary. Individuals and all types of corporations operate as insurers, though no partnerships do. The types of insurers are (1) proprietary, (2) nonproprietary, and (3) governmental. Profit and nonprofit are not good classifications. The "profit" status of an organization relates solely to its relationship with the Internal Revenue Service; nonprofit means a nontax-paying entity. Nonprofit organizations still attempt to have an excess of revenue over expenses. An excess, profit, permanent contribution to surplus, residue, or whatever it may be called, is needed in order for the organization to grow.

Proprietary Insurers Proprietary insurers attempt to make a profit for their owners. Proprietary insurers are either unincorporated or incorporated.

Unincorporated Proprietary Insurers. Perhaps the most famous insurance name in the world is an unincorporated proprietary insurer known as Lloyd's of London. Most people incorrectly view Lloyd's of London as an insurance company. To more completely understand Lloyd's of London, a comparison can be made with stock brokers and their relationship to the New York Stock Exchange (NYSE). Lloyd's is divided into two organizations: the Lloyd's Corporation (similar to the NYSE) and the underwriters at Lloyd's (comparable to brokerage houses). Insuring actually takes place through the underwriters at Lloyd's, comparable to the buying and selling of securities. The service work associated with insurance written—policy typing, claims, statistical work, collections, and disbursements—is handled by the Lloyd's Corporation. In other words, the Lloyd's Corporation provides the physical environment and administrative support to handle the insurance actually written by the underwriters at Lloyd's. Because of consumer confusion about the nature of Lloyd's of London, more detail of their operations is presented.

In the United States, Lloyd's is considered an excess and surplus lines insurer. That is, they write business that is hard to place with a producer's normal insurers. Two states, Illinois and Kentucky, have "admitted" Lloyd's of London. In those states, Lloyd's can write insurance directly through brokers.

The insurance coverage provided by the underwriters at Lloyd's is underwritten by a "syndicate manager," called an attorney-in-fact. When the manager decides to accept a submission, it is accepted on behalf of all members (underwriters) who belong to the manager's syndicate. Each underwriter actually accepts some small percentage of the syndicate's exposure. In return, the underwriter receives a proportionate share of premium and investment income. An underwriter may belong to any number of syndicates. Most underwriters at Lloyd's limit their participation to those lines of insurance with which they feel secure. Syndicates are organized by particular lines of insurance, such as ocean marine hull, aviation hull war risk, motor (automobile liability), and so on. In some lines, multiple syndicates compete for business.

To become an underwriter at Lloyd's requires considerable financial security deposits, character references, and nomination by other underwriters. Until the last decade, only British subjects were eligible to become underwriters. Financial security rests on the deposits. A portion of an underwriter's profits goes into special loss reserve accounts as does a portion of a syndicate's profits. Coupled with the initial security deposit these reserves provide the policyholders with adequate security for their policies. The reserve accounts are administered by the Lloyd's Corporation.

An application for insurance must be submitted to Lloyd's through an approved broker. The broker lists all pertinent details on the submission and circulates a "card" containing the information. The card goes to those syndicate managers who write the line. The card indicates the amount of coverage desired and the premium to be paid. The managers determine whether the rate is acceptable and, if so, accept all or a portion of the submission at the indicated rate. If a policy is not fully subscribed at the stated rate, the broker may have to go back to the managers with a new proposal. It is not unusual to have more than one syndicate participating on any given submission. Like insurance companies, syndicates have "line limits" or maximum amounts of insurance they will write on any given submission.

In total, about 8,500 people are underwriters at Lloyd's. Very few of these are actively engaged in the insurance business. Rather, they treat their position as an investment, placing their confidence in the abilities of the syndicate manager. Only about 300 underwriters are

U.S. citizens, yet Lloyd's derives about 60 percent of their business from this country.

The United States has a few "Lloyd's" type of insurers operating principally in Texas.

Incorporated Proprietary Insurers. One significant type of insurer in the United States is the capital stock insurance company. These are proprietary insurers, that is, for profit in the traditional sense, and they are owned by stockholders who have invested their money, formed a corporation, and seek an investment return. Technically, these stockholders control the corporation by electing the board of directors. As with any corporation, the board then appoints or elects the officers who run the corporation. Usually, key officers determine who will be nominated for the board and submit their nominations to the stockholders. Frequently, officers not only manage the business but also control its operations. Usually, stockholders are only interested in the dividends they receive and the appreciation of the stock price. In the case of incorporated proprietary insurers, stockholders invest in a company that sells insurance rather than in one that makes and sells cars or soap. In the property-liability business, almost three-fourths of the total premium written is handled by stock insurers. Stock insurers are a greater force in commercial insurance than in personal insurance. In life insurance, about one-half of the life insurance in force is with stock insurers. Ownership and control of the organization represent the major difference between proprietary and nonproprietary insurers.

Nonproprietary Insurers Nonproprietary insurers are owned and controlled by their policyholders. Nonproprietary or cooperative insurers can be divided into mutuals, reciprocal exchanges, and miscellaneous cooperatives.

Mutuals. Effective control of a mutual lies with its officers. Typically, all policyholders are entitled to vote for the company's board of directors, but few policyholders exercise this right. Voting is egalitarian; that is, most mutuals will only allow a policyholder one vote no matter how many policies the policyholder has or how much premium is paid. In life insurance, a $1 million policyholder paying $50,000 in premiums a year would have the same vote as a $5,000 term policyholder paying $100 per year. As with stock insurers, executive officers are usually on the board of directors.

There are four types of mutuals: (1) "pure assessment" mutuals, (2) assessment mutuals, (3) perpetual mutuals, and (4) advance premium mutuals.

Pure Assessment Mutuals. Pure assessment mutuals wait until the end of the year to determine or estimate what losses and expenses were incurred. Losses and expenses are divided among the policyholders, and each pays his or her share by an assessment billing. This type of mutual is not common today. Pure assessment mutuals limit the geography of their business and the perils (causes of loss) they will insure. In the middle and late 1800s, this type of mutual was very common. At least one major regional stock insurer, the Westfield Companies, had its beginning as a pure assessment mutual.

Assessment Mutuals. Assessment mutuals charge their policyholders a premium in advance that management feels is sufficient to cover expenses and losses for a normal year of operations. If catastrophes or other events cause the initial premium to be insufficient, these mutual companies may assess their policyholders for the difference. Some charge a low initial premium and tend to write only limited lines in small geographic areas. Others charge higher premiums, write more complicated policies, and rarely assess policyholders.

Perpetual Mutuals. Perpetual mutuals were an important part of the early insurance business—in the 18th and 19th centuries. A few still exist, including the one founded by Benjamin Franklin. Their importance today has diminished because of their inflexibility with regard to the perils and policies written. A perpetual mutual will charge an advance premium, say, twenty times an annual rate. The premium is invested, and investment income from the deposits covers all losses and expenses. When a policyholder sells his or her property, the deposit is refunded. Usually there are no assessments, but charter provisions of the perpetuals do permit assessments.

Advance Premium Mutuals. The final, most important and significant form of mutual is the advance premium mutual. These are the largest mutuals. They issue nonassessable policies, like their stock counterparts. Regulators are reluctant to allow mutuals to issue nonassessable policies unless they exhibit a high degree of financial strength. Companies in this category pay dividends to their policyholders if more money is earned (the excess of revenue over expenses) than is needed to add to surplus. Some of these mutuals, mostly life insurers, regularly pay dividends. In life insurance, it is not unusual for a mutual to pay, in addition to annual dividends, a "termination" dividend when the insured dies or cashes in the policy. Other mutuals of this type pay dividends only in years of unusually high profit. In many cases, these dividends are to be applied only against future premiums and cannot be taken in cash. These mutuals account for more than half of the life insurance in force and about two-thirds of the assets of life insurers. Property-liability companies of this form write about 25 percent of the total industry premiums.

One major factor in property insurance that falls into this category is the factory mutual. Factory mutuals were founded by factory owners who were concerned about safety. Relatively little of the factory mutual's premium goes to pay losses. Most of the premium goes for engineering services to make the property as "fire proof" as possible. Factory mutuals have extensive laboratory facilities in which full-scale buildings can be constructed for testing purposes. This allows for experimentation with construction materials and safety equipment to determine the best mix. It is not unusual for the field representative of a factory mutual to be an engineer. The factory mutuals, primarily insure only very large businesses that are expected to adopt their building engineering specifications.

Reciprocal Exchanges. Reciprocal exchanges are a hybrid of both proprietary and nonproprietary insurers. A reciprocal has two distinct parts, an unincorporated association made up of its members (insureds) and an "attorney-in-fact," usually a corporation, that manages the insurance and business affairs of the association. Each member of the association is actually an insurer of every other member. Unlike Lloyd's, members only insure fellow members. The attorney-in-fact sets and collects premiums, invests the money, pays losses and manages other operations. The attorney-in-fact usually has a contract with the association that allows the attorney-in-fact to retain a portion of the premiums, usually 20 to 30 percent, for expenses. Under the purest form, separate accounts are kept for each member of the association. They are credited with their premium contributions, assessments, if any, and their share of investment income. They are charged their share of the management fee and losses. When a member no longer is an insured, the member is entitled to the balance of the account. Some reciprocals operate with "undivided surplus," and separate accounts do not exist. Under this sytem, no withdrawal rights are available. Like large financially secure mutuals, some reciprocals can issue nonassessable policies. Some are associated with other noninsurance organizations and write insurance only for their members. Most write only a few types of insurance. In some parts of the country (California) and for some occupations (commissioned and noncommissioned officers of the military), reciprocals are a major factor in the business. In aggregate numbers and premiums, however, reciprocals are a small factor.

Miscellaneous Cooperatives. The forms of insurers seem to be unlimited. Many early life insurers were lodges or fraternal benefit societies. These organizations were either formed or had as a part of their basic structure the welfare of their members. Many of these welfare operations became fraternal insurance operations. The insurance organizations of fraternals are a special class and are so treated by the enabling insurance legislation around the country. Because there is an other than insurance relationship, the contract given the insured member does not contain all of the contract. Charters and bylaws of the fraternal are incorporated into the contract by reference. As reciprocals are the exclusive creature of the property-liability side of the business, fraternals are exclusively life and health insurers. They all began as assessment operations. With a tendency for the average age of the members of a fraternal to increase due to a lack of new members, most either changed to a level premium basis or went out of the insurance business altogether. A few assessment types still exist, however.

Some savings banks established in the East in the 1800s offer life insurance in addition to savings plans. Usually the amounts of insurance are small, but state laws have changed allowing up to $50,000 of coverage on a single life. Total volume in force is small, primarily because no agents are employed to sell the policies. Life policies are usually purchased by an individual who requests such coverage from the bank. The small percentage of life insurance in force under this system, less than 1 percent of all the life insurance in force nationally, attests to the need to sell insurance to become a large factor in the business.

The final forms of nonproprietary insurers are the producer or consumer cooperative health expense plans. The two most widely known plans are "the Blues" and HMOs. "The Blues," Blue Cross and Blue Shield, are known as "producer cooperatives" because they historically were formed by hospitals (Blue Cross) and physicians (Blue Shield) with "excess capacity." They are creations of special insurance laws that give them tax exempt status. Customers are not billed a premium based on characteristics of individual insureds or personal loss histories but rather on relative health care costs and health care facility utilization in a given community. This rating method is called "community rating." Traditionally, these organizations were run by boards made up of the providers of the service. Today, insurance regulators are encouraging or requiring that "public" participation be allowed on these boards. Proprietary health insurers typically provide an "indemnity benefit." That is, the insured incurs health related costs and the insurer pays all or a portion of the costs to the insured (or, with a proper release, to the health care provider). The Blues provide "service benefits." These benefits are not stated in dollars but in terms of service to be expected, such as "a semi-private room for 60 days after an accident or illness." Further, the Blues have contracts with the providers of the service to pay the providers directly based on a prearranged price. The Blues compete with commercial insurers and are a major factor in health care. Proprietary insurers feel the Blues are given two great advantages—tax free status and special legislation. The Blues, because of the growing political importance of health insurance, are subject to extreme regulatory examination in rates, forms, and service. Some Blue Cross and Blue Shield organizations have formed life and property-liability insurance subsidiaries and use independent agents as the marketing arm for their operations.

A "consumer cooperative" growing in importance is the HMO or Health Maintenance Organization. The first HMO, formed by Kaiser Industries while constructing the Hoover Dam, set the basic structure for this type of organization. Consumer control is one major difference between HMOs and the Blues. Another major difference is the type of "service benefit" provided to subscribers. The subscriber's total health care program is handled by the HMO. Preventive medicine is practiced: members are encouraged to receive annual physicals as part of the benefit package. Even prescriptions may be covered in plans with a small payment for each prescription. Many HMOs operate large hospitals, extended care facilities, and clinics. Some have special radiation therapy facilities for their subscribers. The HMO usually contracts with a group of physicians to provide necessary services. If a physician with the necessary expertise to perform open-heart surgery, for instance, is not on the staff, the HMO can go outside for an expert. Physicians are paid a salary and, in some cases, a bonus based on reduction in budgeted expenses. Hospital utilization rates show greater efficiency in HMO operations than regular hospitals. Detractors claim, among other things, that the major defect is that the patient does not have a free choice in selection of the physician.

HMOs can be "open," with services available to members and nonmembers alike, or "closed," with services available to members only. The federal government is encouraging the HMO type of health insurance system, and only the passage of time will permit a determination of its contributions and success.

Governmental Insurers Governmental insurers are active in both the life-health and property-liability insurance businesses. Traditionally, governmental insurers came into existence when there were perils that were considered not commercially insurable. Exposures considered too few in number to combine (the lives of military personnel in wartime), or not similar (nuclear exposures), or not definite in time, place, or amount (war), or catastrophic (war, nuclear) or, finally, not accidental from the insured's point of view (building in a flood plain), cannot be practically handled by commercial insurers. Yet if there is a good reason from a public policy point of view for providing some kind of insurance protection, the government can become the "insurer of last resort" and spread the risk of these isolated exposures over the entire population of the United States by using the general revenues of the tax structure to pay losses.

The government also becomes an insurer for loss exposures that fall on the general population, sometimes called "fundamental risks"—such as war exposures. Insurers are better equipped to handle exposures on a home, a business, or an automobile—"particular exposures." Finally, even if an exposure is commercially insurable, if the insurance business does not provide coverage, or provides it at a price deemed "excessive," the government may become the insurer.

Governmental insurance may be offered by federal or state governments depending on the impact of the particular problem being addressed. Competition from public insurers may exist or the government may hold a "monopoly." And, finally, the government may or may not use the distributive or administrative capacity of private insurers.

Examples. Insurance against the failures of banks and savings and loans were once considered "fundamental," catastrophic, and not calculable by commercial insurers. Consequently, the federal government offered such coverage under the Federal Deposit Insurance Corporation and Federal Savings and Loan Insurance Corporation. These "insure," subject to maximum limits, that the depositor's savings will not disappear if a bank fails.

Federal crop insurance is available to farmers for large hail or windstorm losses. Crop insurance is commercially insurable, if underwriters watch their "book of business" and geographically spread such risks. Yet the market for private crop insurance is relatively small. There are other federal insurance programs for a multitude of exposures.

Federal programs for riot and flood insurance are examples of the "insurer of last resort" and cooperation with the existing private insurance mechanism. A brief description now will help clarify the role of governmental insurers. In some of these cases, insurers pool premiums to cover losses (like the FAIR plans), but if losses become excessive, the government is a reinsurer for catastrophic losses. In others, like flood insurance, the government is the primary insurer, but uses agents and brokers to distribute or sell the coverage. In a third case, the health insurance portions of OASDHI or "social security," the government is again the insurer, but uses the administrative abilities of insurers to handle loss payments and statistics.

Insurer Organizations: A Summary There are three basic types of insurers—proprietary, nonproprietary or cooperative, and governmental or public. Proprietary insurers are owned and operated to make a profit. Nonproprietary insurers are owned and controlled by their policyholders. Governmental insurers have primarily developed to provide insurance coverage against losses caused by commercially uninsurable perils. Exhibit 1-2 graphically displays the various types of insurer organizations.

Types of Distribution Systems

Many different categories of insurance distribution systems are possible. The classification system used here stems from the contractual and ownership relationships between the producer, the client, and the company. This classification system divides all distribution systems into four categories: independent agency system (American agency system); exclusive agency system; direct writers; and mail order. It will be necessary to recognize that some distribution systems mix the elements of two or more of these categories.

Independent Agency System Independent agents are "independent" in the sense that they are not employees of insurers. Instead, they have contracts with insurers to generate new business and to renew and service existing accounts. Their compensation is based on what they sell, and is determined by various commission arrangements. If an independent agency principally represents the insured, it is called a brokerage firm. For this program, brokers are considered members of the independent agency system. Independent agents set their own time schedules, pay their own expenses, and operate their own businesses. They "own" the business they produce in the sense that if the relationship between the agency and the insurer is dissolved, the agent has the right to change the client's insurer. The insurer has no right to try to keep the insured—the renewal business belongs to the agent. In fact, the renewal customer is the most valuable asset of an agency. The independent agency system is a unique development of our country. In the 1800s, America was "specie poor," that is, coin and currency were relatively scarce. Insurers have to operate, sooner or later, on a cash basis. Agencies became an efficient vehicle for the collection of cash. Agencies helped to make the insurance business a viable and valuable financial intermediary.

The independent or American agency system also developed from the need to avoid catastrophic exposures and to increase sales for insurers. Many foreign-based insurers established branches in the United States. With an office in New York, it was almost impossible to develop business "in the west," as Pittsburgh, Cincinnati, Cleveland, and St. Louis were known in the early 1800s. Domestic insurers also needed to spread their business over large geographic areas to avoid the catastrophic bankruptcies that plagued the business during the 1800s.

Exhibit 1-2
Types of Insurers

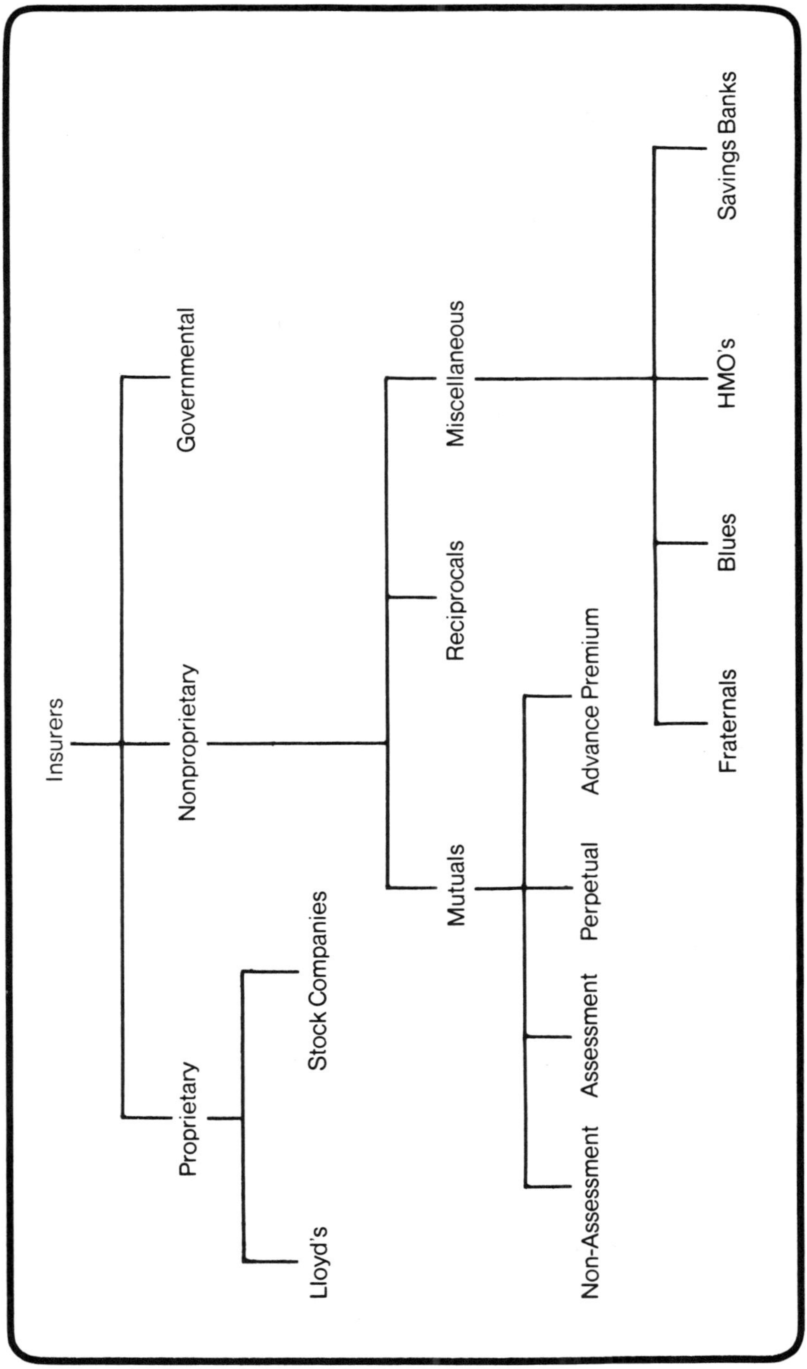

Exhibit 1-3
Distribution of Agencies by Annual Premium Volume — The Independent Insurance Agents of America, Inc., 1973*, 1975**, 1978*** 1981**** and 1982****

Premium Volume	Percentage of Agencies				
	1973	1975	1978	1981	1982 (Est.)
Less than $199,999	30%	23%	18.3%	11%	7%
200,000—299,999	18	17	12.0	8	8
300,000—399,999	12	13	9.3	7	8
400,000—499,999	8	9	9.2	8	8
500,000—749,999	13	13	14.9	16	16
750,000—999,999	6	8	10.3	14	14
Over 1,000,000	13	15	23.9	34	39

* Adapted with permission from Stuart V. d'Adolf, "Profile of the Independent Agent," *Independent Agent*, January 1975, p. 18.

** Adapted with permission from Stuart V. d'Adolf, "Who Is the Independent Agent?" *Independent Agent*, January 1977, p. 14 and January 1979. The totals do not equal 100% because some of the respondents did not indicate their premium volume.

*** Adapted with permission from Stuart V. d'Adolf, "Who Is the Independent Agent?" *Independent Agent*, January, 1979. The total for 1978 does not equal 100% because some respondents did not report their premium volumes.

**** Adapted with permission from "Profile of the Independent Agent," *Independent Agent*, January 1983, p. 36. Note: The percentages may not add to 100% due to the failure of some respondents to provide premium data.

Mostly the bankruptcies came after great conflagrations such as the New York fire of 1835, the Chicago fire of 1872, and the Boston fire of 1873. American and foreign-based companies alike needed to expand to the west. But communication was a problem. Canals, railroads, the telegraph and, eventually, the telephone, improved communication, but there was still no way a New York office could sell in Cincinnati. Three alternatives existed: (1) ignore the west and concentrate on local growth; (2) open a "western office"; or (3) appoint an "agent." Many companies did ignore the west and their growth suffered. Others opened western offices. Others appointed agents who would represent them in the west. These early agents had to be "independent." A company could not afford to pay salaries to untested producers without controlling their sales efforts. The solution was to compensate based on the business generated, and require each producer to be responsible for his or her own expenses. The independent agent grew and became the prototype for the American Agency System.[5]

The size of independent agencies is shown in Exhibit 1-3. The smaller agency, under $500,000 in premium, is becoming a less important factor in metropolitan agency operations but remains important in rural areas. Merger and growth can be seen in the comparisons of agencies by premium volume from 1973-1982. Commission income as a percentage of premiums has been falling over the same time period, giving further impetus to larger, more efficient agencies.

There are functions other than production that independent agents assume. Some have draft authority from their companies to settle small, and usually first party, losses (losses that only involve the insured). Larger agencies provide loss control, claim, and other services. Many are now active in risk management on a fee basis. Many still prepare and issue policies in their offices. On that business, they also bill and collect premiums from their insureds.

There is probably no such thing as a "typical" independent agent or agency. Because they are independent, they operate in the way the principals or owners of the business desire, not in the way the companies they represent would necessarily prefer. Independence is a valued status of these agencies. Normally, they represent more than one company, although a trend is to represent fewer companies. Commercial Union, Fireman's Fund, and Ohio Casualty are three examples of companies that use the independent agency system.

Exclusive Agency Systems Exclusive agents differ from independent agents in two major ways. First, during their initial training, exclusive agents are usually employees of the company they represent. After the initial training phase, and ignoring the one company representation, agents in this group are independent. They are paid by commissions and must pay their own expenses. Second, exclusive agents represent only one company group. Some companies in fact do not even allow their agents to "broker" business, that is, place business with another insurer. If the exclusive agent's company cannot or does not provide a market for a prospect, the agent must pass the business up. Other companies operating under this system do allow brokerage for those lines of insurance not written by the company. In the case of residual programs, automobile insurance plans (assigned risk plans), all exclusive agency companies must allow agents to participate.

There are advantages and disadvantages to the nonbrokerage rules some companies impose on their agents. On one hand, it can be argued that without access to brokerage markets, some good personal and commercial lines accounts are lost. Many insureds prefer to deal with only one agent or agency. If a company does not write a line of insurance and does not allow brokerage, the client may take the business to another agency. On the other hand, some companies maintain that concentration of the producer's efforts in those lines actively written by the insurer will give the agent significant marketing strengths. Agents can concentrate on those lines written and become "experts" in those lines, providing better client service.

Commission rates vary between first and subsequent years in an exclusive agency. First-year business may bring a commission of 15 percent; renewal business may bring an 8 percent commission. By comparison, independent agents generally receive the same percentage on new and renewal business. If exclusive agents were allowed to represent more than one company, shifting the business at renewal would generate greater commission income. Restricting agents to one company not only eliminates moving business, but also accounts for the rapid growth of this type of distribution system. Producers are encouraged by the commission structure to constantly seek new business.

Finally, the ownership of renewals is different for exclusive agents than it is for independent agents. In many cases, producers have no renewal ownership rights. In others, there is a limited ownership that usually expires when the contract between the company and the producer expires. The exclusive agent may be compensated for the "files" in this case, but not to the extent that an "independent" agent would be if he or she sold the agency. State Farm is an example of a company using the exclusive agency system.

Direct Writing System The direct writing system was the original root from which the independent agency system branched. In the early 1800s an insurance company did not typically appoint agents locally. Companies would spring up around the heart of the transportation business. At key points along canals, navigable rivers, and junctions in railroads, companies would establish their home or branch offices. Rates were published in local newspapers (with rates significantly higher in late summer and early fall to coincide with increased demand for insurance on goods shipped). It was not unusual to find the insurance operations tied to a shipping company or, in fact, to find individuals willing to write insurance for their personal account, much like a Lloyd's without all of the financial and technical backup. Today, direct writers do not operate in this manner. They have recognized the value of people "selling" insurance rather than waiting for "drop-in" business.

Most direct writing producers are employees of their companies, not independent entrepreneurs. These producers do not "own" the business they write. Renewals belong to the insurer, even during the period of employment. Compensation arrangements range from salary only to commission only. Some pay a salary and bonus or salary and commission-based bonuses. Commission rates, if involved, follow the exclusive agency pattern in that they are higher in the first policy period and lower thereafter, encouraging the producer to concentrate on developing new business. Liberty Mutual is one example of a company that uses the direct writing distribution system.

One important factor for both exclusive agency and direct writing producers is that they are usually relieved of many administrative functions—policy issuance, premium collections, and claim functions. In some cases, companies will allow the producer to settle small first-party claims, or to provide minor premium auditing or loss control services. One key ingredient in company relationships with their producers is to actively encourage development of new business. Relieving the producer of nonselling activities, and compensating at a lower renewal rate, helps accomplish this goal.

Mail Order Systems In mail order distribution systems the producer is not a factor. Insurance companies using this system claim that not only is the expense portion of their business lower (through the elimination of producer commissions or salaries) but that through pre-underwriting, the loss portion is also reduced. By concentrating on a group of potential insureds who are considered "above average," an insurer can offer a lower premium. Many companies have been successful in this method. United Services Automobile Association (USAA) (which concentrates on commissioned officers in the military) and Government Employees Insurance Company are two examples. Mail order companies operate almost exclusively in personal lines. The products are standard, service (such as claims) can be handled by independent adjusting firms, and price becomes the main competitive feature. Because of the pre-selection of insureds through mailing lists with certain characteristics, rating methods are simplified, allowing more efficient use of in-house personnel and equipment.

Mixed Systems In recent years, some companies have tried different types of systems. Allstate, an exclusive agency company in metropolitan areas, is appointing independent agents in those rural locations in which their direct writing system cannot work. One independent agency company, the Insurance Company of North America (now a part of CIGNA), tried a mail order insurance business through a subsidiary. It is not clear why this idea failed. In any event, that company does not now have its direct mail operation. One chief executive officer for a predominantly direct writing company has publicly stated that if a product or service that can be handled by his company is brought to his attention, he would use whatever marketing system was the most effective in distributing it. Because of this aggressive attitude, his company uses all four methods for various products.

Distribution Systems and the Producer There are advantages and disadvantages to all of the distribution systems and to combinations of them. In the end, the best system is the one that works best in a specific situation.

Too often, consumers, representatives of the federal government, and others judge insurance distribution systems on one criterion—price. This approach ignores other important factors such as service and product innovation.

Though no one distribution system has an overall advantage to the consumer with regard to a combination of price, service, and product, from the point of view of the producer, the mail order system must be the least attractive—it does not use producers. Any judgment made on the other three systems must be based on the producer's goals, desires, and personality. Exhibit 1-4 compares the key elements for producers under these systems: compensation, status with insurer, ownership of expirations, and service performed by the producer. The advantage one producer sees in his or her system may be a strong disadvantage to another producer. For instance, the regular salary of the direct writer may be attractive to some, whereas others would rather have relative freedom in their activities and accept a commission for the business they generate.

Checkpoints

1. Name and describe two types of proprietary insurers, two types of nonproprietary insurers, and two types of public insurers.
2. Explain how a reciprocal exchange resembles (a) Lloyd's of London, (b) a stock insurer, and (c) a mutual insurer.
3. List and describe the major types of property-liability insurance distribution systems.
4. Differentiate among the types of property-liability insurance distribution systems from the point of view of the producer.

SUMMARY

The chapter began with a survey of basic insurance definitions and principles. These definitions and principles serve as a foundation to a study of insurance policies—the "product knowledge" which, along

Exhibit 1-4
Producer Based Insurance Distribution Systems

	Compensation		Status with Insurer	Expiration—Ownership by Producer	Producer Services
	Commission	On Renewal			
Independent Agency	Yes	Same	Independent contractor	Yes	Claims, loss control, others
Exclusive Agency	Yes	Lower	Independent contractor Salary during training	Possible	Limited claims
Direct Writing Agent	Possible or bonus based on production	Lower (if any)	Salary and bonus	No	None

with "market knowledge" and "selling skills," makes up what is frequently called the sales trilogy, the three elements necessary for successful sales in any field.

These basic definitions and principles were followed by an overview of the insurance business's nature, contributions, and organization. The two primary functions of insurers—providing protection against financial loss and acting as financial intermediaries—are the sources of the economic and other contributions of insurance to society.

The insurance business generates economic benefits to society as well as economic costs. The unique nature of the insurance business was examined through an analysis of an insurance transaction as it compares to a comparable industrial transaction.

To examine the organization of the insurance business, the types of insurers and the types of distribution systems used by insurers were defined, analyzed, and surveyed. The advantages and disadvantages, from the producer's point of view, of each type of distribution system were examined.

Chapter Notes

1. C. Arthur Williams, Jr., George L. Head, Ronald C. Horn, and G. William Glendenning, *Principles of Risk Management and Insurance,* Vol. I, 2nd. ed. (Malvern, PA: The American Institute for Property and Liability Underwriters, 1981), pp. 232-238.
2. Williams, Head, and Glendenning, p. 224.
3. Irving Pfeffer, *Insurance and Economic Theory* (Homewood, IL: Richard D. Irwin, 1956), p. 53.
4. George Leland Bach, *Economics,* 9th ed. (Englewood Cliffs, NJ: Prentice-Hall, 1977), p. 210.
5. The first trade association of independent agents occurred on April 18, 1838, in Cincinnati. The organization was known as the General Board of Fire Underwriters of Cincinnati. Today it is known as the Cincinnati Insurance Board.

CHAPTER 2

Management and Sales: An Introduction

INTRODUCTION

This chapter has two objectives: first, to introduce producers to basic management concepts that can be applied to the operations of an agency and to the sales function; second, to introduce producers to some basic sales techniques. The material presented here is merely an introduction to these subjects. A detailed discussion of agency management principles will be found in AAI 83—*Agency Operations and Sales Management.* Sales techniques can be *introduced* in a textbook, but they cannot be *learned* through reading alone. Producers are encouraged to take courses that specialize in the analysis and application of sales techniques.

THE MANAGEMENT PROCESS

Management has been defined as achieving objectives through others.[1] *The management process* is a series of steps taken by one or more managers to achieve objectives through others. The steps in the management process are

1. *Planning*—establishing the purpose and direction of the organization and how they are to be achieved.
2. *Organizing*—determining the way in which the organization's work will be divided into manageable units.
3. *Staffing*—selecting qualified personnel to perform the work.

4. *Directing*—bringing about action toward achieving the organization's plans.
5. *Controlling*—measuring results against the plan and making those changes that are necessary.

The management process is a series of related steps which are performed in order. Controlling, the final step in the process, leads to revised planning, the first step in the process. The management process represents a continuous cycle.

All management functions derive directly from the three basic elements with which all managers must work: *ideas, things,* and *people.* These elements lead to the three kinds of activities that all managers perform: conceptual thinking or planning (ideas); administrating or organizing (things); and leadership—staffing, directing, and controlling—or influencing personnel to achieve desired results (people). Exhibit 2-1 illustrates the sequential steps in the management process and relates them to the three elements with which all managers work.

Planning (Conceptual Thinking—Ideas)

Conceptual thinking is the basis of planning in the management process. At the root of every organization is an idea—the organization's primary purpose, the organization's reason for existing. Clarifying this idea and determining ways to achieve the organization's purpose are the results of planning.

An individual might open an insurance agency with the idea that the business is "to sell insurance." In time, it may become clear that it is possible for the agency to sell insurance and lose money. Through this experience, the individual might change the organization's idea from just selling insurance to include making a profit and plan ways to conduct the business aimed at achieving this revised purpose.

Planning includes the activities of establishing a mission and setting strategies, goals, objectives, budgets, policies, and procedures. Not all of these activities are necessarily performed at the same or at all organizational levels, depending on the size and nature of the organization. Exhibit 2-2 outlines the planning step in the management process.

Organizing (Administration—Things)

Once an organization's plan has been set, it is necessary to determine what work must be performed and how to divide that work into manageable units *before any staff is acquired.*

Exhibit 2-1
The Management Process*

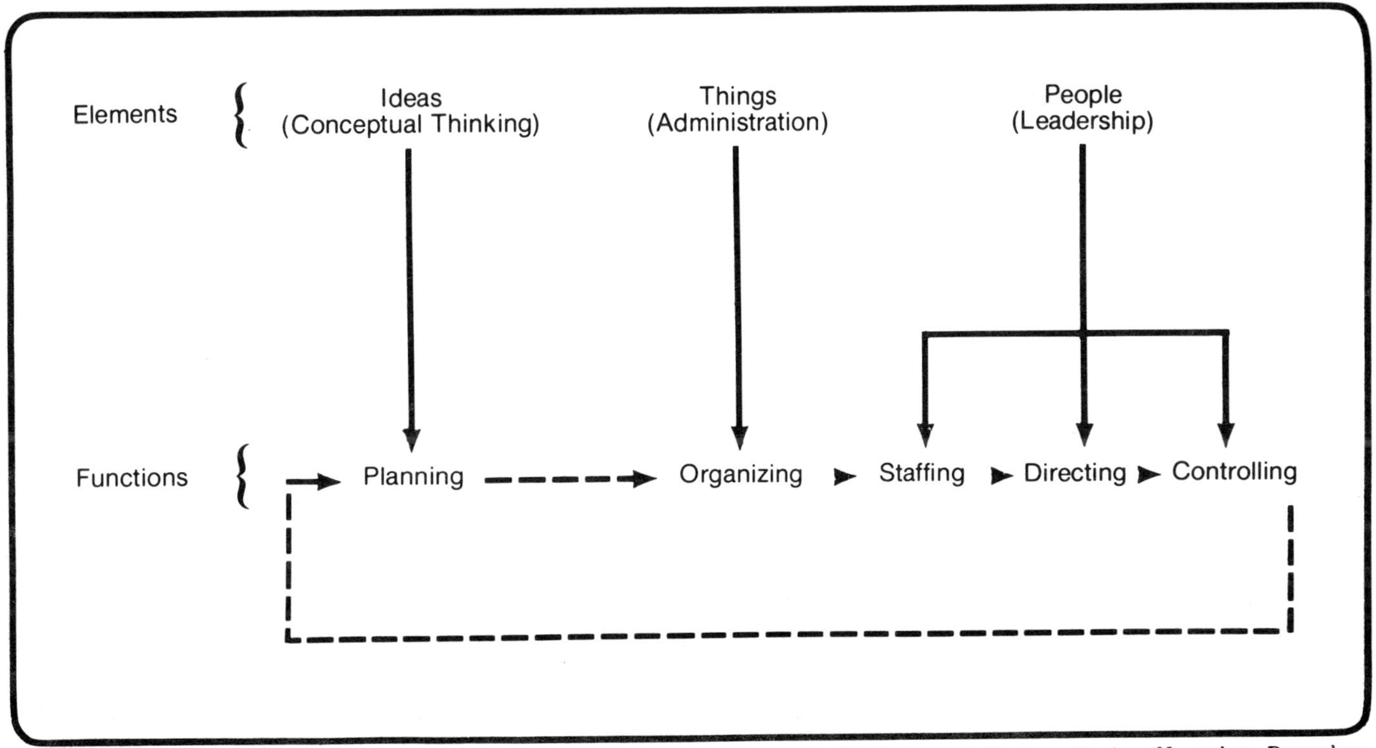

*Adapted with permission from R. Alec Mackenzie, "The Management Process in 3-D," *Harvard Business Review* (November-December 1969), pp. 80-87.

Exhibit 2-2
Idea Phase of the Management Process*

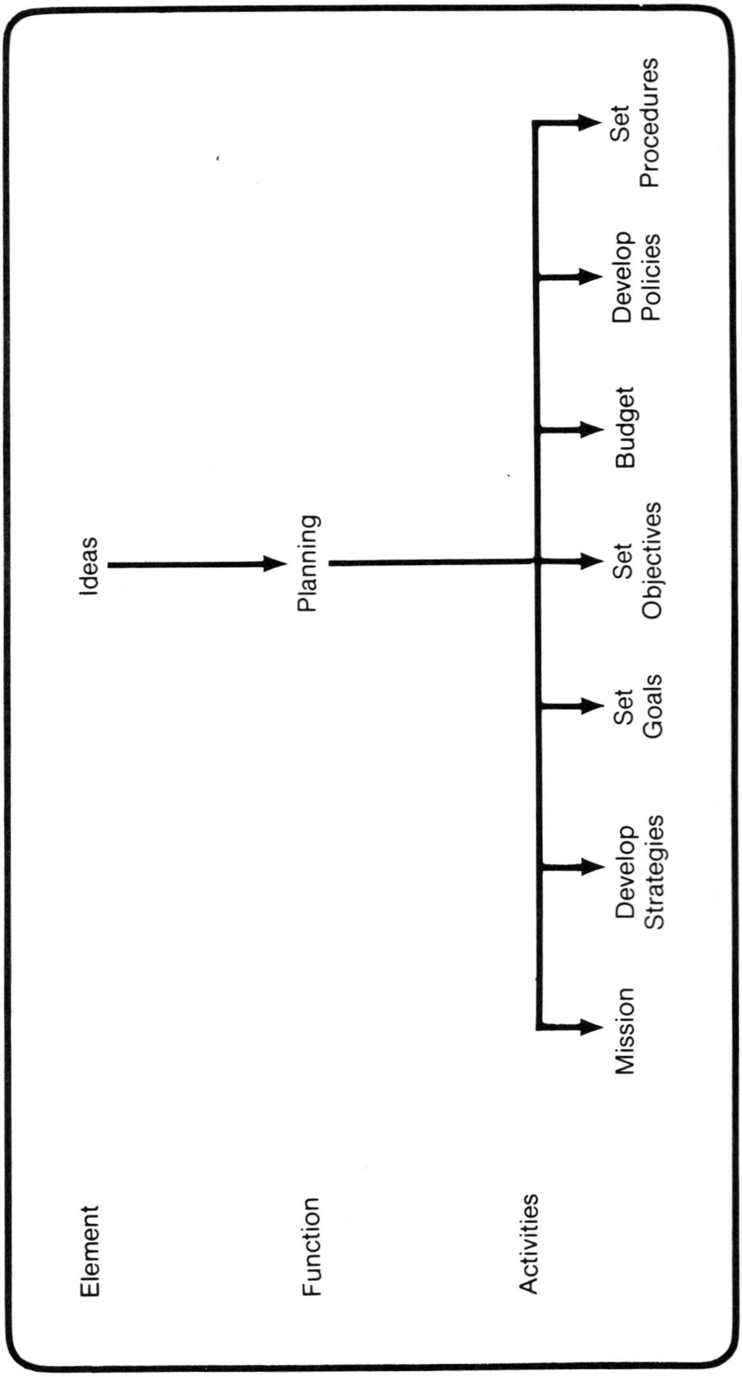

*Adapted with permission from R. Alec Mackenzie, "The Management Process in 3-D," *Harvard Business Review* (November-December 1969), pp. 80-87.

Exhibit 2-3
Things Phase of the Management Process*

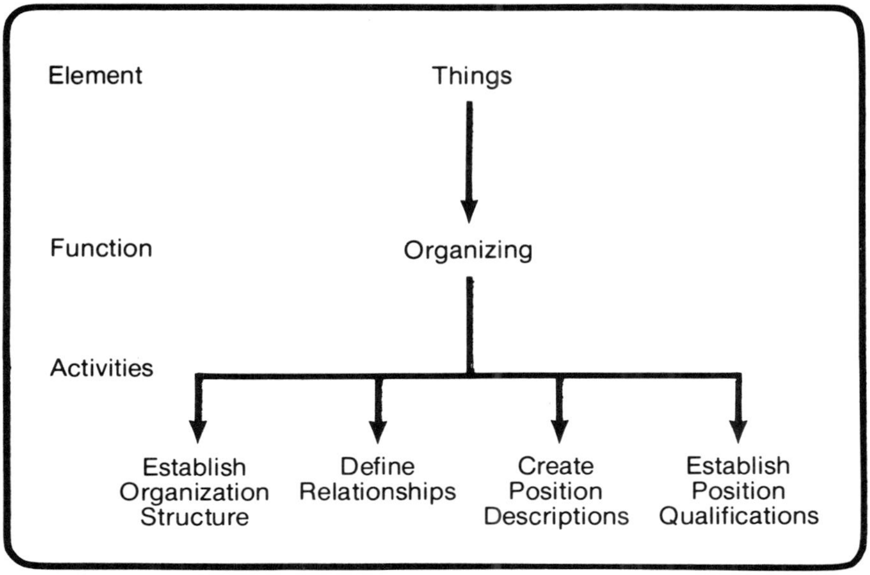

*Adapted with permission from R. Alec Mackenzie, "The Management Process in 3-D," *Harvard Business Review* (November- December 1969), pp. 80-87.

The organizing function in the management process includes the activities of (1) establishing an organizational structure, (2) defining relationships, (3) writing position descriptions, and (4) determining the qualifications for the personnel who will fill the positions. All of the activities in the organizing step in the management process are not necessarily performed at the same or at all organizational levels. Exhibit 2-3 outlines the activities related to the organizing step in the process.

Staffing, Directing, Controlling (Leadership—People)

Leadership means influencing people to achieve desired objectives. Leadership includes the three final functions in the management process: staffing, directing, and controlling. Exhibit 2-4 outlines the activities related to these last three functions.

Exhibit 2-4
People Phase of the Management Process*

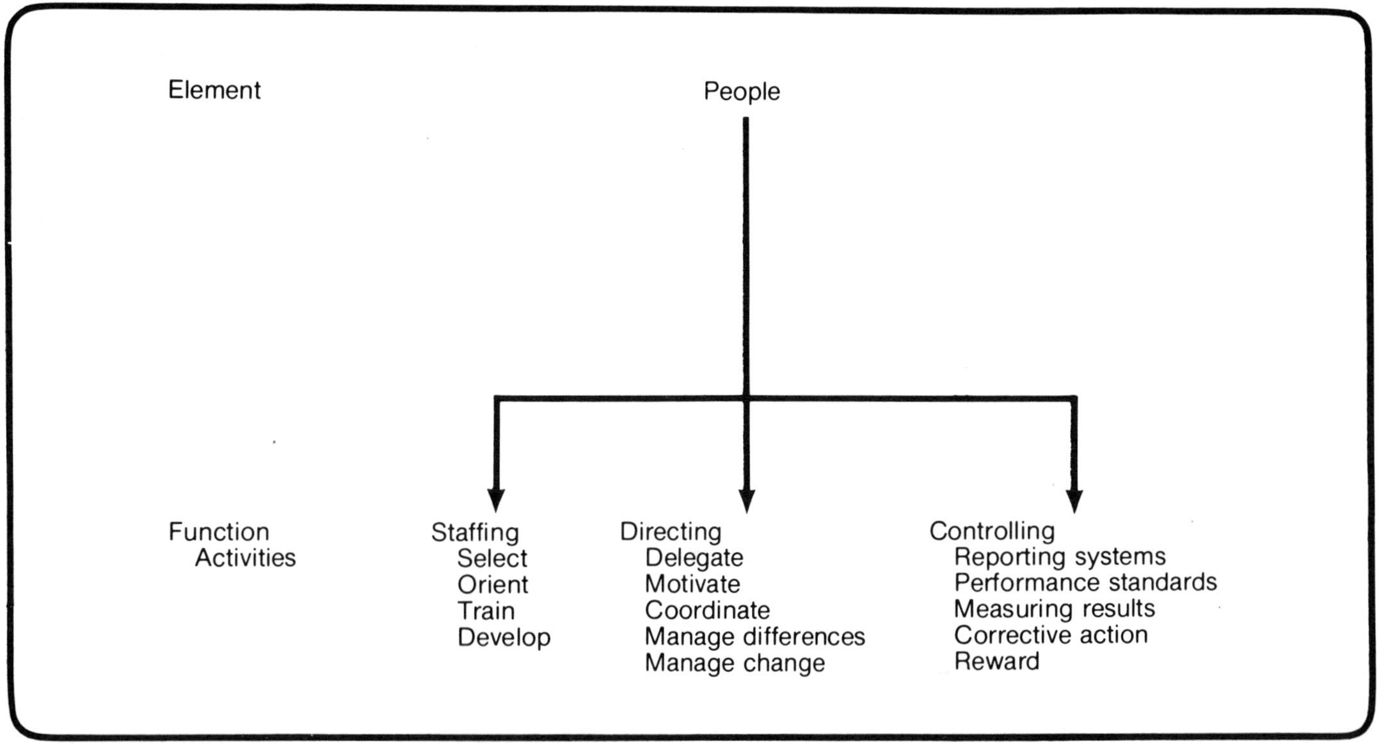

*Adapted with permission from R. Alec Mackenzie, "The Management Process in 3-D," *Harvard Business Review* (November-December 1969), pp. 80-87.

THE MANAGEMENT PROCESS AND THE INSURANCE AGENCY

The management process is as applicable to the activities of an individual insurance producer as it is to the overall activities of General Motors. The intention here is to show, in general, how the process can be applied to (1) the management of an insurance agency and (2) the management of the sales function. While it is true that many producers have little to do directly with the overall management of an agency, it is necessary for producers to realize that an agency's planning, organizing, staffing, directing, and controlling all support producers' sales and service efforts.

Agency Management

Planning The individual or individuals responsible for the management of an agency *plan* in order to make the agency profitable. The heart of planning is to know the purpose of the organization with regard to its customers. A *mission statement* is necessary to communicate the overall purpose of an agency. A mission statement, once determined, will rarely change unless the organization changes its focus. For example, Shell Oil has as its mission statement, "To meet the energy needs of mankind." A mission statement is broad and does not mention any specific products or profit levels.

Once the mission statement is drawn, planners develop *strategies* or ways to accomplish the mission. A strategy is a long-term path toward the mission and is more specific than a mission. *Goals* follow strategies and are the final target for the planning period. In a typical agency plan, goals would be established for one to five years (a usual length of an agency plan). *Objectives* are milestones toward goals. Any goal could have two to ten objectives supporting it. Objectives are necessarily shorter in range than goals.

Budgets are the allocation of scarce resources—money, people, and time. Budgets determine what agency resources will be available to accomplish goals and objectives. *Policies* are statements of general operating rules. For example, to reach a goal of "zero accounts receivable," an agency may develop a policy of "bill on binder." *Procedures* are specific instructions on the way things are to be done. They establish specifically how certain work is to be accomplished.

It is clear that the planning function in the management process may produce the need to alter the organization of the agency. In this way, planning leads directly to the second step in the process, *organizing.*

Organizing Those activities traditionally associated with the organizing step in the management process—establishing an organizational structure, defining working relationships, writing position descriptions, and determining the qualifications necessary for the personnel who will fill the positions—presuppose the formation of a new and relatively large business. But those activities can be adapted for use by small, ongoing firms. Perhaps an example will help show how.

A small, predominantly personal lines agency situated in the suburbs of a large city may, during the planning step of the management process, decide that the agency would like to grow by beginning to write small commercial businesses that are becoming numerous in the vicinity of the agency. Neither of the agency's two partners has had much experience writing commercial lines. They therefore decide to try to recruit an additional producer who has had experience with small commercial accounts.

This decision precipitates a look at the agency's structure, a need to define and redefine relationships, a need to create at least one position description, and a need to determine the qualifications the partners would like to find in the person who will become their part-time producer. All this should be accomplished before recruiting begins and before any additional staff is acquired.

The acquisition of a new producer alters—though slightly, perhaps—the structure of the agency's organization: an additional block must be drawn on the organizational chart, if there is one, and thought must be given to the physical arrangement of the agency's office space so that the producer will have a place to work, phone, store supplies, and so on. Additionally, working relationships will have to be defined. To whom will the producer report—one or both of the partners? Who will perform the clerical work generated by the producer? It will also be necessary to make up and, perhaps write down, a position description that will clearly state the producer's duties. Will the commercial-lines specialist be expected to place the business he or she writes? Will the principals make calls with the producer or should the producer be given a free hand? Finally, a written list of desirable qualifications should be prepared before recruitment of the additional producer begins.

This relatively simple example should help to illustrate the flexibility inherent in the management process. After all, that process is less a rigid model that managers *should* follow than an analysis and description of what managers *do,* consciously or unconsciously, formally or informally. Most of the activities described in the example would be accomplished if one of the partners said to the other: "Look, if we find the producer who can bring in the kind of business we want, he can share my desk and Sally can do his typing and take his calls, but I want you to place his business, keep an eye on him, and pay him." On the other hand, the same activities would have to be performed in a much more formal and complex way if a large brokerage house decided to open for business in a new state. In either case, though, organizing leads directly to the people-oriented functions in the management process, the last three functions in the process, *staffing, directing, and controlling.* These are the functions that were earlier identified with the leadership aspect of management.

Management of Agency Personnel

Staffing, directing, and *controlling,* the third through fifth functions in the management process, are the people-oriented functions in the process, the functions that call on a manager's ability to lead. An agency must be staffed to handle the business written efficiently and profitably by people who are directed to perform specific tasks that contribute to the agency's ability to achieve its plans. The agency's activities must be controlled in order to determine whether or not plans have been met and in order to introduce changes in the way the agency does business if plans are not being met.

Staffing The organizing function in the management process may have created new positions and identified the qualifications which would be desirable attributes of the people who are to fill those new positions. Fundamentally, *staffing* means *hiring people to fill these positions.* Staffing includes attempting to locate potential employees who have the qualifications desired, screening those potential employees, and, eventually, filling the positions by hiring those potential employees who seem to be the best available for the job. In addition, new employees must be made familiar with the agency's office and operations through a formal or informal orientation. Some degree of training is usually necessary before new employees become fully competent, contributing members of the agency's staff. Managers who are good leaders look to the future by developing employees. That is, they encourage employees to increase their knowledge and skill so that they can eventually make greater contributions to the firm and derive greater financial rewards and self-satisfaction from employment. One significant trend in the agency business has been the development of women in the business. More than ever before, women are developing in insurance agencies—moving out of clerical positions to become producers or agency managers.

Directing Directing, the fourth function in the management process and the second people-oriented management function, means *influencing the agency's entire staff to perform in ways that should* *lead to the achievement of the agency's plan.* Directing is probably what most people have in mind when they use the term managing.

The activities associated with directing include: *delegating*—spreading authority and responsibility throughout the staff of the agency; *motivating*—inspiring members of the staff to perform well through example and communication, *coordinating*—seeing to it that the various staff members perform separate functions which are directed toward the plan; *managing differences*—handling problems among staff members despite coordination efforts; and *managing change*—making transitions which occur in the way the agency operates as smooth for staff members as possible.

The manager who uses one individual to place all the business generated by the agency must delegate a significant amount of authority and responsibility to this individual. This necessary delegation of authority and responsibility does not, however, relieve the manager of all responsibility for the placement function. Instead, the manager is responsible for:

- motivating the "placer" to perform in an effective and efficient way,
- coordinating the placer's job with producers and clerical workers—insuring that the placer makes helpful suggestions when producers generate business that is difficult to place, for instance, without dictating to producers the kind or amount of business they write
- settling differences which will perhaps inevitably arise between this individual and producers, and
- leading the placer to accept the need for two individuals performing this function or leading the placer to become active in sales.

Perhaps the major point to be made about directing is that it reflects the manager's responsibility for the total operation of the agency but also reflects the realization that a manager cannot and should not perform all of the functions necessary for the agency's success.

Controlling The final function in the management process, controlling, leads directly to the first function in the process; that is, controlling results in and contributes to planning. *Controlling* means *comparing actual results against projected results throughout the planning period and taking the action suggested by this comparison.*

In order to control, a manager needs information. Information is gathered through the establishment and use of reporting systems and through the establishment and application of performance standards to every job performed in the agency. The information gathered in these ways must be analyzed in order to determine results to date. These actual results can be measured through comparison with projected results. This measurement of results provides the basis for corrective action and the basis for rewarding producers and other agency employees.

This discussion of the application of the management process to agency operations has been necessarily general and introductory. A detailed discussion of agency operation management appears in AAI 83. At this point, it is only necessary that producers know what the steps in the management process are, what these steps mean, and how these steps support and benefit a producer's sales and service efforts. It may be helpful to now discuss a few specific ways that some successful producers have put management ideas to work for them.

The Management Process and the Producer

There is no one correct way to manage an insurance agency. Different but valid ideas about how to sell insurance and provide service to clients require different applications of all steps in the management process. Various managerial emphases are necessarily reflected in operations. Frank J. Howard, CPCU, of Brandow-Howard-Cohler & Rosenbloom, Inc., in Minneapolis, Minnesota, has been successful in directing agency support personnel to increase the effectiveness of his personal sales efforts. Employees flag the file of each personal-lines client who has purchased a single coverage—homeowners, for example. Frank Howard takes the time to review these flagged files and then arranges to discuss the total insurance needs of each of these pre-identified clients. This discussion reveals details concerning the life-style, recreational activities, vacation plans, family background, community involvement, and business interests of each of these clients, often disclosing gaps in the client's insurance program. After drawing the insured's attention to these gaps, Frank Howard is frequently able to convince the client of the benefits of using one agency to handle an entire, coordinated insurance program.

Through this method, Frank Howard found that one of his clients housed the treasury of a community fund-raising endeavor at home in cash, that the insured owned a snowmobile, that the insured used rental cars regularly, that the insured owned a yacht, that the insured had greatly underestimated the value of jewelry housed at home, and that, because of political and community activities, the insured was exposed to libel and slander losses. Because agency personnel flagged this file, Frank Howard had the opportunity to put together a customized insurance program and significantly increase the amount of premium dollars generated by this single client.

One large Cincinnati agency is organized in such a way that new producers do not service an account after it has been sold. Instead, a "servicing producer" accompanies the producer on the initial sales call. Generally, after the sale is closed, the servicing producer delivers the policy. The sales producer goes on to the next account. In this way, sound customer service is assured and clients do not have the disquieting feeling that they have been deserted after the sale has been made.

Management Advisers, Inc., of Indianapolis, Indiana, has an organizational structure that stresses staff specialization. The agency is made up of numerous separate departments—marketing, sales, placing accounts, and customer service. The agency attributes its success to the effective use of personnel through specialization. The agency has a sales manager who has the overall responsibility for the sales function. The agency hires producers with sales ability and relies on the rest of the organization to provide producers with technical backup and support.

Producers must be comfortable with the management system and style used in the agencies. If an agency runs smoothly, producers are freed of many worries and can devote their time and energies to their specialty—selling.

Checkpoints

1. Describe the functions in the management process.
2. Explain where the management process
   a. begins,
   b. ends,
   c. flows.
3. Explain if the management process is the same for an agency and insurance company.
4. Explain if all agencies should operate in the same way.

SALES MANAGEMENT

Sales management—the application of the management process to selling—is considered part of a broader field, marketing management. *Marketing is human activity directed at satisfying needs and wants through exchange processes.*[2] Marketing management has been defined as

> . . . the analysis, planning, implementation, and control of programs designed to bring about desired exchanges with target markets for

> the purpose of achieving organizational objectives. It relies heavily on designing the organization's offering in terms of the target market's needs and desires and using effective pricing, communications, and distribution to inform, motivate, and service the market.[3]

Clearly, producers are frequently and heavily involved with many aspects of marketing management. The nature and amount of that involvement will vary widely depending on the size and the kind of marketing organization with which the producer is associated. Distribution is a primary and constant marketing management function performed by producers. Product design, on the other hand, has been traditionally viewed as an insurer function—though producers can and do influence product design. In addition, producers can do much to customize insurance products through the imaginative use of deductibles and endorsements or, in some cases, through the preparation of manuscript policies.

The emphasis here will be on applying the management process—planning, organizing, staffing, directing, and controlling—to the sales element in marketing management, that is, to the distribution of insurance products and services through "... promotional presentations conducted on a person-to-person basis with the buyer."[4]

Sales Planning

Producers and their activities are affected by two types of sales planning—agency planning and personal planning. The planning which is usually performed annually for an entire agency begins with the mission and strategies for the agency. Agency-wide goals, objectives, budgets, policies, and procedures, all stem from and are intended to contribute to the achievement of the plan. The sales planning an individual producer performs should be a coordinated part of agency-wide plans. In a small, one-producer agency, agency planning and personal planning are basically one.

Agency Sales Planning An example will make clear the relationship between agency planning and individual planning. A relatively large agency might set as its sales goal the production of enough business during a year to generate $1 million in commission income. It is possible that one objective aimed at achieving this goal would be the installation of a minicomputer and the automation of much of the agency's billing and other clerical systems so that the office could profitably handle the paper flow from this volume of business. The agency manager might devote much time and energy to the achievement of this objective. The sales manager, however, would be given the $1 million commission income figure as the agency-wide sales goal. It would be up to the sales manager to work with the agency's individual producers to see to it that the sum of the producers' personal sales goals will result in achievement of the agency's sales goals. *How* the sales manager achieves the coordinated overall goal will vary from agency to agency. Some sales managers may never inform producers of the agency-wide goal and encourage producers to set personal goals on their own. Other sales managers may meet with all the producers in the agency as a group, announce the agency-wide goal, and assign a personal sales goal to each producer. In either case, responsibility for achievement of the personal sales goal will rest with the individual producer. For this reason, personal sales planning is an important part of each producer's job.

Personal Sales Planning The personal sales planning an individual producer performs should include the phases of all management planning—establishing a personal mission statement; developing strategies, goals and objectives; preparing budgets; developing sales policies; and setting procedures. But much of this may be accomplished in a very flexible, informal way.

Whether the producer or the agency's management sets the producer's overall sales goal for the year, once that figure is set it is necessary to establish subordinate, more specific objectives which will contribute to the achievement of the overall goal. These objectives should be expressed in terms of amount of business and kind of business and should be reviewed periodically throughout the annual planning period—quarterly, perhaps. These specific sales goals and objectives should be directly tied to and coordinated with market analysis, segmentation, and targeting.

A *market* is a collection of potential clients that can be subdivided into distinct groups on the basis of criteria established by the producer. A *market segment* is a specifically defined portion of a market. *Market segmentation* is the process of dividing a market into smaller groups of similar prospects. *Product targeting* is designing a special product for a market, a special approach to a market or both. For instance, a producer's auto insurance market might include everyone who drives a car and lives within a pre-defined geographical territory. Each individual in this group would be a *suspect* for auto insurance. In marketing, a *suspect* is defined as a member of a market. The producer, however, may intend to sell auto insurance only as part of a complete personal-lines insurance program. If so, it would be necessary to further subdivide the auto insurance market to target members of it who are also homeowners or tenants. In addition, if a personal umbrella policy is to be part of the personal-lines program offered by the producer, a minimum annual income of, for instance, $30,000, might be an additional market criterion established by the producer. Ultimately, the producer will have targeted a relatively narrow group of *prospects,* those suspects whom the producer intends to approach.

A second look at this example may underscore the relationship between agency sales planning and personal sales planning. It is possible that selling a complete personal-lines program was one of the strategies devised through agency planning. If this is the case, it is possible that the producer was assigned the goal of selling fifty personal-lines policies during the year on a "top-down" basis, that is, the producer's goal was set by the agency's management. On the other hand, it is possible that the producer set as part of a personal sales plan the goal of generating 40 percent of the producer's annual commission income through personal-lines sales on a "bottom-up" basis, that is, the personal-lines goal was set by the producer and approved by the agency's management. In either case, achieving the goal remains the producer's responsibility and personal sales planning should help the producer fulfill this responsibility.

The flexibility and informality inherent in personal sales planning can also be seen through consideration of this example. For instance, it is possible that the producer set this personal-lines goal because of a sales *strategy,* a way of achieving the goal, the producer wishes to use. It could be that one of the producer's commercial-lines accounts is a large manufacturing firm which recently moved into the producer's area. Because of the producer's relationship with the management of this firm, the producer plans to achieve part of the new personal-lines goal by offering the agency's personal-lines insurance program to the executives and managers of this manufacturing firm. If so, the producer's prospects would be clearly and narrowly targeted as the members of the managerial staff of one of the producer's commercial-lines accounts.

Should the producer fail to meet the goal through these prospects, it would be necessary to formulate a new strategy that would result in a new kind of market segmentation, transforming an additional number of suspects (those homeowners and tenants in the area who drive cars and earn $30,000 or more per year) into prospects (perhaps those homeowners and tenants in the area who drive cars, earn $30,000 or more per year, and place some portion of their personal-lines business through the producer).

Exhibit 2-5 illustrates another example of market segmentation and targeting. The outer circle in Exhibit 2-5 represents a segmented market—in this case, the individuals with a residence exposure. That market is further segmented into (1) residences that qualify for homeowners insurance, (2) residences valued at more than $100,000, and (3) the target market, residences valued at more than $100,000

Exhibit 2-5
Residence Insurance Market

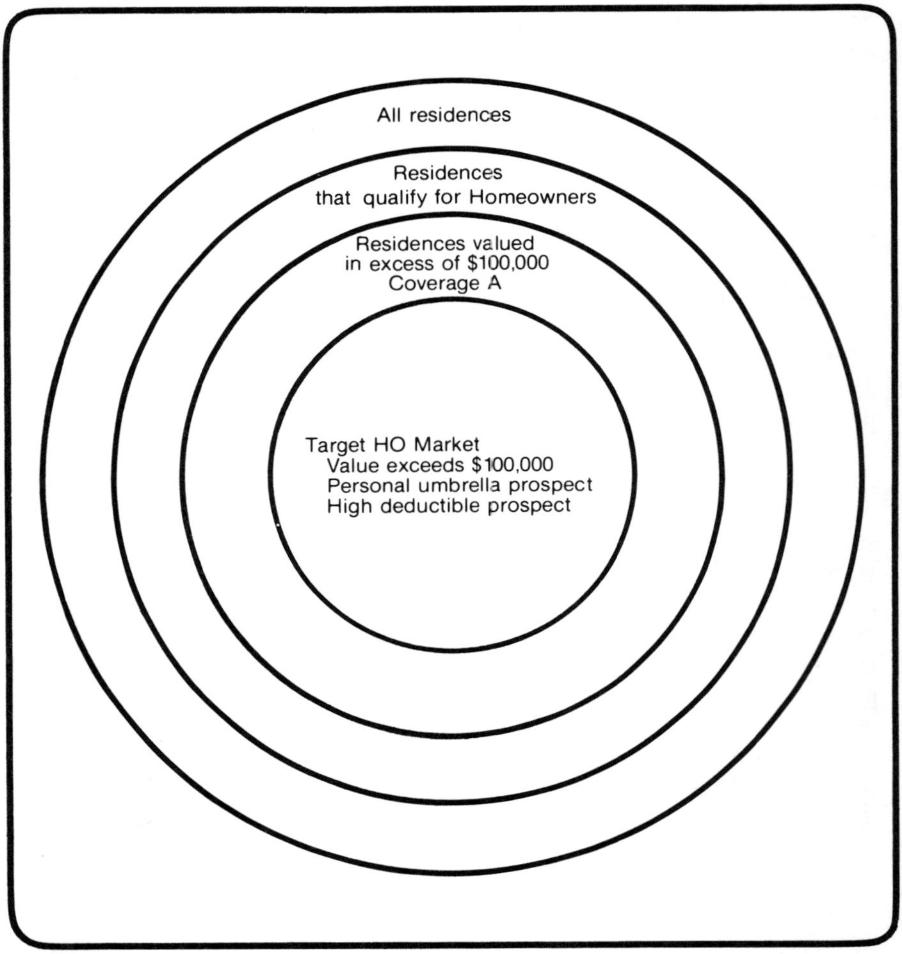

whose owners need catastrophe (umbrella) liability coverage and can afford a high deductible.

Personal sales planning should coordinate strategies, goals, objectives, budgets, policies, and procedures with market analysis, segmentation, and targeting. Sales strategies, goals, and objectives should guide market segmentation to targeting prospects. Once prospects are identified, a sales approach must be devised. The producer may decide to approach some prospects with a cold call, dropping in unannounced. The producer may choose to first approach other prospects with a letter. There are literally dozens of ways producers introduce themselves, their organizations, and their products and services to prospects. The agency's and the producer's sales procedures and policies should help shape the way the producer approaches prospects.

Sales Planning and Market Segmentation Cases The effectiveness of sales planning and market segmentation can probably be made most clear by relating actual cases of their use by successful producers and agencies.

The McTeague Agency in Reynoldsburg, Ohio, used Welcome Wagon as a market segmentation device. The agency arranged with Welcome Wagon to deliver a welcome gift from the McTeague Agency to all individuals who moved into pre-selected neighborhoods. Through pre-selection of the neighborhoods, the agency was able to segment the market so that the agency's gift and message reached those individuals whom the agency wished to approach as personal-lines prospects. After the Welcome Wagon visitor called on a home, the McTeague Agency was provided with a card by Welcome Wagon which stated the results of the visit. Bill McTeague reports that the Welcome Wagon approach was a good way for him to "get his feet wet" in the business while simultaneously generating profitable business.

Very general approaches can be useful, too. Ellis Crotty Powers & Co., an agency in Dallas, sends an attractive brochure to a wide audience of potential clients. The brochure describes all the services available through the agency and is accompanied by a letter that states when a producer will call. The same agency also uses market segmentation, however, and designs approaches specifically for use with some market segments. For instance, the agency developed a mailing list of approximately 600 contractor prospects. Each of these prospects received a complimentary monthly newsletter specifically designed for the construction business from Ellis Crotty Powers & Co. (The agency purchased the newsletter from Insurance Marketing Services, Inc.) The newsletter serves several purposes. It introduces the agency to contractors by providing a service. It establishes the agency as a source of information and expertise. And, perhaps most importantly, it associates the agency in the mind of prospects with the construction business and the bonding and insurance problems which arise in the construction business. After prospects received the newsletter for a pre-determined period of time, the prospect was approached either through a cold call or a letter requesting an appointment.

Planning and market segmentation can also aid and be aided by an agency's advertising efforts. The Bennett-Shade Agency in Decatur, Illinois, uses billboards to inform the public that the agency is interested in personal-lines business. The bulk of the billboard is used to identify the agency. About one-third of the billboard provides a specific personal-lines message which changes every sixty days. Through this changing message, the public is informed of the various types of personal-lines exposures and comes to identify these insurance needs with the Bennett-Shade Agency. The agency's producers are able to obtain identification rapidly by enclosing a reproduction of one of the billboards with a letter to a prospect that states that the producer will call on a specific day.

These examples are just a few of the ways planning and market segmentation have been effectively used to help agencies and producers devise approaches to prospects which contribute to the achievement of sales goals.

Checkpoints

1. Define:
   a. marketing
   b. marketing management
   c. sales management
   d. face-to-face (or personal) selling
2. Explain if the management process is useful in sales management.
3. Describe planning in sales management.
4. Define:
   a. markets
   b. market segmentation
   c. suspects
   d. prospects

Organizing and the Producer Organizing is dividing all the work which needs to be performed into manageable units. For the producer, organizing applies to both the producer's personal activities and to those activities that may be performed by agency staff members who either report to the producer or who perform functions closely tied to the producer's activities—placing the business the producer writes, maintaining files on the producer's clients, and so on. In either case, the producer's aim must be to organize in such a way that the producer can (1) devote the time to selling which is necessary if sales goals are to be met, (2) efficiently obtain the information the producer needs to sell the agency's products and services (renewal dates, mailing list of prospects, and so on), and (3) provide—directly or through others—the desired level of service to clients. Perhaps the most important aspect of organizing for the producer is that the producer should be familiar with the agency's personnel and operations so that the producer can perform effectively both through selling and through delivering service to clients, one of the best ways to sell renewals and keep the producer's clients on the books.

Staffing and the Producer Most producers devote little time to staffing. In a small agency, there are few positions to fill. In a large agency, staffing is usually one of the duties of the agency manager. Nonetheless, producers should be aware of their responsibility for orienting, training, and developing those agency employees who work for or with them. Achievement of personal sales goals, to a large extent, depends on the quality of the agency's clerical, administrative, or technical personnel.

Directing and the Producer Directing can play an important role in the producer's ability to achieve sales goals. Some producers successfully direct agency staff members to perform important background and backup work to their sales efforts. Market segmentation and targeting, direct mail approaches to prospects, and the image of the agency projected through telephone conversations and personal contacts between clients and the agency's staff are all important functions that may be delegated by the producer. If delegated functions are to be performed properly, the producer must take some responsibility for motivating employees and coordinating their duties.

In addition, directing—like all the functions in the management process—can be applied by producers to their personal sales effort. The producer can strive toward self-motivation and coordination of efforts. Many producers establish systems of rewards for self-motivational purposes. For instance, a producer may establish a quarterly long-weekend vacation as a personal reward for each quarter in which personal sales goals are achieved. An awareness of the need for the coordination leads some producers to keep excellent records of sales calls which may reduce duplicative efforts and eventually suggest new sales strategies. Producers should be aware of the elements in directing—delegating, motivating, coordinating, managing differences, and managing change—and recognize that these management activities can be profitably applied to an agency's staff and to the way producers approach the sales function.

Controlling and the Producer Though control of an agency's overall sales function often rests with a sales manager, producers must control their individual efforts to achieve the personal sales goals set through planning. Personal sales goals aid in the development of personal performance standards—standards which may directly or indirectly determine a producer's financial rewards.

Producers should establish and maintain a personal record that details how many letters or phone calls its takes to get an appointment, how many appointments it takes to make a sale, the average premium per sale, and other information that will be useful as a measure of results. Such a record will help producers analyze the way they spend their time, the effectiveness of their sales strategies, and also contribute to future planning sessions.

Consider the Producer Activity Record that appears in Exhibit 2-6. From previous experience, it is determined that it took the producer 815 phone calls to reach 635 people who had previously been contacted by mail. Appointments were made with 293 people who were sent letters during the quarter and with 40 individuals who had been contacted in previous periods and who had provided the producer with expiration dates (X-dates) but who had not yet been called on by the producer. The producer learned the expiration dates of 173 people who were contacted by mail during the period but who did not grant appointments. Sales were made to 98 people who had received letters and granted appointments during this period and to 77 people who had received letters and made appointments in previous periods. The average premiums on sales to both these groups were about the same.

A Producer Activity Record of this type can help producers set performance standards, measure results, take corrective action when necessary, and serve as the basis for a personal system of motivational rewards. The record can help in the development of performance standards that reflect the next period's goals, too. For instance, assume the producer's sales goals for the next quarter were 100 sales from that quarter's letters and 100 sales from prospects with previously obtained expiration dates. The performance standards that should achieve these objectives appear in Exhibit 2-7.

If it took 635 letters to arrange 293 appointments that resulted in 98 sales, it can be projected that to achieve 100 sales during the next quarter should require 649 letters resulting in 299 appointments. Similarly, to achieve 100 sales from prospects with known X-dates should require 182 appointments from the 285 such prospects on file. If results improve, that is, if a greater number of sales result from fewer appointments, an adjustment can be made in future plans to reflect this change. On the other hand, if results deteriorate, corrective action may be necessary and the kind of action necessary may be suggested by the Producer Activity Record.

Producers should use measures and controls that reflect the strategies, goals, and objectives developed in planning. Constant checks on progress toward goals will contribute to the achievement of those

Exhibit 2-6
Producer Activity Record

1/1/X1 — 3/31/X1

Activity	Result	Percent
Letters sent	635	100.0
Phone calls to addressees (includes call backs)	815	128.3
Appointments from letters	293	46.1
Non-appointment X-dates	173	27.2
Appointments from X-dates	140	63.9
Previous period—219		
Sales from letters	98	15.4
Percent of appointments	98/293	33.4
Sales from X-dates	77	55.0
Average premiums from letters	$318	
Average premiums from X-dates	$309	

goals. Controlling, the last function in the management process, contributes to planning, the function with which the process begins, thus completing the cycle and beginning the cycle again.

SELLING

Selling requires product knowledge, market knowledge, and knowledge of selling techniques. Much of AAI 81 and 82 is devoted to product knowledge. The discussion of sales management in this chapter should aid producers in developing market knowledge. The remainder of this chapter will introduce selling techniques. However, selling techniques must be practiced and evaluated to be useful. Producers are encouraged to invest in a course that concentrates on the development of selling techniques.

Exhibit 2-7
Producer Performance Standards

4/1/81—6/30/81				
Activity			Result	Percent
Sales from letters			100	
Ratio of sales to appointments previous period				33.4
Appointments needed,	$\frac{100}{.334}$	=	299	
Ratio of appointments to letter				46.1
Letters needed,	$\frac{299}{.461}$	=	649	
Sales from X-dates			100	
Ratio of sales to appointments previous period				55.0
Appointments needed,	$\frac{100}{.55}$	=	182	
Ratio of appointments to X-date files				63.9
X-date files needed,	$\frac{182}{.639}$	=	285	

Selling and the Producer

Salespersons add a dimension to the products and services they sell. In many cases, when consumers see all products as similar or undifferentiated (substitutes for each other), the salesperson can make the product different. Similarly, a producer who uses a professional approach to solving client problems can make seemingly undifferentiated insurance policies actually different through the service performed. As a general statement, a professional approach is one that applies the salesperson's product to satisfy customer needs.

Selling Techniques There are three different selling techniques. Each can be found in insurance selling.[5] No one technique is necessarily better than another. The planning and goals of individual producers determine the selling technique that should be used. Further, no one producer uses one technique to the exclusion of the others.

Order Processing. When customer needs are immediately recognized by the customer, order processing is an excellent technique. It can be successfully used in the insurance business at renewal. It should be used with caution, however, for it may lead producers to miss potential sales opportunities. In order processing, the producer identifies a need (renewal of automobile insurance), points out the need (calls the client or sends a bill), and takes the order (renews the policy).

Creative Selling. Persuasion is paramount in creative selling. Client needs that are not obvious to the customer must be brought to the customer's attention in a logical way. The producer shows how the suggested policy meets those needs. Creative selling is used most frequently in a risk exposure based sale. A customer's needs are highlighted and a package is designed for those needs. Creative selling is the kind of selling that will be analyzed and discussed here.

Missionary Selling. Missionary selling is indirect selling that establishes the goodwill of an organization through technical services to clients and potential clients. Its most frequent use in insurance is through consulting or risk management services, often provided on a fee basis. The goodwill of the agency is established when customers are provided with technical or operational assistance.

Calling on Prospects When the time for face-to-face contact arises, there are two methods to employ. The first method involves initial contact with a prospect by letter, telephone, or telegram. Then, an appointment is made with the prospect. The producer may make this face-to-face contact alone or with another representative of the agency. To add technical backup, joint calls may be used in training new producers, or to introduce office personnel to a client with whom they may deal in the future.

The second method is to call on a prospect without an appointment, or "cold calling." Cold calls are difficult to make, but they provide the producer an opportunity to "practice" selling and may generate business.

The right method is the one that fits the producer's plans. Successful producers recognize both methods as effective when used properly—to fit plans and meet the goals of the producer.

Joint Calls. For the new producer, it is a good idea to make joint calls. The joint call allows a new producer to see how a successful producer sells, allows the successful producer to guide, coach, and criticize the sales techniques of the new producer, and it has other potential benefits. Staff members who will service the account can go along for introduction. The adage "two heads are better than one" serves as the impetus for a team call. Milford Robinson, CPCU, of Management Advisors, Inc., reports:

> We rely heavily on the joint call approach. The joint call can be of one or two types. The first is one in which two partners from our agency make a call on a prospect or insured to take full advantage of the "two heads are better than one" philosophy. This type of call is made purely for effect and to add a second party to back up the producer in any area where he may not feel totally adequate. The other type of joint call is one in which, again two people are present, but one of the two is a person who will be making the call—the other is there simply as an observer. This is most often done with the producer and the sales manager, but quite frequently may be done with a senior producer and a relatively new producer. The second party's function on these calls is to make mental notes of the primary producer's actions and approach so as to give him a reading on those things which he did well and those things which he, in the opinion of the second party, did not do well. We find this exercise to be both effective in terms of sales success and enjoyable on the part of the two people involved in the sense that it does give them an opportunity to see someone else in action. Often both the observed and the observer benefit from the experience.

Cold Calls Milford Robinson reports that the majority of their joint calls are also cold calls. Milford Robinson understands that cold calls are the least effective method of approaching customers, but "it does work occasionally and, more importantly, gives the salesperson and sales manager an opportunity to develop confidence and experience in selling the insurance service in the most difficult sales situation."

For an individual producer, the cold call gives the opportunity to practice sales techniques, but can also be a "time filler." It is a technique that can be used effectively by either the new or experienced producer. Jim Franklin, Jr., was an experienced producer in Georgia. He moved to Florida and joined the Lanier Upshaw Agency in Lakeland. As Jim Franklin did not need to spend a substantial amount of time learning coverages, he chose to fill his time by making cold calls in the Lakeland area. He had no personal contacts in the town. He spent his first two months with a tape recorder in his car exploring the cities in the area. He placed names and addresses of businesses into a recorder, later extracting them and arranging them not only in alphabetical order but also cross-referencing them with a particular part of town. Jim Franklin reports:

> My pride and joy was my "black book" that all this information ended up in ultimately. Each prospective business account was listed in its appropriate section with pertinent information such as owners' names, addresses, telephone numbers, and a brief summary of the business itself. Keep in mind that I had physically seen each prospect and could summarize as far as housekeeping, etc. If I happened to be in the northeast section of town with a spare hour or so of time, I

> could look in the northeast geographic section of my manual, select one or two prospects that were nearby, turn over to the alphabetical information on the prospective business and then make the call with the necessary confidence to achieve an expected level of success.

Jim Franklin entered in his "black book" the date of call, the results, and the name of one person with whom he spoke. His goal was to obtain expiration dates of current policies and the name of the present agent and company. Within twenty-four hours after the call, he sent a personal follow-up letter, thanking the prospect for the visit. He then could give a quote on the business. He found the cold call method successful and recounts:

> During the first four months, I made slightly over 500 calls and secured approximately 150 expiration dates. The surprising thing I found was that contractors, small manufacturing plants, etc., were much more receptive to accepting quotes on their insurance program than the small retail stores. In retrospect, I feel that any person can make cold calls if he prepares himself psychologically for the possibility of rejection. If he realizes beforehand that out of every ten calls made, he will pick up between three and four expiration dates, the unpleasantness of rejection is greatly diminished.

Jim Franklin knew that his reward would be the ultimate generation of sales. But he also realized that it would take a relatively high number of cold calls to generate a sale. For new producers, with time available, deciding to make five cold calls each week can be a worthwhile goal. But it may also be useful to combine goal setting with a personal system of motivational rewards. That is, a producer may establish, in advance, a reward—an afternoon off or dinner at a special restaurant, for example—if the goal of making five cold calls within one week is achieved. Some producers find personal motivational reward systems useful in many of their activities.

Needs Based Selling The premise of a face-to-face sales call is that the customer has a need the salesperson's product can fill. If there is no genuine need, the sales call is inappropriate. The customer does not necessarily know a need exists. It is up to the salesperson to uncover the need, but the total sale must satisfy the customer's need. To satisfy the need, the salesperson points out an applicable feature of the product. When a product feature can be applied to the customer need, the feature becomes a benefit for the customer—the need is satisfied and the customer is motivated to buy. Selling techniques should be designed to uncover as many needs of the customer as possible so that the salesperson can close and complete the sale.

To illustrate the difference between a *product feature* and a *product benefit,* consider a standard porcelain covered metal cooking container suitable for home canning of fruits and vegetables. Such a device could be perceived to have the following *features:* (1) constructed principally of metal for use on any cooking surface, (2) covered with porcelain for heat distribution and reduction of oxidation, (3) containing a wire basket to separate glass canning containers from the heating surface, and (4) sufficient size to handle up to seven one-half gallon glass containers. Each of these items is a feature, *an attribute of the product.*

In order to make a needs-based sale, the salesperson must *use these inherent features of the product to satisfy a need of the customer* considering such a purchase. A customer looking for a pot large enough to make homemade soup, for instance, would not be interested in the capacity of the container as it relates to canning but more as it relates to the volume of soup that could be made at any one time. Therefore, the feature of holding up to seven one-half gallon containers *would not* be a benefit for this particular customer. However, a customer whose pot just rusted through after two years of use would see the porcelain covering as a benefit. The customer canning principally in half-gallon sizes would be very interested in the large capacity. When a *product feature suits an individual's need, the feature is a benefit.*

Motivation theory suggests that one cannot motivate by appealing to a satisfied need. For instance, all people have a need for food, but it would be difficult, if not impossible, to motivate someone by offering a seven-course dinner immediately after he or she completes an excellent meal. A satisfied need cannot be used to motivate; only unsatisfied needs are motivational.

The Flow of a Sales Call Any face-to-face sales call will have identifiable parts to it. First, the salesperson must present benefits (product features that satisfy a prospect's needs), work with the prospect's reactions to the benefits, and finally, close the sale. Each part of the sales call requires a separate skill. A skill is defined as *applied knowledge.*

Individual Selling Skills

Presentation of Benefits Ideally the producer will have some knowledge of the insurance needs of the prospect prior to the call. The preexisting knowledge may have come from the producer's study of the prospect or from some other source. But some needs must exist. Unless the prospect has a need and the producer's product can satisfy the need, there is no reason to make the call.

Prospect Mentions a Need. In the purchase of insurance, the prospect must feel comfortable with the producer and have trust in the producer and the services offered. If a prospect mentions a need, it is a good idea to assume that some level of trust exists. When the prospect mentions a need the producer can satisfy, a sound psychological idea is to agree that the need is important and then mention how the producer or the insurance policy offered will meet the need.

By agreeing with the prospect's need, the producer is "tied" to the service offered. A relationship is built between the parties. The producer is showing concern and consideration for the prospect's point of view. The agreement shows the prospect that the producer is listening and understanding the needs. It reinforces the producer's role as the need satisfier, and shows the prospect that the insurance producer and service offered are needed.

For illustrative purposes, assume a producer is trying to sell a personal umbrella liability policy to Ms. Jones, a corporate vice president who earns $40,000 a year. The producer is also trying to sell an accountant an office package. Both of these situations will be used to show how statements could be used.

In the sales call with Ms. Jones, she may say, "I do a substantial amount of traveling to our plant in Mexico. As you know, American auto insurance is not valid there, but I still need protection." The producer introduces a benefit by saying, "You are wise to recognize that a judgment in Mexico can be as destructive to your financial health as one here in the United States. That is why the umbrella we offer has worldwide coverage. We would respond to a Mexican judgment as we would to one in Texas." The accountant may be less specific in his statement: "It takes a long time to create worksheets and audit trails. Yet, their existence is vital to my work with my clients." The producer can respond to the implied need, "The expense to reconstruct detailed financial records can be enormous if all were destroyed. Crowley Fire and Marine has available a valuable papers option that would help you by paying for the costs of recreating those documents." These statements illustrate how opportunities to serve the prospect and to build the necessary empathy and trust between the producer and the prospect can be used to make the sale.

Prospect Does Not Mention a Need. On a cold call or in any communication where a producer is before the customer for the first time, it may not be possible to have customers state their needs. But even on a cold call, an assumed need can be stated. Perhaps the salesperson is familiar with problems people in the prospect's business have. This could come from information developed during the market segmentation activities of a producer, prior research on the company or person, a newspaper article, a conversation at a party or any one of a number of sources. The more accurate the assumed need is, the more likely the customer or prospect will be receptive to it.

When the producer must assume a need in order to present a benefit, it is best not to aim remarks directly at the prospect, because if the assumption is incorrect, the relationship between the prospect and producer is diminished. For the vice president, the producer may say:

> Ms. Jones, many successful executives have worked hard to build up an estate. An accident caused by a successful person can bring on a lawsuit and a judgment in an amount not only exceeding primary insurance limits, but also larger than average because of the obvious success of the individual causing the accident. The personal umbrella policy of Crowley Fire and Marine is designed to protect these people for an amount of $1 million dollars in excess of whatever primary limits exist.

The statement was related to executives in general. Ms. Jones was not referred to personally. The insurer (it could have been the agency) was introduced, and a feature of the umbrella was introduced. There was no listing of all provisions (features) of the policy. The statement was a rifle approach at an assumed need. The same technique might be used with the accountant:

> Mr. Smith, a lot of CPAs would rather spend their valuable time serving their clients than watching over the detail of their own operations. My agency, along with Crowley Fire and Marine, has designed an insurance plan for the offices of professionals that is so complete CPAs can concentrate on their profession and know that their own operations are protected.

Again, details are left unmentioned at this point. Mr. Smith is given the feature of time savings—time to concentrate on what he does best.

There is one other time this type of statement can be used in a sales call, — when the prospect becomes reluctant to talk. Generally, a good sales presentation allows prospects to bring up *their* problems and *their* needs. The salesperson responds with corresponding benefits.

When prospects do not want to talk, however, the producer must introduce new features of the product.

Asking Questions Another vital skill a producer must learn is when and how to ask questions. Questions are of two types—nonleading questions or leading questions.

Nonleading Questions. A nonleading question is one that allows the prospect to respond in any manner on any subject. The purpose of the nonleading question is to urge the customer to talk.

Needs selling establishes the producer as the problem solver for the prospect. Needs selling requires that needs be identified so that the producer may respond to them. When a prospect is talking freely or the producer feels that the prospect is about to reveal an important bit of information, the nonleading question is appropriate. For instance, Ms. Jones says, "Well, it sounds good, but one thing bothers me." It appears Ms. Jones has some unsatisfied need and is willing to talk about it. The producer could respond with a nonleading question such as, "Oh?" or "What would that be?" The two samples show that the response is open for the prospect. It encourages the prospect to talk and reveal his or her concern.

Leading Questions. A leading question calls for a specific, limited response. The producer uses leading questions to guide the prospect to a selected subject of considerations.

In some cases, a prospect may be reluctant or unwilling to talk. In other cases, based on prior knowledge or an assumption of need, the producer wants to guide the prospect to a specific topic. In these situations, the leading question is ideal. The best questions are based on clues to subject areas the prospect is interested in. The clues may be picked up in conversation, by observation, or they may come from pre-call research. The leading question must be based on an intelligent guess at what interests the prospect. For instance, the accountant has become reluctant to talk, but the producer knows that a client of the CPA has recently had a large uninsured business interruption loss. Based on that knowledge, the producer can construct a leading question toward the prospect's business interruption exposures:

> Do you ever encounter problems in which a successful business goes out of operation because a fire (tornado, ice storm, or whatever) makes it impossible to continue vital day-to-day operations?

Responses to leading questions are usually short, in many cases limited to a simple "yes" or "no." The producer has selected the topic of discussion and guided the prospect to that subject. The area of discussion should be one that the producer's policy or service can handle. If the prospect responds:

> You know, I just had a situation where a client of mine had a fire. Fire insurance could replace the building, but because the client was a dairy, it could not deliver milk for three months. It had to go out of business because its customers needed milk and went to another dairy. My client could not get that business back in time to save the company.

At this point, the producer can respond by agreeing and illustrating how business interruption insurance could protect the CPA's business.

As a general rule, initial questions should be nonleading. The producer should try to get the prospect to reveal needs and talk openly. If the prospect is not talking, questions should become leading; but when the prospect begins to open up again, the questions should return to the nonleading type.

Rarely does a producer find a prospect who responds favorably to being "led by the nose" with leading questions. Agility in moving from leading to nonleading questions and back again is an essential skill in selling. The need for this agility and the use of the right words reinforces the necessity for the producer to take a sales course and not rely on the description of skills presented here.

A final comment on questioning relates to the universality of the skill. Psychologists, social workers, family counselors, and marriage counselors all agree that communication among individuals is the most vital aspect of living and growing together. Knowing how to question and when to ask the proper type of question is a universal skill that can improve office, family, and community relations. Properly learned and executed, it is an efficient way to learn the problems and needs of anyone or any organization.

Prospect's Reactions The selection of an appropriate question necessitates that the producer be constantly aware of the reactions of the prospect. If the reaction is one of cooperation, a nonleading question can be used. If the reaction is reluctance to talk, the leading question is more appropriate. A flexible set of sales skills will also allow producers to enter any sales call without having to rely on a "canned" sales presentation. In order to be flexible, identification of customer reaction is vital. There are five reactions that will be found in analyzing sales calls:

1. Agreement
2. Disbelief
3. Indifference
4. Objections
5. Delay

Agreement. When the prospect agrees that features presented are suited to his or her situation and there are no questions, the reaction appears to be one of agreement. At that point, the producer should close. Closing will be discussed later. This assumes that some benefits have been mentioned and accepted as relevant by the prospect. There is no need to attempt to relate each feature of the policy or service being sold to the prospect. Just enough benefits should be present so that the producer feels comfortable. Exactly what constitutes "enough benefits" will vary from producer and from situation to situation. When the salesperson feels there is agreement, closing should occur.

Disbelief. Disbelief is doubt—doubt that the policy can or will perform as indicated. When disbelief is encountered, some form of proof will have to be offered by the producer. A simple, "I will show you it is true" will not suffice. Psychologically, it is best to first rephrase the feature under discussion. This shows that the producer is listening carefully, considering the prospect's needs and problems, and understanding that the prospect's needs are paramount.

After rephrasing the feature, proof can be offered. The producer should include any facts, figures, testimonials, or other objective information that shows the prospect that the policy will perform in the manner indicated. The producer should not use personal proofs such as, "It has been my experience..." or "In my case..." as that tends to personalize the doubt and make the situation potentially argumentative.

If a proof is rejected, the producer must find out why. A nonleading question should be used to determine why the proof was rejected. A proof can be rejected for a number of reasons. The prospect may not like or approve of the proof source cited, the testimonial given, or any number of similar reasons. A prudent producer would, in that case, switch to a different proof source for the second proof statement.

In our previous example, Ms. Jones may have indicated that she heard American insurance was not valid in Mexico. A proof statement handling that disbelief could be:

> Ms. Jones, if you are considering catastrophe liability insurance, it is important to know if the coverage is truly worldwide. Here is a copy of the policy. You can read here in the contract that there are no territorial limitations as there are in the auto policy. What that means to you is that if the limits of your auto policy purchased in Mexico prove to be inadequate, this policy will pick up the next one million dollars.

Perhaps the accountant does not believe that a business interruption form is available without having to reveal what he considers proprietary income information:

> I can understand why in a competitive business like yours you would not want to reveal billing information. Here is an article from the *Journal of Information* that describes the type of policy I am offering—one in which you select your monthly business interruption indemnity amount. The article goes on to say that the selected amount is the policy limit at time of loss. You can see then that your privacy is protected and your profits insured.

Proper proof is the best response to doubt.

Indifference. The attitude of "who cares?" is perhaps the most difficult reaction to deal with. When a prospect is not interested, it means either that the prospect does not see a need for your policy or service or that the prospect is happy with his or her current producer. In this case, the producer must use questions to uncover areas of need or areas of dissatisfaction with the current product. The prospect is not interested and must be led to areas of need or dissatisfaction. By definition, *leading the prospect* means using leading questions. If there are no perceived needs, the prospect cannot openly discuss those things that cannot be seen. If the prospect is happy, nonleading questions will reveal the happiness and not disclose areas of dissatisfaction.

Leading questions, based on educated guesses as to needs or possible areas of dissatisfaction, are essential. Pre-call research would be helpful in determining the types of needs or areas of dissatisfaction that may exist. No one wants to admit a mistake in a purchase. Therefore, leading questions must be tactfully stated.

Objections. When salespersons meet, one universal topic of conversation is how to handle objections. When objections arise in a sales call, they must be dealt with immediately. Ignoring objections allows the prospect to concentrate on the objection and ignore other comments the producer may be making. Objections fall into two classifications, each requiring a different technique. Objections may arise because of a *misunderstanding* or because of a *real disadvantage* of the producer's products or services. In either case, the first step is to rephrase the objection in the form of a question. The rephrasing shows attention but not agreement.

If an objection is a misunderstanding, it should be answered immediately after rephrasing the objection. If the objection is based on a real disadvantage, the objection should be restated in the form of a question in which the positive benefits are stressed. In other words, an objection based on a real disadvantage is a reason for the prospect not to buy. Stressing benefits takes the prospect through the policy and in effect shows that there are strong advantages to the prospect that outweigh this one disadvantage. In stressing benefits, use those that have been accepted—that are important to the prospect.

No one objection is inherently a misunderstanding or a real disadvantage. Assume that both Ms. Jones and Mr. Smith respond in the following manner, "I don't like your policy because it costs too much!" The cost objection is a misunderstanding for Ms. Jones and a real disadvantage for Mr. Smith. To handle Ms. Jones's objection the producer may say:

> If I understand you correctly you think the price is too high. Well, I am happy to tell you that this million dollar umbrella policy will have an annual premium of only $150.

The misunderstanding was treated by rephrasing the objection and giving a direct answer. Mr. Smith could be handled this way:

> You think the premium will be excessive, is that correct? Mr. Smith, do you agree that the value of "all-risks" coverage is better than named perils?
> Well, yes.
> And having all of your coverages in one package policy not only provides a rate credit, but also simplifies your handling of the insurance?
> Yes . . .
> Would it not be more expensive to go out of business because of no business interruption insurance—like the dairy?
> Well, sure . . .
> And Mr. Smith, isn't there real value to you in the valuable papers endorsement to this policy?

The technique could be continued until the producer is satisfied that Mr. Smith does see that the premium is reasonable for the total package of protection offered.

Delay. Many times the comments a prospect makes do not help a producer identify the prospect's reaction. Maybe the prospect says, "Well, I don't know. Let me think it over." Or, "I'll run this by a friend of mine. Call me next week." Obviously there is not agreement. But should this attitude be classified as disbelief, "who cares," or objection? In cases like this, or whenever the producer is not really sure of the prospect's attitude, it is appropriate to determine why the prospect is delaying. To determine the prospect's reaction, a series of questions is necessary. Whether they are leading or nonleading questions depends on the situation. The producer must uncover the reason for the delay and then handle the reaction. If the producer does not determine and handle the underlying attitude, there will be no opportunity to close.

Closing Closing is what the sales call is all about. Closing does not necessarily mean the sale is made. Rather it means that the *objective* of the sales call has been met. The objective of each call is based on the producer's marketing plan. It is not unusual in the property-liability business to make two or more calls on a prospect, each with a different objective. The first call could be to introduce the producer and to get expiration dates of current policies. The second call could be designed to obtain copies of current policies. The third call could be the sales call. It is important to have an objective for the call in advance. The techniques and words used in the closing depend on the objective.

Many successful salespersons say that if you can get the prospect to agree throughout the call, the sale will be made. Begin to close by summarizing those features of the policy or service that have been accepted by the prospect (start the head nodding yes), then request a commitment. Only the features that have been accepted by the prospect are summarized, not all of the features of the policy. Using the closing to introduce new features is inappropriate as it gives the prospect the opportunity to direct the conversation away from the commitment. Closing properly can be powerful. Ms. Jones, for instance, has expressed no further needs. The producer may close by saying:

> Ms. Jones, we have discussed the personal umbrella liability policy—how it adds a million dollar layer of protection on your existing coverage. It covers you worldwide—even in Mexico. It expands your homeowners protection from bodily injury to personal injury. It even provides you a million dollars of coverage where you do not now have coverage. All of this for only $150 a year! Ms. Jones, what is the name of your automobile insurer and what are your limits on the auto policy?

Note that both the summary and the requested policy application information flowed into each other. Some feel it is a good idea to use one of the benefits as part of the commitment request. Others feel it is better to give the prospect an alternative between two actions, both of which would mean the prospect will buy. Both of these ideas can be seen in the closing statement for the accountant:

> The beauty of your office facilities can be assured with the coverage I've described, Mr. Smith. "All-risks" coverage will mean it will be replaced for almost any cause of loss. The office package is simple in design and contains cost savings features for you. With the valuable papers endorsement your client's records and yours can be reconstructed. And if your office is destroyed, your payroll and profits are covered while you are spending time getting back into full operations. Do you want a $50,000 or $60,000 limit on your business interruption?

Concluding Comment The types of sales techniques described here will be found in almost any selling course available to producers. The important aspect of any sales approach is that it should increase the "batting average" of the producer by making the sale of a policy or service fit the needs of the prospect. It will be well worth the investment of time and money to take a course in the application of sales techniques.

Good training will help the producer become and remain successful. Selling is not easy. All of us "sell" at one time or another in our lives. Exhibit 2-8 lists eight major causes of failure. It will be clear from the list that this program can deal with *some* of these causes of failure—particularly the third most common cause, inadequate product knowledge. Courses in applied sales techniques can deal with others. Some of these causes of failure, however, can only be handled by an individual producer.

Checkpoints

1. Explain the three types of selling techniques.

Exhibit 2-8
Why Sales Personnel Fail*

Cause of Failure	Percent
Lack of initiative	55
Poor planning and organization	39
Inadequate product knowledge	37
Lack of enthusiasm	31
Salesman not customer-oriented	30
Lack of proper training	23
Inability to get along with buyers	21
Lack of personal goals	20

*Reprinted with permission from Louis E. Boone and David L. Kurtz, *Foundations of Marketing* (Hinsdale, IL: The Dryden Press, 1977), p. 370.

2. Contrast the two methods of face-to-face selling approaches.
3. Identify typical sales skills.
4. Explain the difference between
   a. leading and nonleading questions.
   b. customer reactions.
   c. a policy feature and a policy benefit.
5. Explain how use of the marketing management process can overcome two causes of sales failure.

SUMMARY

Management is achieving goals through others. The management process is an analysis and description of how managers achieve objectives through others. The functions in the management process are (1) planning, (2) organizing, (3) staffing, (4) directing, and (5) controlling. These functions can be directly related to the three elements with which all managers must deal—ideas (planning), things (organizing), and people (staffing, directing, and controlling). These three elements give rise to the three primary facets of the manager's job—conceptual thinking, administration, and leadership.

The management process can be applied to agency management and sales management. In either case, the process can be adapted to increase the effectiveness of agency-wide activities and activities performed by an individual producer. Use of the management process draws attention to the need to coordinate these two sets of activities. The planning phase of sales management relies heavily on market analysis, segmentation, and targeting.

Successful producers require product knowledge, market knowledge, and selling techniques. The second section of this chapter focuses on selling techniques. While selling techniques can be introduced in a textbook, producers are encouraged to take courses that analyze and critique producers' applications of selling techniques. The fundamental aims of face-to-face selling are to uncover and identify client needs and to satisfy those needs through specific features of the products and services offered. These aims are often achieved through the careful use of leading and nonleading questions. In addition to product knowledge, market knowledge, and selling techniques, successful producers often must have certain character traits—particularly initiative and persistence.

Chapter Notes

1. This discussion uses the updated classic formulation illustrated by R. Alec Mackenzie, "The Management Process in 3-D," *Harvard Business Review* (November–December 1969), pp. 80–87.
2. Philip Kotler, *Marketing Management,* 3rd ed. (Englewood Cliffs, NJ: Prentice-Hall, 1976), p. 5.
3. Kotler, p. 7.
4. Louis E. Boone and David L. Kurtz, *Foundations of Marketing* (Hinsdale, IL: The Dryden Press, 1977), p. 318.
5. Boone and Kurtz, pp. 368–369.

CHAPTER 3

Legal Concepts and Liability

INTRODUCTION

Insurance is closely tied to the legal system. The concept of negligence involves a court's determination of whether one's action is reasonable and prudent, often the direct issue in liability insurance. The concepts of agency and other contractual agreements form the basis for producer relations between the insurer and its representatives. Ownership, legal title, and possession form the basis for insurable interest. Such topics are a major concern in property insurance. A producer must possess a reasonable understanding of certain legal topics in order to function effectively. All too often the producer is called upon to give advice and make a judgment for the client in an area that requires a reasonable understanding of tort law and legal liability. Chapter 3 will help provide this background.

LEGAL FOUNDATIONS OF TORT LAW

A legal wrong is an unjustified invasion of a legal right for which there is a legal remedy. There are two broad classes of legal wrongs: criminal and civil.

A criminal wrong is a wrong against society, and remedies include fine and imprisonment. A civil wrong is a wrong against individuals, and remedies include damages awarded the victim and court-ordered injunctions to prevent further injury. Some actions are viewed as being both civil and criminal wrongs. A speeding driver, for example, could be involved in a criminal action for vehicular homicide and could also be

Exhibit 3-1
Types of Wrongs

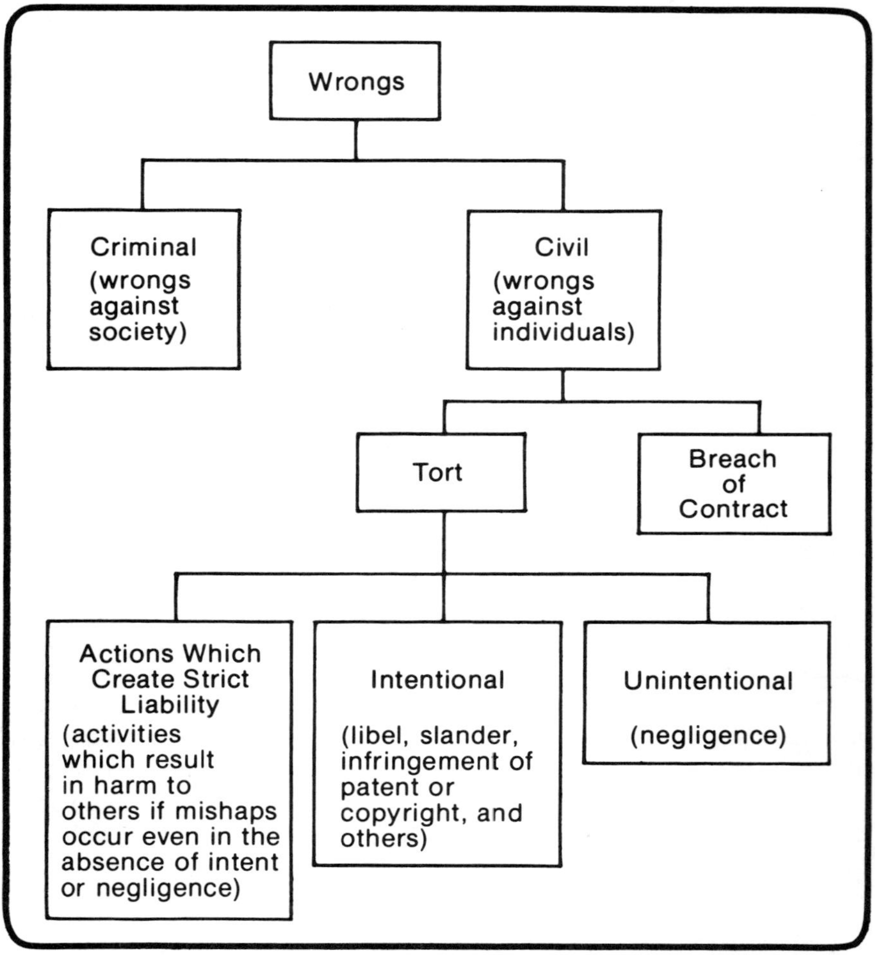

involved in a civil action for recovery of the victim's medical expenses and other damages.

There are two broad classes of civil wrongs: torts and breach of contract. "Broadly speaking, a tort is a civil wrong other than breach of contract, for which the court will provide a remedy in the form of an action for damages."[1] Exhibit 3-1 graphically organizes this information.

These ideas have their basis in English common law which is a body of legal principles deriving its authority from ancient customs as interpreted by court decisions.[2] Most English-speaking countries have legal systems based upon common law. The basic concept is that current court decisions should derive from previous decisions in a logical fashion whenever the circumstances underlying each are similar. The idea is not to develop a comprehensive body of specific written laws covering nearly every subject, as do Napoleonic civil codes. Rather, the idea underlying common law is to develop, through successive judicial decisions, a logical body of general principles against which specific cases are compared. This is not to say that the legal precedent established in some previous case will forever be observed. Often two previous similar cases will seem to have reached opposite conclusions. One court may well attach a greater importance to one case than to the other while another court, in another jurisdiction, could come to an opposite conclusion. Circumstances change, and a precedent may no longer be considered legally, socially, or equitably valid.

Common Law and Statutes

Often court decisions based on common law are superseded by specific laws passed by some legislative body. Federal and state statutes are created by the Congress and state legislatures. Local ordinances are passed in village town meetings and council halls. These statutes then become the precedent for future common law decisions and have the effect of altering and adapting the legal system to the emerging needs of society.

The extent of these statutes depends upon the body passing them. For example, one state may pass a law altering the concept of negligence in automobile operations through a no-fault law which will affect drivers living and operating their motor vehicles in other states.

Essential Elements of a Tort

A tort is a civil wrong, other than a breach of contract, for which the law provides a legal remedy. In order to support an action in tort, four elements must be present. All four are necessary. If any one is lacking, no tort has occurred. Conversely, if all four are present a tort has taken place. These essential elements are:

1. One party must have the right not to be harmed and the other party has a duty to refrain from causing harm. This must be a noncontractual right; otherwise it would place the situation under contract law. Thus, there must be the existence of a right not to be unreasonably harmed and the existence of a duty not to harm unreasonably.

2. There must be either a violation of the right to be free from harm or a breach of the duty not to harm.
3. There must be some harm (damage or injury) that has come to the holder of that right (the victim). This harm must be the direct result of the breach of duty required of the other party (the tortfeasor).
4. There must be no justification for the violation of the victim's right or any valid excuse for not complying with the duty ordinarily owed the victim.

Legal Rights and Remedies

With these four elements present, a situation exists wherein someone had a legal right, someone violated that right (committed a tort), and a legal remedy existed to redress that violation. Violations of rights against which tort law provides protection are:

1. Bodily injury
2. Loss of personal freedom
3. Loss of property
4. Undue interference with an economic right or advantage
5. Damage to public esteem
6. Interference with intrafamily relationships
7. Undue psychological trauma

For the legal rights that tort law protects, the law provides two major remedies: direct action on the part of the victim and judicial remedy.

Direct Action Direct action by the victim must be reasonable in view of the harm. An example might be the right to defend oneself against physical attack in a reasonable way. A victim must use an amount of force considered reasonable in view of the amount of force of the attack. Shooting someone to prevent a slap in the face is an example of unreasonable force. A storekeeper may legally take action against the owner of an auto parked illegally in his or her lot by having the car removed. A person robbed can pursue the thief in order to recover stolen property.

Direct action must be reasonably prompt. Failure to pursue direct action as soon as possible compromises that right, and the victim must then seek a judicial remedy.

Judicial Remedies The law provides legal remedies as an essential element in the definition of tort. If direct action did not or will not result in a remedy, judicial action is required. Three legal remedies exist. The court can:

1. award monetary damages.
2. grant an injunction.
3. require restitution.

Money damages are normally *compensatory,* that is, reasonably related to the extent of injury involved. Damages can also be symbolic or nominal in amount, legally indicating the existence of the tort. *Nominal* damages could be awarded in situations such as simple trespass where no damage to the land was involved. Damages can be *punitive* or far in excess of the actual monetary harm involved when the court views tortious behavior as being particularly repugnant. Usually, punitive damages are awarded in addition to compensatory damages and are labeled as such.

An *injunction* is a court order requiring that a present activity be stopped or that a contemplated future activity not be undertaken. An injunction is used when monetary damages are not adequate to redress the wrong. An injunction might be issued to prohibit future trespass. Often, an injunction is a temporary measure used until an issue is resolved by the court. In a boundary dispute, injunctive relief may be granted to prohibit cutting trees near the property line until that boundary has been precisely established.

Usually, the victim must prove that money damages would be an inadequate remedy in order for an injunction to be granted. In the boundary dispute illustration, money damages, if the boundary dispute is ultimately adjudicated in favor of the victim, would not be an adequate remedy for the loss of the beauty and shade of mature trees wrongfully cut. An injunction would be used before the trees are cut.

Restitution is the return of specific property by court order. Although this term has the general meaning of compensating for a wrong, in terms of tort law its meaning is precise: return of property. No amount of money could remedy the loss of an antique which has sentimental family interest. The return of this family heirloom is the only possible remedy.

Invasions of Rights Protected by Tort Law

There are many ways in which entities can be harmed. People are entitled to reasonable assurances by our system of law that they will be reasonably safe and secure from harm. Some of the harms against which tort law provides protection include battery, assault, false imprisonment, and loss of property.

Battery and Assault *Battery* is an intentional touching of another person without that person's permission or the taking of some other privilege in a manner offensive to the person touched. The word battery is often used in conjunction with the term assault. *Assault* means the threat of battery; that is, putting someone in fear that he or she will be physically harmed. Assault is the threat; battery is actual physical contact.

False Imprisonment *False imprisonment* is the wrongful interference with someone's freedom of movement. One need not be put in jail to have suffered false imprisonment. Preventing a person wrongfully suspected of shoplifting from leaving the store is an example of false imprisonment.

Both battery and false imprisonment are tortious only when the act occurs without the victim's consent. Also, the rights of a person to freedom from bodily injury and to freedom of movement carries with them the right to use reasonable force in self-defense.

Loss of Property People are entitled to the quiet enjoyment and exclusive use of their property. This includes both peaceful possession of that property and rights to any profits arising from its use. Real property is subject to the torts of trespass and nuisance.

Trespass is defined as unlawful, intentional entry onto land by a person (walking on the land) or by an object (dumping trash on someone's property). A *private nuisance* is something which unreasonably interferes with one's use of his or her real estate. It is an intangible interference such as loud noises, smoke, dust, or fumes.

Personal property is subject to the torts of conversion and trespass to chattels (personal property). *Conversion* is an intentional interference with the owner's legal title to personal property. An example of conversion would be an attempt to sell something to which another had title.

Trespass to chattel is an intentional act that interferes with the owners's right to have physical control over an object. Thus, conversion involves interference with an owner's legal claim to the property, and trespass involves interference with an owner's right to control the property.

Undue Interference with an Economic Right or Advantage Economic activity, honestly done, is protected by tort law. Just as the enjoyment of property is protected, so also are honest efforts to acquire property. Deceit, inducing breach of contract, and disparagement are examples of undue interference with an economic right.

Deceit is a conscious misrepresentation of a material fact intended to induce another to rely on the misrepresentation which causes harm to that entity. Deceit is an undue perversion of the truth of a material fact, acted upon by the victim to the victim's detriment.

Parties to a contract have a right to the enforcement of contractual promises. Under tort law, one who acts intentionally to induce another to breach a contract has committed a tort. A football player's agent who encourages the player not to honor his contract, for example, would be committing a tort.

Disparagement is defined as any unprivileged communication to the public that

1. is known by the maker to be false,
2. is derogatory to the victim's title to its property, the quality of its goods or services or to its business activities generally,
3. is intended to discourage the public from dealing with the victim, and
4. causes direct economic harm to the victim.

Damage to Public Esteem Often damage to one's reputation does not result in direct economic loss, yet one's reputation is of inherent value and worthy of protection. Two rights established under tort law must be protected: the right to be protected from the spread of falsehoods which would be injurious, and the right to be protected from the spread of confidential information which, even though accurate, would subject the entity to derision.

Defamation is an unprivileged false communication to third parties, by word or deed, which tends to expose an entity to hatred, contempt, or ridicule or to cause it to be shunned by those whom the communication foreseeably reaches.[3]

Invasion of privacy is a tort that involves a person's right to be let alone. Invasion of privacy occurs if any of the following four specific rights are violated:

1. to be physically secluded
2. to prohibit one's name or identity from being used to promote products or causes without permission
3. to prohibit *private* information about oneself from being publicized
4. to prohibit *public* information about oneself from being publicized in a misleading manner

Interference with Intrafamily Relationships A family has a right, protected by tort law, to the enjoyment of the family's service, affection, and companionship. Spouses have the right of sexual relations. Interference that disrupts these marital or family relationships can be the basis of tort action.

Historically, common law has viewed the wife's legal identity as being absorbed my marriage into that of her husband. They became one person under the law. As a consequence, the husband enjoyed a greater measure of protection than did his wife. A husband, for example, possessed the rights to his wife's consortium or the right to her sex, service, and society. Should she be injured negligently, in addition to her own claims against the negligent party, the husband had a separate claim for his loss of her sex, service, and society. Yet most jurisdictions did not recognize the wife's loss of her husband's services. Recent court decisions have reduced this inequity.

Parent-child relations are based on the rights of parents to the services, company, and affection of their children who are still dependent members of the household and not emancipated. It is a tort to wrongfully deprive a parent of this service, company, and affection.

Undue Psychological Trauma The most common cause of legal action in this category is where some nonphysical injury occurs as a direct result of another tort. Pain and suffering resulting from an auto accident is one example. Nervous breakdown suffered as a result of false imprisonment or defamation of character is another.

Psychological trauma which is not associated with another recognized tort is less widely accepted by courts but does exist. Involved are such torts as assault, infliction of mental distress, malicious prosecution, or wrongful civil proceedings.

Breach of Duty=Invasion of a Right

To review, there are four essential elements of a tort: existence of a right or duty; invasions of that right or a breach of that duty; resulting harm from the invasion or breach; and no justification for the invasion or the breach. The following discussion involves the second of these essential elements: intentional torts, actions that impose liability, and unintentional torts (negligence).

Intentional Torts An intentional tort requires actual intent to invade the rights of the victim or an intentional undertaking which would reasonably be expected to result in injury. In such cases, a high degree of moral blame is assessed against the perpetrator because of the intentional nature of the act or the deliberateness of the injury. Battery is an intentional tort against a person's freedom from bodily injury. Conversion is an intentional tort against the freedom to enjoy one's private property.

Strict and Absolute Liability There are activities that have been determined by legislation or common law to create liability without regard to fault. Workers' compensation is the classic example of no-fault liability created by legislation. Products liability, through the common law process, is approaching no-fault liability. However, it is still necessary for the plaintiff to show that there was some kind of a defect in the product that caused the injury. There are important legal distinctions between what constitutes strict liability and what constitutes absolute liability. For purposes of this course, those distinctions are set aside and both strict and absolute liability are treated as one. The important criterion here is the "standard of care" exercised. Under both strict and absolute liability, the degree of loss control is immaterial. A loss occurred. Society has deemed that the injured party is entitled to compensation by a mechanism that is "quick and fair."

Activities that give rise to liability normally involve situations in which harm to others would result should a mishap occur. In some cases, these situations also involve substantial benefit to society when the activities are performed without problems. Because of the possibility of harm involved, the person conducting the activities is held responsible to see that such harm does not occur. Moreover, because a person undertaking such activities is usually in a better position to understand the potential dangers involved in an especially hazardous situation, it is reasonable to hold that person strictly accountable should someone be harmed.

Activities that impose strict or absolute liability include:

1. Performance of a reasonable activity in an unreasonable setting. An example might be the storing of large quantities of a highly flammable substance in a highly populated area.
2. Allowing the spread of an intentionally started fire. This is not a reference to arson but rather supposes a situation such as a man burning leaves or trash or perhaps a farmer burning waste growth off his fields. The spread of fire is not completely controllable. A freshening wind, a miscalculation of the speed with which the flames will spread, could lead to severe damage to others. Anyone, therefore, who deliberately starts a fire must be responsible for any damage done by its spread.
3. Keeping animals known to be dangerous or those presumed to be dangerous. Wild animals, regardless of the length of time in captivity, are known to be dangerous. A person whose business is providing wild birds or animals for use in promotional activities, for example, is held liable should one of the animals injure someone.
4. Exposing one's employees to injury or disease is a liability situation. Society has decided that it is unfair to expect workers to bear the costs of illnesses and accidents associated with the production of goods and services. Thus, the loss of wages, medical expense, and rehabilitation costs associated with these occurrences are instead borne by the employer, to be added to the cost of the product and paid ultimately by the consumer of that product. The employer is held liable for the employee's affliction, regardless of fault.

5. Damaging persons or property on the ground while operating an aircraft is another area where strict liability is assessed. This is an outgrowth of the concern in the early days of aviation of the extremely dangerous nature of flying. The law recognizes that aircraft do fly over other people's property and that (barring an action for an intentional flight at an unreasonably low altitude which is considered a trespass) in most situations the owners of the property overflown have no effective method to prevent it. This being so, the aircraft's operator must be held accountable for any injury or damage to those on the ground.
6. Producing or marketing goods or services that contain an inherent defect also imposes liability. If a soda bottle explodes, creating a loss, "reasonable care" is not allowed as a defense, and the plaintiff is relieved of the duty to prove a defect in the manufacturing process. Similarly a trucking firm specializing in transporting dynamite can be held liable should an accident happen. A manufacturer of fireworks is involved in an inherently dangerous process and must be held liable for any accident.

Checkpoints

1. Explain how our system of law has developed.
2. List the essential elements of a tort.
3. List the harms against which tort law provides protection and the remedies which tort law provides to persons suffering such harm.
4. Explain the term "strict liability" and describe several activities in which strict liability is imposed.

Unintentional Tort (Negligence) Actions that involve imposed liability and intentional torts are situations viewed by the law as particularly serious. Negligence, the third classification of torts, differs in that it involves a careless rather than purposeful invasion of another's rights. Negligence is the most common tort with which people are generally involved.

Negligence is the failure to use that degree of care which a reasonable person in the same situation would use in order to avoid injury to another. Negligence has been defined as: "The omission to do something which a reasonable man, guided by those considerations which ordinarily regulate the conduct of human affairs, would do, or doing something which a reasonable and prudent man would not do."[4] This definition is called the "prudent man rule." The elements of a tort are present in the definition. Negligence can arise from what a person does or from what a person fails to do. The actions of a prudent man against which one's actions are measured are those considerations that "*ordinarily* regulate human conduct." The criteria against which one's actions will be measured are contemporary and therefore subject to change. Comparisons will be made against what is considered appropriate in this society, in a local area, at this time.

The prudent man against which one is measured is intended to be a peer. An attorney's actions will be measured against those of another attorney, a brain surgeon's actions will be measured against what a reasonable brain surgeon would have done in similar circumstances. Thus, a person whose only medical training was a course in first aid would not be held to the same level of expertise as a medical doctor.

One consideration inherent in such comparisons is that the higher the level of experience, education, or skill involved, the higher the standard of care against which actions will be judged. Thus a producer who advertises in the yellow pages under the heading "Insurance Consultant" could very well be raising the standards of performance against which his actions may be judged. An action considered reasonable when completed by a producer could be considered unreasonable or negligent if performed by a consultant.

The common law characteristics of a negligent act are:[5]

1. The act is that of a nonreasonable, nonprudent man.
2. The act is one of a person who fails to live up to a standard of duty.
3. The standard of care is relative.
4. The act is essentially negative: the person has failed to use care.
5. The act has no motive to cause intentional harm. An act with such motive is a crime. Any deliberateness would make it an intentional tort.

Basically, for right of action for negligence to exist, there must be:

1. a legal duty to use care;
2. a failure to use care;
3. injury or damage;
4. injury or damage as the direct result of that failure to use care; and
5. no contributory negligence on the part of the injured person (except in comparative negligence states).

If care is not owed, it is not negligence to fail to use care; if no damage results, the failure was of no consequence. The first four elements are necessary in all jurisdictions to prove negligence. Exhibit 3-2 should be of help in understanding the idea of negligence.

The diagram shows that negligence can arise just as easily from nonaction or from a failure to act, as from a negligent or careless act. A person renting boats could well be held negligent for failure to provide

Exhibit 3-2
Negligence

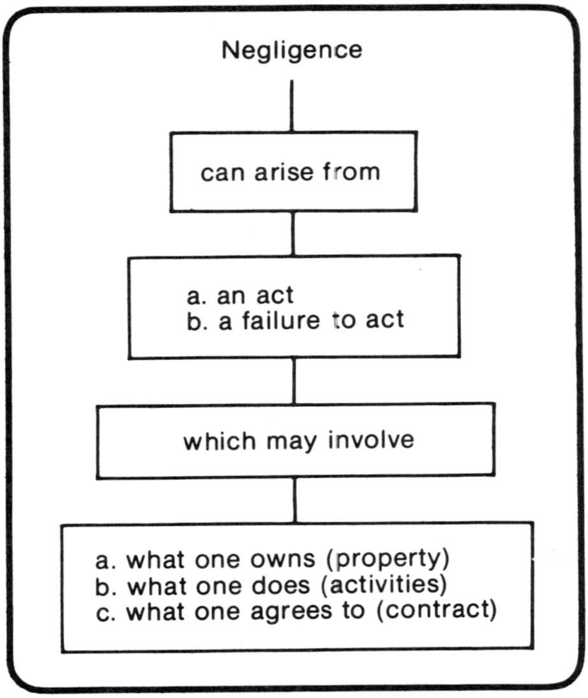

safety equipment in the boats or for failure to provide proper maintenance to make the boats seaworthy. One is not normally required to go to the aid of someone in distress, but a lifeguard at a beach could be held accountable for failure to act to save a drowning customer of that beach.

This diagram indicates that liability can arise from three sources: what you own (property), what you do (activities), and what you agree to (contract).

Property Ownership

The existence of property, both real and personal, creates the possibility that the property could become an instrumentality which injures someone or damages property. Over the years, courts have decided that the care owed people on someone else's land would be that normally provided by a "reasonable and prudent man." Moreover, the level of care required would not necessarily be the same for everyone. The level of care depends on the status of the person entering the land.

Trespassers *Trespassers* are people on another's property for their own purposes without the possessor's permission. Their presence is of no value to the owner. Trespassers actually have temporarily appropriated the property for their own use. In such situations, the law has not placed upon the possessor a duty to use much care. The owner owes the trespasser nothing except not to set traps. Thus, since there is no legal duty to use care, the failure of the owner to provide care is not negligence. The chain of considerations necessary for negligence—legal duty to use care, failure to do so, resulting injury or damage, and so forth—is broken at the first step. So the general idea is that a possessor owes little care to a trespasser.

Two exceptions exist. First, a property owner may not deliberately set a trap. Second, a property owner owes a duty to protect small children who may not understand that they are trespassers.

Suppose, for example, that a person cut across land several times a week on the way to the bus. As he cuts across the garden, a hollow sound is heard when the trespasser steps on an old cistern cover which lies in the path. The person possessing the land had no duty to tell the trespasser that the cistern cover was old, that the wood was rotten and could collapse, sending the trespasser into the cistern. Since the trespasser is not owed this degree of care, there is no obligation to protect him.

But the landowner cannot deliberately trap the trespasser. It would be illegal to set a bear trap, for example, on the path usually taken by the trespasser, cover it with leaves, and hope to teach a person a lesson. This would be an attempt to deliberately harm and would be the use of force out of proportion to the harm inflicted. In Iowa, a landowner, who was frequently robbed, set up a device which would discharge a shotgun when his window was opened. The resulting blast injured the burglar coming through the window and was considered excessive.

The second exception to the idea that a landowner owes no care to a trespasser rests in the principle that all members of society owe a duty to children to protect them from harm. Much of the law involving minors is based on the idea that children must be protected from themselves, from actions which children do not realize will harm them. Property owners owe a duty to small children to keep them safe, even when these children are trespassing. This idea is applied when something exists that the landowner knows will attract children. This attraction, termed an *attractive nuisance,* is something from which children must be protected, because they might be injured by it.

Children too young to read "No Trespassing" or "Warning" signs must be protected. This duty has a higher priority in our laws than does the right of the property owner to enjoy his land in privacy. Thus, an obligation is placed upon the property owner when something exists that should be recognized as attractive to children. The most common example is a swimming pool. A homeowner should realize that a pool would be attractive to children and should also realize that many children cannot swim and could drown. An obligation is owed to protect children from their own inexperience. The landowner should have the pool securely fenced and locked when not in use. Other examples of items attractive to children could be ladders to climb, animals to pet, and machinery to start.

Licensees *Licensees* are people on another's property for their own benefit and who can be assumed to have implied permission. Licensees include door-to-door sales and delivery people, those needing emergency aid or assistance, police and fire officers. Social guests are classified as licensees in most states. The difference between the licensee and the trespasser is in the concept that a licensee, although on another's real property for his or her own benefit, has the property owner's implied or expressed permission to be there.

To licensees, the landowner owes "reasonable" care. Our society recognizes the virtue of work and the necessity of reasonably free and open travel. Commerce requires people to enter the property of others, and these people are entitled to reasonable care. Reasonable care would require the removal of hazards where appropriate or the posting of signs warning of these hazards in cases where their removal is not appropriate.

Invitees The third classification is that of an invitee, someone on property for the mutual benefit of the invitee and possessor of property. An invitee is owed greater than ordinary care. The landowner should actively seek out hazards and remove them. If this is not possible, care should be taken to post signs warning of these hazards. There should be indications of some positive, affirmative action to protect the invitee, action to indicate that care was taken. Invitees would include customers of a commercial establishment, government representatives, public utility workers such as meter readers, and others whose presence would be of benefit to the landowner. Social guests are considered to be invitees in some states.

Although this discussion has largely involved people on real estate, the owners of personal property also have obligations to see that the existence of their property does not harm other people. The existence of machinery discharging fumes or machinery operating at high noise levels can harm others. Some jurisdictions have all but abolished the distinctions among trespassers, licensees, and invitees. Producers should be aware of the status of people on real property in their state.

Activities

The foregoing section involved the existence or use of property which might lead to the detriment of others. One's activities can also negligently injure someone or damage the property of others. Again, in order for there to be negligence, a chain of circumstances must exist. There must be a legal duty to use care in one's activities, a failure to do so, and resulting damage or injury.

In personal activities, one can operate a boat negligently, fish, play golf, ride a bicycle, or perform any of a great number of other activities in a way to harm others. Business activities as well carry with them the obligation and responsibility to the general public not to let these activities harm them. Some activities are potentially so dangerous that strict liability is assessed should damage or injury occur. Under the concept of negligence, the activities involved are not those so potentially harmful as to require absolute or strict liability but rather the day-to-day, ordinary activities of business. To conduct such activities carelessly is to invite a suit for negligence.

Shifting Responsibility by Contract

One can be held liable because of a legal duty *imposed* by the legal system or because of some obligation which is *assumed* under the system. Assumed obligations are transferred from one party to another. Initially, one party had a duty and this duty was assumed by someone else. Because someone agrees to a duty, a failure to perform that duty can lead to an allegation of negligence. This situation involves a "shift" of responsibility from one party to another. It does not mean that any new responsibility has been created by the contract.

As is the case with the existence and use of property and with the activities in which a person is engaged, negligent acts involving obligations assumed by contract can also lead to situations of negligence. A lease of premises agreement might shift the burden for building maintenance from the landlord to the tenant. A subsequent boiler explosion due to faulty maintenance would properly have been appraised as a function and responsibility of the landlord, except that the tenant had assumed this responsibility by contract. The tenant did not have this responsibility until the tenant assumed it. Now he or she is responsible for negligent maintenance of the boiler.

Lease of premises agreements, railroad side tract agreements, and other hold harmless agreements are examples of potential liabilities assumed by contract.

Statutes Affecting Determination of Negligence

The definition of negligence is worded in terms of a "prudent man" and in terms of "those considerations that ordinarily regulate the conduct of human affairs." The definition both explains the concept of negligence and also establishes a criteria (what a prudent man would do in similar circumstances) against which conduct can be measured. Judges and juries are left to decide what a prudent man would have done in similar circumstances.

Such a definition is of great value because it is very adaptable to the changes in our society and in the nation's economic system. But such adaptability is paid for in the vagueness of the definition. Having a more specific definition would make the jury's job much easier, but the concept would be less adaptable to changes.

The vagueness perceived in the definition is sometimes worrisome, and often attempts are made by lawmakers to set up an unequivocal determination of what would constitute negligence. For example, what precautions would a reasonable and prudent man take to protect neighbor children from his backyard swimming pool? Is a four-foot fence enough? Should the fence be chain-link or is a wooden one adequate?

A community could decide to make an effort to answer such questions by passing an ordinance relating to fencing swimming pools. The ordinance could require that all private residential swimming pools be fully enclosed with a chain-link fence at least four-feet in height with a securely fastened gate of the same or similar materials. Now the community knows what a prudent man would do; he would do as the ordinance requires. Such statutes have the practical effect of determining in advance what the conduct of a prudent man would be.

An ordinance requiring all sidewalks to be cleared of snow by 10 o'clock A.M. following a snowfall helps define what a prudent man would do. In a subsequent accident where a pedestrian was injured three days after a snowfall by falling on an icy, snow-covered sidewalk, the task of deciding what a prudent man would do is made easier.

Such local and regional ordinances and statutes adapt the negligence concept to local conditions. Yet, they also have the effect of qualifying and narrowing the concept so that often there is no national consensus as to what a prudent man would do. Some states have modified the common law prudent man concept. These modifications include concepts of contributory negligence, comparative negligence, and last clear chance.

Contributory Negligence The last step in the chain of considerations leading to negligence is that the person injured or damaged was not negligent. The societal ethic involved is that the guilty party must be held responsible; the guilty party must pay. What is presumed as well is that there is an innocent party involved and that the innocent party was harmed by the tortfeasor.

The concept can be applied with relative ease in situations where one party is clearly guilty and one is innocent. When both parties are, to a degree, guilty, the concept begins to break down. This doctrine of contributory negligence has been enacted into statute in many states, sometimes specifically in relation to the operation of motor vehicles. In its simplest form, it states that where each party is to some degree negligent, each must bear its own injury. In an auto accident where one party was drunk and the other was speeding, both would be required by the contributory negligence concept to pay for their own damages. The existence of negligence on the part of both parties breaks the chain.

Comparative Negligence A major defect in the idea of contributory negligence is that the degree of negligence imputed to one party might be very small, yet still be sufficient to require each party to bear the burden of his or her own damages. One party may have been driving recklessly, operating under the influence of alcohol at high speed. The other party may have been operating his or her vehicle only a few miles over the limit. In theory, each was negligent and each should bear his or her own loss. Thus the concept, designed to create equity in situations where both parties were responsible, operated often to the serious detriment of the party who was responsible in a very small way.

Perhaps the "almost innocent" party in the illustration suffered severe injury and damage and the blatantly negligent party suffered only minor injury. The contributory negligence concept requiring each to bear his or her own loss would result in the predominantly negligent party suffering only minor loss while the "almost innocent" party suffered a much more serious burden of expense.

The concept of comparative negligence is an attempt to assess the relative responsibility of the parties involved. Assume Party A was held responsible for 60 percent of the blame and Party B the remaining 40 percent. Then Party A is held responsible for the same proportion of Party B's damages. Depending on the jurisdiction, Party B may be responsible for 0 to 40 percent of Party A's damages. In the first example, the first party could perhaps have been found to be 95 percent to blame and the other only 5 percent negligent. Damages allocated among the parties on this basis would more fairly and accurately reflect the degree of responsibility of each party.

Because comparative negligence statutes appear to operate more equitably, many states have passed them. Difficulties are apparent, however, in their operation. It may be difficult to assess whether negligence is shared and it is asking a great deal more from a judge or jury to go one step further and determine the correct percentage of blame to be allotted to each party. Comparative negligence laws predominate, with about 80 percent of the states having such a law.

Last Clear Chance The *last clear chance* concept is a defense against an allegation of contributory negligence if the plaintiff is held to be contributorily negligent and the defendant had the last clear chance to avoid the accident. When this "last clear chance" was not taken, the defendant's failure becomes the proximate cause of the accident and supersedes an allegation of contributory negligence.

Suppose an auto was stalled in the middle of a turnpike at night and the operator, looking for help, failed to move the vehicle off the roadway. If the vehicle was struck by another speeding motorist who carelessly ignored the flashing lights on the stalled car, then that motorist is said to have had the last clear chance to avoid the accident. It was this failure that was the proximate cause of the accident, overriding the contributory negligence of the plaintiff.

Checkpoints

1. Explain negligence and contrast it with strict liability and intentional torts.
2. What are the characteristics of a negligent act?
3. Explain the qualifications made to the idea that one owes a trespasser no care.
4. Differentiate between comparative and contributory negligence and explain how they affect each party.

Res Ipsa Loquitur One basic tenet of common law is the fundamental idea that a person is innocent until proved guilty. When a plaintiff brings an action, the plaintiff (the complainant) bears the burden of proof. The person charged, the defendant, need not prove an absence of negligence. The other party must prove negligence. Yet there occasionally arises a situation so clear, with evidence so overpowering, that it makes sense to assume the defendant is negligent. This is the kind of situation where, on the surface, no other reasonable explanation exists except to presume the negligence of the accused party.

Quite often there is some physical object involved, which, of itself, is not inherently dangerous. That this object caused harm presumes that some negligent handling of this object must have taken place. A pole holding a window open falls out of the window; a barrel rolls out of a truck; these items usually are not dangerous. If they harm someone, negligent handling must have been the cause. This is why the Latin phrase *res ipsa loquitur* is used. It means "the thing speaks for itself." The object may be harmless, but the situation clearly indicates negligence, so negligence should not have to be proved by the plaintiff.

Often the person harmed by such an event would have a great deal of difficulty in proving a specific act of negligence which caused the accident. Who loaded the truck? Who opened the window so that a strong breeze dislodged the pole? These circumstances are often very difficult for the plaintiff to prove, yet may well involve information readily available to the defendant. It is logical, therefore, to place the burden of proof on the defendant. If the information is available, the defendant can prove lack of negligence; *the burden of proof is shifted to the defendant.* Negligence is presumed until proven otherwise.

This doctrine is usually invoked by a plaintiff trying to demonstrate that negligence existed and may be used if:

1. the incident or object harming the plaintiff would not ordinarily occur unless someone was negligent.
2. the harm was caused by a force or an object which at the time of the incident was in the exclusive control of the defendant.
3. the plaintiff was not also negligent.
4. in some jurisdictions, the evidence of wrongdoing is substantially more accessible to the defendant than to the plaintiff.

The defendant, to rebut this presumption of negligence, can still indicate that one or more of these conditions is untrue. For example, it may be the case that the instrumentality causing the injury was not in the defendant's exclusive control. Perhaps the window pole fell from a hall window accessible to many people and not just the defendant.

Vicarious Liability *Vicarious liability* is the term used in situations where the negligence of one party is imputed to another. Vicarious liability situations often arise in the context of an agent-principal relationship and will be discussed later.

Vicarious liability can arise from specific statutes spelling out this relationship. Some states have passed "family automobile" or "family purpose" statutes wherein the negligent use of the motor vehicle by a family member is imputed to the head of the household garaging that vehicle.

AGENCY

A relationship of *agency* exists when one party represents or acts for another as directed. One party, the principal, delegates responsibilities to another, the agent, who will act under the direct orders of the principal. This relationship can involve an employer-employee relationship when one is acting at the instigation of the other, relations between partners, and between a principal and an independent contractor.

When the words "agent" or "agency" are used in the following discussion, they are used in the legal sense, in the sense that Party A is acting on behalf of Party P. Insurance producers do use the word "agent" to correctly describe their legal position with their insurance companies. But, unless specifically mentioned, "agent" and "agency" here have the broader meaning.

Scope of Agency

The relation between an agent and the principal is usually limited to the authority given the agent by the principal. An agency relationship does not make the principal responsible for any and all acts of the agent. Only those acts undertaken within the scope and intent of the agreement would be involved.

An agency situation is usually set up for a specific purpose. For example, a person agrees to represent an insurance company in the marketing of its product. A real estate agent agrees to act for a homeowner for the express purpose of selling the property. The principal is not involved in other aspects of the agent's activities and is not responsible for these other activities. An insurance company, for example, would not be liable for the negligent operation of a speedboat which one of its agents operated as a hobby.

Dual Agency An agent may not act against the interests of the principal. This requirement suggests that an agent should not represent another party within the scope of that agency. It is difficult for an agent to act with faithfulness when representing two adverse parties. The agent is under an obligation to act with loyalty, in the best interest of the principal. This cannot be accomplished when what the agent would do for Principal X may be to the detriment of Principal Y.

The agent can, however, act for both parties in a transaction when each has the full facts of this representation and when such representation is not adverse to the interests of either. The requirements are for full disclosure and a situation where the agent can maximize the advantage to both parties.

Agency Formation Normally the creation of an agency relationship is deliberate and written. Usually there is agency by appointment with an expressed agency agreement outlining the duties and responsibilities of each party. This is the case with insurance agents.

Such formality is not a requirement. One may agree to be an agent without any consideration for the act. The agreement may be oral.

Sometimes agency is created unwittingly, although usually the arrangement is a deliberate act. If one sends another to the grocery store to make a purchase, an agency relationship has been formed.

Agency by Appointment. Appointment is the usual method of forming an agency relationship. Party P appoints Party A to act on Party P's behalf in a particular area of endeavor, for example, selling insurance, buying property, and so on. There is usually a written agency agreement outlining the duties, responsibilities, limits of authority, and the area of endeavor. Consent is a necessity. Agency is by free choice and the agent must agree to the arrangement. Even in the case of one party going to the store to secure something for the other, agency exists and agreement is there. The first party realizes and tacitly agrees that the act of going to the store is an act done on behalf of another.

Agency by Estoppel. The law may impose an agency relation in some cases even though there was no actual consent between the parties. This is likely to happen in a situation where a principal has created the appearance of agency. Suppose someone acted to suggest or imply that an agency existed and a third party relied upon these acts to his own detriment. In such a case the principal would be estopped (prevented) from denying the agency relationship. Suppose someone had business cards printed indicating that some well-known person was acting in an agency capacity. If a third party acted upon that knowledge, the principal could not then deny the existence of agency. Agency by estoppel is a device to protect third parties from harm when a principal uses agency as a means to deceive.

Agency by Ratification. Should someone hold himself or herself out as the agent of another party, that party can deny it and refuse to confirm any relationship or transaction. But should that party ratify or confirm the transaction, an agency has been established. Ratification is an affirmation of agency authority and this affirmation would cure any defect from lack of authority which has previously existed. Ratification affirms that agency has in fact existed and ratifies and accepts the previous acts as the acts of an agent on behalf of a principal. Normally, ratification would be effective back to the date of the original transaction which implied agency.

Authority of Agents The scope of an agent's authority may be actual or apparent. Actual authority may be either express or implied.

Express Authority. An agent's express authority may be anything legal that is agreed to by the agent and principal. This would include those acts that are necessary to carry out instructions. A "general agent" would have authority to perform all acts that are usual and customary in such capacities. A "special agent" is usually restricted to just those acts that are "essential" to the situation. Most property-liability insurance producers are general agents. Most have authority, within expressed limits, to make or to modify contracts of insurance and to perform all of the other activities necessary in the efficient performance of an insurance agency.

Implied Authority. No agency contract can consider every possible contingency that might arise. Thus, the agreement is broadened by law and by custom to include other acts deemed necessary to carry out the agent's expressed authority. By implication, the agent has some implied authority.

An agent should be able to believe that any actions that are in accord with accepted custom are within the scope of authority granted. It is usual that this authority would track with what other agents in this agent's position would usually have.

Implied authority may also arise from conduct of the principal that could be construed as intending to confer such authority. To illustrate, suppose Agent A has for years been able to bind property exposures without limit on value. Agent A has, by implication, the right to continue to do so until some expression from the company would alter this situation.

Apparent Authority. Few members of the public know the exact extent of the expressed and implied authority relationships that exist between agents and their principals. How many policyholders have seen the agency contract in force between a producer and the insurance company?

Yet third parties cannot always depend upon appearances which are created by the agent. The public must act as reasonable and prudent persons would when acquainted with the customs and nature of the business. The public has responsibility to protect itself. Third parties can rely upon appearances created by the principal. The principal will be estopped from denying that such authority exists when the principal created that appearance.

In general, the public can usually depend upon the law to correct any harm created by defects in agency authority when the agency is operated according to the accepted customs and traditions of that business. The public should always be on guard to note situations that are special or unusual. When an agent acts in a way that appears to be adverse to the best interests of the principal, the third party has the duty to ascertain the extent of the agent's authority by a direct inquiry to the principal. The public can protect itself only by acting in this reasonable and prudent manner.

Duties in Agency Relationships Along with the powers and authority come the duties and liabilities of agency. Again, duties are imposed by the agreement and implied by law. Agency is a *fiduciary* relationship because necessarily there must be a high degree of trust when one is dealing on behalf of another. There must be confidence that this trust will not be breached.

Because of the high degree of confidence and trust involved, the courts must make doubly certain that the agent does not take advantage of the agency relationship. To do this the law imposes a higher standard of conduct on the agent than would be expected in usual business dealings. It is not sufficient for an agent to represent the principal to their mutual advantage. The agent owes a duty to act *primarily for the benefit of the principal.*

This special fiduciary relationship, made necessary by the unique relationship of trust that must exist, requires of the agent:

1. loyalty
2. obedience
3. reasonable care
4. accounting
5. relaying information

If an agent violates these duties, discharge from the agency agreement and a potential liability for damages may result. Breach of these duties is a breach of the implied terms of the agreement, since these duties are necessary to the fiduciary and confidential nature of the relationship.

Termination of Agency The agency relationship existing between an agent and principal can be terminated in several ways: lapse of time, accomplishment of purpose, revocation or renunciation, death or loss of capacity, and impossibility.

Lapse of Time. Often an agency agreement is in effect for a specific period of time. When this period expires, the agency relationship is dissolved. When no time is specified, a "reasonable" time is implied.

Accomplishment of Purpose. If the agent's responsibility is to perform a specific task, then the relationship is finished when the task has been accomplished. Agency exists between a real estate agent and the homeowner when a contract is signed to have the real estate agent represent the owner in the sale of property. When the property is sold and all aspects of the sale are completed, the agency relationship is ended.

Revocation or Renunciation. The principal may revoke the relationship at any time and can do this by any act which indicates that the agent can no longer exercise authority. The agent must be notified. Improper termination may be a cause for action of the agent against the principal for damages, but this does not mitigate the principal's power to end the agency relationship.

The agent can terminate the agreement through "renunciation of authority." Again, doing so may be a breach of contract and may expose the agent to damages, but this does not alter the power of the agent to do so.

This demonstrates the importance of the distinction between the *power* to terminate and the *right* to do so. Because of its fiduciary nature, the efficient operation of an agency relationship requires open, honest, and effective cooperation between two parties. Thus courts may allow damages for improper termination of an agency.

Death or Loss of Capacity. The death of either party automatically terminates the agreement. Since death is a matter of public record, there need be no special notice to the agent or to the public. A major exception to this rule lies in the necessity for banks to accept and process checks and deposits until notified. Checks drawn before death and monies collected before death can still be processed after death until the financial institution receives notification. This allows the ordinary processes of commerce to continue in an orderly fashion.

Impossibility or Changed Circumstances. When the subject for which the agency was formed no longer exists, the agency no longer exists. An agreement with a real estate agent to sell your home is no longer valid when your residence has been destroyed by fire. The property no longer exists in a reasonable form, and the agency agreement is no longer appropriate.

Changed circumstances accomplish the same end. If an agent is appointed to sell the oil from an exploratory well, that relationship ends if the drilling produces a dry hole.

Bankruptcy of the principal is another changed circumstance that would terminate the authority of the agent since all the principal's assets would come under the jurisdiction of the bankruptcy court.

A change of law could terminate agency if the substance or activity which is the basis of agency is no longer legal. A county that voted itself dry would have the effect of terminating an agency agreement involving the sale of alcoholic beverages in that area.

Agency in Property-Liability Insurance

Most of the marketing personnel in the insurance field are referred to as agents. Normally these persons represent the insurer in dealings with the insurance buying public. The scope of their authority and the duties they are obligated to perform can vary greatly. The following terms are widely used in the insurance field.

General Agent General agents have authority, within specified limits established by the agency agreement and common law, to make and to modify contracts of insurance. Such an agent solicits, accepts and forwards applications, agrees to terms, and executes and delivers insurance policies. Such an agent has broad powers to represent the insurance company in a given area and for a specific line or lines of insurance.

Solicitors or Soliciting Agents The authority of solicitors is normally more limited, usually being confined to soliciting applications for insurance from the insurance buying public.

Many specific statutes and state insurance department regulations cover the licensing and the authority of solicitors. If solicitors are allowed, they are usually considered agents of the producer and, therefore, subagents charged with soliciting applications which the producer sends on to the company. Some statutes do make the solicitor a representative of the insurer in the event of dispute between the insured and the company.

The important fact is that the solicitor has less authority and fewer powers than a subagent. Normally there is no authority to do things that are normal for the agent to do. Thus a solicitor usually cannot extend time for payments, or modify or waive any other aspects of the transaction.

Brokers This term is fast becoming a generic term for agents since it is used in many states to indicate any agent who represents a number of different companies. In the strictest use of the term, broker means a person who secures insurance for another party and who is the agent of that party in the transaction, not the agent of the company. Because of this, a great many legal problems can arise, and often there are statutes that specifically spell out the duties and responsibilities of brokers.

Knowledge of an agent is imputed to the principal. Receipt of a premium payment by an agent is receipt of the money by the principal. Since the agent represents the principal, one has, in fact, paid the principal when the agent is paid. But since the broker is really the insured's agent, payment to the broker would not be payment to the company. Because of this, specific statutes have been passed which define the broker as the insured's agent *except for purposes of collecting the premium,* when the broker is considered to be the insurer's agent. Thus, when the broker is paid, the company is normally considered as having received the money. These statutes permit the public to rely on the certainty that payment to their insurance broker is payment to the company. So the broker is the insured's agent for some aspects of the insurance transaction and the insurance company's agent for other aspects of the transaction.

Duties of Insurance Agents

Insurance agents owe to their insurance companies the same duties that other agents owe their principals. However, the agent really represents both parties to the insurance transaction.

The agent's primary allegiance and fiduciary responsibilities are to the insurance company. All information material to the transaction must be transmitted to the insurer, all monies accounted for, and in every way the agent must be the faithful servant of the company. To the client, the agent owes reasonable and informed services in securing the appropriate contracts at an appropriate price. The agent owes the client his or her expertise.

Insurance Professionals

Many insurance agents look upon themselves as professionals, and to a certain extent they are correct. If a profession requires competent performance, high standards of ethical conduct, high standards of education, training, and experience, then, to a degree at least, insurance is a profession. But there are differing levels of professionalism, and certain terms carry different connotations of professionalism. The term "insurance consultant" implies a higher standard of professionalism than do the terms "insurance agent" or "insurance broker."

The important consideration here is the fact that when producers hold themselves to be professionals, the standard of care against which they will be measured is a higher standard. Presumably, a professional charges more (fees) and renders a superior class of service. A listing in the yellow pages under the heading "Insurance Consultant" has the effect of raising the standards of performance against which one is judged. "What would a reasonable and prudent insurance *consultant* have done in similar circumstances?" is a higher standard against which to be judged than "What would a reasonable and prudent insurance *agent* have done in similar circumstances?"

Checkpoints

1. Define *agent* and *principal,* and identify the several ways that agency can be established.
2. Explain how an agency relationship can be terminated.
3. Explain the concept of "changed circumstances."

4. Define "broker" and differentiate between an insurance agent and an insurance broker.

LAW OF CONTRACTS

Commerce and daily life both involve the use of contracts. The insurance agent-insurance company agreement and the insurance policy itself are good examples of contracts necessary in the transactions of insurance. Certain common law concepts as well as specific statutes relate to contracts. Contracts can be defined as "agreements enforceable by law" or as "promises for which the law provides a remedy for breach." For a contract to exist, four elements must be present: (1) agreement; (2) competent parties; (3) consideration; and (4) legal purpose.

Elements of a Contract

Agreement One party (the offeror) must make an offer, and another party (the offeree) must accept it. There must be agreement between the parties. In an offer there must be (1) an expression of the intent to make a contract; (2) sufficiently definite terms; and (3) communicating of these terms to the one receiving the offer. Vague promises such as to "take care of my employees" or "for a few days" are terms too indefinite to be part of most offers.

An acceptance of an offer requires the counterparts to the three elements of the offer. All acceptances must (1) be made by the person to whom the offer was made (same parties); (2) be unconditional and unequivocal (sufficiently definite terms); and (3) be communicated to the offeror.

If these three requirements are not met, there is not acceptance. Perhaps the offeree will counteroffer, which could lead to further counteroffers, until one party makes an offer accepted by the other. At this point, there is agreement among the parties. Only at this point has this essential element of a contract been met.

As a general rule, the insurance agent is not considered as making an offer of insurance protection but rather is soliciting offers for insurance from prospective purchasers. The completed application is considered an offer by the applicant. Issuance of an insurance policy in conformance with the application is considered acceptance. If the policy written is materially different from what was called for on the application, then the policy becomes a counteroffer subject to acceptance by the applicant.

In some cases, the applicant is considered as soliciting an offer from the insurance company if no premium or deposit payment accompanies the application. In such cases the proffered policy is the offer, and the payment of the premium by the client is considered the acceptance.

In property-liability insurance, the client often requires immediate coverage, say at the time of purchase of real estate. Most property-liability agents have the authority to bind coverage so as not to expose the client to a period of time in which there is no insurance coverage on the newly acquired property. Sometimes the client's request for coverage is accepted by the producer's oral statement that the client is covered. Certainly there is an agreement in such cases. The client's request for immediate coverage is (1) an expression of intention to make a contract (2) in definite terms which is (3) communicated to the agent and meets the requisites of an offer. The agent's oral expression, indicating that coverage was granted, is made (1) by the person receiving the offer, (2) in definite terms, and (3) to the offeror, so that agreement exists and the first requirement of a contract has been met. Definite terms for an oral contract of insurance means identifying the perils insured, object or premises, amount of insurance and the names of the insured and insurer.

Given the many difficulties that may arise concerning whether or not a contract of insurance is in force, it is vital that the agent be especially careful to create an actual agreement between the parties. This suggests written rather than oral communications whenever possible. It also suggests that premiums should either be collected at the time of the transaction or that definite arrangements for financing be made. A copy of the ACORD binder form meeting these requirements appears in Exhibit 3-3.

In most life and health situations, the agents *do not* have authority to bind coverage. In most cases, the requirement of an offer and acceptance, that is, agreement, is not satisfied until an application has been presented to the company and acted upon—that is, a policy issued, delivered to the client, and the premium received. Only at this point is there offer and acceptance as a requirement for the formation of a contract.

Competent Parties Another essential element to a contract is the necessity that the parties involved have legal capability or the capacity to contract. One possessing the legal capacity to contract is termed a "competent" party and, conversely, one not capable of entering into a contract is "incompetent."

Incompetency to contract may result if a party is (1) underage; (2) insane; (3) under the influence of alcohol or drugs; or (4) an artificial

Exhibit 3-3
ACORD Binder

SET TAB STOPS AT ARROWS **CAUTION:** Before preparing this binder, refer to the **ACORD** Binder Procedure Guide and applicable company instructions.

acord

INSURANCE BINDER

THIS BINDER IS A TEMPORARY INSURANCE CONTRACT, SUBJECT TO THE CONDITIONS SHOWN ON THE REVERSE SIDE OF THIS FORM.

Binder No.

NAME AND ADDRESS OF AGENCY	**COMPANY**
	Effective m , 19 Expires ☐ 12:01 am ☐ Noon , 19
	☐ This binder is issued to extend coverage in the above named company per expiring policy # (except as noted below)
NAME AND MAILING ADDRESS OF INSURED	**Description of Operation/Vehicles/Property**

PROPERTY	Type and Location of Property	Coverage/Perils/Forms	Amt of Insurance	Ded.	Coins. %

	Type of Insurance	Coverage/Forms	Limits of Liability	Each Occurrence	Aggregate
LIABILITY	☐ Scheduled Form ☐ Comprehensive Form ☐ Premises/Operations ☐ Products/Completed Operations ☐ Contractual ☐ Other (specify below) ☐ Med. Pay. $ Per Person $ Per Accident ☐ Personal Injury	☐ A ☐ B ☐ C	Bodily Injury	$	$
			Property Damage	$	$
			Bodily Injury & Property Damage Combined	$	$
			Personal Injury		$
AUTOMOBILE	☐ Liability ☐ Non-owned ☐ Hired ☐ Comprehensive-Deductible $ ☐ Collision-Deductible $ ☐ Medical Payments $ ☐ Uninsured Motorist $ ☐ No Fault (specify): ☐ Other (specify):		**Limits of Liability**		
			Bodily Injury (Each Person)		$
			Bodily Injury (Each Accident)		$
			Property Damage		$
			Bodily Injury & Property Damage Combined		$

☐ WORKERS' COMPENSATION — Statutory Limits (specify states below) ☐ EMPLOYERS' LIABILITY — Limit $

SPECIAL CONDITIONS/OTHER COVERAGES

NAME AND ADDRESS OF ☐ MORTGAGEE ☐ LOSS PAYEE ☐ ADD'L INSURED

LOAN NUMBER

Signature of Authorized Representative Date

ACORD 75 (11-77)

entity (a corporation) which lacks the authority to enter certain contracts.

In general, the law protects incompetents who are often unable to protect themselves from exploitation by giving them the chance to disaffirm contracts entered into while incompetent. At the same time, an objective of the legal system is to enforce legal agreements and to protect the validity of contracts and other legitimate transactions.

Underage (Minority). At common law, one reaches majority (and therefore gains the capacity to contract freely) at the age of twenty-one. Prior to reaching the age of twenty-one, the law protects minors from themselves—permitting them only to contract for items and services "necessary" to their daily lives.

Many statutes have been passed creating exceptions to these common-law concepts and the Twenty-Sixth Amendment to the United States Constitution, which lowered the voting age to eighteen, served as a great impetus in this direction. These statutes created "majority" at different ages for different purposes. One could be competent to vote at eighteen, but not competent to buy liquor before reaching a higher age.

Certainly the common-law concept that permits enforcement of a contract with a minor for those things "necessary" is in the public interest, for minors must be able to exist and thrive. "Necessaries" include items and services relating to the health, education, work, and comfort of the minor, and minors are liable for the reasonable value of these necessities. The requirement that the minor pay for the reasonable value of the necessary goods and/or services reflects the common law concept that the laws of minority be used as a "shield" to protect them rather than a "sword" to injure someone else.

Any contract for nonnecessities by a minor is voidable by the minor. Generally, a minor may assert minority as a defense against liability in contracts that do not involve the purchase of necessities. A minor may avoid a contract not for necesssaries at any time during minority or within a "reasonable time" after reaching majority. Such a contract is not "void" but "voidable" by the minor. A void contract can be said to "never have existed." A "voidable" contract is enforceable at the option of the minor. A minor has been held not liable under contracts of fire and life insurance by courts which have considered that contracts of insurance are not necessaries. Some jurisdictions, however, have defined a specific age of majority for the specific purpose of purchase of life insurance. The underlying concept is that it is in the youth's best interest to buy when the rates are low and to encourage the development of the traits of thrift and saving.

Because it is not always easy to know what is necessary to a minor's health and comfort, merchants often require that a minor's legal guardians join in any agreement. Then, should the minor disavow, the adult, having also agreed, stands obligated to pay. Even in cases when the minor has the cold cash ready for a purchase, a prudent business will legitimately require the joining of an adult in the transaction.

As well as contract of the necessities of life, minors cannot avoid certain other contracts. If a minor has married or has enlisted in the armed services, the contracts will stand. Minors cannot disavow agreements involving the obligations of a bailbond or for the duties of child support.

Often courts themselves are involved in contracts with minors. An insurance company may require the assent of the courts to any settlement offered a minor in an insurance claim. Court approval may reasonably be sought for a contract involving the performance of services by a child, such as a child actor or performer. Such approval makes subsequent disavowal of the contract by the minor a difficult task.

Insanity. People can be "adjudicated insane," that is, declared insane by a court of law. Any agreement entered into by such persons is void. More troublesome are contracts that persons attempt to avoid on the grounds that they were mentally incompetent, but not "adjudicated insane," at the time the contract was consummated. Contracts of such persons are considered voidable and normally remain in effect until actually voided by the insane party. In such cases, the insane person must show that he or she (1) did not know a contract was being made, or (2) did not understand the legal consequences of what was being done. A requirement is incapacity to contract arising from insanity, idiocy, senility, or some other mental defect. Mere mental weakness or stupidity is not sufficient to avoid a contract.

It is sometimes important to provide for the necessary requirements of an insane person's health and welfare. Contracts for such "necessities" for an insane person are valid. If the agreement was beneficial to the insane person and the other party was ignorant of this situation, the insane party may not disavow it. The insane party may avoid a contract in any instance. The competent party, having entered into the agreement, is bound by it until and unless voided by the other party. Should the contract be disavowed, the consideration (goods, services or whatever) given the incompetent party must be returned to the other party.

Persons Under the Influence of Alcohol or Drugs. Generally, the use of intoxicants or drugs will not invalidate a contract. There is the societal obligation of persons to be bound by their own acts, whether or not such acts were in their own best interests. People should bear the consequences of their folly. Thus, people's foolishness is no reason to escape a legal obligation. Normally, intoxication is not sufficient grounds to void a contract. To void the contract, the same two conditions are required as was the case with an insane person, namely the person was so under the influence of alcohol or drugs that there was no understanding that a contract was actually being entered into or that the consequences of this act were not understood.

Exceptions do exist. If a person were deliberately made drunk or drugged, the party responsible should not be permitted to benefit and the contract can be voided. If a person is adjudicated as an habitual drunkard, this is a matter of public record, and contracts by such persons are voidable. Contracts for necessaries for drugged or intoxicated people are valid.

Artificial Entities. Corporations are created by the state and are considered separate entities in the eyes of the law. As a separate entity, corporations need to enter into lawful agreements and corporations can sue, be sued, commit crimes, torts, enter into contracts, and intentionally breach contracts. The extent of a corporation's competency to contract depended historically upon the powers granted it through its charter.

Traditionally, corporations were given limited powers to conduct activities in specific areas of endeavor. Activities outside the scope of their powers were called *ultra vires* acts; literally "beyond their power." Under this rule, such contracts were voidable by either party if the contract had not already been performed. If fully executed, neither party could avoid the contract.

Today, given the conglomerate movement, the processes of horizontal and vertical integration, and the needs of corporations to diversify, the charter powers are usually broad enough to make allegations of *ultra vires* acts moot. Many states have enacted statutes providing for the protection of stockholders for corporate *ultra vires* acts by permitting suits against the officers of the corporation by the stockholders.

Some specifically licensed and controlled corporations do have limitations placed upon the type of contracts they may make. Banks and insurance companies are good examples of where such restrictions are evident. For example, a property-liability insurer may not be permitted to enter into contracts providing life insurance.

Capacity to Enter into Insurance Contracts.

Insurance Companies. Insurers usually are corporations and may enter into contracts like any other corporation, except for the limitations imposed upon them by their charter powers and by insurance regulations. Normally, insurers must meet financial requirements and be licensed to do business in the fields of insurance and in the areas of the country involved. Statutory law and insurance department regulations together determine the qualifications necessary to do business.

As with contracts of any corporation, an insurance contract that exceeds or is different from the authority granted the insurer may still be enforced against the insurer. Action may be taken by the regulatory authority to revoke its license, and the other party may proceed to enforce the contract as written. The insurer's wrongdoing will not be permitted as a defense in an action on the contract.

The contracts of nonadmitted insurers (those not licensed in a given jurisdiction) are enforceable as well. The problem is the difficulty of enforcement, not a problem of the legal right to sue.

Insurance Agents. Since the act of the agent is considered the act of the principal, it is not necessary for the agent to have contractual capacity. Even a contract entered into by an agent who is a minor, drunk, drugged, or insane cannot later be avoided by the insurer so long as the incompetent agent had the ability to carry out instructions. It is the responsibility of the insurance company not to permit such a person to represent it.

The Insurance Buying Public. Insureds are subject to the same general constraints as other members of the public, such as the requirements for emancipation and competency. Few cases have arisen since the insured can avoid a contract by canceling it or failing to pay a premium when due. In the few cases that have arisen concerning the lack of capacity of insureds, those judged incompetent for any reason generally obtained a refund of the full amount of premiums paid.

Consideration Another requirement for a contract is consideration. Consideration is an exchange of something of value between the parties. It is the thing that one person asks another to do in return for the promise. It is the bargained-for exchange.

Consideration may take several forms. It may be (1) a return promise, (2) an act performed, or (3) a forebearance to act, that is, an agreement not to do something. Consideration must be something of value, that is, there must be "valuable" consideration. A parent might declare: "In consideration of the love and affection I have for my son, I will convey my property located on X Street to him on January 1, 19X1." Such a consideration is neither "valuable" nor reciprocal and so the promise is unenforceable. Sometimes one encounters statements in the agreement that are specifically designed to satisfy the requirement that consideration be present: "In consideration of the sum of one dollar, hereby conveyed, and other valuable consideration, I promise to do the following." Such a statement clearly indicates a money exchange and alludes to other things of value which are involved.

As a consequence of the requirement that consideration be a part of enforceable agreements, promises to make a gift are, normally, not legally binding because it involves a unilateral promise with the intended recipient making no return promise or performing any act that could be considered consideration. Thus no consideration is involved and no legally enforceable agreement exists.

Courts will not be involved in determining the adequacy of the consideration. To do so would involve the court's attempts to measure whether what the parties are exchanging is reasonably equal in value. Exceptions may be made in situations where fraud is indicated, where there is an unequal exchange of identical units, or where the agreement appears unconscionable. That is, where there appears to be an excessively high or excessively low price for a service or goods. Only in such cases as these would the courts inquire into the adequacy of the consideration.

The last thing the courts wish to do is to get involved in determination of the "fairness" of contracts. Given that agreements are entered into freely and that both parties are competent, courts should not interfere relative to the fairness of the exchange. To intervene on one party's behalf would be to the disadvantage of the other. The long-settled rule applies that the courts normally "will leave the parties to a valid contract where it finds them."

Insurance contracts require the presence of consideration just like any other contract. The consideration given by the insurance company is its contingent promise to indemnify the insured upon the occurrence of an event insured against. The consideration given by the insured is payment of the premium or the promise to pay the premium at a later date. In property-liability insurance, prepayment of the premium is not required as a condition of the agreement, but the premium does become an obligation as soon as coverage attaches. When coverage has attached (the policy in full force and effect), the insured is obligated to pay the premium. This implied obligation arises out of the acceptance of the policy, even in the absence of an express agreement to pay the premium.

In life insurance it is normally provided that the insurance will not take effect until the first full premium is paid. There is, however, no duty on the part of the insured to pay any premium beyond the first one. Policies containing provisions for developing cash values also contain provisions to extend the effect of the policy by using these values to continue the contract in force should the policyowner not do so. Thus values accrued in the policy can be returned to the owner in the form of an extended period of coverage.

Genuine Assent Another element of a contract is that there must be real agreement between the parties which is not affected by fraud, duress, concealment, or mistake.

Most contracts are oral and most contracts are performed without recourse to the courts for enforcement of their provisions. Most contracts do not need to be written and, where existence of an oral contract can be demonstrated (perhaps an oral agreement by two parties made in front of competent, disinterested parties), courts find no difficulty in enforcing it.

The existence of some oral contracts may be very difficult to prove, and perjury by a supposed witness could lead to a party having to prove that an oral contract seriously detrimental to that party's interests did not exist. Oral contracts then can more easily lead to situations of fraud. Because of this, all states have enacted Statutes of Frauds which provide that contracts which are particularly susceptible to perjury must be in writing. Six of the most common situations which require that contracts be written are:

1. contracts involving the sale of land;
2. agreements that cannot be performed within one year;
3. promises to answer for the debts of another;
4. promises made in consideration of marriage;
5. promises made by executors of decedents' estates to pay debts of the estate from the executor's own funds;
6. contracts involving the sale of personal property in which the sale price is $500 or more.

By requiring that agreements such as those described above be in writing, fraud, duress, concealment, or mistakes are less likely to be involved. Such requirements place some restriction on what people can do regarding contracts, but inevitably improve commerce between parties. Oral agreements dealing with these situations cannot use the courts to enforce their conditions and so should not be used.

Written Insurance Contracts. Generally, oral contracts of insurance are valid and enforceable. The provisions of almost all of the types of statutes described above do not apply to insurance policies. Even though, for example, a policy is written for a period longer than one year, the contract could well be performed within a year, should a loss occur.

Parol Evidence. Should a contract of insurance be in written form, it will be considered the entire contract. It is reasonable to limit the terms of a contract to those expressed in it and not permit the allegation that additional agreements exist which should modify the written contract. The parol evidence rule therefore prevents the introduction of any prior or simultaneous oral evidence to contradict or vary the terms of the final written contract. Thus, statements made by the producer prior to or at the time of the written insurance contract will not normally be permitted by the courts to vary the written agreement. *Existing* written contracts may be modified orally, however.

Legal Purpose Contracts must be consistent with public policy. If the subject of some agreement between two parties is illegal, society's system of law should not be used to enforce the conditions of that agreement. So, even though there is an agreement, it is not a contract. It is not an "agreement enforceable by law." Thus contracts to commit crimes, contracts harmful to the public interest, agreements calling for excessive rates of interest (usury agreements), and wagering agreements are not contracts because such agreements have no legal purpose.

Insurance contracts must involve a legal subject matter and normally do. Illegality in insurance contracts is not a serious problem. Certain situations do exist, however, which may void the policy.

Insurance obtained on illegal property is not valid. Some property may not legally be possessed (flame throwers, cannons or machine guns, heroin, and marijuana are examples) and cannot be insured. An insurance contract cannot protect one against the consequences of an illegal act.

Public policy requires an insured to have an insurable interest in the life or property insured. This requirement demonstrates that some honest, legal damage can occur to the insured should a loss caused by an insured peril occur. In addition, no insurance contract will remain valid if the wrongful conduct of the insured causes the operation of the contract to violate public policy. Thus arson by an insured would render the contract unenforceable and would preclude recovery under the contract.

Form Required by Law for Insurance Contracts In property-liability insurance, policy form and policy wording may be required by statute or insurance department fiat. In cases where oral contracts are valid, the law presumes the agreement follows any required form and wording.

In life and health insurance no standard form is required, but statutes and insurance department regulations require certain standard provisions be a part of every contract. Thus, although not every aspect of a contract for life insurance is stipulated, each policy must contain certain standard provisions. For example, life insurance policies must contain standard wording and must treat such situations as suicide, grace periods, and incontestable clauses.

Checkpoints

1. Define:
    a. contract
    b. necessaries
    c. assent
    d. age of majority
2. List elements necessary in order for there to be a contract.
3. Define incompetency and identify factors that may make a party incompetent.
4. Define consideration and explain what forms consideration can take.

Unique Aspects of Insurance Contracts

All contracts must have an agreement, competent parties, consideration, and a legal objective. Some must also be in a required form. Insurance contracts must meet all these requirements. But insurance contracts also have features that make them unique, such as that they are conditional, contracts of adhesion, aleatory, unilateral, contracts of utmost good faith, and contracts of indemnity.

Conditional Contracts Insurance contracts are conditional. That is, they are dependent on an uncertain event. Normally, contracts involving a promise must eventually be fulfilled—the work is eventually done, the event ultimately takes place. In property-liability insurance and in term life insurance the contingency insured against may never take place. Thus performance under the contract may never be required and so these contracts are deemed conditional.

Contracts of Adhesion Many contracts are the final product of a bargaining procedure which includes an offer, counter offers, and many changes, until ultimately a final agreement is reached. Price, terms, and conditions are all subject to this bargaining, negotiating process. This is normally not the case with insurance contracts. There may be options and choices available, for example, full coverage or a deductible, named perils or "all-risks" coverage. But by and large, the general form of the contract is fixed. The insured has no opportunity to object to and have removed, for example, lines six and seven of the New York standard fire policy. The insured must either take it or leave it. This is especially true for a required form. The insured must *adhere* to the agreement as written, and so it is a contract of *adhesion.*

This is important to the insurance buying public because of the way in which courts view contracts of adhesion. Courts consistently have taken the position that since the insured had nothing to do with the wording of the contract, any inconsistency or ambiguity should be held strictly against the maker of the contract, the insurance company, and strictly in the favor of the *insured.* This presumes that any difficulty in determining the true meaning of the insurance policy has to be the fault of the insurer and obviously is not the insured's fault.

Adhesion partially accounts for having insurance contracts which do not change very often. To introduce a new policy would be to go through a series of court cases until the new wording has been tested, and in each case the insurance company can count on the courts interpreting any ambiguity in favor of the insured.

Pressures for "readability" are generating new contract forms despite predicted future court actions to define new wording.

Aleatory Contracts The term "aleatory" is related to good or bad luck, especially the risks of bad luck. The concept is that an aleatory contract is dependent upon an uncertain event or contingency as to both profit or loss.

Agreements between parties usually involve consideration that is reasonably equal. No one is willingly going to pay more than is needed nor is anyone going to give a customer much more than is called for. In purchasing a new automobile, for example, the bargaining process goes on, with a compromise being agreed upon which is usually less than the sticker price. At this point the buyer feels that the car is worth the money paid and the dealer feels that enough money was received for the car.

In the typical insurance transaction, this is not the case. The consideration exchanged between the parties is likely to be uneven. Usually, the insured receives more than the premium paid if a loss should occur. On the other hand, should no covered loss occur, the insured receives nothing for the premium except a coverage promise on which the insurance company did not have to make good. Only rarely would the consideration received by each party be relatively even. Because of uneven considerations, insurance contracts are considered aleatory in nature, since the risk of bad luck will largely determine the outcome of the contract.

Unilateral Contracts Insurance policies are called unilateral because only one party to the contract makes an enforceable promise. One party pays a premium, and the other party makes a promise, a unilateral promise. Where both parties make enforceable promises, an agreement would be a bilateral agreement or a promise for a promise. Once a policy becomes effective, the performance under the contract is almost all on the side of the insurer. The insured does agree, as a condition subsequent to the contract, to give notice of loss, separate damaged and undamaged property, and so forth. In the fire policy, for example, the obligation to perform, to pay for the loss, rests entirely with the insurance company if the insured meets the contract's loss conditions.

Contracts of Utmost Good Faith The law believes people should deal fairly with each other, that they should deal in good faith, but given this ideal, the law also obliges parties of a contract to protect themselves. After all, the court cannot spend its time passing upon the fairness and equity of agreements. *Caveat emptor,* or let the buyer beware, is a concept that demonstrates the obligation parties have to protect themselves.

Insurance contracts have been described as contracts of "utmost good faith." Insurance especially involves many aspects which require complete honesty and disclosure of all relevant facts between the parties because the very nature of the contract involves a promise, not a product. In addition, claims often involve human actions or failures rather than a defective product. Also, the consequences of insured incidences often involve people who were not involved in making the product. The beneficiary of a policy must rely upon the good faith of the life insurance company. The general public must depend upon the insurance company to handle a liability claim fairly. The long-term nature of many insurance policies also increases the need for utmost good faith.

Because of these public policy considerations, it is deemed in the public interest to require that the parties to an insurance contract act in utmost good faith. Utmost good faith places upon the applicant, especially, the requirement to disclose all facts material to the transaction. It places upon the insurer as well the obligation to deal with the client in complete honesty.

Concealment. Utmost good faith requires disclosure on the part of the applicant of all material facts relative to the transaction. The failure to disclose all material facts makes the contract voidable by the other party. Many aspects of the transaction involve fact, but failure to disclose all facts is not necessarily important or even required. It is only those facts that are *material* to the contract that must be disclosed. A *material fact* is a fact important to the transaction and one which the other relied upon when entering the agreement. Again, because of the great good faith aspects of the policy and the need of the public to rely upon the insurance transaction, concealment can make the policy voidable.

Warranties and Representations. A *warranty* is a fact regarding the subject of a contract that is either expressed or is implied to be true. To warrant something is to promise the truth of what is said. A *representation* is a statement by one party that is true to the best knowledge of that party. A fact warranted to be true is guaranteed to be true while a representation need only be true to the best of the party's knowledge.

Suppose that somewhere in the retelling of family history someone misinterpreted facts and passed on in error something that later would be a material fact in an insurance transaction (the cause of death of a family member, for example). Were this a warranty situation, the warranty would have been violated. On the other hand, a misrepresentation is a false statement of a material fact, but false within the knowledge of the person making the statement. Misrepresentation has the same effect as concealment. Whereas *concealment* is silence, misrepresentation is a positive statement. In both cases the contract becomes voidable by the other party.

Normally representations are affirmative statements made in connection with the application for insurance and are not normally a part of the contract. It is rare that statements are considered warranties. To do so would place too great a burden upon the applicant and lead to contracts being voided to the detriment of an innocent policyholder. Warranties are found chiefly in marine insurance where, because of the distances involved and the inability of the insurer to inspect the insured object, the company must rely upon the truth of the statements. Such items as the seaworthiness of the vessel, the directness of the route taken by the ship, and the legality of the cargo are subjects the facts of which must be warranted. Here, the simple fact of error breaches the warranty and voids coverage. With a misrepresentation, it must be material, false, and made with the intent to deceive to make the contract voidable.

Contracts of Indemnity To indemnify a person is to restore the person to the same position occupied immediately prior to the loss. To indemnify is to make a person financially "whole" again. The concept is one that considers neither a profit nor a loss but offers a return to the previous situation to the extent possible. The idea is to repair, to replace, or to pay in cash. If the insured suffers a not-paid loss, the insured was not indemnified. If the insured profited by receiving a sum greater than was lost, the insured was not indemnified.

Insurance contracts are meant to be contracts of indemnity, a means through which the injured party is compensated for the loss suffered. The concept is a financial one in that the insurance company will indemnify the claimant by means of a financial settlement. An insurance company, for example, will not usually go into the marketplace to replace a demolished vehicle with another of the same condition, make, and model. Rather, the insurer will pay a financial amount equal to the value of that vehicle excluding, of course, any deductibles.

The concept of indemnity is the very essence of insurance. It is what makes insurance work.

Insurable Interest. To be indemnified, a policyholder must have insurable interest. This is defined as a relationship between the insured, and the event insured against, of such a nature that the occurrence of that event will cause financial loss to the insured. In other words, the insured must have some right, relationship, or interest in the subject covered by the insurance contract and will be hurt financially if a loss occurs. Thus, if the policyholder does not have an insurable interest and therefore will not suffer a financial loss, there cannot be indemnity. To be indemnified, one must have an insurable interest.

The requirement of insurable interest accomplishes three ends: (1) it prevents wagering, (2) it helps to establish the upper limit of a loss, and (3) it reduces moral hazard.

In a wager or bet, one deliberately places oneself in a position to suffer financial loss. If the wrong horse comes in or the wrong card turns up, the bet can be lost and a financial loss is suffered. But with a wager, this possibility of financial loss and gain is deliberately created. In insurance the relationship creating a possible financial loss must be already present and not created deliberately.

Were one to insure one's own house, it is merely taking care of the fact that a loss could well occur which would damage the homeowner. So an insurable interest exists. But if one were to insure a neighbor's house, no real chance for financial loss exists as only the owner would suffer. Thus, only the owner can legitimately purchase insurance and only the owner has an insurable interest (always, of course, subject to the interest of any mortgagee).

Often the maximum limit of a loss is created by the *extent* of the insurable interest possessed by the insured. A person owning a one-third share in a building can reasonably suffer only one-third the value of the building if it is destroyed. Although the total loss is suffered by all owners, a part owner can only suffer the loss of his or her share. Thus, the extent of the interest establishes the extent of that person's loss.

Requiring an insurable interest helps to reduce morale hazard. Morale hazard is some human element, disposition, or inclination likely to increase the probability or severity of loss. Just as a physical hazard (faulty wiring, oily rags) can increase the likelihood or severity of a loss, human actions can also. Carelessness, an opportunity to profit, these kinds of human considerations will cause losses. By requiring a relationship whereby the insured will suffer should a loss occur, the tendency toward carelessness is lessened. By not issuing insurance in situations where a profit is to be made should the accident happen, fewer losses will happen. Thus, requiring the existence of an insurable interest will help reduce the human tendency to cause losses.

Actual Cash Value. In order to be indemnified, one must be able to determine the extent of the loss. What was the value of the property lost? What was its actual cash value? Actual cash value is generally taken to mean the replacement cost of the property minus depreciation and obsolescence. The actual cash value of a ten-year-old roof, costing $2,000 to replace, would be $1,000, given an expected useful life of twenty years. This could be in spite of the fact that the roof cost only $1,000 originally.

Actual cash value is an effort to arrive at the true amount of the loss. In order to be indemnified, one should collect the actual cash value of the property should it be damaged or destroyed.

Sometimes this is very difficult to determine. Antiques often have values that are hard to determine. Many objects have values that can be measured only after an involved process of appraisal. In some cases, it makes sense for the insured and the insurer to come to a prior agreement as to the value of an object. These agreements are "valued policies" and in a sense can be considered an exception to the rule that objects be insured for their actual cash value in order to preserve the indemnity concept. Valued policies are a possible exception, because value normally changes with time and the best determination of value would therefore be at the time of the loss, not when the policy was taken out. Conversely, valued policies can also be viewed simply as a pre-agreement as to what sum would constitute indemnity. Either way, valued policies are commonly used in insurance.

Some states have valued policy laws. Such statutes require that, in the event of a total loss to real (not personal) property, the face amount of the contract must be paid. This is to insure that the policyholder receives the amount of protection for which he or she paid premiums. Such laws would preclude, for example, a company collecting premiums on a value of, say, $100,000 on a factory, then at a total loss saying its actual cash value was only $50,000. If the insured paid premiums on one value then a total loss should result in a payment of that value. Insurance companies are generally uncomfortable with such laws because it places a serious burden to have constantly updated accurate appraisals of insured properties, and this is literally impossible to do. Many view such a settlement in excess of the actual cash value of the property as a violation of indemnity.

So too are policies which insure for the replacement value of property. Indemnification requires that depreciation be taken into account. If the full replacement cost of property is paid in times of rising costs and inflation, it has the effect of replacing old with new.

Yet insurers are concerned with policyholders receiving adequate, satisfactory settlements at the time of loss. If depreciation takes too great a share of the value, the settlement is inadequate for the insured to replace the property. Thus, the property owner faces the necessity of coming up with extra funds to get into a comparable property.

Then, too, people often underinsure and insurers encourage people to insure to value. In this way, insurance companies get a premium that more adequately reflects the risk and values involved. Many insurers use policy provisions that automatically adjust the amount of insurance to reflect the rising value of property.

Another means used by insurance companies to encourage insurance to replacement value is to insert a clause in homeowners policies that permits the settlement of partial losses without regard to depreciation if the policyholder is carrying at least 80 percent of the replacement cost of the dwelling.

Apportionment—Pro-Rata Liability. Another policy provision serving to buttress the indemnity principle is the policy provision for apportioning losses. Differing provisions apply when other additional insurance is involved on real and personal property. Generally, a clause works to limit the company's liability to some proportion of the total loss which that company's coverage bears to the total coverage on that property from all insurers. Such provisions prevent duplicate payments and allocate loss costs equitably among the insurers.

Subrogation. The typical subrogation clause allows the assignment of any rights of recovery the insured may have against the third party to the insurer, to the extent of the insurer's payment to the insured. This helps effect indemnity by preventing the insured from collecting both from the company and from a third party. It also provides equity by permitting the company to be reimbursed for any payment it had to make because of the negligence of a third party. Subrogation ultimately results in the responsible party bearing the loss.

Checkpoints

1. Explain why insurance contracts are called contracts of adhesion.
2. Explain why insurance contracts are called contracts of good faith.
3. Define the term "indemnity" and explain its importance to the insurance transaction.

4. Define insurable interest and explain when it must be present in property-liability insurance.

SUMMARY

The legal foundations of tort law arise from common law as modified by statutes. The essential elements of a tort are a right not to be harmed (or a duty to refrain from causing harm), a violation of the right or duty, damage as a result of the breach of duty, and no justification for the breach of duty. The breach of duty may arise from intentional acts, acts that society considers inherently dangerous, or unintentional acts. Negligence is measured by what a prudent man would have done in a similar situation as modified by contributory, comparative, or last clear chance negligence laws.

Agency arises from an agreement of one party, the agent, agreeing to act on behalf of another party, the principal. Agency is created by appointment, estoppel, or by ratification. Agents have express, implied, or apparent authority from their principals. Agency may be terminated by lapse of time, accomplishment of purpose, revocation, renunciation, death or loss of capacity, impossibility, or changed circumstances.

Law of contracts requires that each contract have certain elements present to be valid. The elements are agreement, competent parties, consideration, genuine assent, and a legal purpose. Insurance contracts, in addition to the essential elements, have certain unique characteristics. Insurance contracts additionally are conditional, contracts of adhesion, aleatory, unilateral, contracts of utmost good faith, and contracts of indemnity.

Chapter Notes

1. William L. Prosser, *Law of Torts,* 4th ed. (St. Paul: West Publishing Co., 1979), p. 2.
2. Henry Campbell Black, *Black's Law Dictionary,* 4th ed. (St. Paul: West Publishing Co., 1968), p. 1457.
3. Kimmerle vs. New York Evening Journal, 262 N.Y. 99, 186 NE 217 (1933).
4. Seymour D. Thompson, *Commentaries on the Law of Negligence,* Rev. ed. (Indianapolis: Bobbs-Merrill Co., 1901-1914), I.2.
5. C. A. Kulp and John W. Hall, *Casualty Insurance,* 4th ed. (New York: The Ronald Press, 1968), p. 52.

CHAPTER 4

Homeowners Insurance

Chapter 3 provided an analysis of general and insurance contract principles. Those principles will now be given meaning through analysis of the homeowners policies. First, however, it is appropriate to develop certain principles of insurance policy contract construction to see how policies may be analyzed.

INSURANCE POLICY CONSTRUCTION

Any insurance policy may be divided into five parts:

1. Declarations
2. Insuring Agreement(s)
3. Exclusions
4. Conditions and Miscellaneous Provisions
5. Definitions

In many cases, policies do not use these specific labels. Still, every clause or provision of an insurance contract fits into one of these categories.

Declarations

The declarations usually appear as a separate form or as the first page of the policy. This declarations section, completed by a computer, typewriter, or handwriting, personalizes the policy as to various aspects of the exposure assumed by the insurer. Information necessary for any insurance policy includes the name and address of the named insured, the policy inception date, the amount(s) of insurance, and the premium. Other information to be entered varies by type of policy—the property and its location or other subject of insurance, identification of lender interests such as a mortgagee or lienholder, deductibles, and physical aspects.

The importance of correct information in the declarations is emphasized by a policy condition which appears in many policy forms:

> Declarations: By acceptance of this policy, the named insured agrees that the statements in the declarations are his agreements and representations, that this policy is issued in reliance upon the truth of such representations and that this policy embodies all agreements existing between himself and the company or any of its agents relating to this insurance.

The courts will protect an insured should the insurer attempt to apply the condition too narrowly. For example, a minor error in the description of the exposure which does not affect acceptability or the premium charged would not provide a supportable basis for the insurer to deny a claim. The declarations should, however, be completed accurately.

Insuring Agreement

The insuring agreement(s) describe the policy coverage in broad terms. If coverage for an accident or loss is to be included, the basis for the insurer to pay must be found in the wording of an insuring agreement. Generally, the insuring agreement(s) appear immediately after the declarations, or at the beginning of the printed provisions of the policy.

Exclusions

The function of exclusions is to narrow to intended bounds the coverage described in the insuring agreements. Exclusions have been classified in numerous ways, but at the risk of oversimplification, all exclusions fill one of two purposes: (1) to exclude because a different form of insurance is more appropriate; or (2) to exclude because the premium charged does not include the exposure for that form of coverage.

For example, a business owner may wish to insure against liability for injuries or damage at the business premises. The insuring agreement might broadly state that any liability arising out of the location is covered. Then, the exclusions would eliminate any coverage for injuries to employees (because the insured should have workers' compensation insurance for such exposure); or for any automobiles, aircraft or boats (because those are subjects for auto, aviation, and marine coverages). In the second category, the exclusions might provide that no coverage exists for damaging property of others in the insured's care, custody, or control, or for pollution or contamination of the air, earth, or water, or for injury or damage intentionally caused by the insured.

Conditions and Miscellaneous Provisions

"Conditions" and "Miscellaneous Provisions" are, from a legal standpoint, distinct from one another. They usually appear together, however, mixed under the title "Conditions" or "General Provisions." Here, the legal distinctions are not important. Insurance policies are *conditional* contracts. The conditions with which the insured must comply, if the insurer is expected to perform, appear here. The insured may be required to give prompt notice of loss of the insurer, to cooperate in various aspects of the claim, to furnish proof of the loss, and to perform or refrain from performing other acts. Other provisions include what have been called "ground rules of the game." Included, for example, are subjects such as how the policy may be canceled, how the policy will apply if other insurance exists, how disputes between insurer and insured will be resolved, and the insurer's subrogation rights. In an ideally constructed insurance policy, no basic coverage provisions should appear in the conditions section, but they sometimes do.

Definitions

In many policy contracts of recent design, a section entitled "Definitions" is included. Here, words and phrases used throughout the policy are given their full definition. Wherever those words and phrases appear, they are printed in bold-face type to remind the reader that a definition applies.

Today, few insurance policies have no forms or endorsements attached. These appendages may modify or add to any of the four basic policy segments. *The provisions of forms or endorsements supersede those of the policy to which they are attached.*

INSURANCE POLICY ANALYSIS

Policy analysis, as used here, means the process of determining if, and to what extent, a specific loss is covered under a specific policy. A method of policy analysis involves posing particular questions in a certain order. One set of questions is used for any "first-party" or property contract, another for a "third-party" or liability contract. The questions contemplate an absence of peripheral problems such as insured's failure to comply with policy conditions, the policy being voidable because of a concealment or misrepresentation by the insured, or the loss occurring at a time not within the policy period. Given those caveats, the questions asked to make a determination on a loss situation under a *property* insurance contract are:

1. To establish whether *any* coverage is provided:
   a. Was the person or organization that suffered the loss protected under the policy?
   b. Was that which was damaged "covered property" and at a covered location?
   c. Was the loss caused by a covered peril?
   d. Are the cause and effect free of all exclusionary provisions?
2. If an affirmative answer applies to all of the above questions, to establish the *degree* of coverage:
   a. What valuation basis applies to the property?
   b. Is there other insurance; if so, how does this policy interact with others?
   c. Does a deductible apply?
   d. What is the limit of coverage?

For a *liability* insurance policy:

1. Does the insuring agreement apply to what happened?
2. Is the person against whom claim is made an "insured"?
3. Does an exclusion apply?
4. Is there other insurance; if so, how does this policy interact with others?
5. What is the limit of coverage?

This method is comprehensive, but not foolproof. For example, liability insurance is normally written without a deductible, but there *can* be a deductible.

It is not necessary to memorize this or any other method of policy analysis. Rather, it is important to develop a "feel" for the important issues and an order in which they should be addressed. Persons who have not learned an organized approach to policy analysis will go about it in a haphazard way. Look at the questions again, but in reverse order. Why be concerned over the amount of insurance if the loss is excluded? Why bother even to look at the exclusions if coverage is not basically provided by the insuring agreement?

Typically, the successful producer has developed a reasonable degree of expertise in policy analysis. Responding authoritatively to insureds' coverage questions is a necessary function. Of more importance, however, is the process of relating contract provisions to an insured's exposures in order to formulate a sound insurance program. Product knowledge and the ability to use it, responsibly and profitably, is the main thrust of the remainder of the AAI 81 course, and all of AAI 82.

HOMEOWNERS INSURANCE

The homeowners program (HO) is regarded as the most popularly received, successful innovation in insurance marketing. Within a brief period after its introduction in the 1950s, virtually all eligible insureds were converted from their separate fire, theft, and liability monoline policies to this modern "package" policy. For the coverage-conscious person who owned several policies, the program offered improved coverage at lower cost. For others, substantially better coverage was provided at a minimal increase in premium cost.

The "standard" homeowners policies in use by most companies are promulgated by the Insurance Services Office (ISO). While a portion of the total market is insured by companies using independent forms, the general framework is the same—to package all nonautomobile property and liability insurance needs for an average family into a single policy. ISO has introduced three homeowners versions since 1974. Since the third version introduced in 1984 has received approval in most states, it is the version examined here. The older ISO programs and individual company plans vary in detail, but few differences will be found in scope.

General

The homeowners policy includes a core of indivisible, mandatory coverages designed to fit the fundamental needs of a typical family. There are six different forms available:

1. HO-1—Basic Form
   This form provides the lowest cost coverage for owner-occupants of dwellings, providing specified peril coverage on the dwelling, other structures, and the insured's personal property, plus liability protection for claims arising from the residence and personal activities. This form has been withdrawn in many states and will not be examined in detail here.
2. HO-2—Broad Form
   The broad form is also for owner-occupants of dwellings and is the same as the basic form except broader specified peril coverage is afforded.

3. HO-3—Special Form
   HO-3 is used for owner-occupants, but coverage on buildings is "all-risks" rather than specified perils. The perils of HO-2 apply to personal property.
4. HO-4—Contents Broad Form
   This form is designed for tenants and other occupants of residential premises (such as apartments) who are not eligible for one of the preceding forms because the building occupied is not owned by them or is ineligible. Except for coverage on structures, it is fundamentally the same as HO-2.
5. HO-6—Unit-Owners Form
   This form is similar to HO-4 but includes some special provisions for exposures inherent in ownership of condominium units and cooperative apartment shares.
6. HO-8—Modified Coverage Form
   This is a "stripped-down" form of coverage for owner-occupants of dwellings, similar to HO-1 but more restrictive, designed for persons who do not meet underwriting standards for the other forms.

As liability coverage is the same under all of the forms, and property covered and not covered is effectively the same in all, the essential difference boils down to what property perils are insured. For owner-occupants, coverage becomes progressively broader from HO-1 to HO-2 to HO-3; HO-8 is a special case. Those for whom HO-4 and HO-6 are designed do not have any choice as to insured perils.

Approximately fifty endorsements are available for optional modifications of the coverage included in the HO forms. With these, a significant degree of flexibility is offered to tailor the policy for most individual needs.

Eligibility Forms HO-1, HO-2, HO-3, and HO-8 may be issued only to the owner-occupant of a one- or two-family dwelling. Rules prohibit issuance to owners who do not occupy (occasional rental to others is permitted), to cover trailers or mobile homes, or to cover dwellings on farm premises. Persons purchasing a dwelling under a long-term installment contract, but without legal title to the property, are eligible in the same manner as titled owners and occupants under a life estate arrangement. Additionally, a dwelling under construction is eligible if the named insured is the intended owner-occupant.

Form HO-4 may be issued to a tenant who maintains a residential premises in any kind of structure. Persons who maintain a residence in a building they own, but which is not a one- or two-family dwelling, are eligible. Only owners of condominium units and cooperative apartment shareowners are eligible for HO-6, although it is not required that the insured be an occupant of the unit.

If a two-family dwelling is co-owned by the two occupants, one of the owner-occupant forms may be issued in the name of one of the two, with the other named as an additional insured to cover that person's interest in the building. Then, the second party may be issued an HO-4. The combination gives both co-owners complete homeowners coverage.

If a portion of the premises is used other than for private residential occupancy, eligibility rules permit (1) not more than two roomers or boarders per family unit and (2) an incidental business occupancy such as an office, private school, or studio.

Coverages and Amounts The HO forms contain the following coverages:

Section I
- Coverage A—Dwelling (not included in HO-4).
- Coverage B—Other structures (located at the same premises as the insured's dwelling under Coverage A) (not included in HO-4 or HO-6).
- Coverage C—Personal property.
- Coverage D—Loss of use.

Section II
- Coverage E—Personal liability.
- Coverage F—Medical payments to others.

The HO package includes all of these coverages—none may be deleted. An amount of insurance is selected for Coverage A (Coverage C when HO-4 or HO-6 applies), subject to certain minimum limits. The limits for other coverages, except E and F, are determined as percentages of the selected amount. The package includes limits of $100,000 per occurrence for Coverage E and $1,000 per person for Coverage F in all of the forms.

The minimum amounts and percentages for Section I are in Exhibit 4-1. For example, an insured choosing HO-3 and desiring $50,000 coverage on the dwelling building would automatically receive $5,000 Coverage B, $25,000 Coverage C, $10,000 Coverage D, $100,000 Coverage E, and $1,000 Coverage F. If any of these limits are lower than needed, increased coverage may be obtained through the use of options.

Declarations A homeowners policy is completed by issuance of a declarations page, attachment of one of the six base forms, and any mandatory or optional endorsements required by rules or optional coverages desired. Insurers tend to individualize the style and format for their declarations page, but the information to be completed must include:

Exhibit 4–1
Standard Limits for Homeowners Coverages — Section 1

Form	Coverage A	Coverage B	Coverage C	Coverage D
HO-1	†	10% of A	50% of A	10% of A
HO-2	†	10% of A	50% of A	20% of A
HO-3	†	10% of A	50% of A	20% of A
HO-4	n.a.	n.a.	†	20% of C
HO-6	$1,000	n.a.	†	40% of C
HO-8	†	10% of A	50% of A	10% of A

†Minimum limits prescribed by individual insurer rules.

- Identification and mailing address of named insured.
- Policy period (usually one or three years).
- Location of residence (if different from mailing address).
- Limit for each Coverage, A through F.
- Premium.
- Identification of form and endorsements attached, by number and edition date.
- Deductible amount applicable to Section I.
- Address of additional locations where insured maintains a residence.
- Mortgagee name and address.
- Countersignature date, agent's signature.

The declarations are of special importance because no reference to a deductible appears in the forms, the provision being wholly contained on the declarations page. The printed statement appears: "In case of a loss under Section I, we cover only that part of the loss over the deductible stated." In most states, the standard deductible is $250. This means that, for Section I losses, no loss payment is due if the insured's covered loss is less than $250, and that amount will be deducted from any loss payment if the insured's loss is over $250.

There are individual state variations which replace or provide options different from the $250 deductible. In addition, there are variations (not necessarily applicable in every state):

1. The $250 deductible may be reduced to $100.
2. The optional $100 deductible applicable to all Section I losses may be supplemented by a $250 deductible for theft losses only.
3. Flat, higher deductibles of $500, $1,000, and $2,500 are available.
4. A special deductible, sometimes called a graduated amount deductible plan, (endorsement HO-274), may be employed with

HO-1, HO-2, HO-3, or HO-8. Under this plan, the deductible varies with the Coverage A limit. The lowest deductible is $300, applying when the Coverage A limit is less than $60,000. The deductible amount ranges upward, reaching $1,200 when the Coverage A limit is from $220,000 to $250,000.

The variety of deductibles offered are valuable tools of both underwriting and risk management. The submission that is unacceptable to an insurer at a low deductible may be accepted at a higher deductible. The insured who is willing to retain a higher deductible than the basic deductible is offered the opportunity to achieve premium savings.

Checkpoints

1. Describe the eligibility for each of the six homeowners forms.
2. Compare the coverage provided by the six forms.
3. List the name of each homeowners coverage, A through F.
4. List the minimum amount requirement for each homeowners form and the percentages of such amounts that apply to other Section I coverages.
5. Identify the Section I deductible variations available in the homeowners program.

Coverage for Dwelling Owner-Occupants—Special Form HO-3

The two most popular homeowners forms are HO-2 and HO-3. The HO-3 was chosen for detailed analysis because it is an "all-risks" contract for some coverages and "specified perils" for others. The other forms for owner-occupants are discussed later, by comparison to the HO-3.

The reproductions from the HO-3 form are presented in generally the same order as they appear in the printed form. There is a degree of reordering, however, where useful. Comments include information on coverage options available, at points where their use would be appropriate. All HO options are reviewed collectively in a later chapter.

The HO-3 is written in the modern, readable, nonlegalistic, "plain-talk" style, as is the case with all forms and endorsements in the homeowners program. The first page of the form contains definitions of words and phrases used throughout. They are printed in bold-face type wherever used.

The first part of Section I in the form describes the "coverages" (A, B, C, and D). Coverage A, dwelling, is:

We cover:

1. the dwelling on the **residence premises** shown in the Declarations, including structures attached to the dwelling; and
2. materials and supplies located on or next to the **residence premises** used to construct, alter or repair the dwelling or other structures on the **residence premises.**
   This coverage does not apply to land, including land on which the dwelling is located. **"Residence premises"** means: (a) the one family dwelling, other structures, and grounds; (b) or that part of any other building: where you reside and which is shown as the "residence premises" in the Declarations.

The "dwelling" by definition includes everything attached to it, such as plumbing, heating and cooling equipment, lighting fixtures, permanently affixed wall-to-wall carpeting, canopies, patio covering and screening, and garages. Detached structures are a subject for Coverage B, and property not affixed to the realty is a subject for Coverage C (except for materials and supplies referred to in b).

The Coverage A limit should be selected with care, giving consideration to all property included in this definition. The Coverage A limit should be not less than 80 percent of the *current replacement cost* of the dwelling in order for losses to be settled at replacement cost.

Coverage B, other structures, reads:

We cover other structures on the **residence premises** set apart from the dwelling by clear space. This includes structures connected to the dwelling by only a fence, utility line, or similar connection.

We do not cover other structures:

1. used in whole or in part for **business** purposes; or
2. rented or held for rental to any person not a tenant of the dwelling, unless used solely as a private garage.

Property commonly found on a residence premises, within this definition, includes a garage, private guest house, swimming pool, fence, tool shed, pump, tennis court, and greenhouse. Other structures which are buildings should be evaluated at current replacement cost as for Coverage A.

The 10 percent of Coverage A that is automatically provided as a Coverage B limit may not be increased, but specific coverage on scheduled structures may be obtained with endorsement HO-48, Other Structures—Increased Limit. For example, if the Coverage A limit is $50,000 (making Coverage B limit $5,000) but the insured desires a total of $15,000 on a detached private guest house, $10,000 coverage could be provided through HO-48.

While Coverage B does not apply to structures on the residence premises that are rented to others (except for a private garage), specific coverage on such structures may be obtained with endorsement HO-40—Structures Rented to Others—Residence Premises. Coverage may also be afforded if an "other structure" on the residence premises is used for certain business purposes by attachment of endorsement HO-42.

The first paragraph of Coverage C, personal property (and relevant definitions) reads:

> We cover personal property owned or used by an **Insured** while it is anywhere in the world. At your request, we will cover personal property owned by:
> 1. others while the property is on the part of the **residence premises** occupied by an **Insured;**
> 2. a guest or a **residence employee,** while the property is in any residence occupied by an **Insured.**
>
> **"insured"** means you and the following residents of your household:
> a. your relatives;
> b. other persons under the age of 21 and in the care of any person named above.
>
> **"residence employee"** means:
> a. an employee of any **insured** whose duties are related to the maintenance or use of the **residence premises,** including household or domestic services; or
> b. one who performs similar duties elsewhere not related to the **business** of an **insured.**

Subject to a limitation in the next paragraph, the full Coverage C limit applies to covered property worldwide. Property owned by others, but being used by the insured, is covered in the same way as the insured's own property. The insured has the option to extend the benefit of Coverage C to guests and residence employees while their property is located at a residence occupied by the insured.

The 50 percent of Coverage A that automatically applies as a Coverage C limit may be increased to any desired amount. The 50 percent is an arbitrary figure deemed to be appropriate for the majority of homeowners. Insureds who can be persuaded to complete a household inventory may find their actual personal property values total more than 50 percent of their Coverage A limit and may desire a higher Coverage C limit.

The Coverage C limit may also be reduced to as low as 40 percent of Coverage A. Credits for such reduction are so small that lowering the automatic limit is generally inadvisable. Insureds are usually too conservative in estimates of their personal property values.

Under the basic forms, personal property should be evaluated by insureds at *actual cash value.* Replacement cost coverage is available as an option by attachment of endorsement HO-90, Personal Property Replacement Cost.

Coverage C provisions continue:

> Our limit of liability for personal property usually located at an **insured's** residence, other than the **residence premises**, is 10% of the limit of liability for Coverage C, or $1000, whichever is greater. Personal property in a newly acquired principal residence is not subject to this limitation for the 30 days from the time you begin to move the property there.

For this 10 percent or $1,000 (minimum) limit on personal property at other residences, which is the exception to the full Coverage C limit applying worldwide, emphasis is on the word "usually." For example, when the insured rents a cottage for a brief vacation period, the insured's property is *not* subject to this limitation. If a secondary residence is owned or rented on a long-term basis, with property *usually* kept there, that property is subject to the limit. The limitation also applies to a student residing in an apartment or dormitory at a school away from home. In most cases, the 10 percent of Coverage C limit is adequate. The 10 percent or minimum $1,000 limit may be increased, however, with endorsement HO-50—Increased Limit on Personal Property In Other Residences, stating a specific increased amount for each such location.

If the insured maintains one or more secondary residences, a separate HO policy is usually advisable. Such coverage should be in the same company that insures the primary residence because of coverage overlaps and applicability of a "duplication of coverage" premium credit.

The Coverage C description continues:

> **Special Limits of Liability.** These limits do not increase the Coverage C limit of liability. The special limit for each following numbered category below is the total limit for each loss for all property in that category.
>
> 1. $200 on money, bank notes, bullion, gold other than goldware, silver other than silverware, platinum, coins and medals.
> 2. $1,000 on securities, accounts, deeds, evidences of debt, letters of credit, notes other than bank notes, manuscripts, passports, tickets and stamps.
> 3. $1,000 on watercraft, including their trailers, furnishings, equipment and outboard motors.
> 4. $1,000 on trailers not used with watercraft.
> 5. $1,000 on grave markers.
> 6. $1,000 for loss by theft of jewelry, watches, furs, precious and semi-precious stones.
> 7. $2,000 for loss by theft of firearms.
> 8. $2,500 for loss by theft of silverware, silver-plated ware, goldware, gold-plated ware and pewterware. This includes flatware, hollowware, tea sets, trays and trophies made of or including silver, gold or pewter.
> 9. $2,500 on property, on the **residence premises**, used at any time or in any manner for any **business** purpose.

10. $250 on property, away from the **residence premises,** used at any time or in any manner for any **business** purpose.

These internal limits on various types of personal property are self-explanatory. Special limits 1-5 and 9 and 10 apply limitations to loss from any peril whereas 6-8 limit the coverage only if loss is by theft.

By endorsement, Special Provisions (HO-300), personal records are added to item 2. The endorsement applies the $1,000 limit regardless of the medium such records are kept on. The limit also includes the cost to research and replace the lost or damaged material.

The limits in 1, 2, 6, 7, and 8 may be increased:

1. The $200 limit on money and similar property may be increased to not more than $1,000.
2. The $1,000 limit on securities and similar property may be increased to not more than $2,000.
3. The $1,000 theft limit on jewelry, furs, and similar property may be increased to $5,000 subject, however, to a limit of $1,000 on any one article.
4. The $2,500 theft limit on silverware and similar property may be increased in increments of $500 to not over $10,000.
5. The $2,000 theft limit on guns may be increased in increments of $100 to not over $6,000.
6. The $2,500 on premises limit for business property may be increased in $2,500 increments up to $10,000. Any increases do not apply to samples, for delivery, or in storage. Such property away from the residence premises is covered for 10 percent of the on-premises limit.

Any or all of the increases may be accomplished with endorsement HO-65, Coverage C—Increased Special Limits of Liability. The standard HO program does not provide for increases in any of the other special limits.

The $1,000 limit on watercraft and equipment affords modest property coverage for an incidental exposure such as a rowboat or canoe; Coverage C perils, however, do not include marine perils. The typical watercraft property warranting special attention is the boat with outboard motor, trailer and various other accessories. While no standard HO option provides for needed coverage, most companies offer an HO endorsement that provides broad coverage on such equipment. If not, the exposure can be handled by a separate inland marine policy. Physical coverages for private watercraft are described in a later chapter.

If the maximum HO limit on jewelry and furs is insufficient to cover the insured's exposure on such property, "all-risks" coverage may be afforded by scheduling individual items with a specific amount on each, by endorsement HO-61—Scheduled Personal Property Endorsement. Silverware (with no specific scheduling requirement) may also be covered under this "all-risks" endorsement if HO limits are not adequate for the exposure, or if broader coverage on such property is desired.

In addition to jewelry, furs, and silverware, the following types of property may also be covered for "all-risks" on the HO-61 endorsement:

Photographic equipment
Musical instruments
Golfer's equipment
Fine arts
Stamp or coin collections

For insureds with gun collections, there is no standard HO basis to provide coverage if the $6,000 maximum available theft limit is inadequate. Many insurers offer a "sporting goods floater" or similarly titled inland marine form. Physical damage on trailers beyond the limited coverage under HO should be handled by automobile insurance.

Coverage C concludes by listing property that is not covered:

> **Property Not Covered.** We do not cover:
> 1. articles separately described and specifically insured in this or other insurance;
> 2. animals, birds or fish;
> 3. motor vehicles or all other motorized land conveyances. This includes:
>   a. equipment and accessories; or
>   b. any device or instrument for the transmitting, recording, receiving or reproduction of sound or pictures which is operated by power from the electrical system of motor vehicles or all other motorized land conveyances, including:
>   (1) accessories or antennas; or
>   (2) tapes, wires, records, discs or other media for use with any such device or instrument;
>   while in or upon the vehicle or conveyance.
>   We do cover vehicles or conveyances not subject to motor vehicle registration which are:
>   a. used to service an **insured's** residence; or
>   b. designed for assisting the handicapped;
> 4. aircraft and parts. Aircraft means any contrivance used or designed for flight, except model or hobby aircraft not used or designed to carry people or cargo;
> 5. property of roomers, boarders and other tenants, except property of roomers and boarders related to an **insured;**
> 6. property in an apartment regularly rented or held for rental to others by an **insured;**
> 7. property rented or held for rental to others off the **residence premises;**
> 8. a. books of account, drawings or other paper records; or

b. electronic data processing tapes, wires, records, discs or other software media;

containing **business** data. But, we do cover the cost of blank or unexposed records and media;

9. credit cards or fund transfer cards except as provided in Additional Coverages 6.

The Special Provisions endorsement (HO-300) deletes number 8 and replaces it with:

8. business data, including such data stored in:
   a. books of account, drawings or other paper records; or
   b. electronic data processing tapes, wires, records, discs or other software media.

However, we do cover the cost of blank recording or storage media, and of pre-recorded computer programs available on the retail market.

The purpose of No. 1 is to prevent overlap between Coverage C and scheduled personal property coverage or other insurance on specific types of property. If some property normally included under Coverage C is covered under the scheduled personal property endorsement or otherwise specifically insured, its value should be excluded in establishing the needed Coverage C limit.

No. 3 prevents overlap with automobile insurance but has the effect of applying coverage to property such as a lawn mower, tractor, unlicensed truck used to maintain the premises, or motorized wheelchair. If coverage is desired on motorized equipment such as go-carts, snowmobiles, mopeds, or trail bikes, it should be provided under an automobile or recreational vehicle type of policy. It excludes CB radios, mobile phones, tape players, and similar property, including media such as tapes, while in a motor vehicle. These types of property may optionally be covered in an automobile insurance policy.

Personal property related to rental of living space to others is excluded under Nos. 5 and 6. The only way provided under the standard HO program to cover such personal property is through use of endorsement HO-308, Landlord's Furnishings, which covers only limited types of property for a limit of $1,000, which may not be increased.

Coverage D, Loss of Use reads:

The limit of liability for Coverage D is the total limit for all the coverages that follow.

1. If a loss covered under this Section makes that part of the **residence premises** where you reside not fit to live in, we cover, at your choice, either of the following. However, if the **residence premises** is not your principal place of residence, we will not provide the option under paragraph (b) below.

a. **Additional Living Expense,** meaning any necessary increase in living expenses incurred by you so that your household can maintain its normal standard of living; or

b. **Fair Rental Value** meaning the fair rental value of that part of the **residence premises** where you reside less any expenses that do not continue while the premises is not fit to live in.

Payment under (a) or (b) will be for the shortest time required to repair or replace the damage or, if you permanently relocate, the shortest time required for your household to settle elsewhere.

2. If loss covered under this Section makes that part of the **residence premises** rented to others or held for rental by you not fit to live in, we cover the:

Fair Rental Value, meaning the fair rental value of that part of the **residence premises** rented to others or held for rental by you less any expenses that do not continue while the premises are not fit to live in.

Payment will be for the shortest time required to repair or replace that part of the premises rented or held for rental.

3. If a civil authority prohibits you from use of the **residence premises** as a result of direct damage to neighboring premises by a Peril Insured Against in this policy, we cover the Additional Living Expense or Fair Rental Value loss as provided under 1 and 2 above for no more than two weeks.

The periods of time under 1, 2, and 3 above are not limited by expiration of this policy.

We do not cover loss or expense due to cancellation of a lease or agreement.

In summary, Coverage D covers extraordinary living expenses of the insured family for the period required to repair, rebuild, or permanently relocate the residence if it becomes uninhabitable because of damage from an insured peril. The insured is given the option, however, to receive the fair rental value of the residence during the repairing/rebuilding/relocation period. If a part of the premises covered by the policy is rented or held for rental, the insured is also reimbursed for the fair rental value for the same period.

The 20 percent of Coverage A which automatically applies for Coverage D is usually adequate for the typical insured. The limit may, however, be increased to any desired amount. This might be considered in special situations such as a large family.

Loss Settlement Having seen what property is covered under Section I, it is appropriate at this point to consider how the property will be valued in any loss payment. Personal property, awnings, carpeting, household appliances, outdoor antennas, and outdoor equipment and structures which are not buildings are settled at actual cash value (ACV) or the cost to repair or replace, whichever is less. Actual cash value usually means, in this context, the cost to replace the item less physical depreciation.

For buildings, if the amount of insurance is 80 percent or greater than the building's replacement cost at the time of loss, losses are settled at replacement cost (cost new without deduction for depreciation). Coverage A and B limits and the cost to repair or replace act as limits for loss settlement.

This clause should provide a strong incentive for insureds to carry not less than 80 percent of full replacement cost for Coverage A—not necessarily in anticipation of the improbable total loss, but to receive full replacement cost of repairs for partial losses. As justification for this departure from the principle of indemnity, consider the underlying reason for the principle. The concept that new should not be given for old is to minimize moral hazard, to avoid any incentive to enrich oneself by destroying owned property. It might be realistic to be concerned over an insured's ability to get a brand new sofa for a tattered one, or a new wardrobe for a closet full of rags. But should there be concern that an insured would damage his or her own ten-year-old roof? Payment without deduction for depreciation will give the insured something better, but the new roof, after all, will only do what the old one did: keep out the rain. So the opportunity is taken to provide the insured with more responsive coverage in the belief that the insurer's position is not likely to be compromised.

If the insured's Coverage A limit is *less than* 80 percent of current replacement value of the building at time of loss, the insured receives a proportionally reduced benefit, but not less than actual cash value. For examples that illustrate full, partial, and no benefit from the replacement cost condition, assume replacement cost of the dwelling is $50,000; covered loss is valued at $10,000 on a replacement cost basis and $7,000 at actual cash value:

Examples

1. If the insured carries $40,000 (or more) Coverage A: insurer pays $10,000.
2. If the insured carries $32,000 Coverage A: insurer pays $10,000 × 32/40(4/5)=$8,000 (that proportion of full replacement cost which coverage amount bears to 80 percent of replacement cost).
3. If the insured carries $28,000 (or less) Coverage A: insurer pays $7,000 (as the formula in (2) produces actual cash value or less).

The loss settlement condition concludes by providing that if the damage is more than $1,000 (modified by the Special Provisions endorsements HO-300—to $2,500) or 5 percent of the amount of insurance on the building, the insured must actually replace the damaged property in order to receive the benefits of replacement cost. The insured can settle on an actual cash value basis with the right reserved to make claim, within 180 days after loss, to collect the difference.

The loss settlement condition is a bonus that makes it attractive for insureds to maintain insurance at not less than 80 percent of replacement cost of buildings. As the 80 percent-or-more test applies *at the time of loss,* in inflationary times a policy with amount properly established at inception may become inadequate during its term.

Through the use of an Inflation Guard Endorsement (HO-243), the amount of each Section I coverage may be automatically increased by an agreed percentage of the original amount annually applied pro rata. The amount of the annual increase may be 4, 6, or 8 percent with other 4 percent increments available. For example, a policy issued at $40,000 Coverage A with 6 percent inflation guard would undergo increases of $200 a month if an annual policy and have a limit of $42,400 at expiration. The Coverage B, C, and D limits increase proportionately, along with Coverage A.

Following the provisions for Coverages A, B, C, and D, the HO-3 special form continues with a section titled "additional coverages." Briefly, the additional coverages provide:

1. *Debris Removal.* Payment is provided for the cost of removing debris of covered property after loss from a covered peril or resulting from volcanic ash, dust or particles when there has been damage to covered property. Five percent of the applicable coverage limit is available as an additional amount if the specific coverage amount is exhausted by payment for the damage.
   This additional coverage, as modified by the Special Provisions endorsement, will also pay, up to an aggregate of $500, for the cost of removing fallen trees that are not covered under the policy if (1) there is resultant damage to a covered structure and (2) the cause of loss is one of the Coverage C perils.
2. *Reasonable Repairs.* Cost of repairs to prevent further damage is reimbursed.
3. *Trees, Shrubs, and Other Plants.* 5 percent of Coverage A may be applied to trees, shrubs, and plants (not over $500 on any one), for loss from perils of fire, lightning, explosion, riot, civil commotion, aircraft, vehicles not owned or operated by a resident, vandalism or malicious mischief, and theft (windstorm is not covered).
4. *Fire Department Service Charge.* Reimbursement of up to $500 is provided for contractually incurred expense of a fire

department service call related to a covered peril if the property is located outside the boundaries of the city or district furnishing the response. This limit may be increased to any higher amount as an optional coverage.

5. *Property Removed.* "All-risks" coverage is provided on property removed to protect it from loss from a covered peril for up to thirty days.
6. *Credit Card, Fund Transfer Card, Forgery, and Counterfeit Money.* Up to $500 coverage is afforded for loss from theft or unauthorized use of credit cards and fund transfer cards, from forgery or check alteration, and from acceptance of counterfeit money. This limit may be increased to as much as $10,000 as an optional coverage. Interest in higher limits of credit card coverage, once very popular, diminished upon passage of a federal law which limits the cardholder's liability to $50 per card if loss of cards is promptly reported to the issuers. Interest has since rekindled, however, with the popularity of fund transfer cards not covered by the law applicable to credit cards.
7. *Loss Assessment.* Loss assessments of a corporation or association of property owners caused by loss to property collectively owned caused by an insured peril is covered for up to $1,000 of the residence premises. This limit of the residence premises may be increased, and coverage for up to two other premises, may be added with endorsement HO-35, Loss Assessment Coverage.
8. *Collapse.* Collapse of a building or part of a building is covered if caused by an insured named peril; hidden decay, insect or vermin damage; weight of contents, equipment, animals or people, rain which collects on a roof; or defects in materials or methods of construction if caused during the remodeling, construction or renovation. Normal settling, cracking, shrinking, bulging or expansion is not covered.

Perils Covered The next major section in the HO-3 form is Section I—Perils Insured Against. In treatment of perils, all property insurance contracts may be classified in one of two ways: specified (or named) perils or "all-risks." In the former category, the peril causing a loss must be specified in an insuring agreement for coverage to exist. If the insuring clause provides for coverage against "all-risks" of loss, a reverse form of analysis applies in that an exclusion must be found to eliminate coverage.

The HO-3 special form grants "all-risks" protection for Coverage A and B and specified or named perils for Coverage C. For Coverage D, the loss of use benefit follows a covered direct loss. Thus, if the dwelling is made uninhabitable because of damage to the structure, Coverage D is "all-risks"; if caused by damage to personal property only, the coverage is specified perils.

The insuring agreement for Coverages A and B states: "We insure against risks of direct loss to property described in Coverages A and B only if that loss is a physical loss to property; however, we do not insure loss" and is followed by the exclusions. The "all-risks" agreement requires many more exclusions than for specified perils to eliminate uninsurable and special perils for which coverage is not intended. It is not considered necessary, for example, to exclude loss which is the subject of an illegal enterprise by the insured, because the courts would not enforce the contract against the insurer as a matter of public policy.

The exceptions following the insuring agreement are:

1. involving collapse, other than as provided in Additional Coverage 8;
2. caused by:
   a. freezing of a plumbing, heating, air conditioning or automatic fire protective sprinkler system or of a household appliance, or by discharge, leakage or overflow from within the system or appliance caused by freezing. This exclusion applies only while the dwelling is vacant, unoccupied or being constructed unless you have used reasonable care to:
      (1) maintain heat in the building; or
      (2) shut off the water supply and drain the system and appliances of water;
   b. freezing, thawing, pressure or weight of water or ice, whether driven by wind or not, to a:
      (1) fence, pavement, patio or swimming pool;
      (2) foundation, retaining wall or bulkhead; or
      (3) pier, wharf or dock;
   c. theft in or to a dwelling under construction, or of materials and supplies for use in the construction until the dwelling is finished and occupied;
   d. vandalism and malicious mischief or breakage of glass and safety glazing materials if the dwelling has been vacant for more than 30 consecutive days immediately before the loss. A dwelling being constructed is not considered vacant;
   e. constant or repeated seepage or leakage of water or steam over a period of weeks, months or years from within a plumbing, heating, air conditioning or automatic fire protective sprinkler system or from within a household appliance;
   f. (1) wear and tear, marring, deterioration;
      (2) inherent vice, latent defect, mechanical breakdown;
      (3) smog, rust, mold, wet or dry rot;
      (4) smoke from agricultural smudging or industrial operations;
      (5) release, discharge or dispersal of contaminants or pollutants;

(6) settling, cracking, shrinking, bulging or expansion of pavements, patios, foundations, walls, floors, roofs or ceilings; or

(7) birds, vermin, rodents, insects or domestic animals.

If any of these cause water damage not otherwise excluded, from a plumbing, heating, air conditioning or automatic fire protective sprinkler system or household appliance, we cover loss caused by the water including the cost of tearing out and replacing any part of a building necessary to repair the system or appliance. We do not cover loss to the system or appliance from which this water escaped.

3. excluded under Section I—Exclusions.

Under items 1 and 2, any ensuing loss to property described in Coverages A and B not excluded or excepted in this policy is covered.

Comments

Exception 1—Excludes collapse losses other than those mentioned under Additional Coverage.

Exception 2a—The freezing exclusion has no applicability if the insured, while away from the residence, takes reasonable precautions against incurring damage.

Exception 2c—A dwelling under construction is eligible for an HO policy for the owner, and this exclusion eliminates the "midnight requisitioning" loss.

Exception 2d—"Vacant" means, generally, not lived in and all personal property removed as well. This situation arises in an HO context when insureds move.

Exception 2e—This exclusion attempts to distinguish the sudden, accidental occurrences causing water damage (covered) from those where ordinary maintenance should have prevented the loss.

Exception 2f—Principally, these exclusions deal with aging and normal maintenance or deterioration. However, water damage from such causes (for example, rupture of a rusty pipe fitting) is covered, including the costs of tearing out and replacing parts of the building to effect repairs.

There are seventeen specified perils applying to Coverage C. The first eight are (1) fire and lightning, (2) windstorm and hail, (3) explosion, (4) riot and civil commotion, (5) aircraft, (6) vehicles, (7) sudden and accidental damage from smoke, but not from agricultural smudging or industrial operations, and (8) vandalism or malicious mischief. Windstorm and hail contains some special limitations:

This peril does not include loss to the property contained in a building caused by rain, snow, sleet, sand or dust unless the direct force of wind or hail damages the building causing an opening in a roof or wall and the rain, snow, sleet, sand or dust enters through this opening. This peril includes loss to watercraft and their trailers, furnishings, equipment, and outboard motors, only while inside a fully enclosed building.

"An opening in the roof or wall" is generally interpreted to include broken windows.

Peril No. 9 is theft and involves several intricacies requiring close attention. The basic coverage wording reads:

9. Theft, including attempted theft and loss of property from a known place when it is likely that the property has been stolen.

This insuring clause wording creates an element of subjectivity. At one extreme, a purely mysterious disappearance loss is not covered; at the other, it is not necessary for the insured to show conclusively that a theft occurred.

There are three basic exclusions relating specifically to the theft peril:

This peril does not include loss caused by theft:

a. committed by any **insured;**
b. in or to a dwelling under construction, or of materials and supplies for use in the construction until the dwelling is finished and occupied; or
c. from any part of a **residence premises** rented by an **insured** to other than an **insured.**

Exclusion (b) ties into the exclusion for Coverage A and B to eliminate any building or personal property theft coverage for dwellings under construction. Exclusion (c) relates to but goes beyond the "property not covered" provisions stated with Coverage C. There, property *regularly* rented or held for rental to others is excluded. For occasional rental, the other perils of Coverage C continue to cover but theft does not. With optional endorsement HO-80, Residence Rental Theft, the absolute exclusion of theft losses while the residence is rented to others may be modified to provide for suspension of coverage only when the residence is *regularly* rented ("regular" versus "occasional" is not defined). With this endorsement, loss is still not covered if caused by the tenant or a member of the tenant's household; and money, securities, jewelry, and furs (which would not normally be left in a residence rented to others) are not covered.

The general theft exclusions are followed by others which deal only with off-premises losses:

This peril does not include loss caused by theft that occurs off the **residence premises** of:

a. property while at any other residence owned by, rented to, or occupied by an **insured,** except while an **insured** is temporarily living there. Property of a student who is an **insured** is covered while at a residence away from home if the student has been there at any time during the 45 days immediately before the loss;

b. watercraft, including their furnishings, equipment and outboard motors; or

c. trailers and campers.

Exclusion (a) further emphasizes the need for a separate homeowners policy on a secondary residence (rather than reliance on the 10 percent of Coverage C which applies) because the theft coverage is suspended when the insured is not residing there. When a family member is a student, in the ordinary situation the theft coverage is not impaired when the student leaves property in an apartment or dormitory. If left for the summer or a similar period, however, with a theft discovered upon return, the loss would not be covered, unless it could be shown to have occurred within forty-five days after departure.

Watercraft and associated equipment and trailers are basically included under Coverage C, subject to special limits of liability. Exclusions (b) and (c), however, eliminate all coverage if the loss occurs away from the residence.

The remaining Coverage C perils provide important additional benefits and are self-explanatory:

10. **Falling objects.**
    This peril does not include loss to property contained in a building unless the roof or an outside wall of the building is first damaged by a falling object. Damage to the falling object itself is not included.
11. **Weight of ice, snow or sleet** which causes damage to property contained in a building.
12. **Accidental discharge or overflow of water or steam** from within a plumbing, heating, air conditioning or automatic fire protective sprinkler system or from within a household appliance.
    This peril does not include loss:
    a. to the system or appliance from which the water or steam escaped;
    b. caused by or resulting from freezing except as provided in the peril of freezing below; or
    c. on the **residence premises** caused by accidental discharge or overflow which occurs off the **residence premises.**
13. **Sudden and accidental tearing apart, cracking, burning or bulging** of a steam or hot water heating system, an air conditioning or automatic fire protective sprinkler system, or an appliance for heating water. We do not cover loss caused by or resulting from freezing under this peril.
14. **Freezing** of a plumbing, heating, air conditioning or automatic fire protective sprinkler system or of a household appliance.
    This peril does not include loss on the **residence premises** while the dwelling is unoccupied, unless you have used reasonable care to:
    a. maintain heat in the building; or

b. shut off the water supply and drain the system and appliances of water.

15. **Sudden and accidental damage from artificially generated electrical current.** This peril does not include loss to a tube, transistor, or similar electronic component.
16. **Damage by glass or safety glazing material** which is part of a building, storm door or storm window.
This peril does not include loss on the **residence premises** if the dwelling has been vacant for more than 30 consecutive days immediately before the loss. A dwelling being constructed is not considered vacant.
17. **Volcanic Eruption** other than loss caused by earthquake, land shock waves or tremors.

Coverage C may be broadened from named perils to "all-risk" by attachment of endorsement HO-15, Special Personal Property Coverage.

Section I—Exclusions The perils section in HO-3 is followed by Section I Exclusions. These apply generally to Section I, in addition to more specific exclusions stated with the perils. The exclusions of general interest:

1. Enforcement of a law regulating construction, repair, or demolition of a building is excluded. The Homeowners program has an optional coverage available (endorsement HO-277) to insure against this hazard.
2. Loss from earth movement is excluded (except fire, explosion, theft, and glass breakage therefrom). Earthquake is an optional HO coverage (HO-54). A deductible of 2 percent of the amount of each coverage applies, minimum $250.
3. Water damage is broadly excluded. The flood and rising water peril may be covered by a flood policy under the Federal Flood Insurance program and available through all insurance agencies. The complete exclusion reads:

3. Water Damage, meaning:
(1) flood, surface water, waves, tidal water, overflow of a body of water, or spray from any of these, whether or not driven by wind;
(2) water which backs up through sewers or drains; or
(3) water below the surface of the ground, including water which exerts pressure on or seeps or leaks through a building, sidewalk, driveway, foundation, swimming pool or other structure.
Direct loss by fire, explosion or theft resulting from water damage is covered.

4. Loss from power failure is excluded if the interruption happens at another location. This exclusion deals principally with

spoilage losses from interruption of refrigeration power. If, for example, freezer contents were lost because lightning struck the power generating source, the loss would not be covered. If the lightning struck the electrical junction box attached to the insured's dwelling, causing the power interruption, the loss would be covered.

5. Loss from neglect of the insured to use reasonable means to save endangered property, and loss from war or nuclear hazards, is excluded.
6. Intentional losses caused by or at the direction of an insured are not covered. If an angry child starts a fire to "get even" with his or her parents, such fire to the premises is not covered.
7. A final set of exclusions applies only to Coverage A and B property:

We do not insure for loss to property described in Coverages A and B caused by any of the following. However, any ensuing loss to property described in Coverages A and B not excluded or excepted in this policy is covered.

a. **Weather conditions.** However, this exclusion only applies if weather conditions contribute in any way with a cause or event excluded in paragraph 1. above to produce the loss;
b. **Acts or decisions,** including the failure to act or decide, of any person, group, organization or governmental body;
c. **Faulty, inadequate or defective:**
   (1) planning, zoning, development, surveying, siting;
   (2) design, specifications, workmanship, repair, construction, renovation, remodeling, grading, compaction;
   (3) materials used in repair, construction, renovation or remodeling; or
   (4) maintenance;
   of part or all of any property whether on or off the **residence premises.**

Section I—Conditions The concluding portion of Section I of the HO-3 special form is "Conditions." There are more conditions that are applicable to both Sections I and II at the end of the form.

Sixteen conditions apply to Section I of the HO-3.

Insurable Interest and Limit of Liability. In keeping with the principle of indemnity, losses are payable to the lesser of the insured's interest in the property or the limit of liability.

Duties After Loss. Prompt notice to the insurer or agent is required. This means as soon as possible under normal conditions. In the case of loss by theft, notification must also be given to the police (or card company if a credit or fund transfer card is involved). The insured must protect the property, make reasonable repairs, and keep records of repair expenses. An inventory of damaged personal property is required showing actual cash value of items lost. Any supporting documents should be attached.

The insured will be required to show damaged property, provide records and documents, and submit to questions under oath. Within 60 days of a request from the insurer, the insured must file a sworn proof of loss. The proof of loss could include the date and cause of loss; the extent of the insured's interest in the property and any lienholders' interests; other insurance which may apply; specifications and repair estimates for damaged buildings; inventory of personal property, receipts for additional living expenses and records supporting fair rental value losses; and any evidence to support a credit or fund transfer card loss.

Appraisal. If the insured and insurer disagree on the amount of loss, either may demand an appraisal. Each chooses an appraiser and the appraisers select an umpire (or the courts may select the umpire if the appraisers cannot). Each appraiser sets the amount of loss. If they agree, the agreed amount becomes the amount of the loss. If they disagree, any differences are submitted to the umpire and the decision of any two of the three becomes binding. The insured and insurer pay for their own appraiser and split the expense of the umpire.

Other Insurance. If other insurance applies, the HO-3 will pay its proportional share of the loss based on combined policy limits.

Suit. If the insured wishes to sue the insurer under the policy, the suit must begin within one year of the date of loss.

Repair or Replacement. Under the "Our Option" condition, the insurer may give notice within 30 days of receipt of the sworn proof of loss of its intention to repair or replace any part of the damaged property with like kind and quality. Insurers have access to sources of personal property such as televisions, silverware, golf clubs and so forth at prices the average insured could not duplicate.

Loss Payment. Losses are payable within 60 days after receipt of the proof of loss and an agreement or judgment on the value of the loss.

Abandonment. The insured cannot abandon property to the insurer.

Mortgage Clause. Important protection applies to a named mortgagee. The insurer issuing its claim check or draft payable jointly to the insured and mortgagee enables the latter to control the proceeds and be assured its collateral is not impaired. The mortgagee is entitled to separate notice of cancellation or nonrenewal (ten days' notice) and may recover to the extent of its interest, even though the insured may not be entitled to recovery because of such things as concealment or misrepresentation in applying for the insurance or failure to comply with a policy condition.

No Benefit to Bailee. The insurer will not recognize any assignment or grant coverage to an organization which holds, stores, or moves property for a fee.

Nuclear Hazard. All losses from the so-called "nuclear hazard" are excluded except direct losses by fire resulting from a nuclear incident.

Recovered Property. If property is recovered after a loss payment, the insured has the option to retain the property or turn it over to the insurance company. If the insured does retain the recovered property, such as a piece of jewelry with historical or sentimental value, the loss payment will be readjusted based on the recovery.

Volcanic Eruption Period. Since volcanic eruption is a covered cause of loss, this condition defines all such eruptions within a 72-hour period as one eruption.

Other Conditions. Remaining conditions of interest include (1) a "pair or set" clause which allows the insurer to settle by repairing or replacing any part to restore the set to its previous value, or by paying the difference between the value of the set before and after the loss; and (2) a provision to pay for safety glazing materials after a glass breakage loss, if required by law.

Section II—Coverages Section II of HO-3 special form begins with the insuring agreements for Coverages E and F.

Personal Liability. For Coverage E, personal liability, the insuring agreement and associated definitions as modified by the Special Provisions Endorsement (HO-300), read:

> If a claim is made or a suit is brought against an **Insured** for damages because of **bodily injury** or **property damage** caused by an **occurrence** to which this coverage applies. Damages include prejudgement interest awarded against the **insured.**
>
> 1. pay up to our limit of liability for the damages for which the **Insured** is legally liable; and
>
> 2. provide a defense at our expense by counsel of our choice, even if the suit is groundless, false or fraudulent. We may investigate and settle any claim or suit that we decide is appropriate. Our duty to settle or defend ends when the amount we pay for damages resulting from the **occurrence** equals our limit of liability.
>
> **"insured"** means you and residents of your household who are:
>
> a. your relatives; or

b. other persons under the age of 21 and in the care of any person named above.

Under Section II, **"insured"** also means:

c. with respect to animals or watercraft to which this policy applies, any person or organization legally responsible for these animals or watercraft which are owned by you or any person included in 3a or 3b above. A person or organization using or having custody of these animals or watercraft in the course of any **business** or without consent of the owner is not an **insured;**

d. with respect to any vehicle to which this policy applies:

(1) persons while engaged in your employ or that of any person included in 3a or 3b above; or

(2) other persons using the vehicle on an **insured location** with your consent.

"occurrence" means an accident, including exposure to conditions, which results, during the policy period, in:

a. **bodily injury;** or
b. **property damage.**

"bodily injury" means bodily harm, sickness or disease, including required care, loss of services and death that results.

"property damage" means physical injury to, destruction of, or loss of use of tangible property.

The definition of "occurrence" is modified by the Special Provisions Endorsement (HO-300) to read, "... accident, including continuous or repeated exposure to substantially the same general harmful conditions, which result...."

In summary, if there is a claim for bodily injury or property damage against anyone who is an "insured" and if no exclusion applies, the insurer will pay damages *for which the insured is legally liable,* up to the policy limit. The insurer has the obligation to defend the insured against claims and the right to conduct the defense in the manner it considers most appropriate. If unsettled or additional claims exist from an occurrence after the policy limit has been exhausted, the insurer's obligation to defend ceases.

The minimum limit for Coverage E is $100,000 per occurrence. Common higher limits, needed by many insureds, are $200,000, $300,000, $400,000, $500,000, or higher.

Coverage E may be extended beyond "bodily injury" to include liability for "personal injury" (false arrest, detention, imprisonment, malicious prosecution, libel, slander, defamation, invasion of privacy, wrongful eviction, wrongful entry) with endorsement HO-82, Personal Injury.

Medical Payments. The insuring agreement for Coverage F, medical payments to others:

> We will pay the necessary medical expenses that are incurred or medically ascertained within three years from the date of an accident causing **bodily injury.** Medical expenses means reasonable charges for medical, surgical, x-ray, dental, ambulance, hospital, professional nursing, prosthetic devices and funeral services. This coverage does not apply to you or regular residents of your household except **residence employees.** As to others, this coverage applies only:
> 1. to a person on the **insured location** with the permission of an **insured;** or
> 2. to a person off the **insured location,** if the **bodily injury:**
>   a. arises out of a condition on the **insured location** or the ways immediately adjoining;
>   b. is caused by the activities of an **insured;**
>   c. is caused by a **residence employee** in the course of the **residence employee's** employment by an **insured;** or
>   d. is caused by an animal owned by or in the care of an **insured.**

Without regard to legal liability for bodily injury, Coverage F pays for medical expenses to persons **other than** an insured and members of the household who are not residence employees and who are injured at the "insured location" or as a result of activities of insureds at other locations. Here is the definition of insured location:

> **"insured location"** means:
> a. the **residence premises;**
> b. the part of other premises, other structures and grounds used by you as a residence and:
>   (1) which is shown in the Declarations; or
>   (2) which is acquired by you during the policy period for your use as a residence;
> c. any premises used by you in connection with a premises in 4a or 4b above;
> d. any part of a premises:
>   (1) not owned by an **insured;** and
>   (2) where an **insured** is temporarily residing;
> e. vacant land, other than farm land, owned by or rented to an **insured;**
> f. land owned by or rented to an **insured** on which a one- or two-family dwelling is being built as a residence for an insured;
> g. individual or family cemetery plots or burial vaults of an **insured;** or
> h. any part of a premises occasionally rented to an **insured** for other than **business** use.

The minimum limit for F is $1,000 per person. Limits of $2,000 to $5,000 are commonly used. A limit higher than minimum is especially indicated if the insured has residence employees.

Additional Coverages. Section II of HO-3 Special Form contains four "additional coverages" which supplement the protection provided by Coverages E and F. Amounts payable in this section are in addition to the E and F limits of liability.

The first additional coverage, claim expenses, provides for insurer payment of expenses of litigation for claims against an insured, including reimbursement of wage loss up to $50 per day when the insured is assisting in investigation or defense of a claim. The second, first aid expenses, reimburses the insured for expenses incurred in securing first aid for others. The third additional coverage reads:

> **Damage to Property of Others.** We will pay, at replacement cost, up to $500 per **occurrence** for **property damage** to property of others caused by an **insured.**
> We will not pay for **property damage:**
> a. to the extent of any amount recoverable under Section I of this policy;
> b. caused intentionally by an **insured** who is 13 years of age or older;
> c. to property owned by an **insured;**
> d. to property owned by or rented to a tenant of an **insured** or a resident in your household; or
> e. arising out of:
> (1) **business** pursuits;
> (2) any act or omission in connection with a premises owned, rented or controlled by an **insured,** other than the **insured location;** or
> (3) the ownership, maintenance, or use of aircraft, watercraft or motor vehicles or all other motorized land conveyances.
> This exclusion does not apply to a motorized land conveyance designed for recreational use off public roads, not subject to motor vehicle registration and not owned by an **insured.**

This provision, sometimes called "voluntary property damage," pays for damage to property of others, without regard to fault or legal liability. The $500 per occurrence limit, with property valued at replacement cost, may not be increased under standard rules. This additional coverage is independent of Coverage E and is not subject to the Coverage E exclusions. As property of others is covered by Section I under certain conditions, exclusion (a) prevents any overlap with Section I. Exclusion (b), viewed in the affirmative, means that coverage *is* provided for damage intentionally caused by an insured under age 13. Exclusions (c) and (d) limit coverage to damage to property of those who are not insureds, tenants, or residents. Exclusion (d) picks up some of the Coverage E exclusions (with damage from use of *any* watercraft, aircraft, or motorized land vehicle excluded).

The fourth additional coverage is for up to $1,000 for a share of any loss assessment charged by a corporation or association of property owners to which the insured belongs, at the residence premises, as a result of a covered occurrence or acts of volunteer officers and directors of the association.

Exclusions. The Section II exclusions are divided into three parts—those applicable to both Coverages E and F, and to each separately. The general exclusions applicable to all Section II coverages provide:

1. There is no coverage for injury or damage expected or intended by the insured.
2. Business pursuits and the rental or holding for rental of any premises are excluded. There are, however, important exceptions to the exclusion:

This exclusion does not apply to:
(1) activities which are usual to non-**business** pursuits; or
(2) the rental or holding for rental of an **insured location;**
    (a) on an occasional basis if used only as a residence;
    (b) in part for use only as a residence, unless a single family unit is intended for use by the occupying family to lodge more than two roomers or boarders; or
    (c) in part, as an office, school, studio or private garage;

The exception to the exclusion means coverage is provided for (1) activities such as entertaining a business client at home or engaging in recreational pursuits with such a person, (2) occasional rental of the residence or regular rental of a portion of the residence such as half of a two-family dwelling or another structure on the premises to not more than two roomers or boarders, or (3) partial use as an office, school, studio, or private garage.
There are three HO options that relate to the business pursuits exclusion.

a. If the residence contains a business occupancy the attachment of endorsement HO-42, Permitted Incidental Occupancies—Residence Premises, is required under Section I. The same endorsement provides coverage for business usage for Section II.
b. If the insured is employed by others (as opposed to being a sole proprietor or a partner in a partnership), liability for the insured's business activities may be covered with endorsement HO-71, Business Pursuits. This coverage is often advisable for employed insureds because standard forms of liability insurance carried by the insured's employer do not normally provide protection to employees as insureds.

c. If incidental farming operations are conducted at the residence premises, liability for such business pursuit may be included by attachment of endorsement HO-72, Incidental Farming Personal Liability.

3. Injury or damage for rendering or failing to render professional services is excluded.
4. The form excludes injury (except to a residence employee) or damage "arising out of any premises owned, rented to any insured, or rented to others by an insured which is not an insured location." The main effect is to exclude coverage for a residence of the insured which at policy inception is not specified in the declarations as an insured location. When the insured acquires an additional residence during the policy term, however, coverage is automatically afforded until expiration.

   The one exposure not included in the "insured location" definition which may be covered under an HO policy is a one-, two-, three-, or four-family dwelling rented by the insured to others. Such rented residences may be included for Coverages E and F by use of endorsement HO-70, Additional Residence Rented to Others. Such residences may not be included for coverage under Section I.
5. Ownership, maintenance, use, loading or unloading of "motorized vehicles or all other motorized land conveyances" are excluded subject to exceptions. A trailer not being towed or carried; a recreational vehicle not subject to registration and not owned, or if owned, on an insured location; a golf cart while playing golf; a vehicle used to service the insured's residence, designed to assist the handicapped, or in dead storage are covered. Entrustment of a motor vehicle or statutory vicarious parental liability using such a conveyance is excluded. A small measure of broadened protection is available with endorsement HO-313, Incidental Motorized Land Vehicles, which retains the main elements of the exclusion but covers an exposure such as a recreational go-cart while being used away from the insured location.
6. Watercraft is treated similarly to motor vehicles in that its ownership, maintenance, use, loading or unloading, entrustment to another by an insured or statutory parental vicarious liability is excluded for certain types of watercraft:
   - owned inboard or inboard-outdrive powered boats
   - rented inboard or inboard-outdrive boats with more than 50 horsepower
   - sailing vessels 26 or more feet in length

- boats with outboard motor(s) owned by an insured totaling more than 25 horsepower unless declared or notification is given the insurer of an intent to insure within 45 days of acquisition. Automatic coverage is provided if such an outboard motor is acquired during the policy period.

The policy does not require notification for coverage to apply during the term of the policy in effect when an outboard motor is acquired. An example of how this provision applies would be an insured having a policy term of 1-1 to 1-1 and acquiring the motor in December, after the renewal policy has been issued. The expiring policy covers because the motor was not owned at inception. The renewal policy covers for up to forty-five days after the date of acquisition, after which date coverage will cease if the policy is not endorsed. The watercraft exclusion has no effect while such craft are in storage. All excluded watercraft may be included for Coverages E and F by attachment of endorsement HO-75, Watercraft, specifically scheduling the boats and outboard motors to be covered.

7. Aircraft are similarly excluded except for hobby or model-type aircraft not designed or used to carry people or cargo.
8. The Special Provisions Endorsement (HO-300) adds an exclusion for bodily injury or property damage arising out of transmission of a communicable disease by an insured.

The exclusions in 4, 5, 6, and 7 do not apply to bodily injury to a residence employee arising out of and in the course of employment by an insured.

The principal exclusions that apply only to Coverage E are:

a. liability:
   (1) for your share of any loss assessment charged against all members of an association, corporation or community of property owners (limited coverage being provided under Section II, "additional coverages");
   (2) under any contract or agreement. However, this exclusion does not apply to written contracts
      (a) that directly relate to the ownership, maintenance or use of an **insured location;** or
      (b) where the liability of others is assumed by the **insured** prior to an **occurrence;**

   unless excluded in (1) above or elsewhere in this policy;
b. **property damage** to property owned by the **insured;**
c. **property damage** to property rented to, occupied or used by or in the care of the **insured.** This exclusion does not apply to **property damage** caused by fire, smoke or explosion;
d. **bodily injury** to any person eligible to receive any benefits:
   (1) voluntarily provided; or
   (2) required to be provided;

by the **insured** under any:
(1) workers' compensation law;
(2) non-occupational disability law; or
(3) occupational disease law;

e. **bodily injury** or **property damage** for which an **insured** under this policy:
(1) is also an insured under a nuclear energy liability policy; or
(2) would be an insured under that policy but for the exhaustion of its limit of liability.
A nuclear energy liability policy is one issued by:
(1) American Nuclear Insurers;
(2) Mutual Atomic Energy Liability Underwriters;
(3) Nuclear Insurance Association of Canada; their successors; or

f. **bodily injury** to you or an **insured** within the meaning of part a. or b. of **"insured"** as defined.

Exclusion a. (1) avoids overlap with limited coverage provided under "additional coverages." The exception to exclusion c. means that if, for example, the insured temporarily occupies a premises or borrows property and it is damaged by fire, smoke, or explosion, and if a liability claim is made against the insured, then liability coverage is provided. As to exclusion d., employers of domestic servants in most states are not subject to the workers' compensation law and protection is afforded through Coverages E and F. If the insured must provide or chooses to provide workers' compensation on employees, Coverages E and F do not apply. Exclusion f. has the purpose of avoiding coverage for intra-family suits in those jurisdictions where such actions are permitted.

In addition to the workers' compensation and nuclear exclusions, Coverage F also excludes injury to a residence employee if it occurs away from an insured location and the employee is not engaged in occupational duties.

Section II—Conditions The HO-3 conditions applicable to Section II:

1. *Limits of Liability.* The Coverage E limit applies per occurrence; the Coverage F limit, per person.
2. *Severability of Insurance.* The condition states: "This insurance applies separately to each insured." This means that policy provisions apply only to the insured(s) against whom claim is made. For example, assume one family member, *A*, intentionally injures a nonfamily member, *X*. *X* sues *A* and *A*'s parent, *B* (the named insured). While coverage would be denied to *A* because the injury to *X* was intentional from *A*'s standpoint, coverage applies to *B* because the injury to *X* was unintended from *B*'s standpoint.

3. *Duties After Loss.* The insured must give prompt notice, complete information about the occurrence, and cooperate with the insurer on all claims.
4. *Duties of an Injured Person—Coverage F.* An injured person seeking medical payments benefits must comply with reasonable conditions to enable insurer verification of the claim.
5. *Payment of Claim—Coverage F.* Payment is not to be considered an admission of liability.
6. Suit Against Us. Conditions must be complied with before the insurer may be sued. The condition also attempts to avoid the insurer being joined in a suit against the insured or from being sued directly by the claimant; however, rules of law in each state actually govern whether such actions are permitted.
7. Bankruptcy of any Insured. The insurer is not relieved of its obligations if its insured is bankrupt or insolvent.
8. Other Insurance—Coverage E. Coverage is excess over other valid and collectible insurance except insurance specifically written to be excess. As compared to the pro-rata condition for Section I, this means other available insurance must be exhausted before this policy may be called upon to pay.

Sections I and II—Identical Conditions The concluding section of the HO-3 special form provides nine conditions applicable to both Sections I and II. The first condition requires all loss to occur during the policy period before coverage applies. Second, coverage is denied to any insured guilty of intentional concealment, material misrepresentation, false statements, or fraudulent conduct. Third, if the insurer adopts a form change which broadens coverage without additional premium, the insured receives the benefits of the broadened coverage. Fourth, all waivers or changes in provisions must be in writing. Requests for appraisal or examination do not waive any of the insurer's rights.

Fifth, the insured may cancel at any time, but the insurer's right to cancel the policy is limited. After the first sixty days of a new policy and from the first day of a renewal, the insurer may cancel only for nonpayment of premium, a material misrepresentation by the insured, or if "the risk has changed substantially since the policy was issued." If the company cancels for nonpayment or during the first 60 days of a new policy, ten days' notice must be given. Otherwise, 30 days is required. If the term is longer than one year, the company may cancel on any anniversary, for any reason, if thirty days' advance notice is given. Sixth, thirty days' notice must be given to the insured if the insurer elects not to renew the policy.

Seventh, no assignment of the policy is valid unless the insurer grants its consent. Eighth, the subrogation condition permits the insured to waive the insurer's rights, if in writing and prior to the loss. Finally, coverage continues to a legal representative of the insured with respect to the premises and property of a deceased insured or spouse-resident of the same household.

Cancellation and non-renewal provisions may be varied by state laws or regulations.

Checkpoints

1. Describe the property covered under each of Coverages A, B, and C under HO-3 special form.
2. List the types of property subject to special limits of liability under Coverage C and specify the special limit of each.
3. Explain how the replacement cost condition applies if coverage on a building is (a) 80 percent or more of full replacement cost and (b) less than 80 percent of full replacement cost.
4. Describe the perils insured against for each HO-3 coverage.
5. Describe the protection afforded by HO-3 Coverages E and F.

Form Similarities

All four of the HO forms available to owner-occupants (HO-1, 2, 3, 5, 8) are identical in:

1. Definitions;
2. Description of Coverages A, B, C, and D (except for a limitation in HO-8, described below);
3. Section I Additional Coverages;
4. Section I Exclusions;
5. Section I Conditions (except HO-8 has a different loss settlement condition, described below);
6. Section II.

HO-1 Basic Form Differences The Coverage D limit is 10 percent of Coverage A rather than the 20 percent for HO-3. The only other difference from HO-3 is in Section I, perils insured against. The HO-1 covered perils are fire, lightning, the extended coverage perils (windstorm, hail, explosion, riot and civil commotion, aircraft, vehicles, smoke), vandalism and malicious mischief, theft, and breakage of building glass.

For these perils, HO-1 contains the following limitations not found in HO-3:

1. Windstorm and hail exclude damage to the *building interior* by rain, snow, sleet, sand or dust, unless the wind or hail causes structural damage.

2. Coverage for damage caused by vehicles excludes any loss caused by a vehicle owned or operated by a resident of the insured's premises.
3. The smoke peril excludes loss caused by smoke from fireplaces.
4. Breakage of building glass is subject to a limit of $100 per occurrence, unless the breakage is caused by another named peril, such as windstorm.

HO-2 Broad Form Differences HO-3 contains seventeen named perils for Coverage C. HO-2 broad form contains those same named perils for Coverages A, B, C, and D (except that damage *by* breakage of building glass is damage *to* such glass in HO-2). Those seventeen named perils provide more limited coverage than HO-3 in the following respects:

1. Like HO-1, interior building damage from wind or hail is not covered unless there is structural damage to the dwelling. This limitation also applies to the "falling objects" peril.
2. Damage by vehicles excludes loss to a fence, driveway, or walk from a vehicle owned or operated by a resident of the insured's premises. This is not as restrictive as the HO-1 limitation.
3. Building damage from accidental discharge or overflow of water or steam from a plumbing, heating, air conditioning system or household appliance (other than from freezing) does not apply if the dwelling was vacant for over thirty consecutive days prior to the loss.

HO-8 Modified Coverage Form Differences The HO-8 is the newest of the HO forms and was introduced to handle special residual situations.

Examples:

1. Applicants not meeting insurer underwriting requirements for other forms.
2. Applicants otherwise acceptable except for the replacement cost feature, such as those on which replacement value exceeds market value or of an obsolete type of construction.

The perils named are the same as for HO-1. The main coverage differences are:

1. Actual cash value basis is applicable to all property—no replacement cost; building losses may be settled at market value if less than ACV.
2. Personal property away from the dwelling is covered only for 10 percent of Coverage C or $1,000, whichever is greater.

3. Theft coverage is limited to $1,000 and covers only at the residence premises. Endorsement HO-303, Theft Coverage Increase, is available to increase the on-premises limit to $3,000 or $5,000, and to add $1,000 coverage for off-premises.

A further limitation imposed for HO-8 is that none of the numerous Section I coverage options, except for alternate deductibles, is available. All normal Section II options may, however, be used.

Coverage for Persons Who Are Not Owner-Occupants—Contents Broad Form HO-4 Contents broad form HO-4 is for tenants of houses or apartments, and owners of buildings other than one- or two-family dwellings who reside therein. With one exception, coverage is identical to HO-3 with elimination of Coverages A and B and provisions specifically relevant to those coverages. The exception is that HO-4 contains one more additional coverage, "buildings additions and alterations." This provision gives the insured the option to apply up to 10 percent of the Coverage C limit to building additions, alterations, fixtures, improvements or installations, made at the insured's expense. An option exists to increase this 10 percent limit with endorsement HO-51, Building Additions and Alterations—Increase.

Coverage for Unit Owners—Form HO-6 What the "condo" buyer owns outright varies by law and the declarations and by-laws applicable to each condominium association. In some, it is only the air space; in others, everything within the unfinished perimeter walls (paint, wallpaper, fixtures, tile, cabinets, partitions, etc.). Other variations may be found. The unit owner has an undivided joint interest with the members of the association in the common elements. A co-op unit "owner" actually occupies the premises under a proprietary lease through ownership of shares in the co-op corporation.

The unit-owners form HO-6 is similar to the contents broad form HO-4, with three principal differences:

1. Coverage A applies to alterations, appliances, fixtures, and improvements that are part of the building and within the residence premises, other real property and structures at the same premises, and property for which the insured has an insurance responsibility under the condo or co-op agreement. The basic form provides broad form named peril coverages, but endorsement HO-32, Unit-Owners Coverage A—Special Form, is available to convert to "All-Risks." Also, the Special Provisions endorsement (HO-300) modifies some of the perils to reflect differences in a residence premises for a unit owner compared to a homeowner.

2. The loss settlement condition gives replacement cost coverage on Coverage A property if the insured actually repairs or replaces.
3. The Section I other insurance condition, instead of specifying pro-rata contribution with all other insurance, provides that the HO-6 is excess over any coverage of the association.

One difficult aspect of arranging proper insurance for the condominium unit owner is the measurement of the additions and alterations exposure. First, it must be determined just what property is at the insured's risk (from the declarations and by-laws). Then, what the original builder paid for cabinets, fixtures, tile, and similar items, at quantity purchase prices, may be wholly irrelevant to the cost of replacing individually. Some developers provide valuation suggestions to unit purchasers; if not, estimates may have to be secured from suppliers, contractors, or others.

Homeowners Options

There is an impressive array of options to enable tailoring of homeowners policies to insureds' precise needs. Many of these were mentioned in the HO-3 form analysis section but there are others. Subject to state exceptions, which may provide for additional options or modify those applicable elsewhere, this section identifies and briefly explains the options which are generally standard. The options are divided into the following categories:

1. Coverage Amounts
2. Section I—Property, Perils, Exclusions, Conditions
3. Section II—Perils, Exclusions, Conditions
4. Unit-Owners Special Options
5. Secondary Dwellings

These options refer to those things which may be done, under standard rules, beyond the selection of a limit for Coverage A (HO-1, HO-2, HO-3, HO-8) or Coverage C (HO-4, HO-6) and the base coverage form. The Section I options are not available with the HO-8 form.

Coverage Amounts

Coverage B. The 10 percent of Coverage A, that applies as blanket coverage for all "other structures" at the residence premises, may not be increased. Specific insurance may be applied to such structures, however, with the Other Structures-Specific Insurance (HO-48) endorsement.

Coverage C. Any amount higher than the automatic 50 percent of Coverage A may be provided, or a reduced limit to not less than 40 percent of Coverage A is permissible. No endorsement is necessary; the applicable net limit is simply entered in the declarations and considered in the rating computation.

Coverage C Special Limits. The endorsement, Coverage C Increased Special Limits of Liability (HO-65) enables application of higher limits for certain types of property subject to special limits:

Property	*Policy Limit*	*Maximum Limit*
Money, gold, coins, etc.	$200	$1,000
Securities, etc.	$1,000	$2,000
Jewelry, furs, stones, etc.	$1,000	$5,000*
Silverware, goldware	$2,500	$10,000
Firearms	$2,000	$6,000

*When the $1,000 limit is increased, a limit of $1,000 continues to apply with respect to any one item.

The policy limit of $2,500 for business property may be increased to a maximum of $10,000 with Increased Limits of Business Property (HO-312).

Credit Card. The endorsement, Fund Transfer Card, Credit Card, Forgery and Counterfeit Money Coverage-increased limit (HO-53), may be used to increase the policy limit of $500. Various limits of up to $10,000 are available.

Personal Property—Secondary Residences. If an insured has personal property usually situated at a residence other than the primary residence described in the policy, Coverage C provides only 10 percent of its limit to such property. The Increased Limits on Personal Property in Other Residences (HO-50) endorsement may be used to provide higher amounts.

Additions and Alterations (HO-4). When contents broad form HO-4 is issued to a tenant insured, an additional coverage permits application of 10 percent of the Coverage C limit to building additions and alterations made at the expense of the insured. With Building Additions and Alterations—Increased Limit (HO-51) endorsement, the policy limit may be increased to any higher amount.

Coverage D. The percentage of Coverage A or C, which applies as a Coverage D limit, varies by form. It may be increased to any higher limit by entry of the selected amount in the declarations and appropriate premium adjustment.

Inflation Guard. Inflation Guard endorsement is used for annual increases of 4, 6, 8 percent or higher in 4 percent increments.

Theft Coverage Increase (HO-8). The limited theft coverage may be increased from $1,000 to $3,000 or $5,000, and $1,000 off-premises coverage may be added, with Theft Coverage Increase (HO-303).

Deductible. When one of the flat deductibles is desired ($100, $250, $500, $1,000, $2,500 or any other permitted by state exceptions), such deductible amount is simply entered in the policy declarations. When one of the graduated amount deductibles (keyed to the Coverage A limit) applies, the endorsement Special Deductible (HO-274) is used.

Section II Limits. The basic limits of $100,000 for Coverage E and $1,000 for Coverage F may be increased to any desired higher amounts without an endorsement.

Section I—Property, Perils, Exclusions, Conditions

Scheduled Personal Property. With Scheduled Personal Property endorsement (HO-61), specific "all-risks" coverage is available on the following classes of property:

Jewelry
Furs
Cameras and photographic equipment
Musical instruments
Silverware and goldware
Golfer's equipment
Fine arts
Postage stamps
Coin collections

Coverage is identical to that provided by a separate inland marine personal articles floater, described in another chapter.

Personal Property Replacement Cost. Coverage may be converted from an actual cash value to a replacement cost basis for personal property, awnings, carpeting, appliances, and outdoor antennas and equipment, with Personal Property Replacement Cost endorsement (HO-290). Antiques, fine arts and stored articles which are obsolete and not in use, remain subject to ACV terms.

Special Personal Property Coverage (HO-3). Endorsement HO-15 changes Coverage C to "all-risks."

Business Occupancy. When a residence contains a non-residential occupancy, the Permitted Incidental Occupancies endorsement (HO-42 if at residence premises, HO-43 if at another residence) is attached. Actually, this is not an option as the endorsement is required when the exposure exists. The endorsement accomplishes the necessary form revisions to include personal property related to the business under Coverage C and to amend the business pursuits exclusion in Section II.

Rented Other Structures. If the insured rents a separate structure on the residence premises to another (a guest house or garage apartment, for example), Coverage B does not cover the structure and Section II does not provide liability or medical payments. With Structures Rented to Others—Residence Premises (HO-40) endorsement, a specific amount of coverage may be applied to the structure and Section II is amended to include the exposure. If the rental includes personal property, there is no way provided in the HO program to extend Coverage C to include such contents, and a separate policy may be necessary.

Rental of Residence. The theft peril in all forms excludes coverage on personal property from any part of the residence premises rented to another. Residence Rental Theft (HO-80) restores coverage for the residence being *occasionally* (undefined) rented to others or for rental in part to a roomer or boarder. Coverage is not extended, however, to theft by the tenant or of money, securities, jewelry, furs, and similar property.

Building Laws. All HO forms exclude loss caused by enforcement of a law regulating construction, repair, or demolition. The endorsement Ordinance or Law Coverage (HO-277) may be used to cover the exposure.

Earthquake. This peril may be covered by attachment of the endorsement Earthquake (HO-54). A deductible of 2 percent of the amount of insurance for each of Coverages A, B, and C applies (minimum deductible $250 in any one loss). Exterior masonry veneer may be included or excluded in the endorsement.

Glass. "All-risks" coverage on specifically scheduled glass is available by Scheduled Glass (HO-68) endorsement.

Building Additions and Alterations—Secondary Residence. Coverage C allows 10 percent of its limit to apply to personal property usually located at the insured's secondary residence. If such a location is rented to the insured, and the insured has made additions or alterations, the endorsement Building Additions or Alterations—Other Residence (HO-49) may be used to apply a specific limit of coverage on the property.

Landlord's Furnishings. Major appliances and wall-to-wall carpeting, in a unit rented to others, may be carried for a $1,000 limit, with Landlord's Furnishings (HO-308) endorsement.

Replacement Cost. The replacement cost provision in forms other than HO-8 sometimes creates a problem for an otherwise wholly acceptable submission. Coverage for 80 percent or more of full replacement value may cause the underwriter to balk, for example, because of a very high insurance amount or home age and obsolescence factors. Yet, there would be no objection to allowing full replacement cost benefits on partial losses. Special Loss Settlement (HO-256) endorsement allows the Coverage A limit to be as low as 50, 60, or 70 percent (as selected), with replacement cost adjustments allowed up to the policy limit.

Section II—Perils, Exclusions, Conditions

Business Occupancy. Endorsement HO-42 amends Section I to cover business property, and Section II is amended to provide coverage for business use of the premises when the applicable endorsement is attached.

Rented Other Structures. The rented other structures discussed earlier above, describes the endorsement to extend Section II coverage to another structure at the residence premises, rented to others.

Residences Rented to Others. Homeowners program rules do not permit Section I coverage on one-, two-, three-, or four-family dwellings rented to others, at a location separate from the insured's residence. Section II may be broadened to include such exposures, however, with Additional Residence Rented to Others (HO-70) endorsement.

Business Pursuits. Section II basically covers only personal activities of an insured. An insured may be covered for liability and medical payments, related to occupational activities; if employed by others. Business Pursuits (HO-71) endorsement grants the coverage, but excludes professional activities other than teaching.

Watercraft. Section II in all forms basically covers boats powered by owned outboard motors of not over 25 horsepower and sailboats of not over 26 feet in length. When the insured has an exposure that exceeds these limitations, coverage is available through the Watercraft (HO-75) endorsement.

Personal Injury. Coverage E protects the insured against claims of others only for *bodily* injury. With the Personal Injury (HO-82) endorsement, coverage may be extended to include the hazards of: false arrest, detention or imprisonment, malicious prosecution, libel, slander, defamation of character, invasion of privacy, wrongful eviction, or wrongful entry.

Farming. Farming is an excluded business pursuit, and if the insured actually operates a farm at the residence premises, the exposure is not eligible for the homeowners program. For only an incidental farming exposure at the residence premises location, however, Section II may be extended to cover with Incidental Farming Personal Liability (HO-72) endorsement. When the insured has farms at other locations, coverage may be provided with Farmers Personal Liability (HO-73) endorsement.

Premises Liability. A person who owns a three- or four-family dwelling and occupies one unit is not eligible for an owner-occupant HO form. Such a person is eligible for a contents broad form HO-4, however, and liability for the entire premises may be provided by Section II through attachment of Three- or Four-Family Dwelling Premises Liability (HO-74) endorsement.

Snowmobiles. Liability and medical payments for operation of a recreational snowmobile may be included by Snowmobile (HO-164) endorsement. This option does not provide coverage for units subject to motor vehicle registration, commercial usage, or in competition.

Motorized Vehicles. A minimal broadening of Section II coverage may be achieved with Incidental Motorized Vehicles (HO-313) endorsement.

Unit-Owners Special Options

Loss Assessment. When a condominium association requires funds, it must look to its member unit owners. Examples of how a member assessment might arise in an insurance context: damage to common elements from an uninsured peril; a large deductible applying to the association's coverage; an uncovered or inadequately covered liability claim. With Loss Assessment Coverage (HO-35) endorsement, the insurer will pay assessments over the $1,000 coverage in the basic policy up to a selected limit (typical: $5,000 or $10,000) based on (1) direct loss to association property caused by a peril included in the insured's policy or (2) an occurrence to which Section II of the homeowners would apply. Regardless of the limit of loss assessment coverage purchased, not more than $1,000 will be paid for an assessment resulting from application of a deductible on the association's insurance. The endorsement excludes earthquake losses, which may be separately covered by endorsement HO-35A.

Additions and Alterations—Perils. The broad form specified perils of Coverage C may be changed to "all-risks" (subject to usual "all-risks" exclusions previously described). Unit-owners Coverage A—Special Coverage (HO-32) endorsement applies.

Rental of Unit. Earlier, in *Rental of Residence,* an option was described to cover occasional rental of a residence premises to others. With Unit-Owners Rental to Others (HO-33) endorsement, an HO-6 may be extended to cover rental with no restrictions on regularity or frequency.

Secondary Dwellings

When an insured owns or rents a secondary residence, the HO

policy for the main residence provides partial coverage. Ten percent of the Coverage C limit applies to property usually kept there (but there is no theft coverage while not occupied by an insured), and Section II includes all private residences of the insured. There are limited situations wherein such protection may be adequate. Generally, however, a secondary private dwelling should be covered with a separate HO-1, HO-2, or HO-3; a rented dwelling or apartment with an HO-4; or a condominium unit with an HO-6.

The second HO policy should be issued in the same insurer as the first because (1) there would otherwise be overlapping coverage situations between the policies and (2) a premium credit applies for the second policy issued in the same company. Section II should be stated to be "not applicable" in the second policy. Rules and coverages are the same as for the initial policy.

Homeowners Sales—Generally

Homeowners sales efforts may generally be placed in one of two categories, both of which are frequently employed by successful producers. There are broad, generalized programs aimed at the entire community. There are also opportunities for targeting sales activities toward segmented portions of the total market.

For the general market, many producers devote a high proportion of advertising and other promotional efforts on homeowners. The acquisition of prospects' expiration dates by mail, telephone, and direct contact is a proven formula. Given the flexibility of the HO program, there is always the opportunity to fashion a better package if the presentation can be timely—the prospect's needs may have changed, or the coverage may not have been arranged with adequate thought in the first place.

If there is one sales aspect of homeowners more strongly emphasized than any other, both to secure and to retain and upgrade accounts, it is a concentration on insurance to value. Because of inflation, the knowledgeable producer is aware that many prospects carry inadequate amounts of homeowners insurance, and locating these underinsureds creates an excellent sales opportunity. Likewise, considerable attention is devoted to maintaining proper amounts for existing customers to avoid vulnerability to competitors. This is accomplished through inflation guard endorsements, periodic contact with increase recommendations, or automatic increases on billing dates.

Homeowners especially lends itself to market segmentation and targeted selling. An affluent neighborhood may be identified where the residents might respond favorably to emphasis on one promoted feature such as replacement cost coverage on personal property or a combination, for example, of valuation service plus scheduling of personal property and high liability limits. A waterfront area where most residents own pleasure boats may be an identifiable market segment to approach with expertise on handling watercraft exposures through the homeowners program. The employees of a large single employer may be identifiable and may be expected to have similar needs at which a sales campaign may be directed. Examples are factory workers or university faculty. Precisely identifiable markets are all residents of rental apartments for HO-4 and all unit owners of condominiums and co-ops for HO-6.

In dealing with the individual prospect, a generalized and rounded approach would suggest analysis of a prospect's existing coverage by answering questions such as:

1. Which is the best form for this person? This is a highly subjective question. Some producers have convinced themselves that HO-3 is best for everyone. A few believe HO-1 is best in virtually all cases because all the added perils in broader forms are frills, not worth the price. There is no "correct" answer as to what is the best form for any insured. After a bit of discussion with a prospect, however, his or her expectations can be measured to some degree, and the form which seems to best coincide would be a logical choice.
2. Is the Coverage A amount adequate (80 percent or more of replacement cost) and is it being kept adequate (inflation guard or automatic increase each renewal)?
3. Are the other limits adequate, especially Coverages C and E?
4. Does the insured have any Coverage C exposures such as jewelry, furs, silverware, or guns, which make any of the special limits inadequate?
5. Are there any special exposures or hazards requiring attention, such as secondary residences? Property such as fine arts which should be separately scheduled? Property rented to others? Occasional rental or residence to others? Watercraft? Business usage of dwelling?
6. Would certain options be especially appropriate for this insured, such as the "all-risk" personal property? Business pursuits? Personal injury?
7. What Section I deductible is most suitable?

Homeowners Sales—Case Study

As an example of analysis and product tailoring, consider the case of John Stewart, executive vice president of Premier Door and Window

Company, a sizable local manufacturing concern. Mr. Stewart is forty-five, married, has one daughter in college, earns a high salary, and is protection conscious.

The Stewarts have a new home in Yourtown; estimated current replacement value is $150,000. They also have a lake cottage with a replacement value of $50,000. At the rear of the main dwelling a small guest house (replacement value $25,000) is gratuitously provided to Mrs. Stewart's mother. Their previous residence in Yourtown is still owned and rented to tenants. Replacement values of personal property have been established as follows:

	At Main Residence	*At Lake Cottage*
General furnishings, appliances, clothing	$75,000	$15,000
Antiques, paintings	$20,000	—
Boat and 50 h.p. outboard motor	—	$8,000
Mrs. Stewart's jewelry	$8,000	—
Mr. Stewart's coin collection	$4,000	—

Based on this information, and after discussion and consideration of the series of questions suggested above, the following program was recommended by the producer:

		Initial Policy	*Secondary Residence Policy*
Form:		HO-3	HO-3
Coverage limits:	A	$135,000	$45,000
	B	13,500	4,500
	C	75,000	18,000
	D	27,000	9,000
	E	300,000	—
	F	2,000	—
Deductible:		$500	$500

The following endorsements were included, all applicable to the primary policy:

Personal Property Replacement cost (HO-290)
Special Personal Property Endorsement (HO-15)
Scheduled Personal Property Endorsement (HO-61)—$20,000 on fine arts, $8,000 on jewelry, $4,000 on coin collection
Other Structures—Specific Insurance (HO-48)—$9,000 on guest house

Inflation Guard (HO-243)—6 percent annual increase
Watercraft (HO-75)—Section II coverage for outboard boat
Additional Residence Rented to Others (HO-70)—Section II coverage for rental dwelling
Personal Injury Liability (HO-82)
Outboard Motor and Boat Endorsement (no standard form—$8,000)

Comments on the recommended program:

1. HO-3 was chosen because it is the broadest peril standard form. When a second policy is issued for an additional residence, the same form as used for the initial residence is recommended for consistency of coverage.
2. Coverage A limits were selected at comfortably above 80 percent of replacement cost. Anywhere from $120,000 to $150,000 would be appropriate for the main dwelling; $40,000 to $50,000 for the cottage. Coverage B may only be 10 percent of A, but must be supplemented at the main residence (see endorsement below). Personal property values under Coverage C are insured to 100 percent, with special types of property handled below (more than the standard 50 percent of Coverage A at the residence, 40 percent minimum at the cottage). Coverage D limits are at the standard 20 percent of A. The $300,000 Coverage E limit was chosen as minimum primary coverage to underlie a personal umbrella policy, also to be written for the Stewarts. This is excess catastrophe coverage, discussed in another chapter. Coverages E and F do not apply in the second policy as the first gives Section II coverage for all private residences of the insured.
3. The $500 Section I deductible was chosen based on discussions with Mr. Stewart, premium comparisons, and the insurer's underwriting requirements.
4. Replacement cost and "all-risk" are provided on personal property in view of the Stewarts' coverage-conscious nature.
5. The scheduled personal property endorsement is necessary for the jewelry and coins because maximum limits for Coverage C would not be adequate for the values involved. The antiques and paintings could have been included in Coverage C, but are covered as fine arts in this endorsement because the coverage is "valued," as explained in another chapter. Additionally, the Section I $500 deductible does not apply to schedule property.
6. The $9,000 specific coverage on the guest house, with the $13,500 Coverage B limit, combine to produce 90 percent of replacement cost.

7. Six percent inflation guard was selected, based on current inflation rates in building costs.
8. As the outboard motor exceeds 25 horsepower, coverage is excluded under Section II and the Watercraft endorsement is necessary.
9. Liability for the rented residence could be covered under a separate policy, but premiums are lower when handled as a homeowners option. Property coverage on that dwelling, however, may not be included, and separate coverage must be effected.
10. Personal injury liability was included, based on Mr. Stewart's wealth and involvement in community affairs.
11. HO Coverage C covers the boat and motor only up to $500, and marine perils are not included. There is no standard endorsement, but it is assumed that the insurer with which this business will be placed offers an HO "all-risks" boat and motor floater endorsement (discussed in another chapter).

Certain other possibilities were considered. Liability for business pursuits was not included because Mr. Stewart is an officer in the corporation which employs him and is thus an "insured" under the liability insurance carried by the employer. No exposure to loss from enforcement of a building ordinance is present. Coverage C special limits on money (other than the coin collection), securities, silverware, furs, and guns are adequate and need not be increased. The 10 percent of Coverage C which applies for personal property of Mr. Stewart's daughter at college was found to be sufficient.

Because there is no single "right" way to deal with the Stewarts' exposures, many would disagree with some details of form, amounts, deductible, and endorsements used. The program suggested is just one approach.

Homeowners Rating

Homeowners is one of the simplest forms of coverage to rate. Differences exist from state to state, but generally a homeowners policy premium is determined as follows:

1. A "base premium" is established from the elements of (a) the territory where the residence is located (a single rating territory may apply for the entire state), (b) the class of fire protection established by ISO as applicable to the location (distance from the nearest fire hydrant or fire station may be a consideration), (c) construction classification of the dwelling (frame, masonry, masonry-veneer, fire resistive), (d) the policy

form desired, and (e) the Coverage A limit (Coverage C if an HO-4 or HO-6). Such base premium includes the remaining Section I coverages at standard percentages and Section II with limits of $100,000 Coverage E and $1,000 Coverage F.

2. The base premium is modified for certain exposures, optional coverages, and any variance from the standard deductible contemplated by the premium tables.
3. Mandatory additional charges apply (a) if there is an incidental business occupancy in the dwelling, (b) for any additional private residences, or (c) if the insured has more than two residence employees.
4. Premiums are added for optional coverages. These are determined either at a rate per $100 or per $1,000 of insurance (for example, to increase Coverage C or provide coverage on other structures) or based on a flat charge (for example, residence rental or Section II increased limits).

Most companies display all rates and premiums for a one-year policy term. Multipliers may then apply for any shorter or longer policy period.

What the Underwriter Needs to Know

Placement of a typical homeowners account is generally trouble-free. The business is considered desirable by virtually all insurers engaged in the line. Completion of the company's standard application, if the submission is not one with special underwriting considerations, will usually suffice.

Depending upon physical features or type of coverage afforded, the underwriter may require photographs of the dwelling and completion of an insurance-to-value form to verify building value. When an application is borderline, narrative comments providing personal information about the applicant and relevant facts about the physical exposures often help the underwriter.

If the application includes scheduled coverage on property such as jewelry, furs, or fine arts, many underwriters require an appraisal to verify values.

Checkpoints

1. Describe how each HO form compares with the HO-3 special form.
2. Identify each of the HO options that may be employed to modify the coverage afforded by the base forms.

3. List the important basic questions that should be answered in order to properly tailor HO coverage to an individual's needs.
4. Identify the rating elements and explain the mechanics involved in establishing a premium for an HO policy.

SUMMARY

The chapter began by discussing the fundamental construction of insurance policies. This discussion led to the development of a way of analyzing policies while stressing the producer's need for expertise in policy analysis.

A method of policy analysis developed. For the homeowners program, examples were used to focus on the connection between detailed policy analysis and the producer's primary function, selling.

To tie together policy analysis and sales, the chapter concluded with a homeowners sales case study and brief discussions on homeowners rating and on what underwriters need to know to write the homeowners business generated by producers.

CHAPTER 5

Automobile Insurance

THE LEGAL ENVIRONMENT

The discussion of the tort system and the concepts of negligence in Chapter 3 generally treated activities of people, what people owned, what obligations they assume under contract, and how these activities lead to liability. All human activities can lead to situations where one party alleges negligence on the part of another. The ownership, maintenance, and use of the motor vehicle is simply a part of the overall liability picture. Its use and ownership can give rise to allegations of negligence that will be handled by the legal system. *Negligence*—the standard of the reasonable and prudent man established as a criterion against which human activities are measured—applies equally to use of the motor vehicle.

Many laws, statutes, and ordinances have been enacted to specifically address the problems of the motor vehicle. These statutes alter and modify some of the common law concepts of negligence and place specific obligations and responsibilities on the owners and operators of motor vehicles. Other changes arise from regulations of federal bureaus like the Department of Transportation, state insurance departments, and state bureaus of motor vehicles. Following are some of the more important statutes and regulations relating to automobile liability that should be known by every producer.

There are several differences in these statutes and regulations from state to state. Every successful producer must be familiar with the specific provisions of the states in which he or she writes personal automobile insurance.

Contributory Negligence

The *contributory negligence* rule is often encountered in relation to automobile liability. Under contributory negligence, when both parties to an automobile accident are negligent, each party must bear its own damages. Contributory negligence rules exist in twelve states.[1]

Comparative Negligence

The *comparative negligence* rule has been adopted in a large number of states and comprises the majority position at the present time. In these areas, the *relative* negligence of each party is determined and the percentage of blame assessed to each. Under the most common version of the comparative negligence rule, the damages recoverable by the plaintiff are reduced by the percentage of the plaintiff's contribution to the accident. Thus, if the plaintiff was judged 20 percent responsible, the plaintiff would recover only 80 percent of his or her damages arising out of the accident. There are other variations of the comparative negligence rule, but a complete discussion is beyond the scope of this book.

Guest Statutes

Guest statutes (or similar rules established by court decisions) are the law in four states.[2] Guest statutes modify the common law doctrine of negligence by altering the *standard of care* a driver owes a guest in the auto. Usually, the standard of care owed would be classified as "reasonable" or "ordinary." But the standard of care owed guest passengers is less!

In order for a driver to be held responsible for injury to guests in states in which a guest statute exists, the driver must be held responsible for "willful and wanton misconduct," "gross negligence," or some other such standard. As a result, it becomes extremely difficult for a guest to pursue an action against the driver. This is the intent of the law—to prevent drivers and guests from colluding to present false claims which insurance companies would find difficult to disprove. Guest statutes apply only to guests. A fare-paying passenger in a taxi or bus would not be considered a guest.

Most guest statutes have been repealed. In recent court decisions, many such statutes were held to be unconstitutional because guests were deprived of "equal protection under the law." Thus, in the majority of states, a driver owes the "reasonable and prudent man" standard of care to guests in the vehicle. However, where guest statutes are the law, guests have little protection unless the driver is judged "grossly negligent."

Vicarious Liability

Normally the person who negligently *operates* a motor vehicle will be held responsible for resultant injury and damage. However, some states have passed statutes under which the owner is held liable for the negligent operation of a car driven with the owner's permission even when the owner is not in the automobile.[3] Other states may impose *vicarious liability* if the driver is acting as an agent for the owner at the time of the accident.

Other Auto Statutes

There are other statutes that operate to alter basic concepts of negligence and reasonable care. Some states issue junior licenses to minors under which the parents or guardians assume a greater responsibility for the reasonable operation of the car than would ordinarily be the case. Unless the parents agree and sign the application, the youth is not granted a license. The object is to provide a greater standard of care to the public, since presumably the parents would not obligate themselves for a child's potential liability unless they felt the child was a careful, prudent driver.

Compulsory Liability Insurance Laws

The State of Massachusetts passed the first state law requiring drivers to carry liability insurance. After World War II, two states (New York and North Carolina) passed similar statutes. Compulsory insurance is viewed as a means of protecting the general public from financially irresponsible drivers. There are problems of enforcement because the law cannot be applied to drivers from other states. In addition, many drivers let their insurance lapse, and drivers of stolen or hit-and-run vehicles are not concerned with observing the law. Such difficulties may be a reason the vast majority of states did not follow Massachusetts and, instead, opted for a different approach, usually a financial responsibility law.

A number of states enacted compulsory no-fault insurance laws. These statutes may require each person, via automobile insurance policies, to indicate compliance with the provisions of that state's no-fault laws.

Financial Responsibility Statutes

The emphasis of financial responsibility statutes is on the need for each driver to be "financially responsible" should an accident occur. In compulsory insurance states, the vehicle owner is required to purchase insurance *before* obtaining or keeping a vehicle registration, but in states with financial responsibility laws an owner need not prove anything until *after* an accident has occurred. After an accident, the owner is only required to prove that he or she is "financially responsible." There are several ways a driver can prove financial responsibility. One way is to show that an automobile liability insurance policy was in force at the time of the accident. Another way is to deposit negotiable securities with the Bureau of Motor Vehicles sufficient to cover all the damages. Finally, some states accept filing of a surety bond as proof of financial responsibility. If insurance is used to meet financial responsibility requirements, a minimum amount of liability insurance will be stated in the statute. The required liability insurance limits vary from state to state in a range of from $5,000/10,000 bodily injury and $1,000 property damage (10/20/5) to $25/50/15.

The objective of these statutes is not to determine fault in an accident. Rather, the state only requires *each* party to be able to show that he or she is financially able to respond.

Should a party be unable to show appropriate insurance in force at the time of the accident or be unable otherwise to prove financial responsibility, that party is usually no longer permitted to operate any motor vehicle in that state. The driver could lose his or her driver's license, and in some cases the vehicle license plates must be returned.

Allegedly, no one else will be injured because the irresponsible driver is off the road, but this is of no value to the innocent uncompensated accident victim. If one party is financially irresponsible and removed from the road, the innocent party still may not be compensated.

Unsatisfied Judgment Funds

Five states (North Dakota, New Jersey, Maryland, New York, and Michigan) have established unsatisfied judgment funds to aid the victims of financially irresponsible drivers. In these states, if the victim obtains a court judgment, and the judgment is not satisfied because the guilty party cannot pay, the victim can recover from a state fund. These laws have limits on the amount of recovery available, ranging from $5/10 to $25/50 for bodily injury. Several of these states permit recovery not only for bodily injury but also for property damage.

The costs of these programs are met by assessing insurance

companies a percentage of premium, by assessing insured drivers, or by assessing uninsured drivers for the right to remain uninsured. Such funds are of limited usefulness, since they provide no protection against unidentified hit-and-run drivers and require a formal court action in order to recover from the fund.

Uninsured Motorist Regulations

A more widely available remedy for injury or damage from uninsured or unidentified drivers is found in statutes and regulations requiring motorists to purchase "uninsured motorist coverage" along with other coverages on their auto policy. This provision results in the insured's own insurance company acting as though it had provided coverage for the uninsured party at the time of the accident in which their insured was injured.

A major disadvantage is the inequity in requiring insured motorists to pay an extra premium to protect themselves from people who are not insured. The results, however, appear to warrant the small additional cost. This coverage is discussed in connection with the Personal Auto Policy.

The No-Fault Concept

The tort system has operated imperfectly in providing reparations for auto accidents. Many difficulties have arisen. Sometimes, it is years before cases involving motor vehicle accidents can be heard in court. By then, witnesses have moved, died, or had their memories dimmed by the passage of time. The costs of court actions are substantial and the percentage of the awards which remains with the lawyers, in the form of contingency fees, means the victim receives only a fraction of the damages awarded by the court.

Why not have everyone involved in an auto accident seek payment from his or her own insurance company? Why not reduce the number of court cases by providing first-party coverage (recover from one's own insurance company) rather than on a third-party (suing the other party) basis? Would this reduce the costs necessary to pay for judges and the expenses of juries? Would this more simple arrangement dramatically reduce the excessive percentage of settlements that go to plaintiffs' attorneys? If all the potential savings were realized, perhaps there would be adequate funds available to pay all injured parties involved in an auto accident, not just the innocent. Courts would be less crowded, justice speeded up, and there would be no need for further expansion of court facilities.

In order to accomplish this, such benefits would have to be

regarded as an exclusive remedy, not just another payment. People would have to give up their prerogative to go to court as consideration for settlements from their own insurance company. Otherwise, it would simply mean another layer of benefits and accompanying costs tacked onto the current system.

The damages a person can suffer as a result of an auto accident can be both economic and noneconomic. Such things as out of pocket medical expenses and loss of wages are *economic* damages and are readily measurable. *Noneconomic* injuries, such as inconvenience and pain and suffering, are not as readily measurable. Even if a person were to receive money for the economic damages, the victim could still go to court and sue for the noneconomic damages and there would be no real savings.

The no-fault system, in order to be successful, would have to exclude the right of a person to go to court to sue for noneconomic damages. The intent of the law is to lessen the need to go to court by having one's own insurance company pay for the economic damages suffered. An important social objective would be met if everyone involved in an auto accident could be reimbursed for economic loss. These goals are not attained by current laws.

No-Fault Thresholds Limiting a person's right to sue is accomplished by instituting a "threshold," a barrier that must be crossed before suit is permitted. A no-fault law may require, for example, that no one can go to court to seek compensation for noneconomic losses unless that person could show expenditure of at least $500 for medical expense. This kind of provision is sometimes referred to as a dollar or monetary threshold. Thresholds are also stated in other ways. Michigan, for example, does not use a dollar threshold, but provides that recourse to the courts is limited to those situations where there is permanent disfigurement, dismemberment, serious impairment of bodily function, or death. This kind of requirement is sometimes called a verbal threshold.

The way the threshold is stated and the monetary amount specified, if any, is extremely important to the rationale of no-fault plans. A very low threshold is no bar to court action and results in only minor reductions in liability suits. In these situations, the premium for automobile insurance, including no-fault coverage, is higher than without no-fault. If thresholds were stated so as to effectively eliminate almost all suits, the premiums could be lower than without no-fault. No-fault, then, can operate to pay all parties to auto accidents and significantly reduce legal expenses. However, a disadvantage is the restriction of the public's right to sue.

Types of No-Fault Laws A *"pure" no-fault* law would completely abolish tort liability for auto accidents and replace it with the right of the parties to collect from their own insurers. There would be no need to prove negligence. The only financial remedy available to accident victims would be claims payments from their own insurers. No pure automobile no-fault plan currently exists in the United States.

Modified no-fault plans do not abolish liability suits but do restrict them to cases involving injuries determined by the threshold specified in the law. Usually, suits are permitted only for noneconomic losses or economic losses in excess of the limits of the law. Assume a no-fault statute required each insured to carry first-party coverage of $10,000 for medical expenses and loss of income. Suits would be permitted only if the economic loss were in excess of $10,000 or if noneconomic losses exceeded specific threshold requirements.

Most no-fault plans cover only bodily injury liability, not property damage liability. There are four reasons for this. First, the amount of damages arising from property damage is normally less than the potential bodily injury loss. Second, the extent of property damage is usually known immediately, whereas the extent of bodily injury may not be known for many years. In addition, there usually is no pain and suffering claim or other noneconomic loss associated with property damage. Third, property damage claims are settled out of court and involve fewer problems than bodily injury claims. The fourth reason no-fault plans usually exclude property damage is that no-fault coverage (first-party) already exists in the physical damage (collision and comprehensive) coverages available to insureds. This covers only vehicle damage and not other property, but the need to go to court to obtain money to have one's own automobile repaired is reduced because many people carry collision insurance.

Thus, because property damage claims can be settled more quickly, for smaller amounts which are more easily estimated, and because such claims are already often covered by first party coverage (collision), the need to extend no-fault laws to cover property damage claims is minimized. No-fault laws offer no savings in this area

Checkpoints

1. Differentiate between the concepts of contributory and comparative negligence.
2. Explain a guest statute.
3. Define "financial responsibility."
4. Explain the purpose and types of thresholds in no-fault plans.
5. Explain a "pure" no-fault system.

Auto Insurance Policy Forms

In 1977, the Insurance Services Office (ISO) introduced the personal auto policy (PAP), a new and simplified auto policy form. Traditionally, the insurance buying public has objected to technical language used in insurance contracts because the contracts were difficult to read and understand. People were annoyed by the "fine print," believing they could not really understand what they were buying.

The insurance industry recognized these problems but remained hesitant to make policy changes. Existing policy forms had been tested in court and there was reasonable agreement as to what the language meant. This was important, because companies knew that any ambiguity or contradiction in a new policy would be construed by the courts in favor of the insureds and against insurance companies.

Forms used in some states are prescribed either by statutes or the department of insurance, and a new form could not be used unless the law was changed or the policy approved. This could mean an insurer would have one form approved for use in one state, but might have to use another form in another state. Yet the general need for a simplified policy continued to be voiced. In response to these needs, the ISO developed the new PAP, stressing simplification, readability, and understandability.

Because of the wide use of the new policy (approved or with approval pending in forty-seven states), the 1985 version of the PAP will be the only auto policy discussed here.

PERSONAL AUTO POLICY (PAP)[4]

The PAP is divided into six parts, to which insurers add their own "jacket" and declarations page:

- Part A—Liability
- Part B—Medical Payments
- Part C—Uninsured Motorists
- Part D—Damage to Your Auto
- Part E—Duties After an Accident or Loss
- Part F—General Provisions

Special endorsements are available to cover such objects as tapes and recording equipment, customizing equipment (special carpets and custom painting), and other situations. Towing and labor cost coverage is also available by endorsement.

Declarations

The declaration identifies the policy number, the parties to the agreement and other considerations specific to this situation—for example, identification of the vehicles insured, area of normal use, names and addresses of persons identified as the named insured, time coverage attaches, term of the policy, what coverages and limits were selected, what deductibles apply, and separate charges for each coverage. All these specifics identify "who, what, and where" in relation to the policy.

Agreement

Each coverage part has its own insuring agreement, but a general insuring agreement appears first, followed by a series of definitions: "In return for payment of the premium and subject to all the terms of this policy we agree with you as follows:. . . ." This twenty-two word agreement accomplishes two important purposes. First, it identifies the premium as the consideration given by the insured and the promise of the insurance company as the corresponding consideration of the company (fulfilling one essential requirement of a legally binding agreement). Second, it incorporates by specific reference all the subsequent terms of the policy.

Definitions

In the policy, the terms defined appear in quotation marks, or boldface, or both, depending on the insurer. A second general statement contains policy definitions:

A. Throughout this policy, "you" and "your" refer to:

1. The "named insured" shown in the Declarations; and
2. The spouse if a resident of the same household.

B. "We", "us" and "our" refer to the Company providing this insurance.

C. For purposes of this policy, a private passenger type auto shall be deemed to be owned by a person if leased:

1. Under a written agreement to that person; and
2. For a continuous period of at least 6 months.

Other words and phrases are defined. They are in quotation marks when used.

The first indication of readability and understandability is the use of "you" and "yours" and "we," "us," and "our" instead of the terms "named insured" and "the company." This paragraph also establishes the status of a leased car. A minimum lease period of six months is specified if the policy is to treat it as an owned vehicle. Next, other terms are defined.

Other Words and Phrases Defined The policy provides the following additional definitions.

D. "Bodily injury" means bodily harm, sickness or disease, including death that results.

E. "Business" includes trade, profession or occupation.

F. "Family member" means a person related to you by blood, marriage or adoption who is a resident of your household. This includes a ward or foster child.

G. "Occupying" means in, upon, getting in, on, out or off.

H. "Property damage" means physical injury to, destruction of or loss of use of tangible property.

I. "Trailer" means a vehicle designed to be pulled by a:

1. Private passenger auto; or
2. Pickup or van.

It also means a farm wagon or farm implement while towed by a vehicle listed in 1. or 2. above.

A ward or foster child is included in the definition of a family member. The language intends to indicate that only vehicles used as private passenger types are normally meant to be covered under a PAP. Those listed fit this description and the "vehicle shown in the declarations" normally must be (a) a four-wheel private passenger, pickup, van, or farm auto that is (b) owned or leased for at least six months by (c) an individual or a husband and wife and which is not (d) rented to others, and is not (e) used in public or private livery.

Eligibility rules are contained in the personal auto manual. They are not part of the contract but are used in order to limit the use of the PAP to private passenger motor vehicles owned by individuals or husband and wife. Two or three wheeled vehicles cannot be insured under a PAP without endorsement, but there appears to be no licensing requirement. A four-wheeled dune buggy or nonlicensed all-terrain vehicle could be insured under a PAP. Motorcycles can be insured by attaching the miscellaneous type vehicles endorsement, and rates for them are shown in the personal auto manual.

Corporations, partnerships, and unincorporated associations cannot buy a PAP. Couples are defined as husband and wife. Unless specifically defined by statute or insurance department ruling, couples sharing a household on any other basis would not fit this definition. If unrelated people live together and jointly own an auto, a PAP may not be issued. They would have to purchase a business auto policy. If only one of the persons owns the auto, it may be insured by a PAP and the other person(s) may be insured by use of a named nonowner endorsement.

Pickups and vans used by farmers and ranchers are eligible for PAP coverage. This continues the historical practice of rating farm pickups as private passenger vehicles.

The definition of a trailer includes the so-called "fifth wheel" type of trailer which rests partially on the bed of a pickup truck. Fifth wheel trailers can be large and usually cannot be pulled by a car. As they can be pulled by a pickup, they are covered under the PAP.

"Your Covered Auto" According to the policy, "your covered auto" means:

1. Any vehicle shown in the Declarations.
2. Any of the following types of vehicles on the date you become the owner:
   a. a private passenger auto; or
   b. a pickup or van.

   This provision (J.2.) applies only if:

   a. you acquire the vehicle during the policy period;
   b. you ask us to insure it within 30 days after you become the owner; and
   c. with respect to a pickup or van, no other insurance policy provides coverage for that vehicle.

   If the vehicle you acquire replaces one shown in the Declarations, it will have the same coverage as the vehicle it replaced. You must ask us to insure a replacement vehicle within 30 days only if:

   a. you wish to add or continue Coverage for Damage to Your Auto; or
   b. it is a pickup or van used in any "business" other than farming or ranching. If the vehicle you acquire is in addition to any shown in the Declarations, it will have the broadest coverage we now provide for any vehicle shown in the Declarations.
3. Any "trailer" you own.
4. Any auto or "trailer" you do not own while used as a temporary substitute for any other vehicle described in this definition which is out of normal use because of its:
   a. breakdown;
   b. repair;
   c. servicing;
   d. loss; or
   e. destruction.

Note *additional* vehicles and trailers will be covered at purchase only if the insurance company is notified within thirty days. A vehicle that *replaces* an auto described in the declarations is covered for liability until the end of the policy term, but physical damage coverage for a replacement vehicle requires notification within thirty days too.

Thus, "your covered auto" includes four categories:

1. the vehicle described,
2. certain newly acquired vehicles for certain coverages,
3. any owned trailer, and
4. a temporary substitute for a vehicle described in the declarations.

Light truck types, such as pickups and vans, are also covered as newly acquired vehicles *only if they are used as private passenger vehicles for pleasure* and not used in any business or occupation. ISO rules permit farm and ranch *business use* of a described vehicle under a PAP. The PAP would automatically grant the broadest coverage provided for any vehicle in the declarations, for such newly acquired vehicles, for thirty days. Exhibit 5-1 shows a summary of PAP applicability based on vehicle type and ownership.

Checkpoints

1. List the six parts of the personal auto policy.
2. List who is eligible to purchase a personal auto policy.
3. List the kinds of vehicles that can be insured under a personal auto policy.

Part A—Liability Coverage

The insuring agreement reads:

> **Insuring Agreement**
>
> **A.** We will pay damages for "bodily injury" or "property damage" for which any "insured" becomes legally responsible because of an auto accident.
>
> Damages include pre-judgment interest awarded against the "insured." We will settle or defend, as we consider appropriate, any claim or suit asking for these damages. In addition to our limit of liability, we will pay all defense costs we incur. Our duty to settle or defend ends when our limit of liability for this coverage has been exhausted. We have no duty to defend any suit or settle any claim for "bodily injury" or "property damage" not covered under this policy.

The policy uses the term "auto accident." Injury or damage must be the result of an accident, something that happened at a specific time at a specific place.

Exhibit 5-1
Summary of PAP Applicability*

PAP = Personal Auto Policy, unmodified.
PAP(m) = Personal Auto Policy, modified by the miscellaneous type vehicle endorsement (PP 03 23).
BAP = Business Auto Policy.
Ind. = Individual H&W = Husband and wife Rel. = Relative.

Vehicle Type	Ownership		
	Ind. or H&W	2 or more Rels.	Other
Private Passenger Auto	PAP	PAP(m)	BAP
Pickup or Van:			
Not used in business	PAP	BAP	BAP
Used in business (except farming)	BAP	BAP	BAP
Used in farm business	PAP	PAP(m)	BAP
Trailer, designed for use with private passenger auto, used with any of above	PAP	PAP(m)	BAP
Miscellaneous Types: All-terrain vehicles, Campers, Dune buggies, Go-carts, Mopeds, Motor bikes, Motor homes, Motorscooters, Motorcycles, Snowmobiles, Vehicles similar to above	PAP(m)	PAP(m)	BAP
All vehicles not described above	BAP	BAP	BAP

*Adapted, with permission, from *Personal Auto Insurance*, Second Edition, FAIA Continuing Education, Florida Association of Insurance Agents, 1982, p. 4.

The insurer, at its option, can either settle or defend any suit. While the insurer must do one or the other, it still has the right to settle any suit without the concurrence of the policyholder. The insurer can also refuse to settle and can choose, instead, to defend any claim in court without consulting the insured. In most cases there will be cooperation between the insured and the insurance company (policy provisions require the insured's cooperation), but the option to settle or defend still belongs with the insurer.

The insurance company's obligation to defend any suit terminates when it has paid out damages to the limit specified in the contract. For example, if four suits were brought against an insured as a result of one accident and the insurer had paid the limits of the policy in the first or second suit, it would not be obligated to defend the insured in any subsequent suits arising from *that accident.* Defense costs are in addition to the limits of liability since they are costs, not damages. However, pre-judgement interest is considered damages and therefore part of the limit of liability. The insurance company could conceivably pay out more in total than the limits of the policy for any one accident. The policy also specifically states that there is no obligation to defend or settle a claim not covered by the PAP. The section continues:

B. "Insured" as used in this Part means:

1. You or any "family member" for the ownership maintenance or use of any auto or "trailer."
2. Any person using "your covered auto."
3. For "your covered auto," any person or organization but only with respect to legal responsibility for acts or omissions of a person for whom coverage is afforded under this Part.
4. For any auto or "trailer," other than "your covered auto," any person or organization but only with respect to legal responsibility for acts or omissions of you or any "family member" for whom coverage is afforded under this Part. This provision (B.4.) applies only if the person or organization does not own or hire the auto or "trailer."

In the PAP *a few definitions change from section to section.* For example, the term "insured" is defined above specifically for the liability section. In the medical payments section, a different definition of "insured" is used. Definitions of "you" and "family member" remain constant throughout the policy.

Coverage for liability is for the named insured, spouse, and family members (as defined) for use of any auto or trailer and for anyone else using the vehicle(s) described in the declarations. Any coverage provided is subject to the exclusion section that follows.

The coverage for other persons or organizations is not as obvious. If some other person or organization is using "your covered auto," that person or organization is covered if there is legal responsibility by a "covered" person for this use. A commonly used example involves a fellow employee's use of the insured's car for the insured's employer. The employer and the fellow employee would be covered.

If the situation is reversed and the insured uses a fellow employee's auto for company business, both the insured and employer would also be covered. These provisions help to handle those situations in which more than one party is named in a suit (if the named insured and his employer or a fellow employee are jointly named in a suit). The PAP extends coverage under the conditions mentioned to cover the other parties.

The supplementary payments section of the policy reads:

> Supplementary payments are in addition to policy limits.
> In addition to our limit of liability, we will pay on behalf of an "insured:"
> 1. Up to $250 for the cost of bail bonds required because of an accident, including related traffic law violations. The accident must result in "bodily injury" or "property damage" covered under this policy.
> 2. Premiums on appeal bonds and bonds to release attachments in any suit we defend.
> 3. Interest accruing after a judgment is entered in any suit we defend. Our duty to pay interest ends when we offer to pay that part of the judgment which does not exceed our limit of liability for this coverage.
> 4. Up to $50 a day for loss of earnings, but not other income, because of attendance at hearings or trials at our request.
> 5. Other reasonable expenses incurred at our request.

Coverage here is $250 for *cost* of bail bonds, but is restricted to bonds required because of an accident, or because of a traffic law violation growing out of the accident where bodily injury or property damage covered by the policy was involved. This means there is no coverage for a traffic law violation unless it was related to an accident.

Should the insurer decide to appeal a court decision and an appeal bond be required, the insurance company must pay the premium for this bond.

According to provision 3, if policy limits were $50,000 for liability coverage and a judgment against the insured for $75,000 is appealed, the interest on the judgment is a supplementary payment until the insurer offers to pay its portion of the judgment ($50,000).

Loss of earnings up to $50 a day will be paid to the insured but only for attendance at hearings or trials. If the insurance company asks the insured to miss work to meet with the insurer's attorneys, for example, no loss of earnings would be paid. Yet any expenses the insured incurs at the request of the insurance company would be reimbursed.

Exclusions Exclusions are important in any insurance policy as they set the boundaries of coverage. The exclusions section of this policy reads:

> **EXCLUSIONS**
>
> A. We do not provide Liability Coverage for any person:

1. Who intentionally causes "bodily injury" or "property damage."
2. For damage to property owned or being transported by that person.

3. For damage to property:
   a. rented to;
   b. used by; or
   c. in the care of;

   that person. This exclusion (A.3.) does not apply to damage to a residence or private garage.

Those situations in which the insurance company will not be providing protection are listed. Intentional injury or damage will never knowingly be covered. A person cannot expect an insurer to pay for an intentionally caused accident. The insurance company also is not providing cargo coverage for property being transported by the persons covered under the policy. Further, the insurance company is not liable if the property involved is in the care of, is used by, or rented to an insured. The insurer will, however, cover liability for damage to property in the care of an insured if the damaged property is a nonowned residence or a garage and if the insured is *liable* for the damage.

The next three exclusions read:

4. For "bodily injury" to an employee of that person during the course of employment. This exclusion (A.4.) does not apply to "bodily injury" to a domestic employee unless workers' compensation benefits are required or available for that domestic employee.
5. For that person's liability arising out of the ownership or operation of a vehicle while it is being used to carry persons or property for a fee. This exclusion (A.5.) does not apply to a share-the-expense car pool.
6. While employed or otherwise engaged in the "business" of:
   a. selling;
   b. repairing;
   c. servicing;
   d. storing; or
   e. parking;

   vehicles designed for use mainly on public highways. This includes road testing and delivery. This exclusion (A.6.) does not apply to the ownership, maintenance or use of "your covered auto" by:
   a. you;
   b. any "family member" or
   c. any partner, agent or employee of you or any "family member."

There is coverage to protect the insured against injury to a domestic employee, unless workers' compensation benefits are in force or are required. The PAP is not meant to be a substitute for workers' compensation coverage. In this regard, the PAP is similar to the liability portion of homeowners policies.

Exclusion 5 states that there is no coverage if the vehicle is being used as a taxi. The intent of the PAP is to provide coverage for the private use of motor vehicles, not when they are being used to carry people or to carry goods for a fee. However, the PAP does not intend to discourage car pooling, and this section differentiates between use of the vehicle as a taxi and its use in a car pool. A taxi is used to make money; a car pool is used to save money and energy by sharing expenses.

Producers should be alert to recognize marginal situations which may not be construed as car pooling. An example might be where one employee regularly takes other fellow employees to work each day and charges a fee higher than a "share the expense" arrangement. If the situation seems to be one where the insured always drives and makes a profit doing it, the producer should point out this exclusion and offer a positive solution such as charging less or buying a Business Auto Policy.

Exclusion 6 eliminates coverage for people in the automobile business. A garage liability policy is needed for such businesses. However, if a son uses "your covered auto" for an errand while working for a gas station, coverage exists.

Exclusion A concludes:

7. Maintaining or using any vehicle while that person is employed or otherwise engaged in any "business" (other than farming or ranching) not described in Exclusion A.6. This exclusion (A.7.) does not apply to the maintenance or use of a:
    a. private passenger auto;
    b. pickup or van that you own; or
    c. "trailer" used with a vehicle described in a. or b. above.
8. Using a vehicle without a reasonable belief that that person is entitled to do so.
9. For "bodily injury" or "property damage" for which that person:
    a. is an insured under a nuclear energy liability policy; or
    b. would be an insured under a nuclear energy liability policy but for its termination upon exhaustion of its limit of liability.

   A nuclear energy liability policy is a policy issued by any of the following or their successors:
    a. American Nuclear Insurers
    b. Mutual Atomic Energy Liability Underwriters; or
    c. Nuclear Insurance Association of Canada.

Exclusion 7 eliminates coverage for nonowned vans or pickups used for business. Owned vehicles of this type are covered for this use, but the PAP manual would not permit a policy to be issued in the first place if such use was indicated. It is possible that an insured borrows a van for use in a business established after the PAP's inception. There would be no coverage in that case for the borrowed van. Coverage for farm use of autos is clearly established.

Exclusion 8 eliminates coverage when no clear belief exists that any person has permission to use a vehicle. The owner does not have to give explicit permission; rather; the belief that permission exists must reasonably be held by the borrower. At the time of loss, it is the obligation of the insured to prove a "reasonable belief" that permission existed.

Exclusion 9 eliminates liability coverage for any accident where an insured was or would have been covered by a nuclear energy liability policy.

The final exclusions of the liability section of the PAP read:

> **B.** We do not provide Liability Coverage for the ownership, maintenance or use of:
> 1. Any motorized vehicle having fewer than four wheels.
>   2. Any vehicle, other than "your covered auto," which is:
>   a. owned by you; or
>   b. furnished or available for your regular use.
> 3. Any vehicle, other than "your covered auto," which is:
>   a. owned by any "family member;" or
>   b. furnished or available for the regular use of any "family member."
>
>   However, this exclusion (B.3.) does not apply to your maintenance or use of any vehicle which is:
>   a. owned by a "family member;" or
>   b. furnished or available for the regular use of a "family member."

Under Exclusion B, three specifics are mentioned. Motorcycles and other vehicles with fewer than four wheels are excluded under the basic PAP.

Also under B, Exclusions 2 and 3 eliminate some exposures. For any vehicle the insured owns but does not list on the policy, there is no coverage. The insured cannot pay for insurance on one auto and expect coverage on several vehicles. For other vehicles furnished or available for the insured's regular use, there is no coverage. This means there is no nonowned coverage where the insured regularly has access to such vehicles. In cases where there is a company owned fleet available for use by an employee, even though the employee might never get the same vehicle twice, the exclusion would stand and there would be no coverage under the PAP. Coverage while driving vehicles furnished for regular use can be provided by attaching the extended non-owned coverage for named individuals endorsement.

Exclusion 3 applies the same restrictions to family members but does not apply to the named insured. Thus, there would be coverage if the insured were to use another family member's vehicle which is not insured under the same PAP. However, the insured's policy would not protect the family member who owned the car.

Endorsements, such as the extended nonowned coverage for named individuals endorsement, can eliminate an exclusion to meet an insured's particular needs.

Checkpoints

1. Explain the limitations on the insurer's obligation to defend claims against the insured.
2. List who is included under the definition of "covered person" for liability coverage.
3. List the expenses the insurer is obligated to pay even if it exhausts the policy limit in the payment of judgments.
4. Explain if the PAP covers the insured's liability for injuries while the car is being used to carry passengers as a part of a share-the-expense car pool.

Limit of Liability The limit of liability section details how much the insurer will be liable for and how often. The section reads:

LIMIT OF LIABILITY

A. The limit of liability shown in the Declarations for this coverage is our maximum limit of liability for all damages resulting from any one auto accident. This is the most we will pay regardless of the number of:
   1. "Insureds;"
   2. Claims made;
   3. Vehicles or premiums shown in the Declarations; or
   4. Vehicles involved in the auto accident.

B. We will apply the limit of liability to provide any separate limits required by law for bodily injury and property damage liability. However, this provision (B.) will not change our total limit of liability.

The limit shown on the declarations page is a single limit per accident. Some financial responsibility statutes are worded to require "per person" as well as "per accident" limits and separate limits for bodily injury and for property damage. In such cases, the PAP will be interpreted to conform to the law. Such interpretation, however, will not change the company's maximum limit of liability. If the insured vehicle is garaged in a state that requires split limits, an endorsement can be used to provide split limits.

For instance, if a PAP is issued for a single limit of $25,000 and state financial responsibility minimum limits are $10/20/5 ($10,000 per person B.I., $20,000 per accident B.I., and $5,000 for property damage liability), the PAP will be interpreted to provide $10/20/5 limits. If the state minimum is $15/30/10, the policy will provide split limits but the insurer will not pay more than the $25,000 indicated on the declarations page. The best solutions are to endorse the policy to provide split limits or sell a single limit well in excess of the state financial responsibility requirement.

Out of State Coverage Most insureds will cross into other states with their cars. This section describes what then may happen to the liability coverage and limits in these words:

OUT OF STATE COVERAGE

If an auto accident to which this policy applies occurs in any state or province other than the one in which "your covered auto" is principally garaged, we will interpret your policy for that accident as follows:

A. If the state or province has:

1. A financial responsibility or similar law specifying limits of liability for "bodily injury" or "property damage" higher than the limit shown in the Declarations, your policy will provide the higher specified limit.
2. A compulsory insurance or similar law requiring a nonresident to maintain insurance whenever the nonresident sues a vehicle in that state or province, your policy will provide at least the required minimum amounts and types of coverage.

B. No one will be entitled to duplicate payments for the same elements of loss.

For example, should the PAP be written with a single limit of $25,000, satisfying the financial requirements of the state of residence, and should an accident occur in another state requiring limits of 15/30/10, the policy, as written, would be interpreted as having limits of 15/30/10. The reference to "province" is a reminder of the availability of coverage in Canada as well as the United States.

Financial Responsibility Sometimes the law requires an insured to show proof of financial responsibility and the insurance company is required to so certify. In such cases the insurer agrees to interpret the policy so that it conforms to the requirements of the law. The policy wording on financial responsibility is:

FINANCIAL RESPONSIBILITY

When this policy is certified as future proof of financial responsibility, this policy shall comply with the law to the extent required.

Other Insurance The section of the policy dealing with other insurance reads:

OTHER INSURANCE

If there is other applicable liability insurance we will pay only our share of the loss. Our share is the proportion that our limit of liability

> bears to the total of all applicable limits. However, any insurance we provide for a vehicle you do not own shall be excess over any other collectible insurance.

The PAP prorates liability coverage in relation to the total limits of liability available. If, for instance, an insured is covered for \$50,000 in one policy and \$100,000 in another valid and applicable auto liability policy, the first policy would pay: $\frac{\$50,000}{\$150,000} \times$ loss, or one-third of the loss up to the policy's limit of \$50,000, and the second policy would pay:

$$\frac{\$100,000}{\$150,000} \times \text{loss.}$$

With regard to a nonowned vehicle, however, the PAP is *excess* over any insurance provided by the vehicle owned. To illustrate, suppose *K* has a PAP issued by Company A covering her owned Pontiac. The limit of liability is \$100,000. *K* borrows *L*'s Toyota, which is insured by Company B, with a limit of liability of \$50,000. If *K* is involved in an accident while driving *L*'s car, the policy covering the *auto* is primary. The policy covering the *driver* is excess. In this case, a \$100,000 loss would be allocated:

Company B (*L*'s policy)	\$50,000 (primary coverage)
Company A (*K*'s policy)	\$50,000 (excess coverage)

Part B—Medical Payments

Under the medical payments (Med Pay) section, if an "insured" incurs a "bodily injury," both as defined in Part B, payment will be made. There is no requirement that the covered person be negligent or liable. Med Pay is a no-fault coverage.

The Med Pay insuring agreement reads in part:

> **Insuring Agreement**
> **A.** We will pay reasonable expenses incurred for necessary medical and funeral services because of "bodily injury:"
> 1. Caused by accident; and
> 2. Sustained by an "insured."
>
> We will pay only those expenses incurred within 3 years from the date of the accident.

Med Pay is designed to be a single peril (auto accident) health insurance coverage for a covered person (defined below). It pays medical and funeral services for up to three years after an auto accident. The three-year period is important because many medical expenses resulting from auto-related injuries may be incurred over a long period of time.

For example, a baby sitter has an auto accident injuring children in his or her care. The sitter may be sued because the children's parents know some medical procedures will not be completed within a short period of time. Orthodontic work, for example, is often not begun until permanent teeth are in place. Thus a young child with injuries to teeth may have to wait a year or more until the time is appropriate to make repairs. With the PAP's three-year period, few situations will require suit because most injuries will be settled under the medical payments provision of the policy.

The Med Pay insuring agreement concludes:

> **B. "Insured"** as used in this Part means:
> 1. You or any "family member:"
>   a. while "occupying;" or
>   b. as a pedestrian when struck by
>
>   a motor vehicle designed for use mainly on public roads or a trailer of any type.
> 2. Any other person while "occupying" "your covered auto."

This definition contains two interesting provisions. First, the term "motor vehicle" is used. Motor vehicle is a general term and any vehicle, such as a large truck or bus, would be considered an auto. However, specifically excluded are those vehicles not designed for primary use on public roads such as a mobile crane.

A second interesting provision lies in the use of the term "pedestrian." Coverage is granted to the named insured or a family member struck by a motor vehicle only if the covered person is a pedestrian.

A covered person in number 2 is a person other than the named insured and family members occupying "your covered auto." The named insured and family members would be covered while operating a nonowned vehicle or while a pedestrian. "Any other person" would be covered only while occupying your covered auto.

Exclusions There are specific exclusions for Med Pay coverage. Many are similar to exclusions discussed in the liability section. For review and brevity only the new or different exclusions will be discussed. Exclusions similar to the liability exclusions are summarized in Exhibit 5-2.

The Med Pay exclusions read:

> We do not provide Medical Payments Coverage for any person for "bodily injury:"
> 1. Sustained while "occupying" any motorized vehicle having fewer than four wheels.
> 2. Sustained while "occupying" "your covered auto" when it is being used to carry persons or property for a fee. This exclusion (2.) does not apply to a share-the-expense car pool.

Exhibit 5-2
Similar Med Pay and Liability Exclusions

Nature of Exclusion	Liability Exclusion Number	Med Pay Exclusion Number
Less than four wheels	B1	1
Livery for fee	A5	2
Workers' compensation	A4	4
Owned, furnished vehicles	B2a,b	5a,b
Family members owned, furnished vehicles	B3a,b	6a,b
Without permission	A8	7
Business, occupation use	A6 and 7	8

3. Sustained while "occupying" any vehicle located for use as a residence or premises.
4. Occurring during the course of employment if workers' compensation benefits are required or available for the "bodily injury."
5. Sustained while "occupying" or, when struck by, any vehicle (other than "your covered auto") which is:
   a. owned by you; or
   b. furnished or available for your regular use.
6. Sustained while "occupying" or, when struck by, any vehicle (other than "your covered auto" which is:
   a. owned by any "family member;" or
   b. furnished or available for the regular use of any "family member."

   However, this exclusion (6.) does not apply to you.
7. Sustained while "occupying" a vehicle without a reasonable belief that that person is entitled to do so.
8. Sustained while "occupying" a vehicle when it is being used in the "business" of an "insured." This exclusion (8.) does not apply to "bodily injury" sustained while "occupying" a:
   a. private passenger auto;
   b. pickup or van that you own; or
   c. "trailer" used with a vehicle described in a. or b. above.
9. Caused by or as a consequence of:
   a. discharge of a nuclear weapon (even if accidental);
   b. war (declared or undeclared);
   c. civil war;
   d. insurrection; or
   e. rebellion or revolution.
10. From or as a consequence of the following, whether controlled or uncontrolled or however caused:
    a. nuclear reaction;
    b. radiation; or

c. radioactive contamination.

The exclusion of medical payments coverage while occupying any vehicle located for use as a residence (exclusion 3) is meant to apply to house trailers, travel trailers, motor homes, converted school buses, and the like "located" as a residence or premises. This does not exclude coverage while such vehicles are being used as motor vehicles. Often people purchase such vehicles and locate them for a period of time at one location, perhaps at a trailer camp or along a river. In such cases the vehicle loses its identity as a vehicle and is a residence.

Exclusions 9 (a) and 10 are similar to exclusion A9 in the liability section. Even if involving a motor vehicle, the insurance company does not intend to provide medical payments for injuries involving nuclear radiation or radioactive substances. The balance of Med Pay exclusions 9 (b, c, & d) exclude losses related to war, insurrection, or rebellion. Losses of this nature are uninsurable due to the catastrophe potential. Exhibit 5-3 is a summary of Med Pay coverage.

Limits of Liability The medical payments section has a separate limit of liability:

A. The limit of liability shown in the Declarations for this coverage is our maximum limit of liability for each person injured in any one accident. This is the most we will pay regardless of the number of:
   1. "Insureds"
   2. Claims made;
   3. Vehicles or premiums shown in the Declarations; or
   4. Vehicles involved in the accident.

B. Any amounts otherwise payable for expenses under this coverage shall be reduced by any amounts paid or payable for the same expenses under Part A or Part C.

C. No payment will be made unless the injured person or that person's legal representative agrees in writing that any payment shall be applied toward any settlement or judgment that person receives under Part A or Part C.

Payments under the medical payments section will be coordinated with benefits payable under the liability (Part A) or uninsured motorist (Part C) portion of the same policy. Payments under this section will be reduced by any payments made under Parts A and C, and the claimant must promise in writing that any coverage B amount paid will be credited if any *future* payment is made under Parts A and C.

This terminology is phrased carefully to make "stacking of benefits" more difficult. "Stacking" refers to an attempt to collect multiples of the policy limits based on the existence of multiple autos covered, claims made, vehicles involved or the like. Insurers are willing to pay full Med Pay benefits, but not multiples of a Med Pay limit.

Exhibit 5-3
Summary of Medical Payments Coverage

The following table shows who is and who is not entitled to receive Medical Payments benefits under a named insured's PAP. Assumption: named insured does not own or have regularly furnished any vehicle which is not a "your covered auto."

How Injured	Person Injured		
	Name Insured	Relative	Any Other Person
1. While occupying named insured's "your covered auto"	Yes	Yes	Yes
2. As a pedestrian by named insured's "your covered auto	Yes	Yes	No
3. While occupying or as a pedestrian by an auto not owned by or regularly furnished to a relative	Yes	Yes	No
4. While occupying or as a pedestrian by an auto owned by or regularly furnished to a relative	Yes	No	No
5. While occupying a vehicle with less than 4 wheels	No	No	No
6. Struck as a pedestrian by a vehicle with less than 4 wheels	Yes	Yes	No

*Reprinted, with permission, from *Personal Auto Insurance: FAIA Continuing Education*, Second edition. Florida Association of Insurance Agents, 1982, p. 54.

Other Insurance This provision intends to make the Med Pay provisions excess when the insured is operating a nonowned automobile. If a policy covering a nonowned vehicle does not provide medical payments coverage, or if these benefits are exhausted, the insured's policy would be primary.

Part C—Uninsured Motorist Coverage (UM)

A major social problem is the injury to people and damage to property caused by motorists who are not financially responsible. Part C of the PAP permits the insured to enter into an arrangement with the insured's own insurer which will pay just as though that irresponsible person had been carrying liability insurance.

Insuring Agreement Because this "arrangement" is complicated, the insuring agreement is more complex than others discussed. The agreement reads:

> **A.** We will pay damages which an "insured" is legally entitled to recover from the owner or operator of an "uninsured motor vehicle" because of "bodily injury:"
> 1. Sustained by an "insured;" and
> 2. Caused by an accident.
>
> The owner's or operator's liability for these damages must arise out of the ownership, maintenance or use of the "uninsured motor vehicle."
>
> Any judgment for damages arising out of a suit brought without our written consent is not binding on us.

The insurer is concerned with protecting its own interests as well as the interests of its insureds. Consequently, the insurance company wishes to have a voice in any decision by their insured to sue the uninsured motorist. This provision makes it plain that should the insured sue and obtain judgment in an action without the consent of the insurance company, that settlement is not binding on the insurance company. This is not to say that the insurer will not pay, but that the existence of or the amount of the judgment does not establish the insurer's liability or the extent of the payment under Part C. The insuring agreement continues:

> **B.** "Insured" as used in this Part means:
> 1. You or any "family member."
> 2. Any other person "occupying" "your covered auto."
> 3. Any person for damages that person is entitled to recover because of "bodily injury" to which this coverage applies sustained by a person described in 1. or 2. above.
>
> **C.** "Uninsured motor vehicle" means a land motor vehicle or trailer of any type:
> 1. To which no bodily injury liability bond or policy applies at the time of the accident.

2. To which a bodily injury liability bond or policy applies at the time of the accident. In this case its limit for bodily injury liability must be less than the minimum limit for bodily injury liability specified by the financial responsibility law of the state in which "your covered auto" is principally garaged.
3. Which is a hit and run vehicle whose operator or owner cannot be identified and which hits:
   a. you or any "family member;"
   b. a vehicle which you or any "family member" are "occupying;" or
   c. "your covered auto."
4. To which a bodily injury liability bond or policy applies at the time of the accident but the bonding or insuring company;
   a. denies coverage; or
   b. is or becomes insolvent.

However, "uninsured motor vehicle" does not include any vehicle or equipment:

1. Owned by or furnished or available for the regular use of you or any "family member."
2. Owned or operated by a self-insurer under any applicable motor vehicle law.
3. Owned by any governmental unit or agency.
4. Operated on rails or crawler treads.
5. Designed mainly for use off public roads while not on public roads.
6. While located for use as a residence or premises.

The term "insured" is defined again in relation to Part C of the policy and differs from the definitions used in Parts A and B. Item 3 under covered person would allow, for instance, a wrongful death payment to survivors of a family member after an accident.

Uninsured Motor Vehicle. The uninsured vehicle definitions include the term "bodily injury liability bond" as well as "bodily injury liability policy" to include any special financial responsibility bonds which a person or organization may have been required to obtain instead of insurance. Some states, for example, require a special bond instead of insurance if a motorist is a self-insurer.

Number 2 of uninsured vehicle presents a different type of situation. For example, say motorist *A* was injured in state *X* where the limits required by *X*'s financial responsibility law were $10/20/5, lower than that of *A*'s home state ($15/30/10). If the injury to *A* was caused by driver *B* carrying only $10/20/5, *B* would be considered an uninsured motorist and these provisions would apply to protect *A*.

Number 3 of uninsured vehicle provides that a hit and run or unidentifiable motorist is also considered uninsured under certain circumstances. An insured or family member struck while walking or while occupying a vehicle, or anyone occupying your covered auto would be covered by UM if the at-fault vehicle was a hit and run or was driven by an unidentifiable motorist.

Number 4 says if the driver causing the accident is insured in an insurance company which denies coverage or is insolvent, the driver is considered uninsured and uninsured motorist coverage applies.

Excluded Uninsured Motor Vehicles The final portion of the UM insuring agreement lists vehicles *not* considered uninsured vehicles. Item one indicates that if the insured or a family member has an uninsured auto, this coverage would not apply. Item two covers those situations where a large corporation, for example, would be permitted by a state to be *self* insured. Such vehicles would not be considered *un*insured.

Many government units enjoy a certain immunity to suit and some have their own formal retention programs. Such vehicles, again, are not considered uninsured, and no benefits would be available under this section.

Vehicles on rails or crawler treads do not come under the definition of a motor vehicle and so are excluded; neither are vehicles used as a premises (see the related discussion in the medical payments section).

UM is also not meant to cover off road farm accidents with farm equipment. Thus a farm tractor would be considered an uninsured vehicle if operated on the highway but not when plowing a field, for example.

Exclusions Again, the exclusions in Part C, Uninsured Motorists Coverage, parallel to a large extent the exclusions for Part A (Liability) and Part B (Medical Payments) as indicated in Exhibit 5-4. The statement on exclusions reads:

A. We do not provide Uninsured Motorists Coverage for "bodily injury" sustained by any person:

1. While "occupying," or when struck by any motor vehicle owned by you or any "family member" which is not insured for this coverage under this policy. This includes a trailer of any type used with that vehicle.
2. If that person or the legal representatives settles the "bodily injury" claim without our consent.
3. While "occupying" "your covered auto" when it is being used to carry persons or property for a fee. This exclusion (A.3.) does not apply to a share-the-expense car pool.
4. Using a vehicle without a reasonable belief that that person is entitled to do so.

Exhibit 5-4
Similar Uninsured Motorists and Liability Exclusions

Nature of Exclusion	Liability Exclusion Number	Uninsured Motorist Exclusion Number
Owned, uninsured vehicle	B2a, B3a	A1
Livery for fee	A5	A3
Without permission	A8	A4

B. This coverage shall not apply directly or indirectly to benefit any insurer or self-insurer under any of the following or similar law:
1. workers' compensation law; or
2. disability benefits law.

Exclusion A2, which is unique to UM, relates to the insuring agreement in this section and is designed to reinforce the insurer's right to be a part of any suit against the uninsured motorist. However, where the insuring agreement says any judgment for damages arising out of a suit brought without the insurance company's consent is not binding on the insurance company, the exclusion states flatly that there is no UM coverage if the claim is settled without the insurance company's consent.

Exclusion B addresses a unique problem. Some states permit a workers' compensation or disability income insurer to sue a negligent uninsured motorist to recover any benefits paid their injured insured. This exclusion acts to prevent such insurers from subrogating and claiming any benefit under UM coverage as an offset against what they paid in compensation benefits.

Limits of Liability The UM limits of liability section of the policy reads:

A. The limit of liability shown in the Declarations for this coverage is our maximum limit of liability for all damages resulting from any one accident. This is the most we will pay regardless of the number of:
1. "Insureds;"
2. Claims made;
3. Vehicles or premiums shown in the Declarations; or
4. Vehicles involved in the accident.

B. Any amounts otherwise payable for damages under this coverage shall be reduced by all sums:
1. Paid because of the "bodily injury" or on behalf of persons or organizations who may be legally responsible. This includes all sums paid under Part A; and
2. Paid or payable because of the "bodily injury" under any of the following or similar law:
   a. workers' compensation law; or
   b. disability benefits law.

C. Any payment under this coverage will reduce any amount that person is entitled to recover for the same damages under Part A.

The minimum limits available for UM are the minimum financial responsibility limits for the state where the car is garaged. Higher limits may be purchased, but they cannot be higher than limits for Coverage A. The phrasing of the first paragraph again indicates an attempt to prevent "stacking" of benefits, in this case UM benefits.

The second paragraph addresses the idea behind uninsured motorists coverage, to provide payment to an insured when injured by a financially irresponsible driver. If the insured receives any settlement from that person or an organization responsible for that person, or from workers' compensation, or a disability benefit *law,* the insurance company will be able to deduct these amounts from its settlement.

The final paragraph coordinates UM benefits with liability benefits. If any subsequent payment is made under the liability section, that payment will be reduced by the amount paid under this coverage. For instance, assume passenger *C* is injured in *A*'s car because of an accident caused by joint negligence on the part of *A* and uninsured motorist *B*. *C* has a right of action against both *A* and *B*. If *C* receives UM benefits for *A*'s policy because of motorist *B*, *C* 's recovery from UM will be reduced by the amount received from *A* 's liability coverage.

Other Insurance The other insurance statement for this part of the policy reads:

> If there is other applicable similar insurance we will pay only our share of the loss. Our share is the proportion that our limit of liability bears to the total of all applicable limits. However, any insurance we provide with respect to a vehicle you do not own shall be excess over any other collectible insurance.

For consistency, this other insurance provision is exactly the same as the other insurance provision of Part A with the exception of one word, "similar."

Arbitration The section of the policy dealing with arbitration for UM coverage reads:

> **Arbitration**
> **A.** If we and an "insured" do not agree:
> 1. Whether that person is legally entitled to recover damages under this Part; or
> 2. As to the amount of damages;
>
> either party may make a written demand for arbitration. In this event, each party will select an arbitrator. The two arbitrators will select a third. If they cannot agree within 30 days, either may request that selection be made by a judge of a court having jurisdiction.
> **B.** Each party will:
> 1. Pay the expenses it incurs; and
> 2. Bear the expenses of the third arbitrator equally.

C. Unless both parties agree otherwise, arbitration will take place in the county in which the "insured" lives. Local rules of law as to procedure and evidence will apply. A decision agreed to by two of the arbitrators will be binding as to:
   1. Whether the "insured" is legally entitled to recover damages; and
   2. The amount of damages. This applies only if the amount does not exceed the minimum limit for bodily injury liability specified by the financial responsibility law of the state in which "your covered auto" is principally garaged. If the amount exceeds that limit, either party may demand the right to a trial. This demand must be made within 60 days of the arbitrators' decision. If this demand is not made, the amount of damages agreed to by the arbitrators will be binding.

After stating earlier that the insurer will not be bound by any court judgment won by the insured against an uninsured motorist, and after specifically excluding coverage for the insured if the suit is settled without the insurance company's consent, the insurance company now establishes a relatively inexpensive and quick method whereby any disagreement between it and the insured can be resolved.

In case of disagreement, either party may demand arbitration. Each party selects an arbitrator. These two select a third, and the decision of two of the three is binding on both parties. Costs are shared equally. The procedure can establish whether coverage exists or the amount of damages or both. In certain circumstances, the right to a trial is also preserved.

Underinsured Motorists Coverage Uninsured motorists coverage will pay only if an *uninsured* motorist is liable; and an uninsured motorist is one who either has no insurance, has insurance in an amount less than the state's minimum financial responsibility limits, or is a hit-and-run driver. The PAP can be endorsed in most states to provide *underinsured* motorists coverage, which pays up to the difference between the Part A limits on the covered vehicle and the Part A limits on the at-fault vehicle, even if the at-fault vehicle had limits in excess of the minimum financial responsibility limits.

To illustrate the operation of underinsured motorists coverage, assume that drivers Innocent and Atfault are involved in an accident because of the negligence of Atfault. Both have policy limits in excess of the state's minimum financial responsibility limits. Atfault's liability limit is $50,000 and Innocent's underinsured motorists limit is $300,000. Innocent obtains a judgment of $150,000 against Atfault, whose liability insurer pays its limit of $50,000. Uninsured motorists coverage would not pay anything, since Atfault did not qualify as an uninsured motorist. However, Innocent's underinsured motorists coverage, endorsed to Innocent's PAP, would pay the remaining $100,000 of damages since Atfault's limit was less than Innocent's limit. Innocent's policy would have paid up to $250,000 if the judgment had been $300,000 or more.

Checkpoints

1. Explain the other-insurance clause of the liability section of the PAP.
2. Explain how the medical payments coverage for "you or a family member" differs from the coverage for other persons.
3. Explain the concept of uninsured motorists coverage.
4. Contrast uninsured and underinsured motor vehicles.
5. Explain who is a covered person under the UM coverage.

Part D—Coverage for Damage to Your Auto

This section, like all coverage sections, begins with an insuring agreement:

INSURING AGREEMENT

A. We will pay for direct and accidental loss to "your covered auto" or any "non-owned auto," including their equipment, minus any applicable deductible shown in the Declarations. We will pay for loss to "your covered auto" caused by:

1. Other than "collision" only if the Declarations indicate that Other Than Collision Coverage is provided for that auto.
2. "Collision" only if the Declarations indicate that Collision Coverage is provided for that auto.

If there is a loss to a "non-owned auto," we will provide the broadest coverage applicable to any "your covered auto" shown in the Declarations.

B. "Collision" means the upset of "your covered auto" or its impact with another vehicle or object.

Loss caused by the following is considered other than "collision:"

1. Missiles or falling objects;
2. Fire;
3. Theft or larceny;
4. Explosion or earthquake;
5. Windstorm;
6. Hail, water or flood;
7. Malicious mischief or vandalism;
8. Riot or civil commotion;
9. Contact with bird or animal; or
10. Breakage of glass.

If breakage of glass is caused by a "collision," you may elect to have it considered a loss caused by "collision."

C. "Non-owned auto" means any private passenger auto, pickup, van or "trailer" not owned by or furnished or available for the regular use of you or any "family member" while in the custody of or being operated by you or any "family member." However, "non-owned auto" does not include any vehicle coverage used as a temporary substitute for a vehicle you own which is out of normal use because of its:

1. Breakdown;
2. Repair;
3. Servicing;
4. Loss; or
5. Destruction.

This agreement is broad. The insurance company agrees to pay for "direct and accidental" loss. To both "your covered auto" and any "non-owned auto." Coverage for nonowned autos tracks with the broadest coverage for any covered auto. Later, in the exclusion section, this statement is subject to some restrictions, but this language covers a wide range of possible perils.

Next, collision is defined. It is necessary to define collision because the insured has the option of insuring against (1) loss by collision, (2) loss by perils other than collision, (3) both, or (4) neither. Collision is defined to include upset. A motorist who failed to negotiate a curve and ended up in a ditch had an "upset" but never actually collided with anything except the ground.

The other loss causes listed are not considered collision, but are "direct and accidental" and so would be covered under the "other than collision" part of the physical damage section, if listed in the declarations.

Part C. of the insuring agreement clearly describes what will be considered a "Non-owned Auto" so that confusion is eliminated.

The insuring agreement continues:

Transportation Expenses
In addition, we will pay up to $10 per day, to a maximum of $300, for transportation expenses incurred by you. This applies only in the event of the total theft of "your covered auto." We will pay only transportation expenses incurred during the period:

1. Beginning 48 hours after the theft; and
2. Ending when "your covered auto" is returned to use or we pay for its loss.

All transportation expenses up to $10 per day and a total of $300, are covered for theft only and beginning after forty-eight hours of such theft. Therefore, bus, taxi and car rental fees are covered. The rental reimbursement/transportation expense endorsement can be added to cover the cost of renting a substitute vehicle following a nontheft loss covered under the physical damage section of the policy. The dollar limits under the endorsement are $15 per day up to a maximum of $450.

Exclusions Exclusions in Part D are extensive and are examined in two parts. The first part reads:

We will not pay for:

1. Loss to "your covered auto" which occurs while it is used to carry persons or property for a fee. This exclusion (1.) does not apply to a share-the-expense car pool.
2. Damage due and confined to:
   a. wear and tear;
   b. freezing;
   c. mechanical or electrical breakdown or failure; or
   d. road damage to tires.

   This exclusion (2.) does not apply if the damage results from the total theft of "your covered auto."
3. Loss due to or as a consequence of:
   a. radioactive contamination;
   b. discharge of any nuclear weapon (even if accidental);
   c. war (declared or undeclared);
   d. civil war;
   e. insurrection; or
   f. rebellion or revolution.
4. Loss to equipment designed for the reproduction of sound. This exclusion (4.) does not apply if the equipment is permanently installed in "your covered auto."
5. Loss to tapes, records or other devices for use with equipment designed for the reproduction of sound.
6. Loss to a camper body or "trailer" not shown in the Declarations. This exclusion (6.) does not apply to a camper body or "trailer" you:
   a. acquire during the policy period; and
   b. ask us to insure within thirty days after you become the owner.

Exclusion 2 lists common losses that are usually not considered "direct and accidental" and so would not ordinarily be covered. If these losses are a result of a theft of the auto they are covered.

Exclusion 3 contains similar wording to both Parts A (exclusion 9) and B (see Exhibit 5-5).

Exclusions 4 and 5 address target items subject to theft often found in autos. With the introduction of more sophisticated and expensive sound systems in autos, the incidence of theft loss increased dramatically. The insurers found themselves paying many losses not anticipated in the rating and so excluded such losses in the PAP. Tapes and records can be insured by an endorsement. The endorsement coverage is limited to $200.

Nonowned campers or trailers or those not listed in the declarations are not covered by Part D. Newly acquired owned trailers are

Exhibit 5-5
Similar Physical Damage and Liability Exclusions

Nature of Exclusion	Liability Exclusion Number	Physical Damage Exclusion Number
Livery for fee	A5	1
Without permission	A8	7
Nuclear	A9	3

covered as of the date of acquisition if the company is notified within thirty days. The reference to "camper body" is to the kind of camping accommodations carried on a pickup.

Remaining Damage to Your Auto exclusions are:

7. Loss to any "non-owned auto" or any vehicle used as a temporary substitute for a vehicle you own, when used by you or any "family member" without a reasonable belief that you or that "family member" are entitled to do so.
8. Loss to:
   a. TV antennas;
   b. awnings or cabanas; or
   c. equipment designed to create additional living facilities
9. Loss to any of the following or their accessories:
   a. citizens band radio;
   b. two-way mobile radio;
   c. telephone; or
   d. scanning monitor receiver.

   This exclusion (9.) does not apply if the equipment is permanently installed in the opening of the dash or console of "your covered auto" or any "non-owned auto." This opening must be normally used by the auto manufacturer for the installation of a radio.
10. Loss to any custom furnishings or equipment in or upon any pickup or van. Custom furnishings or equipment include but are not limited to:
    a. special carpeting and insulation, furniture, bars or television receivers;
    b. facilities for cooking and sleeping;
    c. height-extending roofs; or
    d. custom murals, paintings or other decals or graphics.
11. Loss to equipment designed or used for the detection or location of radar.
12. Loss to any "non-owned auto" being maintained or used by any person while employed or otherwise engaged in the "business" of:
    a. selling;
    b. repairing;
    c. servicing;
    d. storing; or
    e. parking;

vehicles designed for use on public highways. This includes road testing and delivery.

13. Loss to any "non-owned auto" being maintained or used by any person while employed or otherwise engaged in any "business" not described in exclusion 12. This exclusion (13.) does not apply to the maintenance or use by you or any "family member" of a "non-owned auto" which is a private passenger auto or "trailer".

Exclusion 7 serves to exclude coverage for damage to a temporary substitute vehicle when used without permission.

Exclusion 8 relates to the use of the motor vehicle or trailer as a premises. Awnings, cabanas or other equipment related to living space are not logically motor vehicle losses. An endorsement, covered property coverage, available to provide coverage for this property under the PAP.

Exclusion 9 is an extension of exclusions 4 and 5 (this section) to other kinds of sound equipment, that is, transmission and reception devices. The term "permanently installed," however, is more specific here, requiring a through-the-dash installation. A stronger installation is necessary here than for the sound reproducing equipment described in exclusion 4 because CBs and two-way telephones are less likely to be installed in the dash and are more susceptible to loss by theft. An endorsement, coverage for sound receiving and transmitting equipment, may be used to cover this equipment if it is installed in the vehicle but not in the dash opening.

Exclusion 10 is an extension of exclusion 8. Any van, pickup, or panel truck customizing features, interior or exterior, are excluded. An endorsement, customizing equipment coverage, is available to provide coverage for such customizing equipment.

Exclusion 11 excludes loss of or to all types of radar detection devices. The theory is that the primary use of radar detection units is to allow the driver to speed. Insurers do not want to encourage speeding and hence do not insure such units. Exclusions 12 and 13 eliminate coverage for non-owned autos used in automobile businesses or in any other business.

Limit of Liability The limit of liability is clear and simple:

A. Our limit of liability for loss will be the lesser of the:
   1. Actual cash value of the stolen or damaged property; or
   2. Amount necessary to repair or replace the property.

   However, the most we will pay for loss to any "non-owned auto" which is a "trailer" is $500.

B. An adjustment for depreciation and physical condition will be made in determining actual cash value at the time of loss.

The PAP settles losses on the basis of actual cash value (ACV, the cost to replace less depreciation). If an insured would want to insure a vehicle (for example, an antique car) on a "stated amount" basis, it would have to be done by endorsement. Physical damage losses to non-owned trailers are limited to $500.

Payment of Loss The policy spells out the insurer's options with regard to payment of loss this way.

> We may pay for loss in money or repair or replace the damaged or stolen property. We may, at our expense, return any stolen property to:
> 1. You; or
> 2. The address shown in this policy.
>
> If we return stolen property we will pay for any damage resulting from the theft. We may keep all or part of the property at an agreed or appraised value.

Alternatives do exist as to how a damaged or stolen vehicle loss can be settled and these alternatives belong to the insurance company, not the insured. The insurer has the right to decide if it will pay for loss by (1) paying ACV of the vehicle or (2) returning the vehicle and paying to repair any damages. The insurer, not the insured, chooses between these options.

No Benefit to Bailee This clause, unique to Part D, reads:

> This insurance shall not directly or indirectly benefit any carrier or other bailee for hire.

This clause is placed in the policy to reinforce the insurer's right to subrogate against any common carrier, repair shop, or other bailee should they be responsible for the loss. For instance, if a claim is paid because a moving company damaged a car, the insurer could subrogate against the moving company.

Other Insurance The Part D "Other Insurance" clause makes this coverage (1) proportional if other insurance applies to "your covered auto" and (2) excess for a "non-owned auto."

> If other insurance also covers the loss we will pay only our share of the loss. Our share is the proportion that our limit of liability bears to the total of all applicable limits. However, any insurance we provide with respect to a "non-owned auto" or any vehicle used as a temporary substitute for a vehicle you own shall be excess over any other collectable insurance.

Appraisal The appraisal clause is similar to other appraisal clauses. One interesting difference is the last sentence of the appraisal provision contained in the PAP. The entire clause reads:

> **A.** If we and you do not agree on the amount of loss, either may demand an appraisal of the loss. In this event, each party will select a competent appraiser. The two appraisers will select an umpire. The appraisers will state separately the actual cash value and the amount of loss. If they fail to agree, they will submit their

differences to the umpire. A decision agreed to by any two will be binding. Each party will:
1. Pay its chosen appraiser; and
2. Bear the expenses of the appraisal and umpire equally.

B. We do not waive any of our rights under this policy by agreeing to an appraisal.

No other rights are abrogated by agreeing to an appraisal. In other words, if an appraisal sets the amount of a loss in excess of the insurer's ACV determination, the insurer may still elect to repair the vehicle because appraisal is solely concerned with a *determination of an amount of loss,* not the amount payable.

Part E—Duties After an Accident or Loss

In order to process a claim and protect both the insurer's and the insured's rights, duties after a loss or accident are detailed in the policy:

A. We must be notified promptly of how, when and where the accident or loss happened. Notice should also include the names and addresses of any injured persons and of any witnesses.

B. A person seeking any coverage must:
1. Cooperate with us in the investigation, settlement or defense of any claim or suit.
2. Promptly send us copies of any notices or legal papers received in connection with the accident or loss.
3. Submit, as often as we reasonably require:
   a. to physical exams by physicians we select. We will pay for these exams.
   b. to examination under oath and subscribe the same.
4. Authorize us to obtain:
   a. medical reports; and
   b. other pertinent records.
5. Submit a proof of loss when required by us.

The first two paragraphs outline what must be done by the covered person for coverage under any of the four coverage parts. The first paragraph contains a requirement for information the insurer will need to investigate. The second paragraph relates to future actions a covered person must take including physical examinations and examinations under oath.

Following are special duties for those seeking coverage under UM and then Physical Damage reproduced without comment.

C. A person seeking Uninsured Motorists Coverage must also:
1. Promptly notify the police if a hit and run driver is involved.
2. Promptly send us copies of the legal papers if a suit is brought.

D. A person seeking Coverage for Damage to Your Auto must also:

> 1. Take reasonable steps after loss to protect "your covered auto" and its equipment from further loss. We will pay reasonable expenses incurred to do this.
> 2. Promptly notify the police if "your covered auto" is stolen.
> 3. Permit us to inspect and appraise the damaged property before its repair or disposal.

Part F—General Provisions

The PAP with its agreement, definitions, and Parts A, B, C, and D describes coverages provided by the insurance company and lists the applicable exclusions in each section. Section E outlines the duties of the insured after loss or accident. Part F (General Provisions) applies to all coverages of the policy and includes:

1. Bankruptcy of a covered person
2. How the policy may be changed
3. Fraud
4. Legal action against the insurer
5. Subrogation
6. Policy period and territory
7. Termination of coverage
8. Policy transfer
9. Multiple policies

Bankruptcy The bankruptcy provision states:

> Bankruptcy or insolvency of the "insured" shall not relieve us of any obligations under this policy.

This provision helps third-party claimants by not relieving the insurer of any duties to pay if a covered person becomes bankrupt.

Changes The provision on changing the policy reads:

> This policy contains all the agreements between you and us. Its terms may not be changed or waived except by endorsement issued by us. If a change requires a premium adjustment, we will adjust the premium as of the effective date of change.
>
> We may revise this policy form to provide more coverage without additional premium charge. If we do this your policy will automatically provide the additional coverage as of the date the revision is effective in your state.

This provision intends to limit the agreement (contract) between the insurance company and the insured exactly to the written policy and to nothing else. Endorsements may be added. If added midterm, a prorata additional premium will be charged.

Coverage provided under a contract is often improved and liberalized in the insured's favor. Many changes may be made without additional premium charges. If this is done, covered persons will not have to wait until the next policy period to have the advantages nor will they have to cancel their old policy and replace it. The PAP will automatically be interpreted to provide the improved coverage on the date the change would become effective for all of the insurance company's policies in that particular state.

Fraud No insurer knowingly will issue insurance based on false information. Further, conspiracies to defraud insurers are all too common. To protect insurers, the fraud provision is added to the PAP:

> We do not provide coverage for any "insured" who has made fraudulent statements or engaged in fraudulent conduct in connection with any accident or loss for which coverage is sought under this policy.

Legal Action Against Us The provision on legal action against the insurer reads:

> **A.** No legal action may be brought against us until there has been full compliance with all the terms of this policy. In addition, under Part A, no legal action may be brought against us until:
> 1. We agree in writing that the "insured" has an obligation to pay; or
> 2. The amount of that obligation has been finally determined by judgment after trial.
>
> **B.** No person or organization has any right under this policy to bring us into any action to determine the liability of an "insured."

Full compliance means that the insured performs all required duties. All the duties in Part E must have been followed and only then can the insurance company be sued by a covered person. Of course, the insurance company cannot be sued for liability settlement unless a court judgment has been reached or unless the insurer agrees that a covered person insured is legally obligated to pay. This is usually not a problem because in most cases the insurer's lawyers will be involved in defending any suit. But, if the insured is involved in a settlement without the participation of the insurance company, no suit can be brought against the insurer.

Our Right to Recover Payment This provision describes a process known as *subrogation:*

> **A.** If we make a payment under this policy and the person to or for whom payment was made has a right to recover damages from another we shall be subrogated to that right. That person shall do:
> 1. Whatever is necessary to enable us to exercise our rights; and
> 2. Nothing after loss to prejudice them.

However, our rights in this paragraph (A.) do not apply under Part D, against any person using "your covered auto" with a reasonable belief that that person is entitled to do so.

B. If we make a payment under this policy and the person to or for whom payment is made recovers damages from another, that person shall:
   1. Hold in trust for us the proceeds of the recovery; and
   2. Reimburse us to the extent of our payment.

These rights of subrogation apply to all coverages under the PAP. It is especially important that the insured understand these provisions. Suppose the insured had been injured in an accident caused by another driver who was proved to be responsible for the accident. If the insured's insurance company made payment for medical expenses, and the insured collected again from the insurance company of the driver responsible for the accident, the insured must return payments already received from the insured's insurance.

Policy Period and Territory The provision on policy period and territory states:

A. This policy applies only to accidents and losses which occur:
   1. During the policy period shown in the Declarations; and
   2. Within the policy territory.

B. The policy territory is:
   1. The United States of America, its territories or possessions;
   2. Puerto Rico; or
   3. Canada.

This policy also applies to loss to, or accidents involving, "your covered auto" while being transported between ports within the territory listed.

The policy period is shown in the declarations and the policy territory is defined here. The period and territory, as is the case with all of these general provisions, apply to all parts and all coverages provided under the policy.

Coverage during transport applies only to the covered auto (not any nonowned vehicle) and only between the ports of the United States, its possessions and territories, and Canada. If someone ships a covered auto to Europe, it would not be covered, but shipping a covered auto between California and Hawaii would be. There is no coverage in Mexico. An endorsement, Mexico coverage, can be used to provide coverage while in Mexico, but liability insurance must be purchased through a Mexican insurer in order to comply with the terms of the endorsement and the requirements of Mexican law. The endorsement provides coverage only within twenty- five miles of the U.S. border and only for trips of ten days or less in Mexico. Coverage through Mexican insurers is readily obtainable at most border crossing points.

Termination PAPs may be terminated by cancellation, nonrenewal, or automatic termination. Some other termination provisions are also included.

The cancellation provision reads:

A. Cancellation. This policy may be canceled during the policy periods as follows:

1. The named insured shown in the Declarations may cancel by:
   a. returning this policy to us; or
   b. giving us advance written notice of the date cancellation is to take effect.
2. We may cancel by mailing to the named insured shown in the Declarations at the address shown in this policy:
   a. at least ten days notice:
      (1) if cancellation is for nonpayment of premium; or
      (2) if notice is mailed during the first sixty days this policy is in effect and this is not a renewal or continuation policy; or
   b. at least 20 days notice in all other cases.
3. After this policy is in effect for 60 days, or if this is a renewal or continuation policy, we will cancel only:
   a. for nonpayment of premium: or
   b. if your driver's license or that of:
      (1) any driver who lives with you; or
      (2) any driver who customarily uses "your covered auto;" has been suspended or revoked. This must have occurred:
      (1) during the policy period; or
      (2) since the last anniversary or the original effective date if the policy period is other than 1 year; or
   c. if the policy was obtained through material misrepresentation.

Cancellation and termination of auto policies has generated a great deal of discussion and attention from consumer groups. The provisions for cancellation vary from state to state, and the PAP is often endorsed to conform with the regulations of the state in which the insured resides. In the absence of any state provision to the contrary, the above PAP provisions will apply.

The insurance company's right to *cancel* is limited after policy has been in force for sixty days. The insurer can only cancel for nonpayment of premium if the insured or a family member normally using the vehicle has had driving privileges revoked, subject to individual state laws, or if the insured materially misrepresented a fact essential to underwriting.

These provisions do not apply to *nonrenewal.* The insurance company is normally permitted to nonrenew the policy. But even in the case of nonrenewal, appropriate advance notice is required. The nonrenewal provision reads:

B. Nonrenewal. If we decide not to renew or continue this policy, we will mail notice to the named insured shown in the Declarations at the address shown in this policy. Notice will be mailed at least 20 days before the end of the policy period. If the policy period is other than 1 year, we will have the right not to renew or continue it only at each anniversary of its original effective date.

The PAP requires twenty days' notice for nonrenewal, but this too can vary from state to state by statute or by insurance department regulation.

The automatic termination provision of the policy reads:

C. Automatic Termination. If we offer to renew or continue and you or your representative do not accept, this policy will automatically terminate at the end of the current policy period. Failure to pay the required renewal or continuation premium when due shall mean that you have not accepted our offer.
If you obtain other insurance on "your covered auto," any similar insurance provided by this policy will terminate as to that auto on the effective date of the other insurance.

In this case, the insurance company action is the offer; the payment of the premium by the insured represents acceptance. This fulfills one of the requirements for a legally binding agreement. Responsibility for continuing coverage is placed upon the insured.

The other termination provisions affect only insurance on "your covered auto." Nonowned auto coverage, for example, should continue. Of course, if an insured terminates coverage on all owned autos, the coverage for nonowned cars would also terminate. The policy's statement on other termination provisions reads:

D. Other Termination Provisions

1. If the law in effect in your state at the time this policy is issued, renewed or continued:
   a. requires a longer notice period;
   b. requires a special form or procedure for giving notice; or
   c. modifies any of the stated termination reasons;
   we will comply with those requirements.
2. We may deliver any notice instead of mailing it. Proof of mailing of any notice shall be sufficient proof of notice.
3. If this policy is cancelled, you may be entitled to a premium refund. If so, we will send you the refund. The premium refund, if any, will be computed according to our manuals. However, making or offering to make the refund is not a condition of cancellation.
4. The effective date of cancellation stated in the notice shall become the end of the policy period.

At termination, the insured may be entitled to a refund. If the cancellation was on the initiative of the insurer, the refund is the pro rata part of the premium for the remaining part of the policy term. If the cancellation is at the request of the insured, the return premium for policies with an original term of one year or less is 90 percent of the renewal premium. Of greater importance is the statement that a refund is not a condition of cancellation. This permits the insurer to cancel before the refund is made and gives the insurance company time to complete the process of determining the amount of the refund and mailing it, without continuing to insure an unacceptable insured.

Policy Transfer The provision on the insured's ability to transfer his or her interest in the policy reads:

Transfer of Your Interest in This Policy

A. Your rights and duties under this policy may not be assigned without our written consent. However, if a named insured shown in the Declaration dies, coverage will be provided for:
  1. The surviving spouse if resident in the same household at the time of death. Coverage applies to the spouse as if a named insured shown in the Declarations; or
  2. The legal representative of the deceased person as if a named insured shown in the Declarations. This applies only with respect to the representative's legal responsibility to maintain or use "your covered auto."

B. Coverage will be provided only until the end of the policy period.

This provision does not say an insured cannot assign the rights to the contract to someone else. This is sometimes done. But it has to be done with the permission of the insurer.

Multiple Policies The provision on two or more auto policies reads:

Two or More Auto Policies If this policy and any other auto insurance policy issued to you by us apply to the same accident, the maximum limit of our liability under all the policies shall not exceed the highest applicable limit of liability under any one policy.

Throughout the PAP there have been clauses addressing the possibility of having coverage under two or more policies. Authors of the PAP were obviously concerned about the "stacking" of benefits and limits. This general provision aims to prevent "stacking."

Endorsements to the PAP

A major difference between a producer who sells insurance and a producer who manages clients' accounts is the ability to identify and insure the exposures of the client not treated by a basic policy. The PAP was designed to meet the auto insurance needs of most people. Endorsements must be added when an exposure is not addressed by the PAP. Earlier in the chapter, reference has been made to many endorsements. These and others modify coverage to "target" the PAP to an insured's specific needs.

For instance, many insureds feel that they do not need to incur the expense of an automobile club if so-called towing and labor is available under the auto policy. The PAP has such an endorsement, towing and labor cost coverage. Other insureds may wish to rent a substitute auto if any loss occurs to their auto. The PAP will provide transportation expense only with forty-eight hours of a theft, but the rental reimbursement transportation expenses endorsement can be added to provide up to $15 per day with a $450 limit for all losses to an auto. Following is a discussion of other endorsements that producers can use to tailor the PAP to their clients' needs.

Unusual Property Many insureds will have unusual property located in or on an auto insured under a PAP. Much of this property is not insured under the PAP unless it is covered by endorsement.

Audio Equipment and Accessories. Coverage for tapes, records, and the like is available with the coverage for tapes, records or other devices endorsement. This endorsement covers the so-called media used to reproduce sound. The limit is $200. The mechanical and electrical devices used to transmit or otherwise produce the sound from the media may be covered through the coverage for sound receiving and transmitting equipment endorsement.

Alterations to or Special Autos. Customized equipment for or on autos was mentioned earlier. The customizing equipment coverage endorsement is available to cover such equipment. This endorsement limits liability to actual cash value or a stated amount, whichever is less, subject to a deductible. The endorsement covers carpeting, TV receivers, murals, decals, and the like. It does not cover CB radios or other items meant to be covered by other endorsements. For example, the covered property coverage endorsement intends to cover property designed to create additional living facilities up to a stated amount.

To provide stated amount coverage for any auto, the coverage for damage to your auto (stated amount maximum limit of liability) endorsement is available. This endorsement makes any auto subject to a maximum stated limit as well as its actual cash value or the cost to repair or replace.

A miscellaneous type vehicle endorsement is available to provide coverage for a motorcycle, motor home, golfcart, or other similar vehicle. A snowmobile endorsement is also available.

Changing Limits In addition to the variety of limit of liability available under the PAP, special limits are available by endorsement.

Split Limits. Part A of the PAP can become a split-limit policy through the use of the Split Liability Limits endorsement. For UM coverage, the split through the use of uninsured motorists limits and split underinsured motorists limits perform a similar function.

Other Liability Coverage. The underinsured motorists coverage endorsement may be used to raise an underinsured motorist's liability limits up to the limits an insured would select.

Other Types of Endorsements The PAP may be modified to provide some coverage while the auto is in Mexico through the Mexico coverage endorsement. This endorsement is a "gap filler" and, to be valid, the insured must also purchase insurance from a Mexican insurer for the exposures in Mexico.

The extended nonowned coverage for named individual and the named nonowner coverage endorsements are available to cover nonowned exposures.

Endorsements and Selling The discussion of endorsements here refers only to those of ISO. Each producer must look to the insurance company or companies he or she sells for to see what endorsements are available and will be written by the insurer. These modifications to the basic policy can adapt the insurance to fit a producer's market. For example, a producer who wishes to insure a group of motor homes could approach that market with a product which includes endorsements covering customization, communications equipment, or other property designed to make such vehicles more "livable."

By modifying the PAP the producer is not only more adequately covering his or her insured's exposures, but is also generating more premium volume. Both the insured and the producer are thus better served.

Checkpoints

1. Explain how glass breakage is treated in the PAP.
2. Explain how the physical damage coverage under a PAP covers damage to a nonowned car.
3. Describe the transportation expense coverage under the PAP.
4. Describe the policy territory in which losses must occur in order to be covered by the PAP.

RATING AUTOMOBILE INSURANCE

Many factors, such as government regulation and public policy considerations, affect rates.

Rate Regulation

In general, the objectives of insurance rate regulation are to:

1. Promote reasonable rates
2. Maintain adequacy in rates
3. Make certain that the rates do not *unfairly* discriminate against any individual or any class of insured

Reasonable Rates The reasonableness of rates can be determined from the earnings of the property-liability companies. Total earnings from underwriting in recent years has been only a minimal percentage of total premiums. Skyrocketing costs of repair parts, auto body and repair shop labor, jury awards, and increasing insurance company expenses have required rate increases that have not generated large underwriting profit.

Rate Adequacy Insurance regulators are less concerned with rate adequacy than reasonableness. Most state insurance commissioners are sensitive to public opinion, and rate increases are never popular. Cases where regulations required insurance companies to raise inadequate rates are few. The concept of rate adequacy has been approached in many states by creation of a state guarantee fund that is supported by mandatory insurance company contributions and guarantees that policyholders and claimants of a bankrupt insurer will be reimbursed for any loss suffered.

Rate Discrimination Perhaps the most difficult problems in rate regulation deal with rate discrimination. The term "discrimination" has taken on an unsavory connotation, associated with prejudicial treatment of minorities. A dictionary defines the word as, "To make a clear distinction, distinguish, differentiate."[5]

The regulatory intent with regard to rate discrimination is that insurance companies should not *unfairly* discriminate. Obvious differences among the exposure of insureds which lead to different claims experience must be noted and used to alter rates so that each class of insured pays its fair share.

There is criticism levied against insurers by metropolitan area consumer groups who insist that poor urban auto owners are being charged too much while affluent suburbanites who commute into the city and clog the city streets are not paying enough. Such criticism has resulted in some leveling of insurance rates, that is, lowered urban rates and increased suburban rates.

Some groups also insist that age, sex, or marital status should not be used in rate determination. Some insurance companies, however, insist that such factors are relevant to rate determination and are appropriate. There is an unfortunate trend to eliminate some rate classifications based on age, sex, and marital status which are highly objective, verifiable, and statistically significant rating factors for auto insurance.

Automobile Rating—Primary Factors

Generally, automobile rates are promulgated on a class basis. That is, similar exposures are grouped, and rates sufficient to cover the group's loss experience are charged to each member of that group. To differentiate among members of a class would be "unfair" discrimination. In most states, classes are formed on the basis of (1) age, (2) sex, (3) geographical location, (4) type of use, and (5) marital status.

Age Insurance companies generate statistics on the basis of age. These show younger drivers tend to drive more miles, to drive faster, to experience greater loss frequency and severity than other age groups. The differences ascribed to age are most evident at age eighteen or under (perhaps reflecting a lack of driving experience) and seem to disappear by age twenty-eight or thirty.

Sex Females do not use vehicles as much as males. Certain cultural influences can be seen as the cause of these differences. Males are more likely to drive on dates than females, for instance. An interest in machinery and in racing lead more young men than young women to buy high-performance cars. Young married women are less likely to be in the labor force than their husbands and so are less likely to be driving in rush hour traffic. When couples travel by car, the males usually do most of the driving.

The result is that there are more accidents involving young men than young women as a percentage of their total numbers. Insurance company automobile rates reflect this.

Geographical Location Average loss severity and frequency vary from location to location. Jury awards reflect different opinions as to the extent of monetary awards for injuries or death. One locality may spend more money on roads and highways, improving areas with high accident frequency. One state may stress vehicle safety through compulsory periodic vehicle inspections. One area may vigorously enforce traffic laws and be successful in reducing the number and severity of auto accidents. Another area may be sparsely populated without the traffic density which promotes accidents. All these factors combine to make driving location an important factor in the cost of providing automobile insurance.

Generally, automobile claims experience is charged to the location where the vehicle is garaged. A commuter involved in an accident in the city would have the incident charged against the experience of the suburb where the car is *garaged,* although some insurers are now basing rates on where the car is principally *driven.*

Marital Status Marital status has an effect on how, where, and when the automobile is used. Unmarried persons are more likely to use their vehicles at night and in circumstances which involve entertainment and alcohol. Moreover, single people without family responsibilities often prefer expensive "sports" autos, and these cars are often high-powered and present a greater exposure.

The importance of the relationship between marital status and accident frequency diminishes as age increases and is not an important factor for people beyond ages in the late twenties. The difference between the use of a motor vehicle by an unmarried versus a married woman is considerably less than the difference between unmarried and married males.

Automobile Rating—Additional Factors

While rating classes are formed on the basis of the classifications discussed, other factors also affect loss statistics. These factors are not normally thought of as fundamental differences important enough to be part of the classification. Instead, they are treated as modifying credits in most states. These secondary factors vary from insurer to insurer but generally consist of (1) driver education credits; (2) good student discounts; (3) fleet or multiple-car discounts; and (4) merit rating discounts and surcharges.

Driver Education Formal courses that stress knowledge of traffic laws and emphasize defensive driving techniques are designed to reduce accidents among young people. Usually, insurance companies do not grant rate credits unless the course involves road experience with a qualified instructor.

Discounts are in the 10 to 15 percent range and apply only to youthful operators. The effects of driver education courses wear off after a few years, suggesting that there is little difference in claims experience between those taking such a course and those not taking one, after each driver has gained experience on the highway.

Good Student Discounts Rate credits in the 10 percent range are often granted to "good students." Those students maintaining a B average, or its equivalent, are given this discount. Experience shows that these students experience fewer accidents, probably because they spend more time with their studies and less time in their cars. Again, such rate credits apply only to youthful drivers. When the driver is no longer in school as a full-time student, the rate credit is discontinued.

Fleet or Multiple-Car Discounts Rate discounts for multiple autos in the same household are derived from two considerations. First, there is a "quantity discount" because it is less expensive to insure a number of vehicles under one contract than to issue a separate policy for each. There is one billing, one policy to issue, and one policy to record in company and agency records. The insurance company can pass on some of the savings involved to the insured.

Second, when there are a number of vehicles, each is normally used less. When a family has one car, it will be used extensively by all licensed family members. When a family acquires a second car, it normally will receive less use than the principal vehicle. Often, the second car is older and less expensive and is used by the family only to meet neighborhood needs for transportation. Long trips and trips where the whole family is involved will be made in the newer car. The second car is used to take kids to school and go on household errands, and it usually sees less use than the family's principal car.

If a third vehicle is purchased, the use of all three vehicles is usually reduced. One or more of the cars will be in the garage most of the time, given the pattern of use by the typical United States family. Since the use of each vehicle is normally less when more than one car is owned by a family, the rates charged can also be less.

Merit Rating Plans Most consumers believe that they should pay premiums based on loss experience. Those with an accident record have a greater probability of future losses, and equity suggests they should pay more. Allocating a greater proportion of the premium to those who have had accidents makes sense to most consumers (until they have a loss). Rates based on historical losses seem fair and just. Further, a greater premium for poor loss experience is an incentive for loss control practices. Consequently, "merit" or "safe driver" plans are offered by many insurance companies.

In theory, the plans would work as follows, assuming no insurer expenses or profit:

1. Assume there are one thousand drivers in one class. Past experience indicates that claims payments attributable to this class will be $100,000 in one year. If every insured were charged the same rate, each would pay $100, that is, $100,000 divided by 1,000 drivers.
2. Assume 85 percent of these drivers are accident free and have earned a discount.
3. Assume these safe drivers are given a discount of 15 percent from the "normal" or $100 premium.

Exhibit 5-6
Illustrative Rate Calculation

Amount needed to pay claims	$100,000
Discounted premium ($100 less $15) charged to 85% of the drivers (850 drivers × $85 each)	72,250
Balance of premium to be met by drivers having accidents	$ 27,750
Premium for each driver having an accident ($27,750 ÷ 150)	$ 185

4. Assume the 15 percent of the drivers who had the accidents must pay extra (the amount necessary to raise the $100,000 needed to pay the claim).

Exhibit 5-6 shows the calculations.

When the majority (85 percent) of insureds receive a small rate discount ($15.00) for accident free driving, the drivers having an accident pay a significantly higher premium ($185.00) reflecting those losses.

This may see like an unfairly high premium, yet closer examination shows the people who caused the accidents ($100,000 worth) paid only $27,750.00 in premiums and those who were accident free paid over 70 percent of the costs. In practice, the rate differences are not as great. The surcharges are not as high as the example indicates. The theory behind the rate difference, however, is the same. Good drivers pay less, drivers involved in accidents pay more.

Usually, insurers use a three-year experience period. That is, should a chargeable accident or claim occur, that experience will make a difference in the premiums charged to the insured for thirty-six months. Not all accidents or claims result in an extra premium charge. If an insured is "not-at-fault" and collects from another party, the insured's own company will not raise his or her rates. If a parked car is struck by a hit-and-run driver, for example, an insurance company would not assess "points" (extra premium) even if it paid a claim.

Any valid indication of poor driving or loss control practice may indicate higher auto rates. For instance, some insurers charge points for both accidents and serious traffic violations. Parking violations and other minor errors usually will not affect the rate.

The higher premiums charged to these drivers are justified not only because they had accidents but also because experience indicates that drivers with poor driving records will continue to have a greater accident frequency. The past helps predict the future, especially in automobile accident experience.

DIFFICULT-TO-INSURE AUTOMOBILE BUSINESS

Insurance must operate profitably. "Profitable operations" means insuring exposures with loss expectations in line with premiums charged. Prospects with greater than average exposures cannot be insured at average or "standard rates." One of two things must be done. Either the insurance company must refuse to accept or renew this kind of business (or not accept business identifiable as substandard when it is offered) or charge this class of business a higher premium.

Canceling business, not accepting business, or failing to write the business causes many problems. First, all states have laws that either require auto insurance or establish insurance as the best, most practical method of compliance with the law.

Second, driving is a privilege granted by government. The government should decide who may drive and who may not. Insurance companies should not make such social decisions. If a person cannot buy automobile insurance, that person cannot enjoy the privilege of driving. Yet, in these circumstances, the insurance companies are placed in the position of deciding who can or cannot drive.

In order to avoid such situations, the insurance business has moved to allow almost every licensed driver to purchase insurance adequate to comply with the law. Thus, if the law permits a person to operate a motor vehicle, that person can purchase insurance coverage that provides at least the standard of financial responsibility which the law requires. Insurance does this in one of two ways: through so-called substandard insurers or through auto insurance plans (commonly referred to as assigned risk plans).

Substandard Auto Insurers

Rates for automobile insurance in substandard auto insurers are based on a loss expectancy higher than the average exposure. Typically, this market is serviced by specialty insurance companies whose primary business is substandard auto policies. The rate structure of these specialty insurance companies produces a rate that is higher than "standard rates" of insurers dealing in the "normal" automobile insurance market. Often, these rates are 150 to 200 percent higher than the standard market. The policy form used in the substandard market is normally an ISO form such as the PAP, although some insurers use the standard commercial auto form.

In addition to specialty insurers, the substandard automobile market is also serviced by many producers who "wholesale" or broker this coverage to other producers. This permits a producer to use insurers of substandard business without the necessity of directly representing a specialty insurer. Commission rates for substandard business may be lower than for standard.

The substandard market is not new and, in fact, predates the existence of many state assigned risk plans. Even after state plans were instituted, many did not provide physical damage coverages, and producers sought substandard insurers in order to find physical damage coverage for their clients who purchased liability coverage through the assigned risk plan.

Today, insurers of substandard business are an alternative to the automobile insurance plans, with a rate structure that often differs from state plans. For example, rates for substandard business are often tied to the number of traffic violation "points" an applicant has received. State plans are more likely to compute surcharges to "standard" rates, based upon chargeable accidents. Because of these differences, a producer may be well advised to get a rate quotation from an insurer of substandard automobile business in cases where the state plan premium seems exorbitant.

Automobile Insurance Plans

Given that auto insurance rates are not altogether free to reflect the exposure in each case, it seems inevitable that some drivers with poor driving records will have trouble securing auto insurance. From a societal point of view, it is important that drivers be able to purchase auto insurance for their protection and the protection of the public. The various state financial responsibility and automobile no-fault laws require insurance availability if they are to be effective. Therefore, special plans of some nature have been established in every state.

"Assigned Risk Plans" When an applicant for auto insurance has been rejected by two or more private insurance companies, the producer submits an application to the manager of the plan. The manager ascertains if the applicant is eligible for coverage under the plan and, if so, in an "assigned risk plan," the applicant is assigned to an insurer licensed to do business in that state. The insurer is obligated to accept the applicant and issue a policy. Assignment of applicants is rotated among the insurance companies in proportion to the amount of automobile business each insurer does in the state.

Participation in the plan by a driver can be denied only in extreme cases. Normally, this involves such things as illegal use of the vehicle, habitual drunkenness or drug use, narcotics dealing or an applicant who is an habitual violator of the law. In each case, the causes for rejection must be extreme. The objective of these plans is to provide coverage for every licensed driver. Only a tiny percentage of applicants are rejected by the plan.

Once the applicant is assigned to an insurer, that insurance company will compute premiums based upon surcharges added to standard premium for the class to which the applicant belongs. These surcharges can range from zero (in cases where the applicant has a good driving record but is in an undesirable class, perhaps too young and inexperienced or too old) to as much as 200 percent.

This assignment is normally for a three-year period, and at renewal the insurance company sends the insured a notice as to what the premium will be for the next twelve months. After three years, the driver can return to a standard insurer. If standard insurers still reject the applicant, the same procedure must be repeated and the applicant again assigned to an insurer.

Usually, the driver can purchase full coverage, including medical payments and physical damage coverage. There is usually a limit on the amount of liability coverage offered. Some plans provide only the minimum limits required by that state's financial responsibility or no-fault law.

Other Auto Insurance Facilities Many people believe that there is a social stigma associated with the assigned risk type of automobile insurance plan. To avoid this perceived stigma, the insurance business developed two additional plans for providing automobile insurance for those drivers who have difficulty obtaining it in the voluntary market—joint underwriting associations (JUAs) and the reinsurance facilities (RFs).

JUAs and reinsurance facilities are similar in one respect. The premiums, expenses, and losses of the substandard insured are pooled and shared by all participating insurers. The two plans differ primarily in the methods of administration.

Under a reinsurance facility, each insurer must provide coverage for every licensed driver who applies for such coverage. Coverage for those drivers who do not meet a particular insurer's underwriting standard is transferred to the reinsurance facility, and the premiums, expenses, and losses for those drivers are shared by all insurers participating in the reinsurance plan. In a JUA, there are a limited number of servicing insurance companies (fourteen in Florida) who issue all of the policies for drivers placed in the plan. The servicing insurers also adjust claims and provide all other services required under the policies they issue. The premiums, expenses, and losses are shared by participating insurers on the basis of their respective shares of the standard automobile insurance business in the state under both JUA plans and reinsurance facilities.

Loss Results of Auto Insurance Plans The loss experience of persons in state plans has exceeded the premium paid, with each insurance company absorbing its share of these losses through its participation in the plan. All the overhead and administrative costs associated with the plans are shared by the insurance companies on the same basis. Producers, too, share by handling this business at a low commission rate.

RISK MANAGEMENT IN PERSONAL AUTO INSURANCE

The risk management concept requires examination of all of a family's exposures, including all motor vehicle exposures. The advantage to the producer is plain because risk management necessitates account selling and leads to larger accounts. The account also becomes less vulnerable because other producers no longer have bits and pieces of a family's insurance, persistency is increased, premium income is increased, and the producer has the satisfaction of knowing that the client is being well serviced.

The producer's obligations and responsibility are also plain. The producer must do a good job of surveying the family's exposures and of designing a program that provides the protection needed by the family. A questionnaire that is useful in ascertaining the family's motor vehicle exposures appears in Exhibit 5-7. With this information, the producer is in a good position to discuss the coverages available, to discuss the use of deductibles, and to recommend the coverages the producer feels will best protect the family.

SUMMARY

Private passenger automobile insurance accounts for about one-third of the total property and liability insurance premiums in the United States. Consequently, it is a major source of commission income to producers. The personal auto policy, a simplified language policy, is intended to provide all of the automobile insurance protection needed by the vast majority of American families. The policy and the many

Exhibit 5-7
Personal and Family Risk Questionnaire

Personal and Family Automobile Risk Questionnaire

Name __________ Phone # Home __________ Work __________
Address __________ City __________ Zip __________

1. Members of your household including yourself and unmarried children at school

	Name	Birthday Mo	Da	Yr	Relationship	Social Security Number	Drivers License	Occupation
A.								
B.								
C.								
D.								
E.								
F.								

Note: Consider the words "You" and "Your" in the following questions to mean any of the above members. Please explain any "Yes" answers.

2. ______ What is the total number of automobiles owned or leased by you including vans, pickups and motor homes that are not used for business?
3. ______ Are any of these automobiles *not* protected by liability insurance?
4. ______ Are any of these automobiles garaged or kept at a location other than your residence address?
5. ______ Are any of these automobiles leased from others?
6. ______ Are any of these automobiles frequently driven by others who do not live in your household?
7. ______ Are any of these automobiles used in a "Share the Expense Pool"?
8. ______ Are there any non-owned automobiles furnished to you or made available to you for your use?
9. ______ Are you employed or engaged in any way in the selling, services, parking, roadtesting or delivering of motor vehicles?
10. ______ Do you ever drive a commercial type vehicle in your occupation or business?

11. ______ Do you ever rent automobiles, trucks or trailers on a short-term basis for your personal use?

12. ______ Do you ever operate motorcycles or vehicles having less than four wheels?

13. ______ Do you ever carry your employees in your automobile?

14. ______ Do you ever use your automobile to carry persons or property for a fee? (Other than in a "Share the Expense Car Pool")

15. ______ Have you had a moving violation in the past three years?

16. ______ Has your drivers license been suspended in the last five years?

17. ______ Have you been involved in an automobile accident in the past three years while you were driving a motor vehicle? (Regardless of who was at fault)

18. ______ Do you ever drive outside the United States?

19. ______ Do you carry more than one insurance policy on any of your automobiles?

20. ______ Do you race any motor vehicles or use them in any type of a contest?

21. ______ Are you ever not covered by workers' compensation while you are employed?

22. ______ Are you not covered by hospitalization or a medical insurance plan?

23. ______ Do you every tow trailers with your automobiles?

24. ______ Are you physically impaired, have diabetes, a serious heart ailment or subject to epileptic seizures? (Licensed drivers only)

25. ______ Does any of your automobiles have cracked or broken glass or existing body damage?

26. ______ Are any of your automobiles equipped with any of the following items that are not permanently installed in the dash opening or console of your automobile?

A. ______ Car Radio	C. ______ 2 Way Mobile Radio	E. ______ Scanning Monitor
B. ______ C B Radio	D. ______ Mobile Telephone	F. ______ Tape Deck

27. ______ Have any of your vehicles been modified or do you intend to modify any of them in the following ways?
    - A. ______ Equip with non-standard or extra-wide tires?
    - B. ______ Engine or carburetor modified to improve performance?
    - C. ______ The body altered, customized or raised?
    - D. ______ Have a special paint job?

Continued on next page

28. ______ Do you customarily park any of your vehicles at the street curb overnight?

29. ______ Are any of your vehicles equipped with an anti-theft alarm?

If any of your automobiles are a pickup or a van, please answer questions 30, 31 and 32.

30. ______ Does it have any of the following:

A. ______	Detachable Camper?	I. ______	Decals or Graphics?
B. ______	Cooking Facilities?	J. ______	Sun Roof?
C. ______	Sleeping Facilities?	K. ______	Special Windows?
D. ______	Awning or Cabana?	L. ______	Camper Body?
E. ______	Carpeted or Paneled Walls?	M. ______	Fiber Glass Top?
F. ______	Furniture or Bar?	N. ______	T V Receiver?
G. ______	Captains Chairs?	O. ______	T V Antenna?
H. ______	Custom Murals or Paintings?	P. ______	"Fifth" Wheel?

31. ______ Do you plan on adding any of the above?

32. ______ Is it ever used in your business or occupation?

If any drivers are under age 25, please answer question 33.

33. ______ Are any full-time students? (If "Yes," give name of school, driving distance from your home to school and student's grade average)

34. ______ Do you own a travel or camping trailer?

35. ______ Do you own a boat which is trailerable?

36. ______ Do you ever rent and use travel or camping trailers or motor homes.?

37. ______ Do you ever rent boat trailers to haul a boat?

Description of Owned Vehicles

Unit	Make	Model	Year	Identification Number	Cost
1					
2					
3					
4					

endorsements associated with it can be used to provide coverage for passenger cars, pickup trucks, vans, golfmobiles, motorcycles, trailers, snowmobiles, and a variety of other vehicles.

Chapter Notes

1. *Best's Recommended Insurance Attorneys, 1985 Edition.* Oldwick, NJ: A.M. Best Company, 1985, pp. 8T–14T.
2. *Best's Recommended Insurance Attorneys,* pp. 2T–7T (Alabama, Georgia, Nebraska, Oregon).
3. *Best's Recommended Insurance Attorneys,* pp. 2T–7T.
4. The ISO form displayed and discussed here is copyrighted and is used with the permission of the Insurance Services Office.
5. William Morris, ed., *The American Heritage Dictionary of the English Language* (Boston: Houghton Mifflin Company, 1976).

CHAPTER 6

Other Personal Coverages

INTRODUCTION

Life for an insurance producer would be simple if the only insurance contracts needed to service the public were homeowners (HO) and personal auto policies (PAP). Even though the HO and the PAP policies provide adequate insurance coverages for many individuals and families, there are others with exposures (needs) that cannot be met this simply. In many cases, the HOs must be endorsed to reflect the precise needs of the client. If neither program adequately addresses those needs, other policies must be issued to complete the protection.

To complete a family's personal property-liability risk management program, other coverages are often needed such as dwelling forms other than the homeowners, flood insurance, inland marine floaters for special personal property, coverage for recreational vehicles, snowmobiles, motor homes, motorcycles, boats, airplanes, as well as a personal umbrella policy. Some of these extra coverages can be integrated by endorsement onto other contracts. Some must be written separately. All must be considered by an alert producer, and inquiry into the possible need for such coverages is a standard part of the risk management approach.

This chapter begins with unusual vehicle exposures and, in some instances, reviews some PAP and homeowners endorsements in addition to special policies available to treat these unique exposures. Next, personal exposures that can be treated with inland marine policies are discussed. Watercraft, aircraft, flood insurance, and personal catastrophe (umbrella liability) are discussed. The growing area of "second stage packages" precedes the concluding section on the Dwelling Program.

INSURING OTHER VEHICLES

The personal auto policy (PAP) provides adequate coverage for private passenger cars and pickups not used commercially. These types comprise the vast majority of vehicles used by American families. Other types of vehicles, such as minibikes, mopeds, motorcycles, recreational and off-road vehicles, customized autos, classic and antique autos, require special handling.

Minibikes and Mopeds

These are small, often unlicensed, two-wheeled vehicles designed for special purposes. Minibikes are small versions of the motorcycle designed for off-road use. Minibikes are often used by children (aged ten to sixteen) and are frequently used in groups exploring trails or at organized meets where a course is followed and where travel over the course is timed.

Mopeds, on the other hand, more closely resemble bicycles and can be operated by a small motor or by pedaling. Unlike the minibikes, mopeds may be used on public roads but usually are not licensed. State laws vary, and some states define mopeds in terms of maximum permissible speed (usually twenty or twenty-five miles per hour) or maximum permissible horsepower (usually one or two horsepower). If these limits are exceeded by the capacities of the machine, it must be licensed and operated as a motorcycle.

Mopeds vary considerably from motorcycles. Normally, mopeds can be pedaled and do not have turn signals, battery operated lights, or other required standard features of motorcycles. If licensing is required, safety accessories (lights and turn signals) usually must be added.

There is no coverage for either minibikes or mopeds under the unendorsed PAP. There is limited coverage provided under a homeowners policy, but the coverage is restricted to on-premises use. This limited coverage might be of some value to the owner of a minibike but would hardly be of value to a moped owner. Moreover, such protection is limited to liability coverage. This lack of coverage for off-premises use can represent a serious, untreated exposure for the insured. Careful questioning at the initial sales interview or at the time of periodic account reviews can reveal the exposure. At that time, the producer should be very certain that the client is aware of the exposure.

If not endorsed to the PAP, the best method of insuring minibikes and mopeds is to obtain "motorcycle" coverage. Most insurance companies that write motorcycle insurance also quote rates for these vehicles. Some companies, however, have developed a special recreational vehicle policy used with mopeds, minibikes, dune buggies, and other off-road vehicles. Motor homes are sometimes written on this form as well because in some states all these vehicles come under the financial responsibility or no-fault laws. It is best to obtain guidelines from insurers on insuring these vehicles.

Motorcycles

Motorcycles are often insured by specialty insurance companies and may present problems of placement for the producer. While these vehicles are eligible for coverage under the PAP by endorsement, many insurers do not actively seek this business.

There are two reasons for this lack of insurer interest. First, the typical motorcycle operator is male and youthful, both characteristics which have led to high claims experience. Second, because of their instability and light vehicle weight, motorcycles expose the riders to extra hazards. Injuries are often serious because motorcycle riders have none of the protection afforded by an automobile, with its padded surfaces and restraint system. Even specialty insurance companies that write motorcycle insurance are often reluctant to sell medical payments coverage. The coverage most often available is a liability and physical damage policy.

Some states have exempted motorcycles from no-fault laws because the premiums for medical payments coverage would be prohibitive to the average cyclist. In those states, the motorcycle owner is treated as though the no-fault law did not exist and must operate the cycle with the standard liability insurance.

Some motorcycle coverage is available from standard insurers. An adult with an automobile or two and a homeowners policy, who buys a motorcycle, would have less trouble securing insurance than a sixteen-year-old newly licensed driver purchasing a motorcycle. At the other end of the scale, there are situations where even the specialty insurance companies are not willing to insure a cyclist, and coverage is provided by the state's Automobile Insurance (assigned risk) Plan.

Policy forms used for motorcycles are not uniform. They may contain special provisions or endorsements which differ from insurer to insurer.

Recreational and Customized Vehicles

The rapid increase in the number of recreational vehicles on America's highways has created a large new market for personal lines producers. The term "recreational vehicles" is very broad, including motor homes, campers, snowmobiles, all-terrain vehicles, and others. Although such standard policies as homeowners and the personal auto policy make provisions for insuring some recreational vehicles, many such vehicles are insured under nonstandard policies issued by specialty insurers.

The homeowners policies provide $500 of coverage for damage to trailers not used with watercraft. This description is sufficiently broad to include a camper trailer, but collision coverage is not included and the dollar amount is not adequate for most such trailers. A homeowners endorsement, Coverage C-Increased Special Limits of Liability, is used to increase most of the other internal limits on specified property under the homeowners, but it does not mention trailers.

The homeowners policy also provides liability coverage for a camper trailer except when being towed by a motor vehicle. The personal automobile policy provides liability coverage while a trailer is being towed by an insured motor vehicle. Trailers may also be insured for physical damage under the personal automobile policy by listing them on the declarations page and paying the appropriate premium. Physical damage coverage for recreational vehicles is written on a stated amount (not ACV) basis by attaching the Coverage for Damage to Your Auto (Stated Amount) endorsement to the personal auto policy.

Camper bodies designed for use with pickup trucks also can be insured for physical damage under the personal auto policy. They are automatically covered under that policy for liability when being hauled by an insured vehicle. They are covered for liability under the homeowners policy when not being hauled by a motor vehicle.

The only motorized vehicles covered under the homeowners *forms* for physical damage are those that service the insured premises and are not licensed for road use and those designed for assisting the handicapped. Service vehicles are also covered for liability under the homeowners but only while on the residence premises. Vehicles for the handicapped (e.g., battery powered wheelchairs) are covered on and off the residence premises while golf carts are covered off premises when being used for golfing.

The "Snowmobile" endorsement can be used to provide off-premises liability coverage under homeowners policies for specified snowmobiles provided they are not subject to motor vehicle registration. The endorsement does not provide coverage if the snowmobile is (1) used to carry persons for a fee, (2) used for business purposes, (3) rented to others, or (4) used in a prearranged or organized race.

The ISO PAP endorsement, miscellaneous type vehicle endorsement, can be used to provide both liability and physical damage coverages for motorcycles, motor homes, golf carts, and other miscellaneous vehicles. Physical damage coverage is provided on a stated amount basis. The ISO Snowmobile endorsement provides coverage for snowmobiles under the personal auto policy.

Some specialty insurers offer policies especially designed to provide liability and physical damage coverages for snowmobiles and other recreational vehicles. Such policies usually are modifications of automobile policies. Some policies require that the snowmobile be used principally off public highways and exclusively on ice or snow. Others are less restrictive. Some cover all equipment used exclusively with the snowmobile, while others restrict the coverage to equipment permanently attached to the snowmobile. Some provide physical damage coverage on a trailer used to haul the snowmobile, while others do not. The exclusions also vary widely from one insurance company to another. Producers must exercise considerable care in the selection of policies because of these variations.

Several insurers also modify automobile policies to meet the special needs of owners of pickup camper bodies, camper trailers, travel trailers, motor homes, and similar vehicles. Such policies also may be used to cover customized vans or coaches. Such policies provide physical damage coverage on (1) the vehicle, (2) permanent equipment therein, and (3) furniture and equipment used with the vehicle. Personal property and household furnishings used in camping are covered under the personal effects insuring agreement of some such policies.

These specialized policies can be extended to provide liability coverage for nonmotorized vehicles while parked, but this coverage is needed only if the insured does not have comprehensive personal liability or homeowners policy. Liability coverage for nonmotorized vehicles while being towed is provided under the liability insurance on the towed vehicle.

The special recreational vehicle policies provide liability coverage on motorized vehicles (such as motor homes) both while being operated and while being parked. Comprehensive physical damage coverage and collision coverage are provided on a stated amount basis for the recreational vehicle and its equipment. Personal property coverage usually is for specified perils, frequently fire, extended coverage, vandalism and malicious mischief, and flood.

The customizing equipment coverage endorsement can be used to provide stated amount physical damage coverage under a personal auto policy on an "all-risks" basis for customizing equipment such as carpeting, insulation, furniture, bars, television receivers, cooking or sleeping facilities, height-extending roofs, murals, paintings, and similar items. This endorsement specifically excludes TV antennas, awnings, cabanas, and equipment designed to provide additional living facilities. However, those items can be covered under the PAP covered property coverage endorsement. Sound reproducing equipment and records or tapes for use therewith are also excluded, though these can be covered under the coverage for tapes, records, or other devices endorsement to the PAP. Sound reproducing equipment is covered automatically under the personal auto policy if it is permanently attached to the vehicle. Sound receiving and transmitting equipment (CB radios, two-way mobile radio, mobile telephones, and so on) is also excluded but may be insured by attaching the PAP coverage for sound receiving and transmitting equipment endorsement if the equipment is permanently attached to the vehicle.

Antique and Classic Automobiles

Antique automobiles are usually over twenty-five years old. Classic cars may be less than twenty-five years old, but possess special value because of unusual styling or mechanical features. Liability coverage for antique and classic cars does not present any special problems. It is regularly available under standard policies. Rate credits may be given for liability coverage for antique cars driven only in parades and other special events. In fact, many of the applications for coverage on these types of automobiles require the insured to warrant that the car will only be used in such show events.

While securing liability coverage presents little or no problem for the producer, there can be problems when attempting to secure physical damage insurance. This potential difficulty stems from the fact that these cars generally are appreciating in value rather than depreciating. The traditional definition of actual cash value ("replacement cost less depreciation") no longer has valid meaning as the vehicle's current value may have reached the point where it exceeds the original cost new.

One solution to the problem is to use the PAP stated amount endorsement to establish the vehicle's value. Critical to the use of this approach is a current appraisal of the vehicle. Since the endorsement permits the company to pay either the stated amount or the actual cash value, whichever is less, an up-to-date appraisal will establish the vehicle's actual cash value and lessen potential valuation problems at the time of loss.

While many perceive antique and classic car insurance as a limited market, some producers have taken a more aggressive posture. Chief among the methods used to get to the potential buyers are securing booth space at exhibits and placing ads in periodicals that appeal to collectors. In fact, those ads usually contain an application that also allows the prospective insured to self-rate coverage; these ads/applications also contain the warranty of the vehicle's use.

Checkpoints

1. Explain the special problems involved in insuring recreational vehicles and the methods available to cope with these problems.
2. Explain the extent to which homeowners policies cover recreational vehicles.
3. How can insurance be provided for loss or damage to carpeting, furniture, and other customizing equipment installed in a van?

INLAND MARINE FLOATERS

Introduction

Men's clothing sales personnel *take orders on* suits and sell neckties. Many customers come to a men's store intending to buy a suit. When writing the order, a clerk will often ask, "Do you need some ties to go with your new suit?" Usually, the customer does, and the clerk adds ten or twenty dollars to the sale while helping the customer fill his needs. It may be that some stores increase their income more by *selling* ties than by *taking orders* on suits.

Selling inland marine floaters is a bit like selling ties. Insurance buyers generally know they need homeowners insurance, and often intend to make the purchase when contacted by a producer. However, they may not realize they also need inland marine floaters. *Selling* inland marine floaters when taking orders for homeowners insurance enables the producer to increase commissions while providing better service to, and protection for, the client.

Homeowners insurance does not cover all loss exposures involving personal property. The conscientious producer should always point out the coverage exclusions and limitations of the homeowners policy. In addition to providing the client with information necessary to understand the insurance purchase, this practice reduces the chance that the producer will be accused of failing to properly explain the coverage. Many of the needs not met by the homeowners alone can be met with inland marine floaters.

Needs Met by Inland Marine Floaters

The homeowners program is intended to provide most nonautomobile property (and liability) insurance needs "for an average family." The homeowners policies restrict coverage for some personal property loss exposures faced by only a few homeowners. To include coverage in all homeowners policies for loss exposures not found in many homes would raise the premium on all policies to provide coverage for only a minority.

The astute producer can use inland marine floaters to meet the following special needs for personal property insurance coverage:

- Coverage for property limited by the homeowners
- Coverage for property excluded by the homeowners
- Coverage for property with valuation problems
- Coverage for property particularly susceptible to loss by other than the usual named perils
- Coverage for high-valued personal property

Inland marine floaters are extremely flexible. Certain coverages, such as jewelry coverage, are written routinely, but other client situations create special needs not met by a standard insurance form. Both common everyday exposures and unusual one-of-a-kind exposures can often be met with inland marine floaters.

Coverage for Property Limited by the Homeowners The homeowners policies contain limitations for certain property and, in some cases, for certain property lost by theft. Exhibit 6-1 summarizes the limitations and the allowable increased limits that may be purchased. On a homeowners policy with a $250 deductible, a family with more than $1,000 of jewelry faces the chance of losing *more than* the $250 deductible if jewelry is stolen. As indicated in Exhibit 6-1, homeowners policies do permit modest increases in these coverages. Beyond these optional increased limits, a different coverage is needed.

Coverage for Property Excluded by the Homeowners Completely excluded from coverage under the homeowners policies is the following:

> **Property Not Covered.** We do not cover:
> 1. articles separately described and specifically insured in this or other insurance;
> 2. animals, birds or fish;
> 3. motor vehicles or all other motorized land conveyances. This includes:
>   a. equipment and accessories; or
>   b. any device or instrument for the transmitting, recording, receiving or reproduction of sound or pictures which is

Exhibit 6-1
Homeowners Property Limitations and Allowable Increased Limits

Property Limited	Homeowners limitation	Homeowners allowable increased limits by Endorsement HO-65
Money, banknotes, bullion, gold, silver, platinum, coins, and medals	$ 200	$1000
Securities, accounts deeds, evidences of debt, manuscripts, etc.	$1,000	$2,000
Watercraft and its trailers, furnishings, equipment, and outboard motors	$1,000	——
Nonwatercraft trailers	$1,000	——
Grave markers	$1,000	——
Theft of jewelry, watches, furs, precious and semi-precious stones	$ ~~500~~ 1,000	$5,000 with $1,000 per article limit
Theft of silver or silverplate ware, gold or goldplate ware and pewterware	$2,500	Up to $10,000 in $500 increments
Theft of guns	$2,000	Up to $6,000 in $100 increments

operated by power from the electrical system of motor vehicles or all other motorized land conveyances, including:
(1) accessories or antennas; or
(2) tapes, wires, records, discs or other media for use with any such device or instrument;

while in or upon the vehicle or conveyance.

We do cover vehicles or conveyances not subject to motor vehicle registration which are:

a. used to service an **insured's** residence; or
b. designed for assisting the handicapped;

4. aircraft and parts. Aircraft means any contrivance used or designed for flight, except model or hobby aircraft not used or designed to carry people or cargo;
5. property of roomers, boarders and other tenants, except property of roomers and boarders related to an **insured;**
6. property in an apartment regularly rented or held for rental to others by an insured;
7. property rented or held for rental to others off the **residence premises;**
8. a. books of account, drawings or other paper records; or
   b. electronic data processing tapes, wires, records, discs or other software media;
   containing **business** data. But, we do cover the cost of blank or unexposed records and media;
9. credit cards or fund transfer cards except as provided in Additional Coverages 6.

The first exclusion clarifies the relationship between homeowners insurance and other coverage on personal property. When an article is specifically insured in an inland marine floater, there is no coverage under the homeowners for that same article. The full value of the article should be insured in the floater. It would *not* be correct to insure a $2,500 ring for $1,500 in a jewelry floater, relying on the homeowners policy to provide the other $1,000 of needed coverage. According to exclusion 1, the homeowners does not cover the ring if specifically insured either by endorsement to the homeowners or a separate policy.

Some of the other excluded exposures are usually covered by auto insurance, aircraft insurance, or business insurance. The homeowners exclusions merely prevent duplicate coverage in these situations. However, there may be unusual circumstances in which a homeowners client has a substantial personal property loss exposure not covered by the homeowners policy, because of these exclusions or by any other policy. In many such cases, an inland marine floater can often provide the necessary coverage.

Coverage for Property with Valuation Problems Unendorsed homeowners policies provide coverage for unscheduled personal property valued at actual cash value. For all covered personal property, the policy will pay replacement cost minus depreciation. Although this approach works well for most kinds of property, it has deficiencies. Antiques and works of art can be particularly difficult to value. For instance, a baby crib actually used by the now-famous poet and editor Dr. Warren Hope may be worth thousands of dollars to collectors of such memorabilia. However, this forty-year-old piece of baby furniture would probably have an actual cash value approaching zero, because it is fully depreciated for practical purposes. An inland marine floater, written on a valued basis, could help resolve this problem.

Because the homeowners policy deals with *unscheduled* personal property, other practical problems could result following a loss. When an insured owns unusual, high-valued items that have been stolen or completely destroyed, it is sometimes difficult to prove that these items actually existed, or that they were as valuable as claimed. For example, Elliot may have inherited a sterling silver candelabrum, which he stored in the back of his closet. If this candelabrum is stolen, Elliot may have difficulty convincing a claims representative he really had such an item. This difficulty is reduced when the high-valued item is specifically listed and described on a floater policy. Such problems are further reduced when the insurance company is also furnished with a copy of an appraisal signed by a qualified appraiser.

Property Particularly Susceptible to Loss by Other Than the Named Perils The special personal property coverage endorsement (HO-15) in conjunction with an HO-3 form provides "all-risks" coverage on unscheduled personal property. The vast majority of homeowners policies provide personal property coverage on a named-peril basis. Some property is susceptible to damage by perils not named in the homeowners forms. For example, it is not uncommon for a diamond to fall from its setting and be lost. The prongs supporting a diamond gradually wear until they become very thin. Sometimes a prong will hook on a thread, or will bump against a hard object and bend, making it easy for the stone to fall out. There is no named peril in homeowners policies covering such a loss, but it would be covered under an inland marine floater.

Other types of property also need special treatment. An expensive oriental rug, for example, is insured under the homeowners policy like any other rug in the house. However, a dropped jar of grape jelly or other spillage might irreparably damage this expensive item. Again, none of the homeowners named perils applies, but an "all-risks" inland marine floater would cover such a loss.

High-Valued Property Homeowners policies typically provide coverage on personal property equal to 50 percent of the amount of insurance on the dwelling. For most families, this amount of coverage is sufficient. There are cases in which the value of contents in a home exceeds this 50 percent limit. A musician, for example, might have a $10,000 organ and a $6,000 piano, along with other personal property, in a home insured for $100,000. These musical instruments are not excluded by the homeowners policy, but the combined values of the instruments and other contents may exceed the $50,000 Coverage C limit; or, stated another way, the presence of the high value items decreases the amount of insurance available for the other personal property items. The homeowners limit can be increased, but it is often considered more desirable to purchase specific "all-risks" coverage on these few, high-valued items by using an inland marine floater.

How Inland Marine Floaters Meet These Needs In most cases, an inland marine floater meets more than one of the coverage needs discussed. For example, jewelry is (1) high-valued property, (2) especially susceptible to loss from certain perils not covered in the homeowners, and (3) subject to coverage limitations in the homeowners forms. After discussing the construction or format of the inland marine policies and endorsements, important general coverage provisions applicable to most inland marine floaters will be addressed. Finally, coverage on specific types of property will be analyzed.

Policy Construction

Inland marine coverage can be written either as a separate policy or as a supplement to a homeowners policy. When there is no homeowners policy, a separate floater policy is the only possible approach. Coverage and rates are usually the same whether a personal articles floater policy or a scheduled personal property endorsement to the homeowners policy (HO-61) is used.

Which is better, a separate policy or a homeowners endorsement? There are arguments on both sides of this question. A single homeowners policy with the scheduled personal property endorsement has some advantages in terms of simplicity. On the other hand, frequent changes to the schedule of personal property will create frequent changes in the homeowners policy premium. When a mortgagee is involved in the transaction, the simplicity of a single policy can create a penalty because of the complexity of the premium paying arrangement. (Mortgagees may collect monthly installment payments from the homeowner and hold them in "escrow" until the premium is due. The mortgagee then remits the premium. The size of the monthly installment payment to the mortgagee is based on the annual homeowners premium and every change to the endorsement schedule changes the homeowners premium.)

When written as an endorsement to the homeowners policy, the inland marine floater contains only those provisions necessary to add the desired coverage(s); it does not include general coverage clauses already found in the homeowners policy. When written as a separate policy, an inland marine floater has two components: (1) the "floater policy," a type of policy jacket and (2) the floater form. The "floater policy" contains general provisions and information applicable to all inland marine floaters. The floater form contains provisions applicable only to the type of coverage being written. For example, the floater policy may serve as a "jacket" for any of many different floaters, including a personal articles floater, personal effects floater, or personal property floater.

Because the "floater policy" or jacket contains a declarations page and provisions common to all inland marine floaters, these common provisions will be analyzed first.

Agreement The floater policy agreement is similar to the general agreement found in other modern language policies:

> We will provide the insurance described in this policy in return for the premium and compliance with all applicable provisions of this policy. Throughout this policy, "you" and "your" refer to the "named insured" shown in the policy and "we," "us" and "our" refer to the company providing this insurance. In addition, the word "insured" means you, your spouse and relatives of either who are residents of your household.

General Conditions The first three general conditions read as follows:

1. **Conformity to State Law.** When any policy provision is in conflict with the applicable law of the State in which this policy is issued, the law of the State shall apply.
2. **Concealment or Fraud.** We do not provide coverage for any insured who has intentionally concealed or misrepresented any material fact or circumstance relating to this insurance.
3. **Loss Settlement.** Unless otherwise stated in this policy, the value of the property insured is not agreed upon but shall be ascertained at the time of loss or damage. We will not pay more than the least of the following amounts:
   (a) the actual cash value of the property at the time of loss or damage;
   (b) the amount for which the property could reasonably be expected to be repaired to its condition immediately prior to loss or damage;
   (c) the amount for which the article could reasonably be expected to be replaced with one substantially identical to the article lost or damaged; or
   (d) the applicable amount of insurance.

Conditions 1 and 2 are also found in other places and need no special explanation. Because inland marine floaters are often used to insure property with valuation problems, Condition 3 requires closer examination. Note that the policy will pay *not more than the lowest of* (a) actual cash value, (b) repair cost, (c) replacement cost, or (d) amount of insurance. The phrase "could reasonably be expected" provides some benefit to insureds, because the insurer must be "reasonable" in establishing a repair or replacement cost figure. This loss settlement provision applies to all kinds of property insured in an inland marine floater unless a special valuation provision applies—as is the case with some kinds of property, discussed later.

Inland marine floaters are often used to insure pairs, sets, or parts—such as pairs of earrings, sets of golf clubs, or parts of a camera. General condition 4 relates to these coverage situations.

4. **Loss to a Pair, Set or Parts**
   (a) Pair or Set. In case of a loss to a pair or set we may elect to:
      (1) repair or replace any part to restore the pair or set to its value before the loss; or
      (2) pay the difference between actual cash value of the property before and after the loss.
   (b) Parts. In case of a loss to any part of covered property, consisting of several parts when complete, we shall pay for the value of the part lost or damaged.

In case of loss involving insured property consisting of a pair or set, insured may not be paid on the basis of a total loss because one part of a pair or set is lost or damaged. Instead, the insurer may elect one of the two options above. The insured *may* receive more than 50 percent of the value of a pair when one part is lost. If, for example, a pair of antique salt and pepper shakers is valued at $1,000 and the salt shaker is broken, the remaining pepper shaker may be valued at only $200 without its mate. In that case, the insured could recover $800 from the insurance.

When an owner of property consisting of several *parts*—such as a movie projector—sustains loss to any part of such equipment, the only option available to the insurer is to pay for the value of that part of the property which has been lost or damaged.

The loss clause determines if insurance on an item continues after a loss:

5. **Loss Clause.** The amount of insurance under this policy shall not be reduced except for a total loss of a scheduled article. We will refund the unearned premium applicable to such article after the loss or you may apply it to the premium due for the replacement of the scheduled article.

For example, if Kim's Minolta camera suffers a broken lens when Kim falls from his photographic perch in a tree, the amount of insurance on the camera would be unaffected. If the camera is stolen, Kim's insurance will pay for the camera. Kim then has the choice of taking a refund on the premium for the rest of the policy period or adding his replacement camera to the schedule in place of the one previously insured. Although this may seem to be a minor point, clients sometimes become concerned over issues like this. If Kim's camera was stolen one month after he paid $50 to purchase a year's worth of insurance, he might think he was due a refund for the next eleven months of coverage he will not use. According to the loss clause, he would qualify for such a refund.

The next five conditions are similar to those found in other policies, and do not require extensive discussion. These conditions specify the duties of the insured and insurer following a loss. If there is disagreement as to the *amount* of the loss, an appraisal procedure is spelled out. If both parties comply with the policy provisions but the insured is unsatisfied with loss settlement, the insurer may be sued provided the action is brought within one year.

Conditions 11 and 12 involve situations that could sometimes be confusing to the producer or to the insured.

11. **Claim Against Others.** In the event of loss which we believe may be collectible from others, we must pay in the form of a loan to be repaid out of any recoveries from others. You will cooperate every way possible to assist in such recovery from others and we shall, at our expense, take over your rights against others to the extent of our payment.
12. **Insurance Not to Benefit Others.** No person or organization having custody of the property and to be paid for services shall benefit from this insurance.

These two conditions preserve the insurer's right to subrogate against other parties responsible for the loss. In some situations, any *payment* by the insurer to the insured would make it impossible for the insurer to subrogate. This is particularly true when the loss is caused by a trucker or other carrier using a carefully worded bill of lading that says, in effect, "If you collect from your insurer, we owe nothing." To get around this problem, the insurer gives the insured a "loan" that does not have to be repaid unless the damages are recovered from others. The insured does not have to wait until other avenues of recovery have been attempted. The insured gets a "loan" as indemnification for the damaged or destroyed property, but will not need to repay the "loan" unless recovery is successful.

Conditions 13, 14, 15, and 16 are not unusual. Condition 13 avoids duplicate coverage when there is other insurance; Condition 14 is a typical cancellation provision; Condition 15 states that policy changes must be in writing; and Condition 16 (liberalization clause) automatically broadens the policy if the insurer adopts a policy revision that would broaden the coverage for new business without an additional premium.

General Exclusions The inland marine floater policy excludes coverage for loss caused by war or nuclear hazards. No other exclusions are found in the floater policy jacket.

The Personal Articles Floater (PAF)

When the personal articles floater (PAF) is attached to the inland marine floater jacket, these forms contain all the coverage provisions necessary to provide coverage on nine different classes of personal property:

1. jewelry
2. furs
3. cameras
4. musical instruments
5. silverware and goldware
6. golfer's equipment
7. fine arts
8. stamp collections
9. coin collections

A floater policy may be written to cover any single category of the nine or any combination of the nine. For instance, a floater may cover only one class of property and be a "jewelry floater."

Coverage for items in each of the PAF classes applies only when an amount of insurance and premium for that class is shown on the floater. When the class of personal property contains the statement "as scheduled," the specific items of insured property must be shown in the "schedule" on the policy. This *requires* the producer to provide a complete application showing all types of property to be insured and providing a proper description of each item scheduled. The PAF application is discussed later.

The personal articles floater provides insurance for "...risks of direct loss to property described only if that loss is a physical loss to the property." The only exclusions, in addition to the general exclusions already mentioned and a few applicable to certain types of property, are: wear and tear, gradual deterioration, inherent vice, insects, and vermin. This extremely broad coverage is applicable anywhere in the world for most insured items and is not subject to a deductible.

Jewelry The highest premium volume in any of the classes eligible for personal inland marine coverage is in the jewelry class.

Eligibility. Individually owned personal jewelry consisting of articles of personal adornment composed in whole or in part of silver, gold, platinum, or other precious metals and alloys, whether or not containing pearls, jewels, or semi-precious stones, is eligible for this coverage, according to the rating manual. Pens, pencils, flasks, smoking equipment, cigarette cases, trophies, and similar items may also be insured as jewelry. However, this category does not include silver, silverware, platedware, bullion, gold, and other precious metals and unmounted gems.

Coverage. No additional exclusions affect this coverage. Most jewelry items are immune to damage by insects and vermin. Wear and tear, gradual deterioration, or inherent vice (such as the natural tendency of silver to tarnish) would not be covered.

A *newly acquired property* provision provides some automatic coverage for newly acquired jewelry, provided the new jewelry is reported to the insured within thirty days and an appropriate premium paid. Coverage is limited to 25 percent of the amount of coverage on jewelry or $10,000, whichever is less. For customers who have extensive jewelry schedules and frequently add new items of jewelry, this feature can be of special value.

Selling Jewelry Coverage. The item most commonly covered in a personal articles floater is a diamond engagement ring. If a prospect for homeowners insurance is *wearing* an engagement ring or other expensive jewelry, this prospect has a need for an inland marine floater. In other cases, discussing the jewelry limitation in the homeowners policy can uncover the need for specific coverage on jewelry. Some producers have successfully sold inland marine floaters by following up on engagement announcements in the newspaper.

Inflation in recent years has increased jewelry prices so rapidly that many people do not realize how valuable their jewelry has become. One insured was recently surprised to learn that the engagement ring he bought for $285 in 1966 was worth $2,500 in 1985!

Submissions for jewelry coverage should usually be accompanied by a recent bill of sale or a qualified appraisal from a gemologist or jeweler. A good jewelry description contains:

1. the general description, setting forth the character of the metal and the manufacturer's name, if applicable
2. the weight and depth of the stone
3. the color of the item
4. flaws or degree of perfection of stones

The producer should become familiar with the appraisal requirements of the insurers represented, and also with qualified local appraisers to whom clients can be directed.

Furs This classification includes imitation furs and fur rugs, garments consisting principally of fur, or garments with fur trim.

Coverage. No additional exclusions or limitations affect fur coverage. Furs are susceptible to loss by wear and tear, gradual deterioration, vermin, and insects. The client should be informed that coverage does not apply to such losses. Newly acquired furs are covered on the same basis as newly acquired jewelry.

Selling Fur Coverage. All persons owning furs valued at $250 or more are prospects for this coverage. It is an attention grabber because the minimum premium is low. Special attention should be paid to valuation. New furs can be valued at purchase price, with values established by a bill of sale. Proper valuation of older furs depends a great deal on their condition. While depreciation tends to pull the value downwards, inflation tends to increase the value of a used fur. For fur garments more than one or two years old, current appraisals are desirable and can be obtained from many reliable furriers.

Cameras Coverage for items in this class is not limited or excluded by homeowners policies. However, cameras and related equipment are especially susceptible to perils such as breakage, and this coverage feature can be a good selling point.

Eligibility. This category includes much more than the typical device for taking snapshots. Projection machines, sound recording and playback equipment, and even films, binoculars, telescopes, and microscopes may be insured in this category.

Coverage. There are no special exclusions or limitations applicable to camera coverage, and newly acquired property is covered subject to the limitations previously discussed. Coverage is so broad as to include loss caused by accidentally dropping a camera over the side of a boat.

Selling Camera Coverage. Anybody owning expensive camera equipment should be a prospect for this coverage. Many families today have at least a modest camera, and the use of sophisticated camera equipment is becoming increasingly common. Many sales can be generated simply by asking if the client owns any cameras, projectors, or tape recorders.

Whereas jewelry and furs must be scheduled, it is usually permissible to include 10 percent of the total amount of camera insurance to cover miscellaneous items on a blanket basis. This makes it easy to provide coverage on camera bags, tripods, filters, and other miscellaneous photographic paraphernalia not valuable enough to schedule.

Musical Instruments and Related Articles of Equipment Musical instruments are not limited or excluded by the homeowners policies. However, musical instruments are usually susceptible to damage by perils not generally covered in the homeowners. Moreover, musical instruments are sometimes high-valued items that require special insurance for that reason.

Eligibility. It is important to determine whether the prospect will ever "play for pay." The policy contains the following warranty: "You agree not to perform with these instruments for pay unless specifically provided under this policy." This warranty can and should be deleted, for an additional charge, whenever a "play for pay" exposure is involved. Otherwise, the musician will not have the intended coverage.

An inland marine floater can also be used to insure generally immobile musical instruments such as organs.

Coverage. No special exclusions apply to mobile musical instruments, and newly acquired instruments are covered. However, organs not of a mobile nature are not covered for:

> Loss or damage caused by mechanical or electrical breakdown or failure, repairing, adjusting, servicing or maintenance operation unless fire or explosion ensues and then only for the loss or damage by such ensuing fire or explosion.

Selling Musical Instruments Coverage. Prospects for musical instruments coverage are the owners, both professional and amateur, of expensive musical instruments. Band members, orchestra players, and even collectors of rare instruments should be interested in this coverage. Electronic amplification equipment used with some instruments is also eligible for coverage and should not be overlooked. As with cameras, up to 10 percent of the limit of coverage for items in this classification may be used to provide blanket coverage for music, cases, drumsticks, spare parts, and the like.

Except for those items insured blanket, the schedule should include complete descriptions of the instruments covered, including serial numbers whenever possible. It is usually desirable to obtain bills of sale or appraisals on instruments valued at $1,000 or more.

Silverware, Silverplated Ware, Goldware, Goldplated Ware, and Pewterware The increases in silver and gold values of recent years have created a coverage need that did not previously exist. Homeowners policies did not limit coverage for these items until the Homeowners 76 forms were introduced. Rapid increases in silver and gold values have changed this, leaving many homeowners grossly underinsured.

Eligibility. Certain types of property are not eligible for coverage under the silverware classification because they are insurable as jewelry. Pens, pencils, flasks, smoking implements, or jewelry are in this category.

Coverage. Although silverware and the like may be scheduled, there is no policy provision requiring scheduling. In fact, it may often be impractical to list and specifically describe each knife, fork, and spoon in a set of silverware. When coverage is written blanket, newly acquired property would be covered, but the total amount of coverage is not automatically increased. No special exclusions or limitations affect silverware coverage.

Selling Silverware Coverage. Many clients are unaware of the policy limitations that create a special coverage need, and this creates a good sales opportunity for the alert producer. In many cases where a homeowners policy has been written for years by another producer, the other producer may have made no specific attempt to inform customers of the homeowners limitation on silverware and related articles.

Silverware coverage prospects are those owning silverware, but it is not obvious who these prospects may be. Many families inherited numerous items of silverware used only on special occasions or preserved as heirlooms. In many cases, the value of these items has not been recognized. Tactful probing may be necessary to discover a silverware exposure, but it may be particularly helpful for the producer to concentrate on identifying silverware exposures when using the risk management approach.

Golfer's Equipment Avid golfers often own high-valued equipment. Although the exposure is not excluded by homeowners policies, it is often desirable to purchase specific "all-risks" coverage with no deductible.

Eligibility. Coverage may be written on golf clubs, clothing, and equipment.

Coverage. Golfer's equipment may be scheduled, but blanket coverage is also permitted. Some coverage provisions are of particular interest. Street clothing is covered while contained in a locker while the insured is playing golf. And, because golf balls have been known to mysteriously disappear from a golf course, coverage on golf balls is limited to loss by fire or burglary. Although not specifically stated in the policy, it seems logical to assume that golf clubs *intentionally* damaged, bent, or destroyed by a frustrated golfer would not be covered. Given the occasionally frustrating nature of the game, perhaps this could be considered "inherent vice" or, at the least, wear and tear.

Selling Golfer's Equipment Coverage. All golfers who own equipment valued at $200 or more are prospects for this coverage. A good place to look for insurance prospects on a pleasant day is at the golf course (perhaps this is the reason so many insurance producers are avid golfers).

When insuring a particularly expensive matched set of clubs, it may be desirable to schedule the clubs at a value agreed to by the underwriter, to reduce the difficulty of establishing value on this "set" after the loss.

Fine Arts Rare, historic objects or items of artistic merit are difficult to value. One-of-a-kind items are irreplaceable at any price. It may seem unreasonable to insure something that cannot be replaced. Nevertheless, the owner of a rare, historic, or artistic item has lost something of monetary value when the item is damaged or destroyed.

Eligibility. Private collections of paintings, etchings, pictures, tapestries, art glass windows, and other bona fide works of art of rarity, historical value, or artistic merit are eligible. This would include valuable rugs, statuary, marbles, bronzes, antique furniture, rare books, antique silver, manuscripts, porcelains, rare glass, and bric-a-brac. Dealers, art galleries, art institutions, museums, and the like are not eligible for fine arts coverage under the personal articles floater.

Coverage. Several PAF exclusions apply only to fine arts.

> If fine arts are covered:
>
> (a) damage caused by any repairing, restoration or retouching process;
> (b) breakage of art glass windows, glassware, statuary, marble, bric-a-brac, porcelains and similar fragile articles. We cover loss by breakage if caused by fire, lightning, aircraft, windstorm, malicious damage, theft, explosion, earthquake, flood or collision, derailment or overturn of conveyance;
> (c) loss to property on exhibition at fair grounds or premises of national or international expositions unless the premises are covered by this policy.

Losses that can be prevented by proper care are excluded by (a). Fragile articles are particularly susceptible to breakage, the reason for exclusion (b). This exclusion can be eliminated for an additional premium. When an item is particularly susceptible to breakage, the owner usually exercises loss prevention measures, and the breakage losses do not cause great problems for insurers.

The loss settlement condition of the PAF replaced the loss settlement clause of the inland marine floater policy. As a result of this condition, fine arts are insured on a "valued basis."

> (a) Fine Arts—We will pay the amount shown for each scheduled article which is agreed to be the value of the article.
> In cases of loss to a pair or set, we agree to pay you the full amount of the set as shown in the schedule and you agree to surrender the remaining article or articles of the set to us.

When fine arts coverage is written, the insurer and the insured agree *in advance* what the scheduled article is worth, and this amount is stated in the policy. This, then, is the amount paid in case of total loss. When part of a pair or set is destroyed, the insured does not have to negotiate with the insurer to determine how much the set or pair is worth without the destroyed article. The policy contains a provision, applicable to fine arts only, that will seem unfair to the insured and is in need of an explanation before a loss occurs. If a fine art, which is part of a pair or set, is damaged or destroyed while the other item(s) are untouched, the company has the right to (1) pay the full amount for the pair or set and (2) take possession of the remaining undamaged pieces. For example, an insured has two matched Ming vases insured as a set for $30,000. Should one be broken, the other—now the only one of its kind in the world—will increase in value and perhaps substantially so. However, the company can pay the insured the full $30,000 and take possession of the remaining vase. The way to avoid this situation is to insure each vase separately.

The premium for fine arts insurance is based in part on the fire contents rate at the location of the property. The producer should accurately state the address when completing the application. The policy states, "this premium is based on your statement that the property insured is located at the following address." The insurer could deny coverage if the address is misstated or the insured moves the property to another location during the policy term.

Unlike other property insured with the PAF, "fine arts are covered only while within the limits of the Continental United States, the State of Hawaii and Canada."

Newly acquired objects of art are covered for their *actual cash value* for up to 25 percent of the amount of insurance for fine arts scheduled, provided they are reported to the insurer within 90 days. It is in the insured's best interest to report newly acquired fine arts as soon as possible in order to obtain *valued* coverage. The insured also agrees when moving fine arts that the covered property will be packed and unpacked by competent packers.

Selling Fine Arts Coverage. A surprisingly large number of people collect antiques, own heirlooms, or develop a collection of one kind or another. Often, these items are objects of which the individual is particulary proud. It is often difficult to determine what is an antique and what is junk. Objects with sentimental value and objects with no outstanding quality other than age are not necessarily appropriate for fine arts coverage. It is often desirable to obtain a bill of sale or appraisal to use as a basis in establishing fine arts values. In some cases, collector journals provide some basis for values.

Although not excluded from coverage by the homeowners policy, the valuation approach of the homeowners, whether with or without the personal property replacement cost endorsement, to fine arts is not particularly appropriate. Moreover, it is often desirable to provide broader coverage for fine arts than the named perils of the homeowners. These are compelling reasons to suggest fine arts coverage when a prospect raises a question as to how an item of antique, historic, or artistic value should be insured.

In some cases, an item may be eligible for coverage as fine arts or under another classification of the PAF. In such cases, a determination should be made by considering whether actual cash value or valued coverage is desired. A genuine Stradivarius violin should be insured as fine arts. An ordinary violin should be insured as a musical instrument. An old fiddle used by a new music student is probably adequately covered by the homeowners.

Stamps and Coin Collectors Different rates are used for stamps and for coins, and the PAF separates them into different classifications:

8. **Postage Stamps** including due, envelope, official, revenue, match and medicine stamps, covers, locals, reprints, essays, proofs and other philatelic property, including their books, pages and mountings, owned by or in custody or control of the insured.
9. **Rare and Current Coins,** medals, paper money, bank notes, tokens of money and other numismatic property, including coin albums, containers, frames, cards and display cabinets in use with such collection, owned by or in custody or control of the insured.

Because these two classes have a great deal in common, they will be discussed together.

The term *philatelic* simply refers to stamp collecting, or *philately*. *Numismatic* refers to coin collecting.

Eligibility. The eligibility rules in the ISO manual repeat the description from the policy.

Coverage. Five special exclusions limit "all-risks" coverage on stamp and coin collections:

4. If either of the classes of property, Postage Stamps or Rare and Current Coin collections, are covered:
   (a) fading, creasing, denting, scratching, tearing, thinning, transfer of colors, inherent defect, dampness, extremes of temperature, gradual depreciation, or any damage from handling or being worked upon;
   (b) disappearance of individual stamps, coins or other articles unless the item is described and scheduled with a specific amount of insurance, or if the item is mounted in a volume and the page to which is attached is also lost;
   (c) loss to property in the custody of transportation companies; nor shipments by mail other than registered mail;
   (d) theft from any unattended automobile unless being shipped as registered mail;
   (e) loss to property which is not an actual part of a stamp or coin collection.

The unattended automobile exclusion may be deleted for an additional premium. Blanket coverage is permitted for up to $1,000 or stamps and coins worth not more than $250 per unscheduled stamp, coin or other individual articles or any one pair, strip, block, series, sheet, cover, frame, card, or the like. In effect, each stamp or coin with substantial value should be scheduled while those of less value may be insured on a blanket basis.

These provisions tie in with the special loss settlement provisions applying to stamp and coin collections:

> (b) Postage Stamps or Rare and Current Coin Collection—In case of loss to any scheduled item, the amount to be paid will be determined in accordance with the 3. Loss Settlement provisions, under General Conditions in the policy.
>
> When coins or stamps are covered on a blanket basis, we will pay the cash market value at time of loss but not more than $1,000 on any unscheduled coin collection nor more than $250 for any one stamp, coin or individual article or any one pair, strip, block, series, sheet, cover, frame, or card.
>
> We will not pay a greater proportion of any loss on blanket property than the amount insured on blanket property bears to the cash market value at the time of loss.

Selling Stamp and Coin Collection Floaters. Stamp and coin collecting are popular and many collectors need protection. They can best be identified by routinely asking all homeowners insurance prospects whether they have any stamp or coin collections. The producer should remember that most people, when asked if they have a coin collection, envision an extensive, organized collection and will answer no. However, countless numbers of people save "wheat back" Lincoln pennies, silver coins, bi-centennial quarters, and so forth in jars and, while not a "collection" as such, the value could be substantial.

Once the existence of the collection has been established, it is often a good idea to have the collector prepare a schedule of the stamps or coins and their values. Many times the collector is surprised to discover the values that have accumulated and, by this process, recognizes the need for special insurance.

Floater Coverage by Homeowners Endorsements In all nine categories of the PAF, similar coverage is available by use of the scheduled personal property endorsement (HO-61). A producer may consider using the PAF as an entry to the personal lines business of a prospect. By doing a professional job of the PAF, the producer has a reason to call at HO renewal—to get the HO account and replace the PAF with an endorsement to the HO.

When a producer submits an inland marine floater to an insurer in the manner suggested, it is a good idea to attach a note indicating that, at renewal, the producer intends to supplement the PAF with other personal lines business from this applicant. If the underwriter sees future profitable business, he or she will be more likely to act promptly and positively on the "naked" or unsupported-by-other-business PAF. The producer should then follow up and solicit the remaining personal lines business.

Personal Effects Floater

In contrast with the personal *articles* floater, the personal *effects* floater covers the insured property *only* while away from the insured's home premises. The personal effects policy is intended to provide coverage for *baggage* carried by tourists. The insured property is shown as:

> ... personal effects such as are usually carried by tourists and travelers, belonging to and worn by the insured and/or his wife and their unmarried children permanently residing together.

The coverage is provided on a worldwide and "all-risks" basis, with only a few exclusions. The demand for this form has declined since the introduction of the homeowners policies, which also cover the insured's personal property worldwide.

Personal Property Floater (PPF)

Before the widespread use of homeowners policies, the amount of off-premises coverage for personal property was severely limited under dwelling and contents fire policies. On-premises coverage was named perils, usually for fire and extended coverage.

The personal property floater was developed to overcome these shortcomings. The personal property floater is a broad policy covering the insured's personal property anywhere in the world. Furniture, clothing and similar unscheduled personal articles are covered under a blanket amount of insurance. Valuable individual items (such as jewelry, furs, etc.) may be scheduled with a specific amount of insurance on each item.

Demand for the personal property floater has declined as the popularity of homeowners policies has increased. However, the personal property floater is still attractive to a few middle or upper income families who live in apartments or condominium units. It is the only way they can obtain "all-risks" coverage on all their personal property, both on premises and off.

Exhibit 6-2
Property Possibly Needing Inland Marine Treatment

Antique autos	Money
Air conditioners	Mountain climbing equipment
Archery equipment	Phonograph records, tapes, and cassettes
Bicycles	Power mowers
Bowling equipment	Religious vestments
Camper units and camping equipment	Scuba gear
Collectibles	Securities
Contact lenses	Silverware
Dentures	Skiing equipment
Dogs	Snowblowers
Fishing equipment	Snowmobiles
Flags	Tennis equipment
Garden tractors	Trailers
Golfmobiles	Trophies
Guns	Watercraft
Hearing aids	Wedding presents
Jewelry	Wheel chairs
Microscopes	Wigs

Other Inland Marine Floaters

The personal articles floater may be used to provide broad coverage on nine classes of property. The personal effects floater is appropriate to insure the baggage of some travelers. The personal property floater provides "all-risks" coverage on a blanket basis. Other situations for which inland marine floaters are appropriate are almost without limit. For some classes of property, many insurers have preprinted coverage forms and published rates. For other classes, a special policy may have to be prepared, and the underwriter may rely solely on judgment to develop appropriate coverage provisions and rates. These oddball cases provide the opportunity for creativity in determining coverage needs and negotiating appropriate coverage and rates. Sometimes the producer will even have a hand in preparing the policy language to be used.

It would not be possible to develop an exhaustive list of property for which inland marine floaters are appropriate. Exhibit 6-2 illustrates the variety of situations possible.

Submitting a Personal Inland Marine Application

Many insurers accept the ACORD Personal Inland Marine Application, shown in Exhibit 6-3. Other insurers require different applications that contain much of the same information. The ACORD application will be used here as the basis of discussion.

The ACORD application has been designed so it can be used either for a homeowners endorsement or a separate inland marine floater policy. The ACORD *Personal Inland Marine Procedure Guide* suggests the producer record the information on the application during the initial interview, printing legibly. This eliminates the need for subsequent retyping and reduces the chance of error in describing or valuing an object of insurance.

The two blocks at the top of the application contain general information which requires no special elaboration here.

The *applicant information* section provides important underwriting information. In many cases, the underwriter is providing coverage on high-valued property for a relatively low premium, and must rely almost entirely on the insured's "word" if the property is allegedly stolen or destroyed. Underwriters are particularly concerned that inland marine applicants be of good moral character. Information regarding the age, marital status, and occupation of the applicant and spouse provide some insights into the status of the individual and the loss exposures that individual faces. In the "occupation" block, it is more helpful to provide descriptive information than job titles. For example, "Department manager of retail store" provides more information than "Manager." The location of the property other than at the mailing address also helps the underwriter assess any hazards involved.

Information in the *limits/premiums* section of the application will eventually appear on the policy itself. For each type of property to be insured, the *total amount* of coverage for that class should be indicated in the "amount of insurance" column. The rate can be obtained from the rate manual for the state or territory in question. The amount of insurance multiplied by the rate will equal the premium.

When fine arts are insured, the rate is based in part on the fire contents rate where the property is located. For fine arts, an amount of insurance should be shown at each insured location rather than a total amount.

The *rating information* section of the application requires information regarding the type of dwelling, its construction, the number of families, the fire protection class, the fire contents rate, and any coinsurance percentage applicable.

When wedding gifts are to be insured, the amount of insurance

Exhibit 6-3
ACORD Personal Inland Marine Application

ACORD **PERSONAL INLAND MARINE APPLICATION**

SET TAB STOPS AT ARROWS

DATE

PRODUCER

APPLICANT

MAILING ADDRESS (INCLUDE ZIP CODE)

COMPANY | POLICY NUMBER | ☐ NEW ☐ RENEWAL

CODE | SUB-CODE

EFFECTIVE DATE	EXPIRATION DATE	BILLING PLAN	PAYMENT PLAN
		☐ AGENCY ☐ DIRECT BILL	

APPLICANT & LOCATION INFORMATION

AGE	MARITAL STATUS	OCCUPATION	SPOUSE'S OCCUPATION	OTHER

LOCATION OF PROPERTY (IF DIFFERENT FROM ABOVE) ☐ ADDITIONAL LOCATION	DWELLING TYPE(S)	CONSTRUCTION TYPE(S)	# FAMILIES (IN EACH)

COVERAGES

#	PROPERTY	AMOUNT OF INS.	RATE	PREMIUM	#	PROPERTY	AMOUNT OF INS.	RATE	PREMIUM
1	JEWELRY				8	COINS			
2	FURS				9	GOLFER'S EQUIPMENT			
3	FINE ARTS				10				
4	CAMERAS				11				
5	MUSICAL INSTRUMENTS				12				
6	SILVERWARE				13				
7	STAMPS				14				

☐ UNATTENDED CAR COVERAGE (Stamps/Coins) ☐ NON-MOBILE ORGAN COVERAGE ☐ BREAKAGE COVERAGE (*ON SCHEDULE)
☐ BROAD FORM PAIR & SET COVERAGE ☐ SAFE CREDIT (IDENTIFY PROPERTY, SAFE CLASS ETC)

TOTAL $

ADDITIONAL RATING INFORMATION

GENERAL INFORMATION

#	EXPLAIN ALL "YES" RESPONSES IN REMARKS	Yes	No	#	EXPLAIN ALL "YES" RESPONSES IN REMARKS.	Yes	No
1	Any protective devices/systems in use?	☐	☐	6	Any coverage declined/cancelled/non renewed? (Last 3 yrs.)	☐	☐
2	Will any property be exhibited?	☐	☐	7	Any other insurance with this company?	☐	☐
3	Will any special restriction/endorsements apply?	☐	☐	8	Did any loss occur during the last 3 years?	☐	☐
4	Will any type of deductible apply?	☐	☐	PRIOR INSURER & POLICY NUMBER			
5	Is any property used professionally/commercially?	☐	☐				

REMARKS:

SCHEDULE OF PROPERTY

#	PROVIDE A DETAILED DESCRIPTION OF EACH ITEM, FROM WHOM PURCHASED ETC. IF ADDITIONAL SPACE IS REQUIRED, USE THE SCHEDULE ON THE REVERSE SIDE. BE SURE TO ATTACH ALL REQUIRED APPRAISALS/BILLS	PURCHASE/ APPRAISAL DATE	AMOUNT OF INSURANCE
1			

ACORD 81 (7/80)

PLEASE COMPLETE REVERSE SIDE

Continued on next page

SCHEDULE OF PROPERTY (CONTINUED)

#	DESCRIPTION	PURCHASE/ APPRAISAL DATE	AMOUNT OF INSURANCE

BINDER/SIGNATURE

INSURANCE BINDER		IF THE "BINDER" BOX TO THE LEFT IS CHECKED, THE FOLLOWING CONDITIONS APPLY:
☐ COVERAGE IS NOT BOUND ☐ BINDER		This Company binds the kind(s) of insurance stipulated on the reverse side. This insurance is subject to the terms, conditions and limitations of the policy(ies) in current use by the Company.
EFFECTIVE DATE	EXPIRATION DATE	This binder may be cancelled by the Insured by surrender of this binder or by written notice to the Company stating when cancellation will be effective. This binder may be cancelled by the Company by notice to the Insured in accordance with the policy conditions. This binder is cancelled when replaced by a policy. If this binder is not replaced by a policy, the Company is entitled to charge a premium for the binder according to the Rules and Rates in use by the Company.
TIME ______ M	☐ 12:01 A.M. ☐ NOON	

IMPORTANT NOTICE REGARDING THE FAIR CREDIT REPORTING ACT: In making this application for insurance it is understood that as part of our underwriting procedure, an investigative consumer report may be prepared whereby information is obtained through personal interviews with your neighbors, friends, or others with whom you are acquainted. This inquiry includes information as to your character, general reputation, personal characteristics and mode of living. If an investigation is made, you can be assured that it will be handled in the strictist confidence.

If you wish information on the nature and scope of the Customer Report which may be requested, ask your agent for the address of the Company handling your account.

APPLICANT'S STATEMENT: I have read the above application and I declare that to the best of my knowledge and belief all of the foregoing statements are true; and that these statements are offered as an inducement to the Company to issue the policy for which I am applying. (Kansas: This does not constitute a warranty.)

APPLICANT'S SIGNATURE		PRODUCER'S SIGNATURE	

FOR COMPANY USE

should reflect the expected value of wedding gifts to be received (a rough estimate, at best, in most cases). The rating insurance section requires information regarding the wedding date, whether breakage coverage on fragile articles is desired, and any applicable coinsurance percentage.

The "Other" section of the rating information block can help serve as a reminder of the coverage options available.

- The unattended car coverage block should be checked if coverage is desired for theft of stamps and coins from an unattended auto.
- The professional use block should be checked if any cameras or musical instruments to be insured are used professionally or commercially (a musician who "plays for pay" is not covered unless this information has been supplied and is noted in the policy).
- Nonmobile organ coverage is different from coverage on a mobile musical instrument. This box provides the opportunity to indicate whether a nonmobile organ is being insured.
- Breakage coverage may be provided for an optional premium on specified fine arts articles. When breakage coverage is desired, the producer should insert an asterisk on the schedule below beside those articles for which breakage coverage is desired.
- Rate credits are available for items such as jewelry or stamp and coin collections kept in a safe or vault. Even where a rate credit is not granted, underwriters may be more willing to provide insurance on specially valued items protected by a safe. This block provides the opportunity to note whether certain property is kept in a safe.

The *schedule of property* block is particularly important, and some suggestions have been made previously regarding information that should be supplied. The *Personal Inland Marine Procedure Guide* provides the following guidelines:

> Give a comprehensive description of each item being insured. If jewelry or fur, use the description on the Bill of Sales or Appraisal. If Cameras, describe each item with a serial number where applicable. Musical Instruments should show type of instrument, name of manufacturer and serial number. Silverware may be scheduled or blanket. Every item of Fine Arts must be individually described with its own amount of insurance. A description of a Stamp Collection may show the number of albums, the countries, the era, first day covers, etc. The Coin Collection must be scheduled. Sports Equipment is covered on a schedule basis, describing the article, manufacturer's name, serial number and any other pertinent information.

The *general information* block requires general underwriting information applicable to all classes of property. Protective devices, if applicable, will help to control losses. Exhibition of valuable property, on the other hand, increases the exposures. Previous refusals to grant coverage may indicate an account with a problem. On the other hand, other insurance with the same insurer may lead the underwriter to look more favorably on the application.

Finally, the applicant's signature on the application minimizes the chance of any future disagreement regarding the insurance applied for. By signing the application, the applicant also indicates that he or she has received and read a copy of the Fair Credit Reporting Act prenotification printed on the back of the application form and reproduced in Exhibit 6-4. Underwriters frequently use an investigative report to obtain information on the prospect. The Fair Credit Reporting Act of 1971 requires an insurer to notify an applicant, in advance, that an inspection report may be ordered. Once the report is written and used by the insurer, the applicant has the right to ask the inspection company about the information it obtained. The inspection company has to inform the applicant of its findings. This information can be challenged by the individual who was the subject of the report. The challenge, or the individual's version of the information, must then be put in the file by the inspection company and passed along to past and future clients who inquire about the same individual.

Insurance companies have set up procedures to comply with the act, and it is important that the producer be familiar with the provisions of the act and the way its mandates are administered by the insurance company. In addition, there may be local or state laws that affect inspections in some areas. Although insureds and producers sometimes become annoyed at these Fair Credit Reporting Act requirements and other procedures imposed by government, these procedures have been established for the *client's protection.* If the client suspects that faulty information has been provided in an investigative report, the client is provided by law with a method of correcting this information. The purpose of the prenotification requirement is to ensure that insurance applicants are aware of their legal rights in this regard.

The Fair Credit Reporting Act notification requirement applies to other lines of insurance as well.

Checkpoints

1. Describe special coverage needs that can be met by using an inland marine floater.

Exhibit 6-4
Fair Credit Reporting Act Prenotification

BINDER/SIGNATURE

INSURANCE BINDER

☐ COVERAGE IS NOT BOUND
☐ BINDER

EFFECTIVE DATE	EXPIRATION DATE
TIME ______ M	☐ 12:01 A.M. ☐ NOON

IF THE "BINDER" BOX TO THE LEFT IS CHECKED, THE FOLLOWING CONDITIONS APPLY:

This Company binds the kind(s) of insurance stipulated on the reverse side. This insurance is subject to the terms, conditions and limitations of the policy(ies) in current use by the Company.

This binder may be cancelled by the Insured by surrender of this binder or by written notice to the Company stating when cancellation will be effective. This binder may be cancelled by the Company by notice to the Insured in accordance with the policy conditions. This binder is cancelled when replaced by a policy. If this binder is not replaced by a policy, the Company is entitled to charge a premium for the binder according to the Rules and Rates in use by the Company.

IMPORTANT NOTICE REGARDING THE FAIR CREDIT REPORTING ACT: In making this application for insurance it is understood that as part of our underwriting procedure, an investigative consumer report may be prepared whereby information is obtained through personal interviews with your neighbors, friends, or others with whom you are acquainted. This inquiry includes information as to your character, general reputation, personal characteristics and mode of living. If an investigation is made, you can be assured that it will be handled in the strictist confidence.
If you wish information on the nature and scope of the Customer Report which may be requested, ask your agent for the address of the Company handling your account.

APPLICANT'S STATEMENT: I have read the above application and I declare that to the best of my knowledge and belief all of the foregoing statements are true; and that these statements are offered as an inducement to the Company to issue the policy for which I am applying. (Kansas: This does not constitute a warranty.)

APPLICANT'S SIGNATURE		PRODUCER'S SIGNATURE	

FOR COMPANY USE

2. Identify personal property coverage limitations of the homeowners policy that create a need that can be met with an inland marine floater.
3. If a pair of diamond earrings is insured for $1,000 in a personal articles floater and one earring is lost, explain how the loss adjustment will be handled.
4. List the classes of property that may be covered on a personal articles floater.
5. Describe the special valuation provisions that apply to fine arts coverage.

Watercraft Insurance

Special inland or ocean marine floaters may be needed because boats have limited protection under the homeowners policies. For example, the homeowners restricts physical damage coverage as follows:

1. There is a limit of $1,000 on watercraft, including trailers, furnishings, equipment, and outboard motors.
2. Coverage is named peril.
3. Windstorm coverage is applicable only when the craft is inside a fully enclosed building.
4. There is no theft coverage on the boat and motor away from the residence premises. Accessories, trailers and other boating personal property are excluded from this coverage as well.

Watercraft Liability Liability coverage for use of watercraft also is limited under the homeowners. Specifically, there is no liability coverage:

f. arising out of:
   (1) the ownership, maintenance, use, loading or unloading of a watercraft described below;
   (2) the entrustment by an **insured** of a watercraft described below to any person; or
   (3) statutorily imposed vicarious parental liability for the actions of a child or minor using a watercraft described below.

   Watercraft:
   (1) with inboard or inboard-outdrive motor power owned by an **insured;**
   (2) with inboard or inboard-outdrive motor power of more than 50 horsepower renting to an **insured;**
   (3) that is a sailing vessel, with or without auxiliary power, 26 feet or more in length owned by or rented to an **insured;** or
   (4) powered by one or more outboard motors with more than 25 total horsepower if the outboard motor is owned by an

> **insured.** But, outboard motors of more than 25 total horsepower are covered for the policy period if:
> (a) you acquire them prior to the policy period and:
> (i) you declare them at policy inception; or
> (ii) your intention to insure is reported to us in writing within 45 days after you acquire the outboard motors.
> (b) you acquire them during the policy period.
>
> This exclusion does not apply while the watercraft is stored.

Note that part (4) of the description of watercraft in the exclusion applies to any boat, provided it is powered by one or more outboard engines owned by any insured. In other words, if the engines are owned by any insured, there is no coverage regardless of whether the boat is owned by, rented to, or borrowed by the insured. Coverage would be provided, however, if the engine is rented to or borrowed by the insured. Coverage is also provided for outboard engines acquired during the policy term. However, there would be no coverage for any liability arising from the use of an outboard engine (or two or more engines) owned by any insured at the inception of the policy if the total horsepower of such engine or engines is more than 25 horsepower.

An HO endorsement can be used to extend the homeowners liability and medical payments coverage to (1) larger outboard engines, (2) boats not more than forty feet in length and powered by inboard or inboard-outboard engines, or (3) sailboats not more than forty feet in length. Boats that do not fall within these specifications cannot be insured for liability under the homeowners policy.

Watercraft Physical Damage The kind of policy used to provide physical damage coverage for boats varies with the kind and size of boat. The limited coverage under the homeowners policy may be adequate for rowboats, canoes, and even for small outboard boats. Larger or more expensive canoes, rowboats, or outboard boats and motors may be insured under an inland marine *outboard motor and boat policy.* Boats powered by inboard engines, inboard-outdrive units, or sail (and even some very large outboard boats) should be insured under a *yacht policy* (a specialized ocean marine policy designed for the specialized exposures of pleasure boats).

Outboard Motor and Boat Policy The inland marine coverage for boats and outboard motors varies somewhat from one insurer to another. The coverage may be either for named perils or "all-risks." Although the policy is intended primarily to cover damage to the insured boat, the policies of many insurers also cover (on a limited basis) the insured's liability for property damage arising from collision while afloat. This collision liability coverage may be limited to a specified dollar amount (such as $500) or to the value of the insured boat and motor. There is no coverage for bodily injury liability.

In addition to the boat and motor, the policy may also provide coverage for the trailer and other equipment used with the boat. The boat, motor, and trailer usually are scheduled on the policy with a specific amount of insurance on each. Other equipment may be insured blanket.

There is considerable variation in the exclusions from one insurer to another, but a few exclusions appear in most policies. Most policies do not cover any loss occurring while the boat is used for any purpose other than private pleasure purposes. If the boat is used for any business purpose or is rented or chartered to others, there is no coverage unless the policy has been endorsed to permit such use. The policy may also exclude any loss or damage caused by the process of refinishing, renovating, or repairing. Loss or damage while the boat is in a race may also be excluded. In addition, the policies contain the usual exclusions of war damage, nuclear damage, wear and tear, deterioration, vermin, and similar causes of loss.

Yacht Policy Boats not qualifying for the outboard motor and boat policy (and even some larger ones that do qualify) should be insured under a yacht policy. A yacht policy provides coverage for both physical damage to the insured boat and the insured's liability to others arising from the ownership, maintenance, or use of the boat.

The coverage for damage to the boat may be either for named perils or "all-risks." Coverage may not apply to loss of spars, sails, or rigging while racing, but some insurance companies will provide coverage for such losses by endorsement for an additional premium. For high-speed power boats, the policy may exclude damage to rudder, shafts, or machinery, unless the damage is caused by burning, stranding, collision with another vessel, or sinking caused by an insured peril. Loss by war, strike, capture, freezing, or similar perils is usually excluded.

Hull coverage of a yacht policy is usually valued for total loss. That is, the amount of insurance stated in the policy is paid in the event of a total loss, regardless of the value of the boat at the time of loss. Partial losses are settled at the cost of repairs, without deduction for depreciation.

The coverage on the boat (hull) also includes a "running down" clause (collision liability). This clause covers the insured's liability for damage to another vessel caused by collision with the insured boat. The limit for this liability coverage is the same as the limit for physical damage to the insured boat, but is in addition to the coverage on the insured boat. Consequently, the insurer may be required to pay twice its hull limit, once for physical damage to the insured boat and again for collision liability.

Another form of liability protection is included in the liability section of the policy, sometimes called protection and indemnity or P&I, and is an unusually broad liability coverage. It covers both bodily injury and property damage liability, usually excluding the insured's liability to provide benefits under the federal Longshoremen's and Harbor Workers' Act. It also covers the insured's liability for the cost of removing the insured vessel if it is sunk in a navigation channel.

Some yacht policies provide lower limits of liability coverage when the boat is being used for water skiing. There may be no liability coverage at all while towing a glider or other device designed for flight. Some policies also exclude liability for damage to property owned by, rented to, or in the care of, the insured.

Coverage is also provided for medical expenses incurred by persons accidentally injured in, upon, boarding, or leaving the insured boat. The medical payments coverage also applies to persons while engaged in water skiing from the insured boat. The coverage usually applies to the insured and relatives as well as other persons.

Yacht policies usually contain restrictions on the geographic area in which the boat can be operated and the season of the year in which it can be used. These provisions are sometimes called the *navigation warranty* and the *lay-up warranty,* respectively. Any use of the boat beyond the specified area or during the season when it is supposed to be laid up would suspend the coverage. Insurers will usually endorse the policy to provide coverage for such use, subject to an additional premium charge. Producers should make clients aware of these warranties and ways to avoid suspension of coverage.

The rates for both the yacht policy and the outboard motor and boat policy depend on the kind, age, and size of boat (or motor), the area in which it is used, and the experience and training of the operators. Rates may sometimes be reduced by increasing the deductible under the policy.

Boats are owned by many middle and upper income families. Producers can segment personal lines to seek clients with boats or yachts and the exposures involved in ownership, maintenance, and use. Extra premium dollars can be generated by sale of appropriate boat policies.

One agent in Chicago uses a simple technique to attract this type of business. He places a small advertisement in the Boat Section of the Sunday *Chicago Tribune* indicating that his agency has boat and yacht coverage available. Not only does he generate a large volume of business this way, he also uses the yacht and boat coverage as an entry to a prospect's *entire* personal lines account.

For producers not familiar with the types of boats in use, Exhibit 6-5 contains drawings and brief descriptions.

Checkpoints

1. Describe the protection provided insured boat owners under an unendorsed homeowners policy.
2. Describe how the protection and indemnity coverage differs from liability coverage under homeowners policies.
3. Compare a yacht policy and an outboard motor and boat policy with regard to (a) physical damage coverage, and (b) collision liability coverage (running down clause).
4. Compare the yacht policy with a homeowners policy with regard to (a) medical payment coverage and (b) indicate at least one kind of liability covered under the P & I section not covered under the liability section of homeowners policies.

AIRCRAFT INSURANCE

Most producers specializing in personal lines and small commercial accounts are likely to have clients with an interest in flying. Aircraft insurance closely resembles auto insurance, yet there are enough differences to indicate caution. These differences will be highlighted.

Liability Coverage Alternatives

Although the insurance contracts used in aircraft are not standard, most have similar provisions and offer the following coverage options:

1. Bodily injury liability insurance, excluding passenger liability
2. Passenger liability insurance
3. Property damage liability insurance
4. Single limit bodily injury and property damage liability insurance, excluding passenger liability
5. Single limit bodily injury and property damage liability insurance, including passenger liability

Normally, one of five coverages or coverage combinations below is selected:

1. Item one only
2. Items one and three
3. Items one, two, and three
4. Item four
5. Item five

Exhibit 6-5
Know Your Boats*

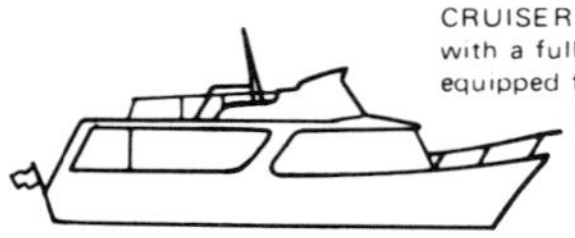

CRUISER a power boat with a fully enclosed cabin equipped for living aboard.

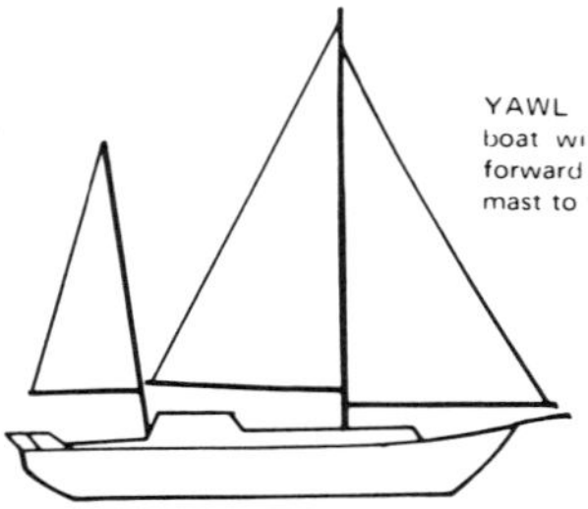

YAWL a two-masted boat with the tallest mast forward and the shorter mast to the rear.

AUXILIARY – a sailing yacht principally propelled by means of sails, but equipped with an inboard engine to provide supplemental power.

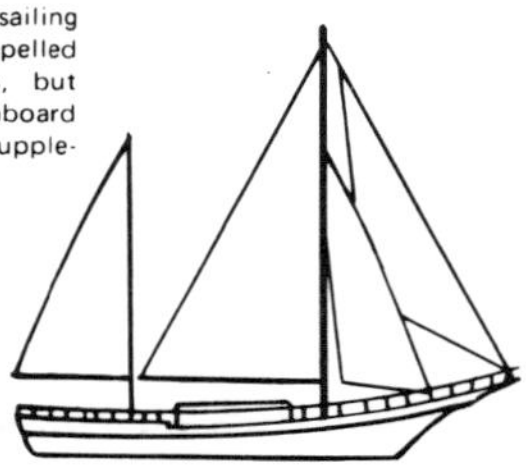

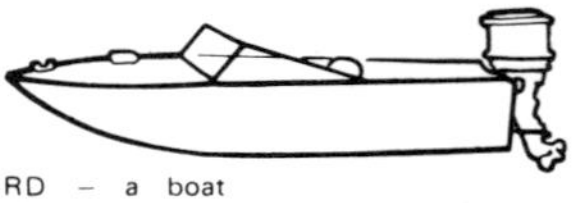

OUTBOARD – a boat equipped with a detachable motor fixed to the stern.

TENDER (Dinghy) - a small boat carried aboard a larger vessel, often used for transporting passengers to and from shore.

CUTTER – a single masted sailboat with the mast placed nearer the center than that of a sloop. It has a single mainsail and usually two headsails.

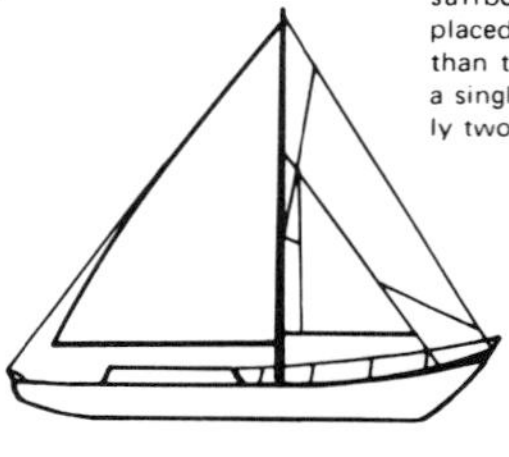

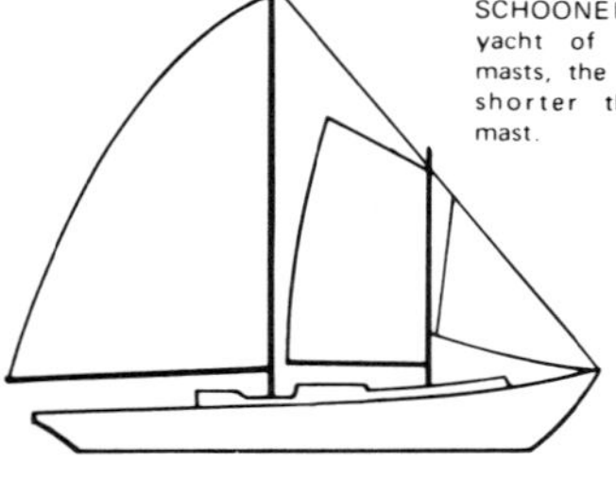

SCHOONER a sailing yacht of two or more masts, the foremast being shorter than the main mast.

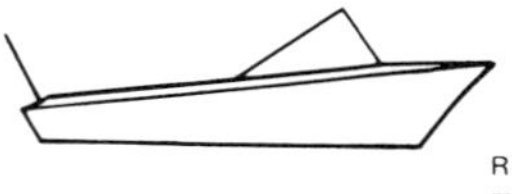

RUNABOUT a smaller motorboat with an open cockpit.

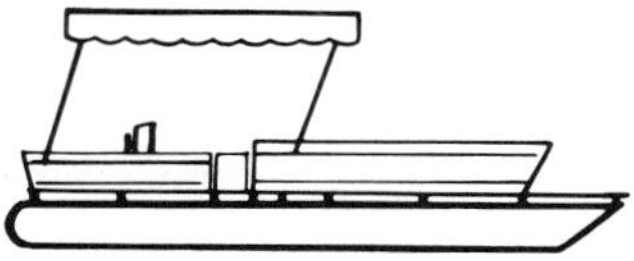

PONTOON BOAT a flat deck placed on pontoons (portable floats), primarily used on inland lakes and waterways.

CATAMARAN a boat with twin hulls side by side, usually sail powered.

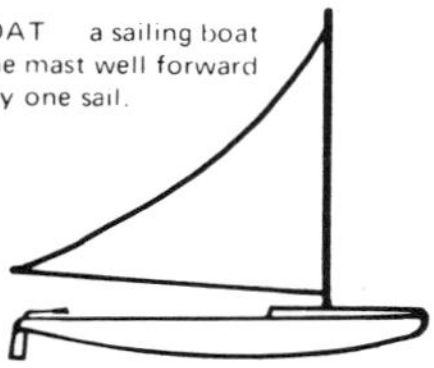

CATBOAT a sailing boat with one mast well forward and only one sail.

JETBOAT an outdrive boat powered by an inboard engine, and equipped with a jet pump to propel the boat. The hull is totally free of any underwater propeller or protrusions.

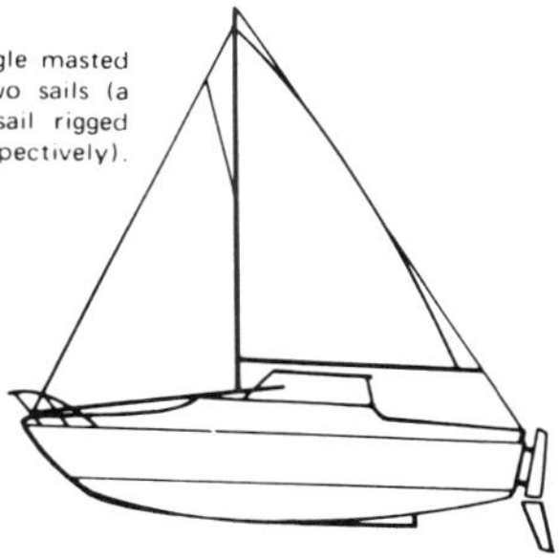

SLOOP a single masted sailboat with two sails (a jib and a mainsail rigged fore and aft respectively).

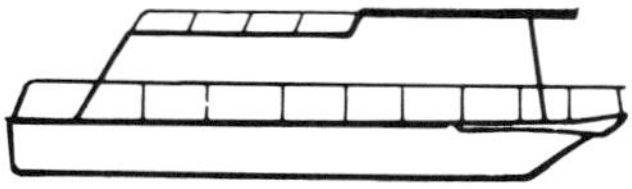

HOUSEBOAT a power boat fitted for use as a dwelling or for leisure cruising, with a super-structure much like a house, and usually flatbottomed.

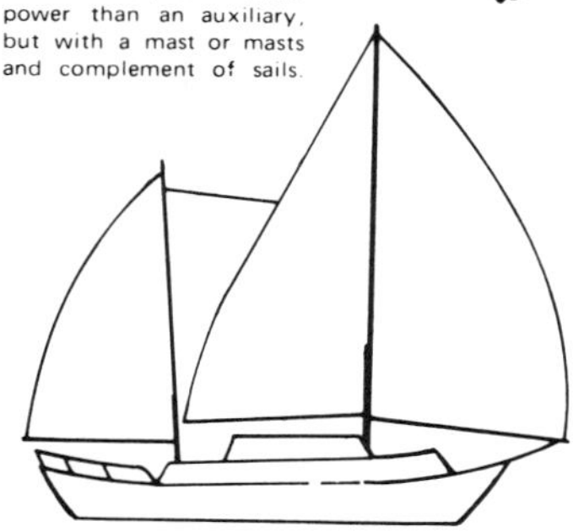

MOTOR SAILER a combination of a powerboat and sailboat, with more power than an auxiliary, but with a mast or masts and complement of sails.

INBOARD-OUTBOARD (also called outdrive, stern drive) Engine to the rear, but inboard, with the drive portion outside the stern.

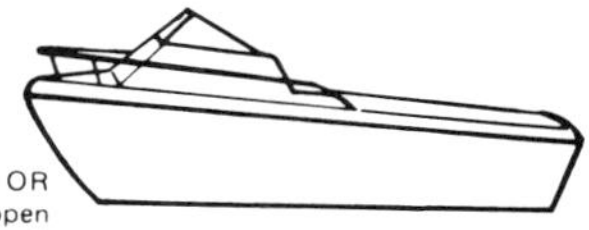

SPORT FISHERMAN OR CUDDY CABIN an open power boat with a small cabin forward.

* Reprinted with permission from Aetna Life & Casualty, Casualty & Surety Division, "Marketing Report—Special Boating Issue," April 1972, pp. 24-25.

In each case, the insuring agreement would provide "occurrence" coverage for all sums the insured would become legally obligated to pay as damage because of bodily injury, sickness or disease, and, if included, of injury to or destruction of property caused by an occurrence arising out of the ownership, maintenance, or use of the aircraft.

Third-party bodily injury liability insurance is offered separately from both passenger and property damage liability insurance. This separation gives the client a choice and an opportunity to pay a lower premium at the expense of incomplete protection. A careful explanation of these options must be given to each client.

Medical Payments

Coverage is similar to that found under the PAP except that the pilot is not covered unless stated in the declarations and an additional premium paid. Coverage is provided for medical expenses, including hospital, ambulance, and nursing services and funeral expenses, up to the limit of coverage selected by the insured, arising from riding in, entering, or alighting from the aircraft.

Coverage is extended to the other aircraft operated by or for the named insured or spouse; however, such coverage is excess over all other valid medical payments coverage.

Use of Other Aircraft

This coverage applies only if the named insured is an individual. It closely resembles the provisions of the personal auto policy and protects the named insured or spouse when using other aircraft operated for the same purposes as the owned aircraft (the same risk classification as the owned aircraft). For members of flying clubs or owners of small businesses, for example, rated in classification one or two above, this extension of coverage for the use of rented or borrowed aircraft is available at an additional premium. Because of the many types of aircraft, such protection is extended only to (1) use of substitute fixed wing aircraft, (2) with a standard airworthiness certificate, and (3) of a type the insured is qualified to operate.

Voluntary Settlement and Seat Accident Coverage

An additional coverage, often written along with the liability coverage, is passenger admitted liability insurance, also called voluntary settlement coverage. This unusual form of protection is comparable to personal injury protection of no-fault automobile coverage. It provides a stipulated amount for damages caused by death or dismemberment of guest passengers, and, for an additional premium, the crew.

Payment under this provision will be made only if the claimant signs a release of liability form, agreeing not to sue. Should such a release not be signed, the claimant must sue and the insured would be protected under the regular passenger liability coverage provided by the policy. Voluntary settlement coverage is a courtesy type of coverage, permitting payment to a claimant without the necessity for suit. The coverage has value because it provides a way to settle, without necessitating a court struggle, in cases where the insured's negligence is doubtful. When this coverage is added, the premium for the passenger liability coverage is reduced.

Although similar to voluntary settlement coverage, seat accident coverage does not require a release of liability. It is usually written as a separate policy and would not affect the premium for the passenger liability portion. This is a voluntary type of courtesy coverage in the broadest sense, since it does not require a release of liability. A claimant could collect under the insured's policy and still sue the insured. It is hoped, however, that this will not be the case.

Aircraft Physical Damage (Hull Coverage)

Aircraft insurance is not standardized, and the producer should check the provisions of the policy before delivering it to the insured. These coverages closely parallel typical automobile physical damage contracts, however, and are relatively easy to understand.

Coverage may be either named perils, "all-risks," or a combination of the two. For example, coverage may be "all-risks" while on the ground and named perils while in flight. Named perils coverage would usually include the perils of fire, explosion, lightning, theft, robbery, or pilferage. However, fire or explosion caused by the collision of the aircraft with the ground, water, or any other object may be excluded. Some insurers do not offer a named perils option.

The hull coverage may also be written to provide coverage while the aircraft is (1) in flight, (2) in motion, or (3) not in motion. One insurer offers the following options:

1. "All-risks" of physical damage to the aircraft both in flight and on the ground;
2. "All-risks" of physical damage while not in flight, but excluding fire or theft resulting from crash or from collision while in flight; or

3. "All-risks" of physical damage while the aircraft is not in motion under its own power.

The first coverage is the broadest and the most expensive of the three; the third one is the most limited. The second insuring agreement listed would cover the aircraft while taxiing to or from the end of the runway but not from the time it begins its take-off run until it ends its landing run. Flight is defined as beginning with the start of the take-off run and ending with the end of the landing run. It does not include taxiing. The third insuring agreement would not cover the aircraft while moving under its own power: it covers the aircraft only while it is stationary or being towed by a tractor or other power source.

Some policies may cover only the actual cash value of the aircraft hull. Others are valued polices and will pay the stated value for total loss. It may also pay the actual cost of repairing partial losses, without any reduction for depreciation of the damaged parts. Some contracts also cover the cost of transporting the damaged aircraft from the site of the loss to the repair site and returning it either to the site of loss or to its home airport, whichever is nearer.

Deductibles are widely used in aircraft hull insurance and are often a percentage of the hull value, such as 2.5, 5, or 10 percent, coupled with a minimum dollar amount stipulated. One deductible amount may apply while in motion with a different one applying while not in motion.

Insurers

Aircraft policies are specialty coverages, and few insurance companies write the business directly. Instead, most insurance companies participate in one of several pools or underwriting groups formed to write aircraft exposures exclusively. As a consequence, producers may not have direct access to underwriters but must work through a pool. This normally means there is no binding authority granted unless the producer handles a considerable volume of aircraft insurance. Moreover, most transactions are sold for cash upon policy delivery, and flat cancellations are not permitted.

Underwriting

Rates charged and acceptability of the submission are affected materially by the purpose for which the aircraft will be used. Aircraft are usually classified according to use. Information about the aircraft required for underwriting purposes appears in Exhibit 6-6. With regard to the pilot information, the most important experience period is the

Exhibit 6-6
Aircraft Underwriting Information

Type of aircraft
- landplane
- seaplane
- amphibian

Airworthiness certification
- acrobatic
- limited
- multiple
- normal
- restricted or experimental
- transport
- utility

Make and model of aircraft
- registration number
- number and horsepower of engines
- date purchased
- purchase price
- schedule of additional equipment, date purchased and value

Information regarding the pilot is of even greater importance. The underwriter will need to have the following information:

Pilot rating
- student
- private
- instrument
- commercial

Pilot experience
- number of flight hours (by aircraft type)
  - dual instruction
  - solo
  - co-pilot
  - first pilot
- kind of flight experience
  - cross-country
  - night and instrument
  - other
- any civil aeronautics regulations violations

most recent (within ninety days) and involving the particular type of aircraft being insured.

Selling Aircraft Insurance

Reviewing Exhibit 6-6, producers can see the need to be proficient in the terminology of aircraft. A few producers can earn their livings by specializing in aircraft insurance. But it takes time to gain the knowledge required to be able to competently sell the right coverage and to fully explain any unusual characteristics of an aircraft to an underwriter. Use of the aviation pools, with their expertise, allows most producers to sell this type of insurance without a technical background. Aircraft pools are sufficient for the exposures of most producers' clients.

PERSONAL UMBRELLA COVERAGE

The size of liability awards has increased sharply in recent years, requiring an equally rapid increase in liability coverage limits. The additional coverage can be obtained by increasing limits under basic liability policies (e.g., personal auto policy or homeowners), purchasing a personal umbrella liability policy to provide coverage over and above the basic liability policies, or both. The umbrella is likely to provide the best protection for the insured since the umbrella policy may also cover some liability loss exposures not covered by basic policies.

Umbrella policy is a generic term used to refer to a broad liability policy intended to provide high limits of coverage in excess of basic liability policies. Umbrella policies may be written either for commercial accounts or for individuals or families. The discussion here is limited to personal umbrellas designed for individuals or families.

Personal umbrella policies are not standardized, and the coverage may vary from one insurer to another. Producers must exercise considerable care in choosing between policies offered by different insurers. The discussion that follows will be general and may not accurately describe any particular insurer's personal umbrella policy. Generally, personal umbrellas are characterized by high limits of liability, broad territorial coverage, excess coverage over primary policies, a "retention" for certain exposures, and broad coverage.

One distinguishing characteristic of personal umbrellas is a high limit of liability. Most such policies have limits of at least $1 million in excess of basic policies, and limits of $2 million to $5 million are common,.

Another characteristic of personal umbrellas is worldwide coverage. This is in contrast with most basic liability policies, that cover only accidents or occurrences that take place in the United States, its possessions, or Canada.

Exhibit 6-7
Underlying Policies Required By a Typical Umbrella Policy

Coverage		Limit
Automobile Liability		$300,000
Comprehensive Personal Liability		100,000
Employer's Liability		50,000
Snowmobile Liability		50,000
Aircraft Liability—	Bodily Injury	
	per person	250,000
	per occurrence	500,000
	per passenger	100,000
	Property Damage	100,000
Watercraft Liability		100,000

A third characteristic of personal umbrella policies is the requirement that the insured carry certain specified primary liability coverages and limits usually referred to as "required underlying insurance." One reasonably typical umbrella policy requires the underlying policies appearing in Exhibit 6-7. Primary coverage for snowmobiles, aircraft, and watercraft would be required only if the insured owns or leases snowmobiles, aircraft, or watercraft.

If the insured carries the required underlying coverage, the umbrella applies as excess over the underlying insurance. If the insured fails to carry the underlying coverage, the liability of the umbrella insurer is not changed. The underlying limits then become, in effect, deductibles, and the umbrella applies as excess over the amount the underlying coverage would have paid if it had been carried. The producer should follow up quickly when he or she learns that an insured nonrenewed or canceled an underlying policy.

A fourth characteristic of personal umbrellas is the existence of a "retained limit" (or deductible) applicable to the losses covered under the umbrella but not covered by the underlying coverages. The amount of the retained limit may vary from $250 to $10,000, depending on the insurer.

A final characteristic of personal umbrellas is very broad coverage. They usually include automobile liability, premises and sports liability, personal injury liability (libel, slander, etc.), aircraft liability, boat liability, employers' liability, and bodily injury and property damage liability from most other sources except those specifically excluded. The exclusions are the key to umbrella coverage and must be reviewed carefully. Umbrellas, for example, usually do not contain the care, custody, or control exclusion which is characteristic of other liability policies.

Umbrella policies usually do not provide any defense cost coverage for losses covered under required underlying coverage. Some do provide defense cost coverage for losses not covered under the required underlying policies, provided such losses are covered under the umbrella.

Some insurers will add professional liability coverage to personal umbrellas written for doctors, dentists, and other professionals. A substantial amount of underlying professional liability coverage is usually required, along with a substantial additional premium.

Two examples will illustrate the relationship between an umbrella, the underlying coverages, and the retained limit. Exhibit 6-8 shows the levels of protection available to an insured with the following policies:

1. $100,000 comprehensive personal liability
2. $300,000 single limit on the PAP
3. $300,000 single limit watercraft liability

The insured, Richard Roe, has a personal umbrella with a policy limit of $1 million and a retained limit of $1,000. The insurer's required underlying coverages for Roe are:

Automobile Liability	$300,000
Personal Liability (including employer's liability)	$100,000

Mr. Roe is involved in an auto accident for which he is held liable. A passenger in the other car obtains a judgment for $1,000,000 against him. The underlying insurer pays its limit of $300,000 plus defense costs. The umbrella insurer pays $700,000 for a total of $1,000,000 for the two insurers combined. If the judgment had been for $1,500,000 the insurers would have paid $1,300,000 combined and Roe would have had to pay the balance, $200,000 personally. If Roe had only a $100,000 limit on his auto policy with a $1,000,000 judgment, the auto insurer would have paid $100,000 and Roe would be responsible for the next $200,000, with the umbrella insurer paying $700,000 or the excess of the judgment over the promised $300,000 auto liability limits.

The second example assumes the same policy as the first example. Rachel Roe, wife of Richard Roe, borrows a Ming vase valued at $10,000 to show at a social event. The vase is broken during the event, and Mrs. Roe is held liable to the owner for its value. Her liability is not covered under her personal liability policy because of the care, custody, and control exclusion, but the "damage to property of others" provision of that policy will pay $500 without regard to liability. Mrs. Roe will pay $500, the retained limit less the $500 paid by the underlying insurance. The remaining $9,000 will be paid by the umbrella insurer. If Mrs. Roe's

Exhibit 6-8
Personal Umbrella Policy

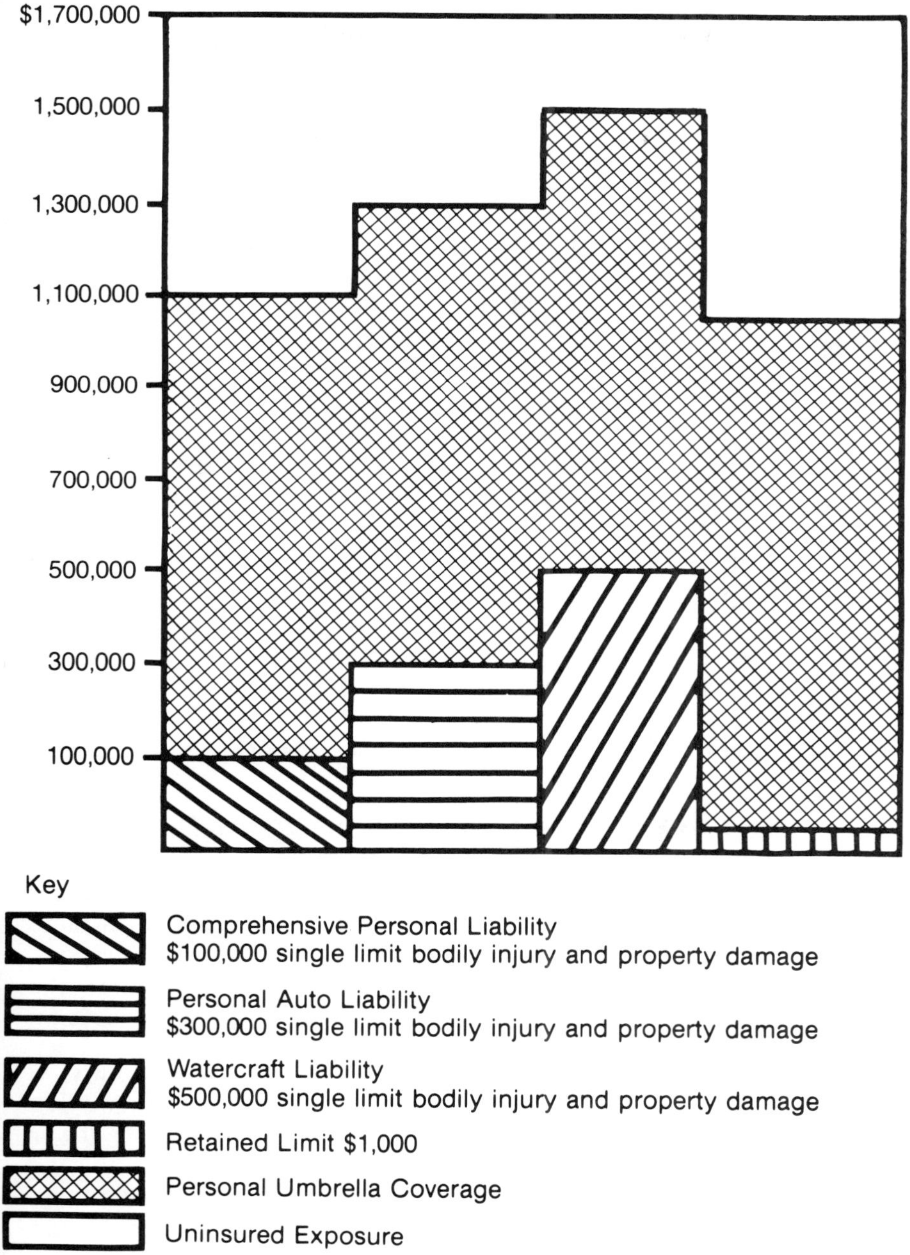

personal liability policy had not included the "damage to property of others" coverage, she would have been required to pay the entire retained limit of $1,000, but the umbrella insurer's liability would be unchanged.

Since umbrellas vary from company to company, many producers try to place the umbrella with the same insurer writing the auto and homeowners. Such a practice will eliminate disputes between different insurers as to how each other's policy should respond and thereby speed up the settlement process. In addition, having the business with a single company can assist the producer in making volume commitments and in achieving greater efficiency in the agency.

Selling the personal umbrella is recommended to all producers. A small brochure can be included in renewal billing to current clients, or the brochure can be introduced in a personal call. The umbrella can also be an entry to prospects. A letter containing a copy of a local and recent "jumbo verdict" can bring the umbrella to a prospect's attention. If an interview is granted, the prospect's entire personal lines account must be discussed to determine underlying limits. Through this discussion, the producer obtains expiration dates of other personal lines insurance the prospect purchases from other producers.

There are a number of selling points for the personal umbrella policy. Most sales points revolve around the distinguishing characteristics of an umbrella discussed. An additional point is the premium: through most insurers, a $1 million umbrella costs less than $150—a small price to pay for such broad catastrophic coverage.

The sales appeal of an umbrella is enhanced for those producers who have access to a "second stage" personal package policy.

DWELLING POLICY PROGRAM

When a residential structure or personal property is not eligible for a homeowners policy, the dwelling policy program may be used to provide "fire" coverage.

Generally, the dwelling policy program is appropriate for the following situations:

1. One and two family dwellings and their contents which are (a) not owner-occupied, (b) not acceptable for HO for underwriting reasons, and (c) to be written for amounts of insurance lower than HO minimums.
2. Residential trailers and mobile homes at a fixed location.
3. Dwellings in the course of construction which the insured is not intending to occupy.

4. All residential exposures eligible for HO are also eligible for the dwelling program. (The dwelling program may be used to provide coverage for underwriting, cost, or other considerations.)

Most states have adopted ISO's dwelling policy program called "Dwelling '77." This program closely parallels the homeowners program covered in Chapter 4 in terms of policy language and format, although the dwelling program offers only three policy forms. Each dwelling form is roughly the equivalent of its homeowners counterpart: the dwelling basic form (DP-1) parallels the HO-1; the dwelling broad form (DP-2), the HO-2; and the dwelling special form (DP-3), the HO-3.

The essential differences between the two programs are:

- The dwelling program does not provide any theft or liability coverages under any of the three forms.
- Replacement cost coverage is applicable only on the DP-2 and DP-3 forms and only on the dwelling and other structures. Losses under a DP-1 are adjusted at actual cash value.
- Contents coverage must be added to all three forms. There is no automatic percentage of Coverage A as there is with the homeowners program.

Given the wide variety of homeowners forms and the ability to customize the coverage to meet the insured's needs through endorsements, the dwelling program has dwindled in its use as a popular means for covering the client's exposures. However, the producer should be aware of the availability of the dwelling program as a limited alternative to the homeowners program.

FLOOD INSURANCE

Coverage for the peril of flood is excluded by homeowners policies, dwelling policies, and most other insurance policies involving property at a fixed location. Flood damage is covered, however, under most auto policies including physical damage coverage "other than collision" or comprehensive, and under most inland marine floaters.

The flood peril has been difficult, if not impossible, for private insurance to handle. Adverse selection is a problem because flood insurance coverage would be purchased only by those with property in areas subject to flooding. The catastrophic nature of floods presents an added problem. Many insureds could be affected by a single flood.

Until 1968, homeowners could not buy flood insurance on their home from any source. When flood struck, they could only hope that the area was declared a disaster area and eligible for federal relief. The

National Flood Insurance Act of 1968 established a flood insurance program to resolve this problem.

Currently, the National Flood Insurance Program (NFIP) provides government underwritten insurance through two mechanisms. A producer may write the business direct through the servicing representative designated by the Federal Insurance Administration (FIA) or may choose to place the business with an insurance company participating in FIA's "Write Your Own" (WYO) program.

WYO is a concept by which FIA seeks to reinvolve the private sector in the NFIP. Insurance companies that sign up for the WYO—and there are currently more than 150 participating—issue and service flood insurance through their own facilities and are allowed to retain approximately 30 percent of the premium to cover expenses. Should the remaining 70 percent be insufficient to cover losses, the companies can seek reimbursement from the government.

It is recommended that a producer investigate to determine if companies that he or she represents are participating in the WYO program. The chief advantages of placing the flood business with a WYO company are (1) the producer may be dealing with a local branch office and personnel he or she is familiar with rather than with someone who is a great distance away, and (2) improved service on accounts. The producer will not gain any rate advantages by placing business with a WYO company since they must offer the same coverages at the same prices as the federal government.

Knowing how to sell flood insurance has become a virtual necessity for the producer handling property insurance for two reasons. First, since 1974, flood insurance has been required by law on certain types of federally backed loans secured by property situated in flood prone areas. Second—from a producer's standpoint perhaps most importantly—failure to recommend flood insurance to a customer is appearing as a frequent source of errors and omissions claims against producers.

Since there are more than 15,000 flood prone communities in the United States, it can be said that there is a viable market for this protection; and the fact that more than 1.9 million flood policies have been sold proves that contention. Familiarity with the National Flood Insurance Program will provide the producer with another marketing tool to use in developing total insurance protection for the client.

Underwriting Rules

Flood insurance cannot be written anywhere in the country nor can coverage be placed on any type of building or contents. Flood insurance can be written only on an *eligible building* or on *eligible contents* within an eligible building located within an *eligible community.*

Exhibit 6-9
Residential Limits of Insurance for National Flood Insurance Program

	Basic Amount	+	Additional Amount (1)	=	Total Coverage
Building					
Single family	$ 35,000		$150,000		$185,000
All other residential	100,000		150,000		250,000
Contents (Per Unit)					
Single family	10,000		50,000		60,000
All other residential	10,000		50,000		60,000

(1) *Additional amounts* of coverage are available only in those communities eligible under the regular program

The above amounts of coverage are set by law; rates are set by Federal Insurance Administration

Community Eligibility Under the National Flood Insurance Program, the federal government, through the FIA, notifies those communities it deems to have a flood problem. The government expresses a willingness to assist in dealing with those flood problems should the community elect to join the National Flood Insurance Program.

Should the community join, it does so under the initial program phase called the *emergency program.* Under this emergency program, a limited amount of insurance at standard rates is available. The amount of coverage available is based on the type of building or contents (see Exhibit 6-9 under the heading of *"basic amounts."*)

While the community is eligible under the emergency program, the FIA arranges for a detailed study of the community and its flood problem. This study results in the publication of a map called a Flood Insurance Rate Map (FIRM).

The publication and acceptance of the FIRM and passage of local flood plain ordinances designed to lessen or eliminate future flooding by appropriate community officials, allows the community to be "promoted" to the second and final phase of the National Flood Insurance Program, called the *regular program.*

From an insurance standpoint, the regular program means more insurance is available. The *additional amount,* as well as the basic amount available under the emergency program, is rated on an actuarial basis (shown in Exhibit 6-9).

Building Eligibility Once the status of the community has been determined, attention turns to the building or contents to be insured. Under current rules of the National Flood Insurance Program, insurance can be written on the building or the contents therein only if the building is walled and roofed (although there is no requirement for a minimum number of walls), affixed to a permanent site, and principally above ground (i.e., at least 51 percent of the building's ACV is above ground). Mobile homes are also eligible for coverage, but they must meet anchoring requirements established by the FIA.

Contents Eligibility Most types of personal property are eligible for coverage under the National Flood Insurance Program, provided they are within a fully enclosed building or, in the case of a building with one or more open sides, sufficiently tied down at the time of a flood to prevent flotation.

Some of the items most commonly damaged by a flood are ineligible for coverage: trees, lawns, shrubs, driveways and walkways, bridges and docks, as well as any other open structures located on or over water.

In an effort to curb losses, FIA has greatly restricted what it will cover in basement areas. Essentially there is no coverage for any items of personal property located in a basement that are damaged by flood waters. FIA will permit coverage to apply, however, to those items necessary for the maintenance and service of the dwelling (e.g., heating and air-conditioning systems, hot water heaters, washers, dryers, and so on). This exclusion is relatively new, and many insureds are not aware of it until after a loss.

The residential form also excludes business property and requires the individual who has business property in the residence to obtain coverage through the separate general property flood insurance policy.

Waiting Period The general rule for the national Flood Insurance Program is that there is a five-day waiting period between the time the individual completes the application and pays the annual or three-year premium and when the coverages go into effect. However, there are three exceptions to this five-day waiting period:

1. If coverage is desired to coincide with the acquisition of a building, it can be made effective the day of closing.
2. During a community's first thirty days of eligibility under both the emergency and regular programs, coverage can be made effective 12:01 A.M. (*local time*) the day following the date of application and premium payment.

3. Increases or additions in coverage on existing policies are effective 12:01 A.M. (*local time*) the day following the date of application and premium payment.

When discussing waiting periods and effective dates of coverage, producers should keep two points in mind: (1) the National Flood Insurance Program uses 12:01 A.M. *local time* in lieu of 12:01 A.M. *standard time;* and (2 under the regulations issued by the FIA the applicant/insured is required to make the full premium payment at the time of application.

Policy Term The National Flood Insurance Program permits a policy to be issued on a one- or three-year prepaid basis. There is no deferred premium payment plan.

Minimum Premium The minimum premium for either a one- or three-year policy is $50.

Important Policy Terms and Conditions

The drafters of the flood insurance policy used in the National Flood Insurance Program essentially took the standard fire policy, and where the word "fire" appeared, it was erased and the word "flood" was inserted.

Definition of "Flood" The policy defines "flood" as a general and temporary condition of partial or complete inundation of normally dry land areas caused by the overflow of inland or tidal waters or the rapid and unusual accumulation or runoff of surface waters from any source. The definition also includes accelerated erosion of coastal areas and mudslides which are caused by accumulations of water on or under the ground.

To better understand what is meant by "flood," the producer must be familiar with the first exclusion. Among other things, the policy will not cover flooding confined solely to the insured premises and those premises immediately adjacent. While this limitation of the term "general" fits nicely into an urban situation, it is usually overlooked when there is rural flooding with a considerable distance between the insured premises and those immediately adjacent.

Sewer Backup Sewer backup is covered only when the proximate cause of the backup is a flood as defined in the policy.

Removal Provision Like the standard fire policy, the flood insurance policy provides coverage for property moved to a temporary location. However, the coverage remains only for flood and only for forty-five days at a temporary location.

Preservation of Property Coverage The policy will reimburse the insured for those reasonable expenses incurred when the insured takes measures to preserve and protect personal property or the structure when flooding is imminent. The flood does not have to occur, but a very real threat must be present to cause the insured to act. In addition, this coverage extension is applicable only when there is coverage on the item(s) being protected.

Replacement Cost The dwelling policy form makes available replacement cost to the owners of single-family dwellings provided that the home is the insured's principal residence (i.e., the insured lives in the dwelling at least 80 percent of the time). Mobile homes are not eligible for replacement cost under the NFIP. Mobile homes and all personal property losses are adjusted at actual cash value.

Deductibles The NFIP has a mandatory deductible applicable to both building and contents. While the base deductibles are $500 on building and $500 on personal property, the NFIP does offer several deductible options which can discount the premium up to 35 percent.

Coverage for Other Structures The NFIP extends up to 10 percent of the coverage on a single-family dwelling to a garage or carport only. This extension is not an additional amount of insurance. Should more coverage be required or the other structure not be a garage or carport, the producer must secure a separate policy.

Cancellation/Reduction of Insurance Clause The insured may cancel or reduce coverage at any time during the policy term, but the premium is considered *fully earned* so long as the insured retains an interest in the property covered at the location described on the declarations page. Since the insured is required to make the full payment at the time of application, the producer cannot use nonpayment as a reason for cancellation and expect to get a refund from the National Flood Insurance Program in those cases where the producer advanced the premium. Cancellation for nonpayment does apply in the case where the producer received a bad check from the insured.

Marketing Set-Up and Other Considerations

The producer has two means available for writing flood insurance. He or she can place the business directly with the NFIP's servicing representative in Maryland or use one of the "Write Your Own" companies. Producers can write the NFIP, P.O. Box 619, Lanham, Maryland 20706 or call 1-800-638-6620 to obtain information on community eligibility, "Write Your Own" company participation, and producer manuals. Specially designed advertising materials are also available at little or no cost.

Marketing Tips For many producers the National Flood Insurance Program can represent a new marketing tool that can lead to other sales. However, producers have been successfully sued by clients for failing to advise properly of flood insurance. Thus, a producer should consider implementing some or all of the following to serve client insurance needs and protect against an errors and omission claim:

- Include "stuffers," available at little or no charge from the National Flood Insurance Program, in routine mailings
- Include mention of flood insurance in advertising (e.g., Yellow Pages ad)
- Review flood files in a manner similar to other insurance lines
- When developing a proposal for a client, include a quote on flood insurance

Adjusting Flood Losses In addition to marketing the program, producers are also responsible for handling the initial reporting and assigning of losses to qualified flood adjusters. A qualified flood adjuster is one who has (1) prior flood adjusting experience, *or* (2) two years of wind and water adjusting experience, *or* (3) five years of general property adjusting experience, and in all cases, (4) the competency to execute small property damage estimates (up to $3,000) without resorting to a separate appraiser for such work.

On those occasions where there is serious flooding, the National Flood Insurance Program may elect to set up an on-site adjusting office. In those cases, the producer would receive the notice of loss from the insured and send the notice to the NFIP storm office for the actual assigning of the adjustment.

Mandatory Purchase Requirement When Congress passed the Flood Disaster Protection Act of 1973, it decreed that any loan secured by real property located in an area identified as flood-prone and within a community participating in the National Flood Insurance Program must be covered by flood insurance. While the law brings almost every type of secured loan under this heading, the most common is a mortgage secured at the sale of a building. The lending institution will normally require the bare minimum of flood coverage for the loan and then only on the building.

For the producer, this represents a unique opportunity. The producer should encourage the client to protect more than the lender's investment with higher limits on contents. While the flood insurance policy does not automatically provide contents coverage, the most severe loss exposure to flood is not to the building but to the personal property within.

PACKAGING PERSONAL LINES COVERAGE

The development of multiple-lines packages, in both personal and commercial lines provides producers with powerful new sales tools. The availability of the packages results in many people buying coverages that they have never bought before. Before the advent of the homeowners policies, few families purchased the residence theft policy or the comprehensive personal liability policy. There was a tendency for those families with greater loss exposure to buy the coverage while those with moderate exposures did not. After the introduction of homeowners policies, virtually all families bought the theft and liability coverages because they were included automatically in the homeowners policy. This widespread purchase of additional coverages is advantageous to both producers and insurers: for producers, it means higher premiums and commissions and fewer uninsured losses for their clients; for insurers, it means less adverse selection with consequent lower loss ratios.

Producers and insurers also find that package policies reduce clerical costs. Instead of issuing, billing, and accounting for three policies, these procedures can now be performed for a single policy. Package policies provide coverage at lower cost and alert producers use this advantage to persuade clients to let the producers handle entire accounts, rather than buying several policies from several producers.

The packaging concept has now evolved to the point where insurers are combining auto, homeowners, umbrella, and other personal lines forms into a single package with the insured receiving a discount for placing his business with a single company. In addition, companies are broadening the protection offered by this "second stage package" as an inducement to sell the concept.

The advantages to producers of the simple and flexible "second stage package" are numerous. An entire account can be written rather than just the auto or homeowners. Producers can either offer clients a discount on existing policies or, for the same premium, offer broader coverages by using discounts on existing policies to buy an umbrella, for example. A producer can bill for one policy and have one file per client with common expiration dates. Further, it is difficult for a competitor to compare rates and coverages since most competitors do not have a similar product to sell.

From a professional liability standpoint, packaging tends to cover exposures otherwise not treated, reducing the producer's errors and omissions exposure. For example, one second stage package offers a common limit of liability for both the auto liability and for the personal liability provided under the homeowners. Since most people carry higher limits on their auto policy than on the liability portion of the homeowners, this common limit usually serves to provide higher liability limits for premises than would have otherwise been provided. Further, there always exists the possibility that coverage could be provided by both the homeowners and the personal auto policy if individually written. Laws do vary from state to state and some gray areas in coverage do exist. Is a moped a motor vehicle? Is unloading the car an "auto" activity or a "homeowners" activity? Does the client really want two different adjusters involved in a claim? All these questions are raised by losses involving two different coverages placed with different companies. A "second stage package" alleviates these problems.

But the most powerful reasons for producers to use a second stage package are greater account control and persistency. A producer who uses second stage packages exclusively for personal lines sales reports 95 percent renewal for this block of business. His personal lines package accounts average $1,800 in premium and 4 out of every 5 not renewed were insureds moving out of the producer's territory.

Innovations in "second stage packages" continue as more insurers begin to compete for this business. For example, mortgage cancellation life insurance has been added to the package. These all-lines packages may have to await further changes in some state insurance regulatory laws, however.

Producers must be constantly alert to be aware of these changes and to evaluate the potential effects of the changes on their clients. The producers who are first to bring these new policies to the attention of their clients are likely to be the ones who write the business and cash the commission checks.

Checkpoints

1. How is aircraft insurance (a) similar to or (b) different from automobile insurance?
2. How does a personal umbrella policy differ from the comprehensive personal liability policy?
3. To whom may flood insurance be sold?
4. What is the difference between the regular program and the emergency program?
5. Explain the advantages of personal lines package policies to (a) the producer, (b) the producer's client, and (c) insurers.

SUMMARY

Virtually any producer can handle the common exposures for most individuals and families. The quality that distinguishes a "good" producer from an "ordinary" producer is the knowledge and ability to identify the uncommon loss exposures to which a particular client is subject, and to properly design an insurance program to cope with those exposures.

This chapter has dealt with the means for insuring some of the less common loss exposures to which many individuals and families are subject. A knowledge of these insurance forms and exposures will help a good producer to get new accounts, protect existing accounts from competition, and write more premiums and earn more commissions in the personal lines field.

CHAPTER 7

Life Insurance

INTRODUCTION

Life insurance offers a large market that, with intelligent planning, can bring substantial commission dollars to producers who sell life insurance. The approach to life insurance sales need not always be an intricate, estate planning approach. Rather, the approach should suit the producer's style of selling and fit into the producer's overall marketing plans. This chapter will acquaint the property-liability producer with the major types of life insurance products and ways to sell them.

Why Sell Life Insurance?

The sale of life insurance fits the concept of risk management. Life insurance is a vital component of total account selling. It suits the buying desires and patterns of Americans. It can put additional dollars in a producer's pocket.

Risk Management and Life Insurance From the standpoint of risk management, the producer can approach life insurance sales in much the same way the producer sells property-liability insurance—by identifying exposures to loss and recommending products to treat these exposures. The more closely a producer can tie an exposure to a product, the easier the sale.

Two methods of life insurance exposure identification will be introduced—the *human life value* method and the *needs approach.* Hybrids of these two can be developed by producers. The discussion of life insurance products to meet the exposure will be on the most common life insurance products available. Social security, group life, credit life, or industrial (home service life) will not be discussed.

Account Selling and Life Insurance It is widely held that the one-policy customer is the least profitable and probably the most "troublesome" client. Life insurance can be used to convert one-policy customers to multiple-policy customers. The sale of life insurance to an existing personal or commercial lines client will also generate greater premiums on that account. Life insurance may turn an unprofitable or marginal account into a profitable one. Finally, since there is an array of "limited peril" health insurance coverages available within property-liability policies (medical payments in automobile and homeowners, for instance), selling life and health insurance allows better coordination of benefits and perhaps can save a client premium dollars.

Consumers *want* to meet all of their insurance needs through one agent and through one group of insurers under a common management. A study of consumers conducted by Lou Harris asked this question:

> Suppose you could obtain all your personal insurance from one agent—would you prefer to buy your personal insurance policies from that one agent, or would you prefer to have more than one agent, depending on the type of insurance you are buying?

Responses to this question were analyzed this way:

> Fifty-six percent of the participants would prefer to buy all of their personal insurance from one agent, while 44 percent prefer multiple agents . . . the future prospects for those agents who are (or will be) in a position to provide "onestop" shopping look excellent. . . . As many as 44 percent of those who now deal with two or more agents report that they would prefer to deal with only one agent. On the other hand, only 22 percent of the respondents who are now dealing with one agent (plus a small number who currently do not deal with any agents) desire to have multiple agents. The conclusion is that the concept of "onestop" shopping for personal insurance is indeed a popular one from the consumer's standpoint and will command a prominent position in the future auto and homeowners insurance marketing system.

This analysis also concludes, ". . . the vast majority (87 percent) of those who want one agent also prefer one company."[1]

Life Insurance and the Producer

Property-liability insurers, through their life affiliates, are developing life insurance sales. Property-liability companies are far more apt to grant favors (accommodations) to producers if significant amounts of life insurance are produced. Yet there is a reluctance on the part of some property-liability producers to enter into the life business. With an understanding of the technical differences between life and nonlife insurance, adequate sales skills, and use of agency client files, there is no reason to ignore life business.

THE NATURE OF LIFE AND HEALTH INSURANCE

Life insurance is usually associated with dying. The association is unfortunate because the life insurance product is used to treat two exposures—dying too soon and living too long. Health insurance can help an insured pay medical bills and supplement income during the recovery period.

The Life Cycle and Mortality

Life Cycle The human life cycle can be described as three economic phases. Most people are "net consumers" until ages eighteen to twenty-two, during the "education" phase of their lives. The work or "net savings" phase runs from the end of the education phase until retirement, about age sixty-five. With retirement, people become net consumers again. During the working phase, people "build surplus." That is, they consume less than they earn. The total assets built in this manner are called the *estate.* Some people want to build large estates to pass on to their heirs, to a charity, to a church, or others. Some people only desire to build an estate big enough to "live on" until they die. In either case, life insurance can be an important part of that estate.

Mortality The "mortality" table excerpted in Exhibit 7-1 shows, for a group of 10 million males at age zero, how many begin each year alive, the number who die during that year, the probability of dying in that year, and the probability of living through that year.

Most of the published mortality tables for life insurance are not used to establish rates for life insurance. That simple fact cannot be overstressed. Mortality tables with the word Commissioners in their titles are used in the life insurance business *exclusively* to establish the liabilities of a life insurer for statutory accounting purposes. The actual rates a company charges are developed from its own mortality experience, the experience of companies operating in a similar manner, or from an expected mortality experience for the company.

Life Insurance Is Not Necessarily Insurance

An insurance plan provides a payment only if a loss occurs. A financial plan accumulates assets whether or not a loss occurs. Term life insurance, plans that cover a limited time period, such as five-year term, twenty-year term, and so on, are true insurance plans. If death does not occur within the prescribed period, the policy does not pay. Insurance plans that pay no matter when death occurs combine a true

Exhibit 7-1
Except from the Commissioners 1958 Standard Ordinary (CSO) Mortality Table (Male Lives)

Age at Beginning of Year	Number Living at Beginning of Designated Year (lx)	Number Dying During Designated Year (dx)	Yearly Probability of Dying (qx)	Yearly Probability of Surviving (px)	Age at Beginning of Year	Number Living at Beginning of Designated Year (lx)	Number Dying During Designated Year (dx)	Yearly Probability of Dying (qx)	Yearly Probability of Surviving (px)
0	10,000,000	70,800	0.00708	0.99292	51	8,689,404	79,160	0.00911	0.99089
1	9,929,200	17,475	0.00176	0.99824	52	8,610,244	85,758	0.00996	0.99004
2	9,911,725	15,066	0.00152	0.99848	53	8,524,486	92,832	0.01089	0.98911
3	9,896,659	14.449	0.00146	0.99854	60	7,698,698	156,592	0.02034	0.97966
10	9,805,870	11,865	0.00121	0.99879	61	7,542,106	167,736	0.02224	0.97776
11	9,794,005	12,047	0.00123	0.99877	62	7,374,370	179,271	0.02431	0.97569
12	9,781,958	12,325	0.00126	0.99874	69	5,859,253	267,241	0.04561	0.95439
20	9,664,994	17,300	0.00179	0.99821	70	5,592,012	278,426	0.04979	0.95021
21	9,647,694	17,655	0.00183	0.99817	71	5,313,586	287,731	0.05415	0.94585
22	9,630,039	17,912	0.00186	0.99814	72	5,025,855	294,766	0.05865	0.94135
23	9,612,127	18,167	0.00189	0.99811	73	4,731,089	299,289	0.06326	0.93674
32	9,439,447	21,239	0.00225	0.99775	82	2,058,541	265,902	0.12917	0.87083
33	9,418,208	21,850	0.00232	0.99768	83	1,792,639	249,858	0.13938	0.86062
34	9,396,358	22,551	0.00240	0.99760	84	1,542,781	231,433	0.15001	0.84999
42	9,173,375	38,253	0.00417	0.99583	92	272,552	72,480	0.26593	0.73407
43	9,135,122	41,382	0.00453	0.99547	93	200,072	57,881	0.28930	0.71070
44	9,093,740	44,741	0.00492	0.99508	94	142,191	45,026	0.31666	0.68334
45	9,048,999	48,412	0.00535	0.99465	95	97,165	34,128	0.35124	0.64876
46	9,000,587	52,473	0.00583	0.99417	96	63,037	25,250	0.40056	0.59944
47	8,948,114	56,910	0.00636	0.99364	97	37,787	18,456	0.48842	0.51158
48	8,891,204	61,794	0.00695	0.99305	98	19,331	12,916	0.66815	0.33185
49	8,829,410	67,104	0.00760	0.99240	99	6,415	6,415	1.00000	0.00000
50	8,762,306	72,902	0.00832	0.99168					

insurance plan with a financial plan. That is, they act as insurance plans *if* the insured dies prior to completing a financial plan. In addition, however, the insured is investing in a plan that will accumulate a determined amount if the insured does not die. It is similar to buying a house.

Permanent Life Insurance Compared with a Home Mortgage In effect, the home buyer says to a mortgage company, "I want a $100,000 house. I do not have the money to buy it. I will put $20,000 down, and pay you $X per month for thirty years. At the end of the thirty years, I will own my house." In effect, the purchase of permanent life insurance says to the insurer, "I want $100,000 no matter when I die. Here is $Y per year. If I reach age 100 (or some other age), pay me the $100,000. If I die before that, give it to my beneficiary." In both cases, equity in an asset is being built up over a period of time.

Life Insurance Rates The development of life insurance rates takes into account mortality, interest, expenses, and profit (including contingencies). Despite the 1958 CSO Table's exclusive use as a valuation table, it will be used here to show how rates are developed.

Pure Death Costs. If an insurer excluded interest, expenses, and profits, the life insurance rate would reflect only pure death costs. The formula for determining the pure death cost per year is: the probability of dying during the year times the face amount of the policy. For all calculations, the face amount will be assumed to be $1,000. The probability of dying is calculated by dividing the number of individuals who die during a year by the number of individuals alive at the beginning of the year. For simplicity, it will also be assumed that premiums are paid in advance and that any death benefits are paid at the end of the year. With these assumptions, the pure death cost for a one-year policy for a male age zero is:

$$\text{Probability of Dying} \times \text{Face} = \text{Pure Death Cost}$$

$$\frac{70{,}8000}{10{,}000{,}000} \times \$1{,}000 = \$7.08$$

The pure death cost for the male age zero is $7.08.

Based again on a one-year policy, the pure death cost for a male age fifty would be:

$$\frac{72{,}902}{8{,}762{,}306} \times \$1{,}000 = \$8.32$$

Net Premiums. No life insurer sells a pure death cost policy. The next step in the ratemaking process is to develop *net premiums* or premiums that also assume an interest rate. Once a premium is received, it can be invested. Since the assumption here is that death claims are not paid until the end of the year, the insurer has the funds invested for a full year. Assume that the insurer earns only 5 percent on invested funds. The net premium for the two policies illustrated would be reduced by interest earnings. According to *present value* tables, if 95.2 cents are invested at 5 percent for a year, the account will contain exactly $1.00 at the end of the year. Therefore, multiplying the pure death cost by 0.952 will give the amount of money necessary at the beginning of the year to pay the $1,000 death claims at the end of the year. The net premium for the one-year policies would be:

$$\text{Probability of Dying} \times \text{Face} \times \text{Discount Factor} = \text{Net Premium}$$

Male age zero:

$$\frac{70{,}800}{10{,}000{,}000} \times \$1{,}000 \times 0.952 = \$6.74$$

Male age fifty:

$$\frac{72{,}902}{8{,}762{,}306} \times \$1{,}000 \times 0.952 = \$7.92$$

The life insurance rate is reduced by including an assumed interest rate on premiums received.

An additional amount to cover such expenses as commissions, medical examinations, premium taxes, home office expenses, a level of insurer profit, and the like, is added to the net premiums.

For life insurance policies that cover more than one year, the process is more complicated, but similar. Each individual year's premiums are summed into a *single premium.*

The single premium is the amount of money necessary today to be sure all benefits will be paid at the insured's death. The single premium is "too high" for most insureds to pay, so it is spread or leveled over a premium paying period.

To determine a level (annual) premium for the premium paying period, actuaries must consider that some insureds will die and not make some future payments and that interest on those premiums will be lost. The resultant level premium is higher than the pure death costs for the early years of the policy and lower than pure death costs in later years.

The single premium mathematically represents an amount the insured should pay for life insurance for the period of protection. The single premium is the *present value of future benefits* (PVFB) promised by the life insurance policy. The leveled premiums are mathematically equal to the single premium and are also known as the *present value of future premiums* (PVFP).

At the beginning of the policy, the present value of future benefits equals the present value of future premiums (PVFB = PVFP). As premiums are paid, death becomes more likely, raising the PVFB. Future premiums are fewer in number, lowering PVFP. The life company must therefore have a balancing figure, called the reserve, which is the difference between PVFB and PVFP, or PVFB − PVFP = Reserve, as shown in Exhibit 7-2. The reserve closely approximates the gradual accumulation of the estate (cash value) mentioned earlier.

Uses of Life Insurance Reasons for buying life insurance vary with the individual. Reasons include paying final expenses, providing income to the surviving spouse and children, making sure the house is paid for, having money for children's education, leaving money to a charity, a school, a fraternity, a political party, or any of hundreds of others. The sales key will be to fit a life insurance policy to a particular need of the insured. It may be as simple as a mortgage redemption policy or it may be a complicated estate plan attempting to distribute assets to heirs, while minimizing income, estate, and inheritance taxes, and leaving some assets to favorite organizations.

Selecting the market to sell is vital. Selling mortgage redemption life insurance requires little technical knowledge. Preparing and selling a complex estate plan may require a knowledge of tax laws and the need to coordinate life insurance with other assets of the insured through attorneys and accountants.

There are business as well as personal reasons for purchasing life insurance. Perhaps the most obvious business reason is to provide insurance on the key individuals in corporations. Imagine a company dependent on the vision, creativity, or skill of one individual—the early days at Polaroid or Walt Disney Studios, for instance. The untimely death of Dr. Land or Walt Disney would have created severe problems for those companies. By purchasing a substantial amount of life insurance, the companies could have a cash cushion to keep "the ship afloat" while new creative people were found and trained. Business uses of life insurance are discussed in AAI 82.

Selling life insurance requires matching the need of the individual or business to the product being sold. The sale of life insurance to

Exhibit 7-2
Policy Reserve Development

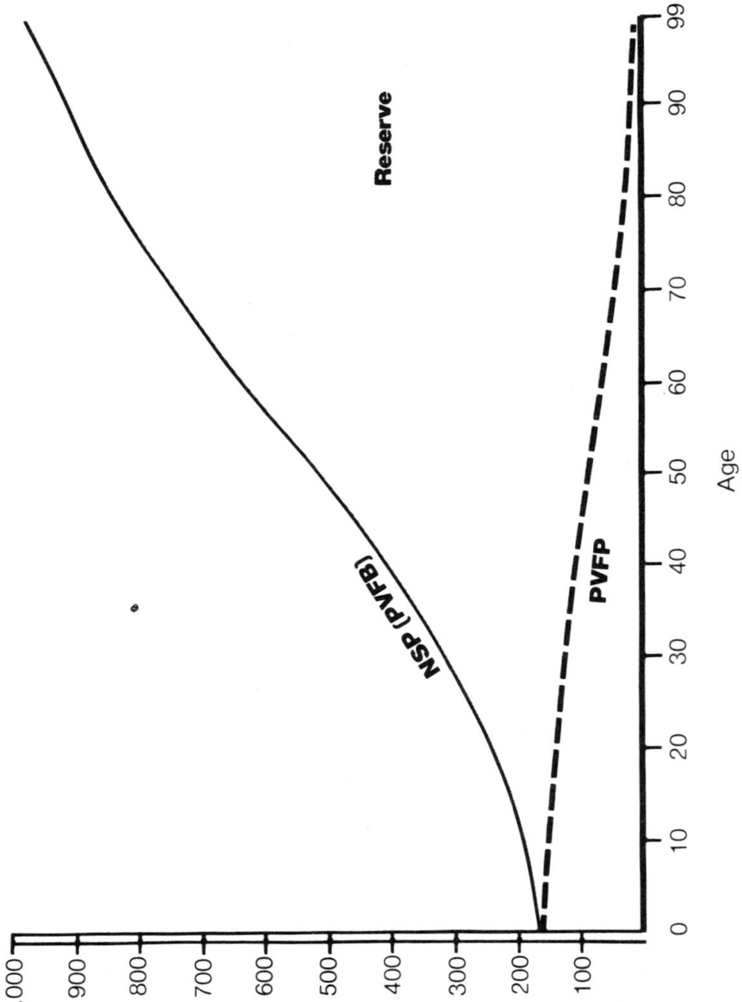

businesses is more complicated. That is why most life affiliates of property-liability companies provide the services of "life field personnel." The life representative can make the sales presentation using the expertise of his home office and his or her own personal experience.

Health Risks and Morbidity

It is likely that prospects can envision the need for health insurance more easily than the need for life insurance. When an illness strikes or an accident occurs, the person involved faces continuing expenses of maintaining a family while ill or injured, increased costs in the form of medical bills and, perhaps, a reduction in income.

Nature of Losses and Perils Health insurance can be subdivided into categories based on losses or perils covered.

Losses Covered. Exhibit 7-3 shows one potential set of categories. Health losses can include the replacement of lost or reduced income, the financing of extra expenses, or both. The need for income replacement can arise from temporary or permanent disabilities. Extra expenses can be divided into hospital expenses, surgical expenses, medical expenses, and major medical expenses. While these four categories are not of great significance, they represent the four types of health insurance

Hospital expenses include costs for services rendered by or in the hospital. They include charges for room and board, laboratory fees, X-rays, and the like. They may also include such nonhospital expenses as ambulance charges.

Surgical expenses are those related to surgical procedures only. *Medical expenses* are nonsurgical, physician-related expenses. Usually, the surgeon or attending physician charges for visits to the patient before and after an operation. These medical expenses usually are not as great as hospital or surgical expenses.

The final form of health coverage, which has been growing in importance, is *major medical expense.* Historically, major medical was sold with a high limit, a large deductible (to have been met by the other three types of expense policies) and a co-payment (with an 80/20 co-payment, the insurance company pays 80 percent and the insured 20 percent of covered expenses). The policy was designed for catastrophic illnesses and covered hospital, surgical, and medical expenses not covered by or in excess of hospital, surgical, and medical expenses. Today, major medical policies have fewer internal limits, a significantly lower deductible, and a smaller co-payment. Insurers and insureds have found that major medical insurance is more efficient and offers broader

Exhibit 7-3
Categories of Health-Related Loss Exposures

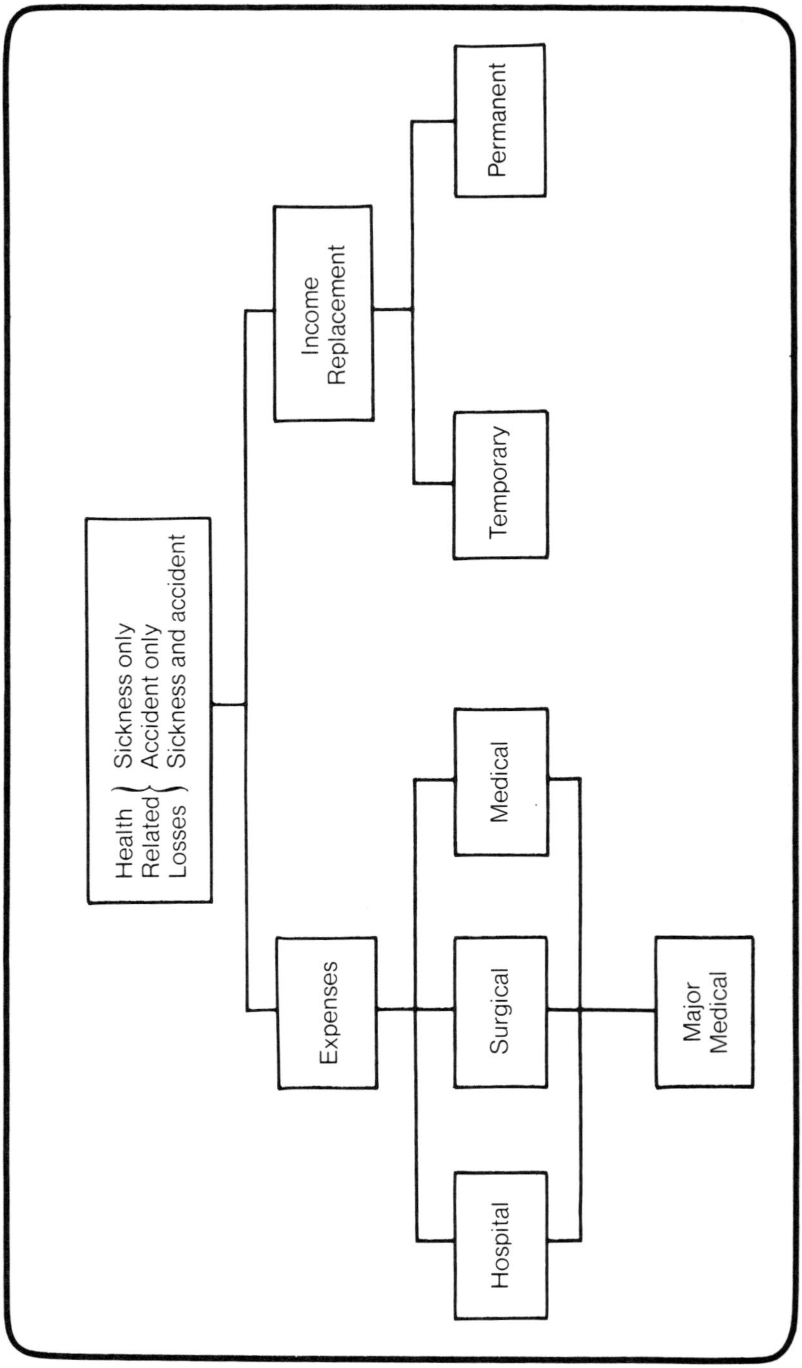

coverage in one policy than maintaining four separate policies for four separate types of loss.

Perils Covered. All of the policies mentioned could have been written to cover sickness only, accident only, or both. Today, the individual health insurance market is not as broad as in the past. Most people obtain group coverage as an employee benefit. But, occasionally, individual health insurance is needed and producers should be willing and able to write such business.

Health Insurance and Sales Opportunities The health insurance prospect needs to protect income and provide for the extra expenses associated with a sickness or accident. Health insurance should reflect income levels, relative medical expense levels in the area, and other applicable benefits or policies the insured may have. For sales to businesses, the group insurance market as an employee benefit is the largest and most competitive. But just as life insurance can be used as an additional benefit for the key employee, health insurance can be used as an additional benefit to help retain that employee. Health insurance can also be used to fund a "disability buy out." In partnerships and closely held corporations it is important to "buy out" the deceased's interest in the firm. Also, it is important to buy out the partner or owner who is totally and completely disabled so that he or she does not act as a drag on the income or prospects of the firm and so that new employees can be brought in to handle those aspects of the business the disabled associate handled.

Generally, the market for individual health insurance is small due to the vast number of people covered under employer-employee group insurance plans. With the expansion of the group technique, even small businesses (fewer than twenty-five employees) have access to health insurance for their employees. However, there are some occupations that do not have group health coverage. Producers who wish to sell significant amounts of health insurance should either become "experts" and work the group insurance market or find markets for good individual health insurance and sell to those without group insurance. Typically, the nongroup market includes farmers, tradesmen, owners of and employees in small companies, or the business health insurance market in which health insurance can be used to fund the disability buyouts.

MEASURING LIFE AND HEALTH INSURANCE NEEDS

In some areas of the insurance business, measuring loss exposures is relatively simple. But how does the producer answer the life insurance prospect who asks, "How much life insurance do I need?" The answers can vary from "Enough to bury you" to "We would have to do a complete estate analysis to determine the answer." Rules of thumb are available, typically ranging from three to five times income. But there are two basic methods for measuring life insurance needs: the *human life value approach* and the *needs approach*. Both can be valuable sales tools. Measuring health insurance needs is more intricate and is not discussed in detail here.

The Human Life Value Approach

Ingredients The *human life value approach* was first described by Solomon S. Huebner, the father of insurance education and founder of The American College and the CLU designation. The human life value approach is a mathematical model, a tool. Like any tool, its effectiveness will depend on how it is used and the validity of the assumptions used. The necessary ingredients for the model are:

1. Average expected income during the working period.
2. The time horizon, or expected working life.
3. Costs of "self maintenance."
4. An interest rate that could be earned, on average, over a long period of time.

Using these four bits of data, the human life value can be determined. But the human life value is just the beginning point which is necessary for determining how much life insurance is needed. From the human life value, current income-producing assets must be subtracted along with the present value of any assets that would be available at the insured's death. The human life value approach can be used in some markets as a powerful sales tool.

An Example The human life value concept considers the human being as a "machine." The human life value is a device that mathematically converts the output of the life (machine) into a "bundle of cash." Because the mechanics of the human life value give an aura of precision, an understanding of the assumptions or subjective measures is vital to the sales presentation. Assume a prospect named Franklin Amour, age thirty-five, is an engineer currently earning $40,000 a year. Frank asks how much life insurance he needs.

The first bit of information needed is Frank's average expected income until retirement. Frank estimates that until retirement he realistically expects to average $55,000 per year. He anticipates working full-time only until age sixty-five. That gives him thirty years in which to earn his $55,000 per year average income. The next bit of information is perhaps the toughest to determine—costs of self maintenance.

The human life value approach attempts to find the amount of annual income that is surplus to the individual—in this case, the excess above what Frank would consume himself. The surplus is the money that goes to the rest of the family and helps determine the overall standard of living for the individual and the family. The surplus will include amounts spent on education for children, automobiles, vacations, clothing, and food for everyone in the family except Frank. It is this "surplus" figure that determines whether or not Frank's financial plans will be met. The items to include in "costs of self maintenance" are any money Frank spends on his portion of housing (he could live less expensively by himself), his clothing, food, the portion of his salary that goes for FICA (social security or OASDHI), federal, state, and local taxes, and all other expenses to maintain Frank as a productive asset.

Perhaps the best way for a producer to determine self maintenance expenses is to ask the prospect to project that figure in percentage terms: "Frank, how much of your income goes to support yourself?" The percentage of gross income Frank brings home is the figure with which to start. His personal expenses and life insurance premiums can be deducted from gross income and restated in percentage terms. Frank believes that 40 percent of his income is "consumed" and the 60 percent available for the family is the "surplus."

To calculate human life value, it is also necessary to ask, "What interest rate could your family consistently earn, with adequate concern for safety of principal, should you not be around to invest for them?" There is no single correct answer to this question. Frank's wife could be a financial wizard, able to earn 12 to 15 percent or more over a long period of time. On the other hand, the family may be conservative, relying totally on accounts in banks or accounts in savings and loan associations. In the latter case, assuming a large sum of money and use of longer term "investment" type savings certificates, they could earn between 5 and 9 percent.

Frank anticipates having an estate in six figures and will use the investment services of a trust department of a bank. He therefore predicts a 7 percent long-term interest rate.

Exhibit 7-4 details the questions and answers used to determine Frank Amour's human life value and life insurance needs.

The next part of the human life value approach is purely mechanical. It involves taking the given information, placing it into the mathematical model, "turning the crank," and receiving the answer. To determine Frank's "surplus," subtract self maintenance expenses from

Exhibit 7-4
Frank Amour's Human Life Value Assumptions

1.	Average expected income	$55,000
2.	Time to retirement	30 years
3.	Cost of "self maintenance"	40 percent
4.	Interest rate	7 percent

"average" income. Since 40 percent is self consumed, 60 percent of $55,000, or $33,000, is "surplus."

The human life value will determine the value *today* of cash that is flowing from the "Frank Machine" in the future. The mathematical table to use is a *present value of an annuity table.* An annuity table is used because the figure to be worked with is an assumed, static flow of cash—$33,000 per year—for a finite period of time—30 years. This particular table recognizes that the income stream over the next thirty years is not worth 30 × $33,000, because one dollar today is worth more than one dollar expected next year.

Exhibit 7-5 contains the array of numbers necessary to use given the 30-year time horizon and 7 percent interest rate. In the "7%" column and the "30" year row, the factor to use is 12.409. Multiplying this annuity factor times the $33,000 ($33,000 × 12.409) results in $409,497. This is Frank's human life value. To state it differently, Frank's family would be *financially indifferent* to having $409,497 today in an account earning 7 percent and drawing $33,000 per year from that amount for 30 years or having Frank generate a surplus of $33,000 a year for the next 30 years, when the account will be at a zero balance. Emotions do not play a part in the determination of a human life value. The family would be in the identical *financial* position in either case. As a money machine, Frank is worth $409,497 to his family.

Since the family needs $409,497 today or Frank alive and working for the next thirty years, life insurance needs can now be determined. Any amount of current life insurance is deducted along with the social security benefits. Any savings accounts and investments are deducted along with the present value of income that would continue if Frank died (income from trust funds, perhaps). Subtracting these amounts from the human life value reveals the amount of life insurance that Frank needs.

To complete this illustration, assume Frank has $50,000 of group life insurance from his employer, an additional $50,000 of individual life insurance. Frank's social security benefits, payable to his wife until the youngest child (age 4) is 18 would average $1,000 a month. The Amours have $5,000 in the bank and $12,000 in company stock. Social security

Exhibit 7-5
Present Value Interest Factors for a One-Dollar Annuity*

Year	5%	6%	7%	8%	9%	10%
1	0.952	0.943	0.935	0.926	0.917	0.909
2	1.859	1.833	1.808	1.783	1.759	1.736
3	2.723	2.673	2.624	2.577	2.531	2.487
4	3.546	3.465	3.387	3.312	3.240	3.170
5	4.329	4.212	4.100	3.993	3.890	3.791
6	5.076	4.917	4.767	4.623	4.486	4.355
7	5.786	5.582	5.389	5.206	5.033	4.868
8	6.463	6.210	5.971	5.747	5.535	5.335
9	7.108	6.802	6.515	6.247	5.995	5.759
10	7.722	7.360	7.024	6.710	6.418	6.145
11	8.306	7.887	7.499	7.139	6.805	6.495
12	8.863	8.384	7.943	7.536	7.161	6.814
13	9.394	8.853	8.358	7.904	7.487	7.103
14	9.899	9.295	8.746	8.244	7.786	7.367
15	10.380	9.712	9.108	8.560	8.061	7.606
16	10.838	10.106	9.447	8.851	8.313	7.824
17	11.274	10.477	9.763	9.122	8.544	8.022
18	11.690	10.828	10.059	9.372	8.756	8.201
19	12.085	11.158	10.336	9.604	8.950	8.365
20	12.462	11.470	10.954	9.818	9.129	8.514
21	12.821	11.764	10.836	10.017	9.292	8.649
22	13.163	12.042	11.061	10.201	9.442	8.772
23	13.489	12.303	11.272	10.371	9.580	8.883
24	13.799	12.550	11.469	10.529	9.707	8.985
25	14.094	12.783	11.654	10.675	9.823	9.077
30	15.373	13.765	12.409	11.258	10.274	9.427
35	16.374	14.498	12.948	11.655	10.567	9.644
40	17.159	15.046	13.332	11.925	10.757	9.779
45	17.774	15.456	13.606	12.108	10.881	9.863
50	18.256	15.762	13.801	12.234	10.962	9.915

*Reprinted with permission from Lawrence J. Bitman, *Principles of Managerial Finance* (New York: Harper & Row, 1976), p. A-14.

Exhibit 7-6
Calculating Frank Amour's Life Insurance Needs

Average Annual Income		$ 55,000
Less: 40% self maintenance (0.4 x $40,000)		22,000
Average Surplus		$ 33,000
Present Value Factor at 7%, 30 years		12.409
Human Life Value		$ 409,497
Less:		
Current Life Insurance	$100,000	
Savings	5,000	
Investments	12,000	
Social Security (OASDHI) $1,000/month at 7%, 14 years ($12,000 x 8.746)	104,952	$221,952
Life Insurance Needs		$ 187,545

would provide $12,000 a year for 14 years. The present value of that is $12,000 times 8.746 (7% column, 14 years) or $104,952. Adding the present value of social security to Frank's other assets (including life insurance) yields a total of $221,952 that would be available today. Frank's human life value was 409,497. Frank's life insurance needs are $187,545. This is the additional amount of cash Frank's family would need if he should die tomorrow to replace the income that Frank would have generated during his expected working years. The calculations are shown in Exhibit 7-6.

At this point, the producer could bring out an application and say, "Frank, should we make it exactly $187,545 or would you prefer $190,000?" From this point, Frank's real interest could be determined.

Some Key Points A couple of points should be kept in mind when using the human life value approach. All of the data used should be based on the client's estimates.

Who Makes Assumptions? To determine a prospect's life insurance needs, producers should ask questions and describe the parameters within which responses to the questions should fall. But producers should not supply the answers. There is sound psychology behind these statements. The amount of life insurance an individual needs should be determined by the individual. It should be the individual's plan, not the producer's. Actively involving the client and forcing the client to supply all of the answers makes the plan the client's. As such, the client is more likely to accept the final answer as his or her own and buy whatever amount of insurance is suggested by the human life value approach. If the producer supplies answers, or injects any answers into the mathematics, the plan becomes less the client's and, thus, easier for the client to reject. The producer should:

1. present the approach and explain its logic,
2. ask the questions,
3. provide any "technical" assistance by suggesting what is involved in the answer,
4. compute the mathematical portions in the client's presence,
5. show the answer and suggest policy alternatives to the client, and
6. let the final and all intermediate decisions rest with the client.

Importance of Assumptions. Mistakes or changes in assumptions can change the results significantly. Suppose Frank's projected "true average income" proves incorrect by $5,000. That would mean his human life value is incorrect by $62,045 (12.409 × $5,000). If Frank's estimate is too high, his life insurance needs decrease by that amount; his life insurance needs increase by that amount if he underestimates. With a present value factor of 12.409, the estimate will vary by $12,409 for each thousand dollar average income variance.

If Frank's estimate of "interest rate" is incorrect, the figures change substantially. Exhibit 7-7 shows the results if the estimated interest rate were incorrect by two percentage points, either high or low. A 2 percent *downward* variation in the interest rate results in a need for an additional $83,976 of life insurance. A 2 percent *upward* variation would result in a decrease of $58,935 in life insurance needed. The interest rate change affected two different figures. The present value of future income and the present value of OASDHI benefits change *in the opposite direction of the interest rate.*

The final factor is the time horizon. Suppose Frank really plans to retire at an age five years earlier or later than he first admitted. Exhibit 7-5, the present value table, shows that the factor changes −0.755 if Frank really retires at age sixty and changes +0.539 if he retires at age seventy. The changes in the amount of life insurance needed become $24,915 less or $17,787 greater if he retires at sixty or seventy respectively.

A change in the "cost of self maintenance" would also change the resultant figures. The point is that if the life insurance needs determined are to be accurate, the assumptions must be as accurate as possible.

Exhibit 7-7
The Effect of Interest Rate Assumptions on Human Life Value Computations

	5%	7%	9%
Average Income	$ 55,000	$ 55,000	$ 55,000
Average "Surplus"	$ 33,000	$ 33,000	$ 33,000
Present Value Factor of X% for 30 years	15.373	12.409	10.274
Human Life Value	$507,309	$409,497	$339,042
Less:			
Current Life Insurance, Savings, and Investments	117,000	117,000	117,000
	390,309	292,497	222,042
OASDHI	12,000	12,000	12,000
Present Value Factor of X% for 14 years	9.899	8.746	7.786
Less:			
Present Value of Social Security	118,788	104,952	93,432
Life Insurance Needs	$271,521	187,545	128,610
	+83,976 (5%–7%)		−58,935 (7%–9%)

Accuracy of the Human Life Value over Time. At this point, it is relevant to ask how the human life value would change over a period of time. Assume that the interest rate and costs of self maintenance remain the same over time. Other regularly occurring changes would be a decrease in the present value factor caused by a one-year-at-a-time decrease in the time to retirement and an increase each year in the average salary figure. Taking the shortening time horizon first, the impact is almost negligible. Exhibit 7-8 isolates the factor for the present value of an annuity of one dollar for years 25-30. The difference between year 30 and year 29 is only 0.131. This would affect Frank's human life value by decreasing it only $4,323 over the five years. In the 28th year, the reduction in Frank's human life value is only $4,653.

There are two factors at work at the same time that increase the amount of insurance needed. As each year passes, Frank's salary may increase at a rate greater than that anticipated in his projection of average income, thus *increasing the human life value.* The second is a

Exhibit 7-8
Present Value Factor at 7 Percent
for Years 25 to 30

Year	PV Factor
25	11.654
26	11.827
27	11.989
28	12.140
29	12.281
30	12.409

reduction in the amount subtracted from the human life value in the OASDHI account. Remember, OASDHI (social security) is *only* included for fourteen years when Frank is age thirty-five and his youngest child is four. When Frank is thirty-six, his youngest child is five, and the maximum period for social security survivors benefits becomes thirteen years. The difference between the present value factors at years 14 and 13 is 0.387, significantly greater than at years 29 and 30. The OASDHI deduction reduces by \$4,644 (\$12,000 × 0.387), more than offsetting the reduction in the human life value of \$4,323 caused by Frank aging a year. The OASDHI increase in human life value added to an increase in the human life value caused by a greater average income means that Frank's life insurance needs will, if anything, increase. The important thing to remember is that changes in assumptions based on the passage of years when the client is relatively young (more than fifteen years to retirement) basically offset each other.

This analysis is based on the facts and figures of Frank Amour. Changes in his family situation, a new child for instance, would change the figures. Any significant change, like a new job with a large pay increase, will affect the human life value and the resulting life insurance.

Best Prospects for the Human Life Value Approach. The human life value approach appeals to those with a scientific bent. Many people mistrust "mathematical models" and will not respond to the technique. The prospects for the human life value approach are limited. Engineers, accountants, architects, and others familiar with mathematical models are the best prospects. The producer using the technique should be familiar with the theory of the method. An insightful question that cannot be answered by the producer will not generate confidence.

Finally, the producer should be aware of the assumptions implied in the human life value approach.

Checkpoints

1. Explain why it is generally in the producer's best interest to sell life insurance.
2. What facts and assumptions are necessary to calculate the human life value?
3. Explain how an increase (or lengthening) of each of the following changes affects the human life value:
   a. Interest rate
   b. Retirement date
   c. Average annual income
   d. Costs of self maintenance

The Needs Approach

Other sales approaches that can identify the amount of life insurance a prospect should have are just as valid as the human life value method and perhaps easier for the prospect to understand. One comprehensive approach is the *needs approach.* A given fact situation will produce approximately the same result through either the human life value or the needs approach. The needs approach requires less mathematical precision. Also, under the needs approach, policy types can be more accurately fitted to certain needs.

The needs approach requires accurate information and coordination with all of the prospect's financial resources. In other words, the producer still must have an understanding of OASDHI, group insurance, and other financial assets at the disposal of the prospect. Finally, the needs approach can be used in a simple fact-finding interview, or it can be made attractive by use of multiple colored graphs and charts.

As the name indicates, the needs approach centers on what the prospect would like to have happen to the family after the breadwinner's death. The needs approach also focuses on the very real probability that the prospect will live on into retirement.

Need Categories There are many categories established by different writers for the needs approach. All are justifiable and provide opportunities for sales. The need categories considered here include:

1. Needs created by *final expenses*
2. Needs for *readjustment income*
3. Needs for income during *dependency*
4. Needs for *capital*

5. *Retirement needs*

In each category, the prospect reveals the personal need for a sum of money to accomplish the prospect's personal goals. These goals can then be matched with resources available. Any deficiency can be made up with a life insurance product that matches the need. The needs approach contemplates not only using income from various sources, but also using existing capital for current "needs."

Final Expense Needs. The first category in the needs approach is final expenses. Burial expense is the most obvious expense in this category, but there are a host of others. Final medical expenses can exceed funds available from private or group health insurance. There may be a variety of bills to pay that are currently outstanding—credit cards and the like. The goal of this category is to free the family of all short-term consumer debts.

Estimating the size of this "final expense need" is not easy. The cost of a funeral is perhaps the easiest to predict. A producer using this approach would be wise to contact a funeral director to determine what current average costs are and how they have been increasing over the last few years. Clearing up consumer debts may also be reasonably easy to estimate. Final illness expenses are the most difficult to estimate. The prospect cannot possibly know the length of the final illness. A prolonged illness would be more expensive than an accidental death. In any event, it is probably a good idea to encourage the prospect to "guess high." Any money left over could be used as an emergency fund (covered in the capital needs section) or for those ever-present unexpected expenses.

For producers who use life insurance in estate planning, the final expenses could well be the largest item if they are dealing with wealthy people and people who wish to leave a considerable portion of their estate to heirs. The one portion of final illness expenses not yet mentioned is *death taxes.* These are the federal estate and state inheritance (or estate) taxes due within a short period of the time of death. The federal estate tax form must be filed within nine months of death. The tax rate is sharply progressive, as shown in Exhibit 7-9. Use of tax avoidance techniques, like the marital deduction, charitable deductions, and the like, can reduce the impact of the taxes. But the wealthier the individual is and the greater the wealth tied up in illiquid assets, like real estate, the more vital it becomes to have cash generated by life insurance to pay death taxes.

It is common for a forced sale of an asset to bring a low, distressed sale price. There may be a very profitable, highly valuable apartment complex or business in an estate. To have to sell it at a reduced price (while the IRS values it at "normal" market price for estate tax

Exhibit 7-9
Unified Tax Rate Schedule for Federal Gift and Estate Taxes *

If the Amount Is:		Tentative Tax Is:		
From	To	Tax +	%	On Excess Over
0	$ 10,000	0	18	0
$ 10,000	20,000	$ 1,800	20	$ 10,000
20,000	40,000	3,800	22	20,000
40,000	60,000	8,200	24	40,000
60,000	80,000	13,000	26	60,000
80,000	100,000	18,200	28	80,000
100,000	150,000	23,800	30	100,000
150,000	250,000	38,800	32	150,000
250,000	500,000	70,800	34	250,000
500,000	750,000	155,800	37	500,000
750,000	1,000,000	248,300	39	750,000
1,000,000	1,250,000	345,800	41	1,000,000
1,250,000	1,500,000	448,300	43	1,250,000
1,500,000	2,000,000	555,800	45	1,500,000
2,000,000	2,500,000	780,800	49	2,000,000
2,500,000	Up	1,025,800	50	2,500,000

*U.S. Treasury Department, Internal Revenue Service.

purposes) places a double burden on the estate planning process. As a general rule, wealthy people with a desire to leave property to future generations face a growing and permanent need for substantial life insurance to make sure their goals can be achieved. This need correctly falls into the final expense need category. The more successful the prospect, the more likely a sale can be made based on having cash available immediately at death to pay federal estate and state inheritance taxes.

Readjustment Income Needs. Readjustment income is the second need category. Readjustment income is the prospect's current "take home pay" for a period of time sufficient for the family to adjust to the absence of the breadwinner, an amount of money provided to allow a transition from the current income level to a reduced income level. Typically this period of time runs from one to five years. The readjustment period should be long enough to allow as normal a home life as possible. Because many households have two working spouses, the period may be very short. Nonetheless, some male prospects may prefer that their wives (assuming the husband dies first) never need to work. Others would actively encourage work or a return to work as rapidly as possible.

If the prospect is covered by OASDHI, funds from that source may cover the readjustment income needs. Assuming that a husband dies, leaving a wife and two or more children, the survivor's payments can be substantial. With "average monthly earnings" (a social security basis for benefit levels) of $1,000, survivor's benefits would be almost $1,000 per month until the first child reaches eighteen (or twenty-two if the child attends a college or university). If only the wife and one child (under eighteen) survive, survivor's benefits could still be in excess of $800 a month. When the last child reaches eighteen (or twenty-two), *all* survivor's benefits cease until the surviving spouse reaches age sixty.

Dependency Income Needs. The dependency income needs category reflects income required while the children are dependent. The period can run from the end of the readjustment period until the children reach age eighteen or twenty-two. More income is needed while the children are dependent than after they "leave the nest." The income level during the dependency period is usually less than that of the readjustment period, simply because there are fewer dependents, but more than that needed for the surviving spouse while living alone. If the insured does not wish the surviving spouse to work at all, the dependency period runs until his or her retirement. On the other hand, if the surviving spouse has a viable career, the dependency period ends when the youngest child reaches age eighteen or twenty-two.

Ages eighteen or twenty-two are selected because children usually go either to work or to college. If an insured wishes to continue payments while the children are in college, the period runs until the youngest child graduates. If not, it can end at age eighteen. With such a wide variety of possible time periods, it again becomes critical to mention the parameters of the need and let the prospect decide what period to use.

Capital Needs. Capital needs is a catchall for many types of needs that require lump sums of money rather than periodic income. The first category of capital needs is an *emergency fund.* The title is descriptive. The money is ready and available for emergencies—uninsured illnesses, accidents, unforeseen housing needs, and so on. The emergency fund should be established to meet all unexpected events which require ready cash.

Money to pay off a mortgage falls into the capital needs category. In this case, the amount is known or can be easily determined. A lump sum can be set aside and used to pay off the mortgage at once, or it can be used to generate the necessary income to make the periodic mortgage payments.

A capital needs fund can be used for any long-term financial obligation. For example, an insured might have bank loans for tuition of children already in school, and the capital needs fund can cover those obligations (as opposed to credit card debt). Also, it may be that a significant amount of stock was purchased under an option, thrift plan, or in the open market, and the stock was pledged to support a loan. In practice, these types of loans become long-term loans and since they are generally "callable" (due if and when the bank determines), they need the protection of insurance. The capital fund can provide for the payment of loans on a car, boat, or vacation home. Some people have even included $500 a year for twenty years for Christmas and birthday gifts (a nice $10,000 sale).

One other use of the capital fund is to reduce the amount of the dependency income fund. If a lump sum is established here to provide money for college, the length of time necessary for dependency needs may be reduced.

Retirement Needs. The final "need" is very personal and shows the prospect that the producer recognizes that not every insured will die during his or her working life. It is the *retirement fund.* The retirement fund can be a lump sum of money to augment retirement payments from OASDHI, private retirement plans, IRAs, and other savings. The retirement fund stresses that life insurance does not necessarily provide only for others, after the insured dies, but is a valuable asset of the insured that can be called on when life should be easy and cares minimal. The fund may provide money to allow the retired insured to play golf three times a week (insurance has been sold on this exact living benefit of life insurance). The fund can contain extra income for other "nice but not necessary" times. The fund should provide a level of income more than sufficient to survive—that is the goal of OASDHI. The key fact to present to the prospect is that the retirement fund should be sufficient so that the insured can receive the "rewards of labor."

Presentation to Prospects Presenting life insurance needs to prospects based on the needs approach can be simple or complex. The final expense and capital needs categories can be totaled to determine a required lump sum. Readjustment and dependency needs can be stated as continuing income, in dollars per year. These dollar per year figures need to be restated in terms of lump sums through the use of present value tables.

For instance, assume a prospect indicates that the family would need $20,000 per year for a three-year readjustment period. According to Exhibit 7-5, the present value of $1.00 for three years at 6 percent is $2.673. Multiplying 2.673 by $20,000 determines that a $53,460 lump sum would be the equivalent of the desired readjustment income. Dependency income requirements should be treated the same way mathematically. These calculations produce two additional lump sum dollar figures to be added to the capital and final expense needs. The total of these four lump sums indicates the financial needs of the prospect should the prospect die.

Retirement income should also be reduced to a single sum. It should not, however, be added to the other four needs, since retirement income will only be needed if the prospect lives on into retirement. The other four needs are necessary if the prospect dies. Life insurance needs are determined from the first four need categories and *then* compared to total needs, including retirement income.

All available financial resources are subtracted from the total of the first four needs to determine life insurance needs. Some financial resources, such as survivor's benefits from OASDHI, are periodic income figures and must be translated into a lump sum. Other resources will be lump sums and can be totaled immediately.

This same method is used to calculate retirement needs. From the lump sum retirement need, subtract anticipated savings, investments, and retirement income (private and retirement benefits of OASDHI) available at retirement. The result, if a positive number, represents the amount of cash values (explained below) to be accumulated through life insurance.

Sales presentations to prospects can be simple or complex. They can even be fun. For instance, an organization in Ohio developed a "game board" where each of the needs is filled with plastic "gold bars" stacked in specific needs slots. These "stacks of gold" make a great visual impact on the prospect. Further, since prospects are making all of the decisions and piling on the gold bars themselves, it creates a strong commitment to attain the goals. It is very difficult for the prospect to reject an amount of insurance recommended because it is "too much." The producer says, "Fine, here are the needs you anticipated. Where do you want to make the cuts?" The method clearly puts the prospect on notice that the plan is personal and is the prospect's responsibility.

Producer Use of the Needs Approach The needs approach has even greater application for the property-liability producer who does not wish to spend full time or even a significant portion of time on life insurance sales. A producer who recognizes the value of some life insurance sales can use any of the needs categories as a portion of market segmentation plans. Using the "Welcome Wagon approach" suggested in an earlier chapter, the producer can determine the approximate value of the house (if the purchase price is not available) and the approximate down payment, with the balance assumed to be the amount mortgaged. The producer can present a "mortgage cancellation" life insurance policy along with proposals for homeowners and auto insurance. Similarly, the birth of a child can generate a sale that would provide a small amount of life insurance on the child (for the child's final expenses) and also help provide money for the child's education if the child survives. As a final example, personal retirement plans can be funded through the use of life insurance.

A producer interested in using the needs approach or one of its variations should check with the field representatives of life companies. They will have material to help make sales in any or all of the need categories. The field representative can even help on sales calls. The important thing is to find out what is readily available and what will fit into a producer's personal marketing plan. There are specific types of life insurance plans to fit specific needs. These will be introduced in a later section of this chapter.

The Health Insurance Need

For a personal sale of health insurance, two items of information are critical: the income of the prospect and the prospect's existing health insurance. It is likely that a prospect will have some health insurance. It is also likely that the plan the prospect has will not cover all needs. There may be significant gaps that can be filled with private health insurance. The most prominent of those gaps is in the Medicare portion of OASDHI. There are expenses that Medicare does not cover. Health insurance is available to fit those gaps.

In disability income insurance, gaps can also occur. A prospect's employer may have a fine long-term disability plan, beginning six months after disability. Yet the employer may only provide sick leave or other benefits for thirty days. The gap between the first thirty days and the end of the six-month period can be filled.

There are a host of other gap fillers available. There are policies for unmet hospital, surgical, and medical expenses. There are plans to supplement current hospital expense policies, recognizing increasing costs. There are even plans (of marginal usefulness) that can pay substantial sums if one particular disease is incurred. These are usually called "dread disease" policies, picking up their title from the public's dread of such diseases as polio (before the vaccines), cancer, heart attack, and stroke.

To sell health insurance professionally requires more expertise than can be developed through this program. No mention will be made of health insurance marketing methods because of their complexity. Yet producers selling health insurance should know the nature and extent of the health insurance products available. Care must be exercised so that the right health insurance product is sold with the proper provisions to meet the needs of the prospect. It may be a good idea to check any sales ideas or presentations with the life insurance field representative before making a sales presentation.

LIFE INSURANCE PRODUCTS

The goal of this section is not to make the producer a full-time life salesperson, but rather to acquaint the producer with various products commonly available to meet prospects' needs. If the producer needs more knowledge of estate planning or life insurance, other educational courses are available. However, no good sales opportunity should be passed up if it fits a producer's marketing plan.

Types of Life Insurance Policies

Essentially there are only three basic types of life insurance policies—term, whole life (permanent), and pure endowment. All available life insurance is a variation or combination of these three basic types. If the insured's needs are or can be met by a particular hybrid of one of the three basic forms, that hybrid is the product to sell the insured. To apply a product to a need requires an understanding of the basic form, its strengths, and weaknesses.

Term Life Insurance Term life insurance is similar to the other products sold by the property-liability producer. It covers a certain object (the insured), for a certain peril (premature death), for a specific amount (the face of the policy), for a certain period of time:

> Life Insurance Company will pay the life insurance proceeds to the beneficiary promptly upon receiving proof that the Insured died during a term period, if premiums have been paid in accordance with the Premiums section.

Term insurance is temporary life insurance. The use of term insurance should be related to needs that are also temporary. For instance, if a person obtains a five-year loan from the bank to help expand business, it is very appropriate to cover that five-year loan with a term life insurance policy for a five-year period. Similarly, if the prospect perceives a need to cover a mortgage to make sure the family has a place to live should premature death occur, a term life insurance policy for the length of the mortgage and related to the amount of the mortgage is appropriate.

On the other hand, suppose a prospect sincerely desires to leave $25,000 to her favorite charity. This desire is permanent in that the prospect wants to accomplish this goal no matter when death occurs. A term life insurance policy is then inappropriate unless the prospect, at the same time, is building specific assets that will pass to the charity at death.

Temporary needs should be covered with temporary life insurance. One exception is when the prospect cannot afford permanent insurance. In that case, it is better to cover the need, even temporarily, rather than to leave it unaddressed. The prospect in that case should clearly understand the obligation to change the insurance to a permanent form when finances allow.

Permanent Life Insurance Permanent life insurance (whole life) is coverage until death. Every permanent life policy will eventually mature in a claim. That fact makes some "internal" features of a permanent life insurance policy different from those of a term life policy. Restated, the probability of a death claim for an insured with a permanent life policy is 1.0.

Permanent life insurance is the only device which is specifically designed to financially provide for eventual death. In effect, the insured says, "I want $100,000 available in my estate when I die." *When* I die, not *if* I die during a specific period of time. As with term life insurance, a portion of the premium is used to fund the contract should death occur early (or prematurely). But a second portion of the premium establishes a fund that will be sufficient to provide the $100,000 *when* the insured dies.

This second portion of the permanent life insurance premium makes up the policy's "nonforfeiture" values. The premium payer maintains the right to any funds accumulated for the eventual death if the life contract is canceled. Nonforfeiture provisions will be discussed later, but it is important to point out that this fund is not of the same nature as a savings account or any other form of "investment." It is more accurate to describe it as a "reserve" or a contingency fund and not a savings or investment plan.

Permanent life insurance is used for permanent needs. If a business desires to retain a key employee permanently, a whole life insurance contract is an appropriate employee benefit. If the owner of a business is also a "key employee," permanent life insurance is appropriate to cover the eventual loss of that employee-owner. Permanent life insurance would be *inappropriate* for covering a five-year term loan, a temporary need.

Pure Endowment A pure endowment is exactly the opposite of term life insurance. The heart of a pure endowment is that the insured *must survive* the term in order for payment to be made. In term life insurance, the insured *must die* during the term for the company to pay.

As a life insurance policy, pure endowments (and the word *pure* is critical, as will be shown) have limited use alone. They are vastly more significant in combination with one of the other two forms of insurance.

A pure endowment policy should be used when survival of the insured is critical to meet the goals or needs of the insured. For instance, a prospect with no surviving relatives and no charities or "heirs" to be concerned about would be more interested in the need for a retirement fund than for any other need. Since this prospect is not concerned with the value or distribution of an estate if death occurs before retirement, a pure endowment policy is appropriate.

Another use of a pure endowment occurs when a prospect has a legal obligation based on a life contingency. A divorced prospect with the obligation to "provide the one living son with $25,000 for college education expenses at the son's attained age of eighteen" could very well cover that obligation by purchasing a pure endowment on the son's life with the benefit to be paid at age eighteen. If the son dies prior to age eighteen, there is no obligation. If the son survives, the obligation exists. A pure endowment is perfect for this highly limited situation.

A series of pure endowments is sometimes salable. Assume a prospect does not want a lump sum when retirement is reached, but would rather have a level income for the balance of his or her life. A series of pure endowments, payable annually, monthly, or in any other mode, is appropriate. This "series of pure endowment payments" is more usually called an "annuity." In the "pure annuity" the periodic payments would cease at the annuitant's death, and each is contingent on the prospect surviving until the next period.

Modifications of Term, Permanent, and Pure Endowments The words "term" and "permanent" life insurance are generic in that there are a host of policies sold as term and permanent policies. Pure endowments, on the other hand, are most likely to be found in combinations with term and/or permanent insurance. Pure endowments are rarely sold alone.

Term Variations. Term life insurance policies can be designed for almost any desired length of time. There are yearly term policies, five-year term policies, ten-year term policies, and twenty-year term policies. There are also term policies to age sixty-five and even a "life expectancy term" life insurance. The *life expectancy policy* runs for a period equal to the average life expectancy of the age of the insured.

The name of the term policy may also express what happens to the face amount of coverage. There may be ten-year *level* term, ten-year *reducing* (or decreasing) term, and even ten-year *increasing* term (the latter is usually in combination with one of the other forms). In the absence of a descriptive name, the amount of coverage is usually level. A five-year term policy would be a level face amount product.

The final set of descriptive term products relates to options available to the insured. A five-year *renewable* term policy would allow the insured to renew coverage, at a higher rate, for at least another five-year period and perhaps up to age sixty-five. A five-year *convertible* policy would allow the insured to convert the policy to a permanent form of life insurance within the five-year period. A five-year renewable and convertible product would allow both conversion and renewal.

The conversion privilege is valuable. If the term period cannot be extended, conversion allows the insured to retain insurance coverage, at higher permanent rates, if the insured should become uninsurable. Renewability is valuable for similar reasons.

Use of these products, again, should fit needs. In periods of mortgage interest rates of between 7 and 9 percent, a decreasing term policy would be ideal for mortgage protection. At interest rates in excess of 11 percent, a combination product of level term for the first ten years (assuming a thirty-year mortgage) and then decreasing for the remaining twenty years would seem appropriate. If a debt exists that increases each year, an increasing term policy would be appropriate.

Permanent Variations. Permanent life insurance policies are usually classified according to the length of the premium paying period or by what happens to the amount of protection. In either case, coverage continues for life; only the premium paying period differs.

Premium Paying Period Variations. *Life paid-up at 65* policies require premium payments to stop at age sixty-five. The once popular *twenty pay life policy* required premiums to stop at the end of the twenty-year period. Even single premium life insurance is sold (one premium payment, but coverage lasts for life). Conversions are not necessary as this is a permanent product. Renewable features are not needed as coverage runs until death. The face will not vary. In some policies, premium levels may change. In this way, insurers are recognizing a need for permanent protection without adequate money to buy it. Initial premiums are set at a low level and gradually increase for five to twenty years until they reach a maximum and thereafter level amount.

The selection of various permanent policies is based on the income situation of the prospect. If a prospect anticipates retiring at age sixty-five, life paid-up at sixty-five may be recommended. The prospect would have permanent protection but pay for it only during working years. A prospect with a large, one-time income (a lottery winner or someone who receives a large inheritance) might even consider single premium permanent life. Someone with a relatively short peak income period, like the professional athlete, may consider a five, ten, or twenty pay life contract.

While all of these premium paying periods may make sense, an astute producer would point out that the same periodic premium for whole life insurance (protection and premiums running until death) would have an additional advantage over the shorter premium paying period insured. Any policy that limits premium paying periods requires that the premiums stop at the end of the premium paying period. Further, any permanent life insurance policy allows discontinuation of premiums at any time. The prospect purchasing a whole life policy with the same annual premium as a twenty pay policy would still be allowed to stop premiums in twenty years. During the twenty years, however, the prospect would have a substantially greater insurance benefit with whole life. At the end of the twenty years, the insured could stop premium payments and would probably still have a paid-up policy (no more premium due) equal to the face of the twenty pay policy. These results are shown in Exhibit 7-10 for a typical stock life insurance company's policies.

Amount of Protection Variations. Two types of permanent life insurance policies offering a varying face of protection while still providing permanent life insurance are cost-of-living policies and variable life insurance.[2]

In the inflationary environment of recent years, companies began providing a cost-of-living policy or rider that automatically increases the death benefit and cash values as prices increase. Although most policies of this type are linked to the consumer price index (CPI), other indexes are used.

Some cost-of-living plans operate by automatically purchasing one-year term insurance whenever the CPI increases a specified amount. If the CPI does not increase (or does not increase enough), no additional insurance is purchased. The face amount never decreases below the face amount of the original policy.

One advantage of the cost-of-living policy is that evidence of insurability is usually not required. Another possible advantage is that the additional protection may not be fully loaded for expenses (since agents' commissions normally are not paid on the additional insurance). These advantages should not imply that all policyowners should request a cost-of-living policy or rider. The policy requires an increasing

Exhibit 7-10
Comparison of Twenty-Pay Life and Whole Life (Premiums and Values Based on $100,000 20-Pay Life Policy Issued in 1978 to a Male, Age 35)*

	Policy	
	20-Pay Life	Whole Life
Annual Premiums	$2,817	$2,817
Death Benefit	$100,000	$185,281

Insured pays $2,817 each year but has an initial additional $85,281 death benefit with whole life insurance.

Assume insured stops premium payments after 10 years or after 20 years.

	After 10 Years	
	20-Pay Life	Whole Life
Annual Premiums	—0—	—0—
Reduced Paid-up Death Benefit	$50,000	$54,472

	After 20 Years	
	20-Pay Life	Whole Life
Annual Premiums	—0—	—0—
Reduced Paid-up Death Benefit	$100,000	$104,128

After paying premiums for 10 or 20 years, the insured still has a greater death benefit with the whole life policy than with the 20-pay life policy. Results may vary based on different life insurers' policies, rates, and benefits.

*This exhibit is based on information provided by Michael Fedyna, FSA.

premium in periods of inflation. Furthermore, an individual's life insurance needs are not necessarily correlated to changes in consumer prices.

Variable life insurance, in general, is any form of life insurance providing a death benefit that may change with time. A narrower definition, however, has evolved. According to the NAIC Model Variable Life Insurance Regulation, variable life insurance is a policy in which the death benefit varies with the investment experience of a segregated investment account maintained by the life insurance company. Under this definition, cost-of-living policies are not considered a form of variable life insurance.

The motivation for a variable life contract arises from a desire for a product based on equity values that shares some of the investment gain with the policyholder. The insurance company may view variable life as a product that will be competitive in the marketplace. The individual may see variable life as possible protection against inflation.

Since the values in a variable life contract depend on the performance of an investment account, there is an inflation hedge only to the extent that the underlying investments keep pace with (or outperform) the general movement in prices. In the past, equity investments have surpassed general price increases in some years, but equity prices and consumer prices have also moved in opposite directions for some years.

According to the NAIC Model Variable Life Regulation, all variable life policies share three important features:

1. Although the policy will provide variable death benefits and policy values, the premiums paid by the policyowner will remain level.
2. It is required that the death benefit be greater than or equal to the original face amount of the policy.
3. Coverage must be permanent.

There is no variable term or endowment insurance. As a general rule, the annual premiums on the variable life coverage must be payable for a minimum of fifteen or twenty years.

At present, variable life policies may follow four designs. All methods depend on an "excess investment return" concept. Basically, this approach involves a comparison between the *actual net investment rate (ANIR)* and the *assumed investment rate (AIR)* In determining the ANIR, all elements of investment performance are considered, including dividends received, and risk contingencies. Death benefits will remain level if the ANIR is exactly equal to the AIR, but the face amount will change when a difference between the two rates develops.

One approach is to provide paid-up variable life insurance at the net rate for the attained age of the insured (if the ANIR is greater than the AIR). In other words, with favorable investment experience, dollars are applied, in effect, to purchase a single-premium policy in the amount that can be purchased at the insured's attained age. Since the additional insurance is being purchased on a single-premium basis, the amount that can be purchased in any one year will be modest, but over time and with favorable investment experience, the total amount of paid-up insurance will accumulate. If the ANIR is less than the AIR, the appropriate amount of paid-up life insurance is deducted from the death benefit, as long as the face amount does not fall below the original amount.

A second method involves purchasing additional insurance that is not paid-up. These purchases are made at net rates based on the insured's original age (not the insured's attained age). With favorable investment experience, larger amounts of insurance will be purchased in the early policy years than would be purchased under the paid-up method. However, as time passes, a smaller amount of insurance will be purchased because the funds available from the excess investment performance must first be used to pay the premiums on policy additions that were purchased in previous years; only the remainder, if any, is available to purchase new insurance.

A third method is the purchase of paid-up term insurance. The regulation does not stipulate the term period, but the term insurance would probably run until the next valuation period.

The fourth method permitted is a combination of two of the three other approaches.

Pure Endowment Variation. Pure endowments are limited in use. They are most frequently sold in combination with other types of life insurance.

Combination of Types There are many potential life insurance products based on combinations of the three types of life insurance. Most are geared either to a specific need of most insureds or are used as "marketing tools or gimmicks" with little or no relation to a need. Examples of each follow. The key marketing consideration for the producer interested in selling some life insurance is that the consumer's need must be matched with the right combination of types of life insurance. If not, dissatisfaction will ultimately result. Combinations used for examples include family income, family maintenance, endowment insurance, universal life, adjustable life and "gimmick" policies.

Family Income Policy. An example of a combination policy designed for a specific need is the family income policy (FIP). The FIP is a combination of twenty-year decreasing term insurance with a basic permanent policy. The goal of the FIP is to provide $10 per month income to the beneficiary for each $1,000 of permanent life insurance for a maximum of twenty years. Payments would begin at the death of the insured and continue up to twenty years *after the date of purchase.* If an insured purchased a policy at age thirty-five and died at age forty, payments of $100 per month (the base policy is a $10,000 face) would be made for fifteen years. At that point, the $10,000 permanent life insurance would be paid. The FIP is designed to fit both the readjustment income and dependency period need for income. It provides a stable income and a lump sum that can be used for "capital" needs.

Family Maintenance Policy. Another combination similar to the FIP is the family maintenance policy (FMP). Instead of monthly payments stopping at the end of the twentieth policy year, the FMP provides the $10 per month per $1,000 face for a full twenty years from the time of death if the insured dies within the first twenty years. Payments can continue for twenty years after the insured's death because a twenty-year level term policy is used in combination with the permanent policy. Again, the FMP is ideal for the readjustment and dependency period.

Endowment Insurance Policy. Another example of a combination policy is the *endowment insurance* (EI) policy (as opposed to pure endowment). The EI policy combines the promises of both the term and pure endowment policies. The face is paid if the insured dies within the policy period *or* if the insured survives the policy period. Remember the obligation of a divorced father to finance his son's education used earlier as an example. The father, instead of placing a pure endowment on the son, could purchase EI on himself. *If* the father survives the period, the company pays the face and the money is available for the son's education. If the son does not survive, the father has access to the money. In addition, if the father dies, the insurance proceeds of EI would be available for the son's education.

An interesting combination of *pure endowment* and permanent insurance occurs in policies typically marketed to juniors and seniors in college. The unique aspect of the policy is that the student does not have to pay the first premium. Instead, the student signs a note for the first year's premium. The note is due in five years. However, the policy includes a five-year *pure endowment* in combination with the permanent policy. At the end of the five years, if the insured is still living and paying premiums (or "surviving and persisting" in the language of life insurance) the five-year pure endowment matures and is sufficient to pay off the note. The insured is *not* getting something for nothing. The premium includes a charge for the pure endowment, but it is spread over the premium paying period. For a college student with a need for life insurance and no current ability to pay, this may be an attractive feature. But the product should be understood and the need should match the policy.

Universal Life Policies. One of the most popular life insurance policies in recent years is the so-called universal life contract. The rationale for developing universal life contracts was to deal with the concept that consumers should "buy term insurance and invest the difference" because of the alleged low rate of return on traditional whole life insurance contracts. Additionally, universal life provides certain flexibilities that are not typically available under traditional whole life insurance policies. Universal life policies are essentially a combinition of one-year renewable for life term insurance and a fund (cash value) into which premiums are paid.

Universal Life Defined. Though there are many variations of universal life contracts, most have an initial required premium (also called a contribution). Sales and administrative charges are deducted from the premium, and the balance goes into a fund. Each month a charge is deducted for pure term insurance covering the difference between the cash value and death benefit amounts. The balance of the premium earns at least the rate of interest guaranteed in the contract. If the insurer earns excess interest, additional interest credits can be added to the cash value. During periods of high interest rates, relatively high interest returns have been credited.

There are two different policy designs for universal life contracts. Under one design, the amount of pure insurance can be a level amount throughout the life of the policy, or, under the other form, it can be the original amount of the insurance less the cash value. A good way to understand the nature of a universal life concept is to compare a typical universal life policy with the traditional permanent life insurance policy.

Under a typical permanent life insurance policy (but not some forms of variable life) the amount of insurance protection and the premium level are fixed at the inception of the policy. An individual who wants additional insurance must take a medical examination, and a new policy will be issued. Under a universal life policy, additional life insurance can be added to the same contract, but a medical examination may be required. Some universal life policies also have cost-of-living options.

Under a traditional whole life policy, the insured normally pays a fixed annual premium, while under a universal life policy the insured can pay a varying premium after the first year. For example, the insured could skip a payment or two, and the funds to pay for the insurance protection would be taken out of the cash value of the contract. The insured could pay lower premiums that just cover the expense charge and the mortality charge. Conversely, if the insured wishes to pay more into a universal life policy, a faster buildup of cash value can be achieved.

Another difference between universal life and permanent life insurance contracts, and term insurance contracts for that matter, is in the area of disclosure of what portion of the premium is paid to the insurance company for administrative and other charges. While such charges typically are not disclosed under traditional whole life and term insurance contracts, they are disclosed under universal life contracts. The annual statement for a universal life policy illustrates premiums paid, expenses charged, cost of term insurance, and the interest credited to the cash value.

Investment Element of Universal Life. The previous excitement and current growth of universal life is probably accounted for more by its investment features than by its life insurance characteristics. Universal life was designed for many reasons, two of the more common from the insurer's perspective being to stem the decline in the amount of traditional whole life insurance being sold and to be able to compete effectively against other savings vehicles to counter the "buy term and invest the difference" philosophy. The proponents of universal life stress the "high current rates" being applied to the universal life cash values compared with the lower rates being applied to the more traditional whole life products. The proponents also argue that the current rates are attractive not only because they compare favorably with other savings vehicles but also because the tax advantages actually provide a significant positive difference compared with other savings vehicles.

The arguments work well in times of high interest rates. Proponents of the more traditional permanent life products argue that if interest rates should drop substantially, universal life products will not be such "high flyers" compared with the more traditional permanent life products.

Adjustable Life Policies. Another combination of life insurance is so-called "adjustable" life insurance (also referred to as "life cycle" insurance). Adjustable life, its proponents claim, is more flexible than other life contracts because adjustable policies can be changed fairly easily to meet an individual or family's changing life insurance needs over time. Death benefits can be increased or decreased. This might be desirable, for example, following changes in a family's situation such as the birth of children. Most adjustable life policies permit changes at the discretion of the policyowner.

The flexibility offered by adjustable life is achieved by permitting switching back and forth between the term insurance and cash value forms of coverage in the contract. It is designed to allow both the coverage and premium to change to meet the insured's desires. An extra premium can be paid, and a cost-of-living agreement can be added. Exhibit 7-11 illustrates how an adjustable life policy might work as an individual's needs change over time.

Exhibit 7-11
Adjustable Life Illustrated*

How they work

Here's one way a man might vary his coverage and premiums from age 25 to 65 with an adjustable life policy.

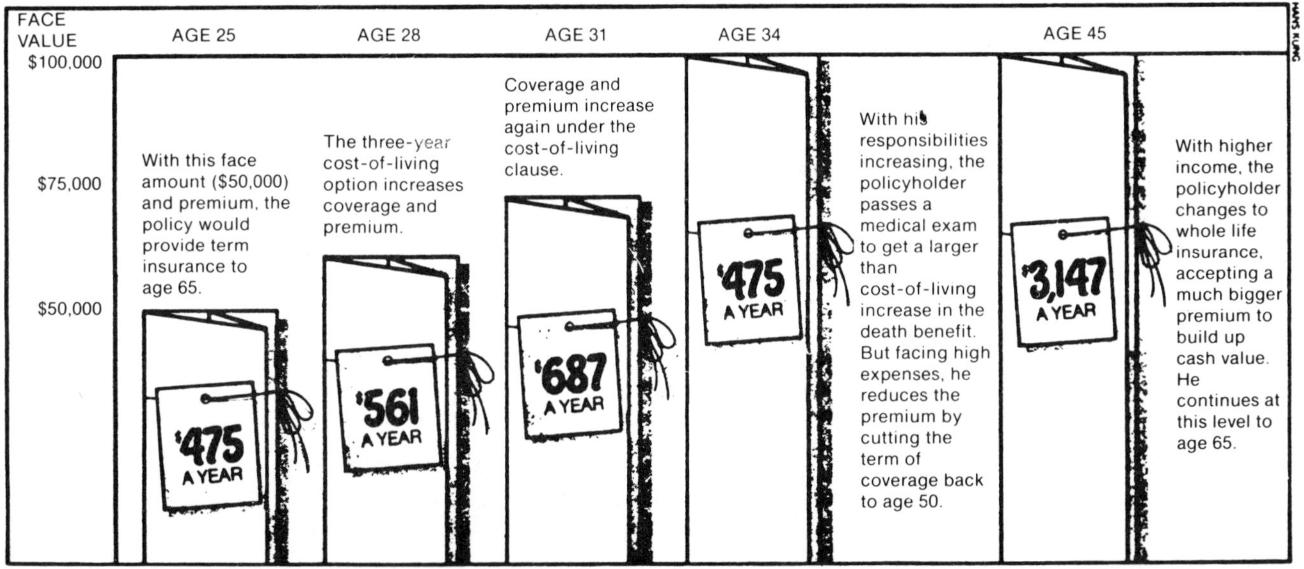

Actual Premiums for comparable coverage would currently be lower.

*Reprinted, with permission, from Minnesota Mutual Life Insurance Co.

Gimmick Combination Policy. The following presentation abridged from an actual sales presentation is an example of a combination of types of life insurance used as a marketing gimmick.

> I have a policy for you that cannot be beat. For each unit of insurance you purchase we offer you a $5,000 death benefit no matter when you die. Because this is a new policy, we offer an additional $5,000 death benefit for the first ten years. Also, if you should die within the first twenty years of the policy, my company will refund all of the premiums you have paid.

An analysis of this policy shows that each unit contains a $5,000 whole life policy with a ten-year term policy of $5,000 and a twenty-year increasing term policy. The increasing term portion increases annually by the amount of annual premiums. Nothing is being given away. Each benefit is charged for and the insured is not "getting a grand opening deal." The objection to this type of policy is misrepresentation in the sales presentation. If the insured has a need for a combined whole life, ten-year level term (not renewable or convertible) and twenty-year increasing term policy, the combination fits the needs. It is hard, however, to imagine a situation that fits this policy. Needs must match policies.

Checkpoints

1. List the need categories used in the needs approach.
2. Explain and give examples of each need category.
3. Explain how to determine how much life insurance a prospect requires using the human life value and needs approaches.
4. Define the type of policy, how it should be used, and an example of:
   a. Term life insurance
   b. Permanent life insurance
   c. Pure endowment
   d. Universal life
   e. Adjustable life

Important Life Insurance Provisions

Because this chapter is designed to acquaint the producer with life insurance, an exhaustive dissertation on each provision will not be presented. Rather, each will be highlighted. Detail can be found in many sources. If life insurance will be a major factor in a producer's overall marketing plan, such detail is vital and should be sought.

Insuring Agreement A simple insuring agreement of a life insurance policy was presented earlier. The agreement stipulates that the insurer requires proof of death, usually a certified death certificate. If premiums have been paid and all provisions met, the full face is payable. Unlike property-liability policies, even if a few premiums have not been paid, there still may be a substantial benefit payable (to be discussed in the nonforfeiture section of this chapter). Permanent forms of life insurance have cash values available, and any loans against the policy will be deducted from the proceeds otherwise payable.

Entire Contract Clause A typical entire contract clause reads:

> *Entire Contract* The entire contract consists of this policy and the attached copy of the application. Only the Chairman, President, Secretary, or a Vice-President of the Company can change or modify the contract, and then only in writing. Any change or modification in the contract can be made only with the written consent of the Owner.

When the insured is presented with the life contract, all portions of the contract are included. Even a copy of the application for life insurance is attached. The provision states which representatives of the company can modify the contract—in this case, those representatives are strictly limited to senior officers. This is different from a property-liability policy in that the life producer never has authority to modify the policy. Company bylaws or other rules or regulations not attached to the policy cannot be applied. Even if policy changes were to be made, they could be made only with the consent of the owner of the policy.

Policy Dates Another interesting difference between property-liability and life insurance is that the life policy is measured against a policy date, not a policy period. For example:

> *Dates* Policy years, policy months, and policy anniversaries are measured from the policy date.

As some of the provisions in a life insurance policy are limited or granted based on the passage of time, this provision is important. Some states allow "back dating" a policy. Back dating establishes an earlier policy date and, when allowed, may grant the insured a lower premium because of an age change. The suicide and incontestible clauses (discussed below) are measured from the date.

Ownership It is possible that the owner of a life policy is a different person from the insured. If a husband purchases a policy on a wife, either could be the owner, but the wife's life would be the insured life. There are estate tax implications attached to ownership of a life policy. More important, the owner has valuable "property rights" in the policy that can be exercised only by the owner. The provision also outlines how a change of ownership can be effected.

Premium Payments A representative premium payment section reads:

> *Payment of Premiums* Premiums are payable, during the lifetime of the insured, at the Home Office, at any Central Service Office, or at the Canadian Service Office of the Company. Each premium is payable on or before its due date as shown in the Premium Schedule.
>
> The premium for this policy can be paid at annual, semi-annual, or quarterly intervals at the company's premium rate in effect as of the date of issue for that interval. The interval can be changed by paying the correct premium for the new interval. Premiums can be paid by any other arrangement made available by the Company.

The actual payment date for premiums and the frequency of the payments are listed on the declarations page of the policy. Changes to payment schedules, less than annual, are allowed. After the policy is issued, paying the premium is the only responsibility of the insured or owner. Because of the substantial property rights in a life policy, the owner is allowed a grace period, typically thirty days beyond the anniversary date, to pay premiums. During the grace period, insurance is in force. If premiums stop, wording of the "nonpayment of premium" provisions will control what happens to the policy. Usually, for term insurance, if the premium is not paid by the end of the grace period, coverage ceases. Because there are cash values at some point in permanent insurance, three options are available to the owner after the expiration of the grace period.

Nonforfeiture Options

These three options are spelled out in the guaranteed values or nonforfeiture provisions section. The three options are known as extended term insurance, paid-up insurance, or cash surrender value. The extended term option is usually automatic unless the policy owner selects another option.

Extended Term Insurance. The first, and the automatically operative provision unless the owner directs otherwise, is that the policy becomes one of "extended term insurance." From the "table of guaranteed values" of a sample policy, it can be seen that if a lapse occurs in year 11, the policy (see Exhibit 7-12) becomes an extended term policy for 17 years, 213 days. The face of the policy would remain as originally issued. If any loans are outstanding, they will reduce the face. Similarly, if there are any "dividend additions," they will increase the face.

Reduced Paid-Up Insurance. The second option is for the owner to accept a reduced face amount of permanent insurance that requires no further premium payments. In year 11 of the sample policy, the reduced paid-up policy would be for $9,900.

Exhibit 7-12
Table of Guaranteed Values*

End of Policy Year	Cash Value	Alternatives to Cash Value: Paid-up Insurance	or Extended Insurance: Years	Days	End of Policy Year
1	. . .	. . .	. . .	. . .	1
2	$ 350	$ 1.025	3	273	2
3	800	2.225	7	135	3
4	1.250	3.350	10	19	4
5	1.700	4.400	12	19	5
6	2.175	5.450	13	254	6
7	2.675	6.475	15	18	7
8	3.150	7.375	15	345	8
9	3.675	8.325	16	273	9
10	4.200	9.200	17	118	10
11	4.675	9.900	17	213	11
12	5.175	10.660	17	286	12
13	5.675	11.250	17	317	13
14	6.200	11.900	17	333	14
15	6.725	12.500	17	316	15
16	7.275	13.100	17	288	16
17	7.825	13.625	17	234	17
18	8.400	14.175	17	173	18
19	8.975	14.675	17	91	19
20	9.575	15.150	17	3	20
Age 60	11.875	17.300	15	212	Age 60
Age 65	14.075	19.025	13	343	Age 65

Life policy; proceeds available at insured's death; premiums payable during insured's lifetime, as shown in premium schedule. Policy is eligible for dividends. Values do not include dividend values or reflect an unpaid loan.

* Reprinted with permission from Insurance Information Institute, *Sample Policy Kit*, p. 412.

Cash Surrender. The owner may decide to give up all insurance benefits and select the cash option. In year 11, that would be $4,675.

Automatic Premium Loan. The need to select one of these options can be avoided (and lapse would not automatically occur) if the owner selects what is known as the *automatic premium loan* (APL) on the application for life insurance. If the APL is elected, at the end of the grace period the insurer automatically borrows sufficient money from the cash value to keep the policy in full force. The true benefit of this selection can be seen when the provisions of reinstatement are understood.

Reinstatement Reinstatement is one of the policyowner's valued rights. Once the grace period for premium payment has passed, a policy may be reinstated if the cash surrender option has not been exercised. Reinstatement entails some major requirements. First, the insured must furnish evidence of insurability—beyond physical acceptability. Second, the reinstatement request must be made within a specified time period, typically within five years. Third, premiums from date of lapse and interest on those premiums at a rate stated in the policy must be paid. In addition, any policy loans and interest on those loans must be paid.

There are several advantages or potential advantages to reinstating a policy as opposed to obtaining a new one. The reinstated policy may have a lower policy loan rate than a new policy would have. Reinstatement avoids new and perhaps more restrictive policy provisions. Finally, the substantial cash values of the old policy are immediately reestablished.

The inability to make a premium payment within the grace period, for one reason or another, is not uncommon. Without APL, reinstatement must take place. Since the reinstatement process may be cumbersome, selection of APL on the original application is recommended.

Misstatement of Age and Sex This is the one provision that will change the limits of a life policy no matter when death occurs. From the mortality table, Exhibit 7-1, it can be seen that the probability of death increases with age after year 10. The misstatement provision allows the company to adjust, up or down, the face of the policy based on the actual age or sex of an individual. If the insured's age was understated, the death benefit decreases; if overstated, it increases. Since females have a lower death rate at all ages, the company will adjust benefits if sex was misstated. The tendency would be to state a lower than actual age, but the provision can work in both directions. Benefits do not cease if age or sex was misstated. They are adjusted based on actual age or sex. Misstatement of sex has no application in those few states that apply unisex rating to life insurance.

Suicide and Other Exclusions In a typical policy, the only excluded cause of death is suicide. And suicide is excluded only if it occurs during the first year (though most states allow two years as a maximum, many companies use only a one-year exclusion). If suicide is contended by the company, the burden of proof rests with the company.

Common law assumes all deaths are not self-inflicted unless proved otherwise.

There are a few other exclusions that *may* appear from time to time in the policies of selected insureds. These exclusions would be based on the vocations or avocations of prospects. Insureds who pilot private aircraft less than 100 hours a year will usually have an exclusion for death in a private aircraft. These exclusions do not apply to commercial airline pilots on their commercial flights.

During time of war, a war-related death exclusion may be attached to new policies of insureds of military age. Neither aviation nor war clauses can be added to an existing policy.

Other restrictions are possible. A stunt car driver, stunt-actors for the movies, a sky diver, and others with unusually dangerous jobs or hobbies may have policies issued with exclusions based on these jobs or hobbies. If death occurs as the result of an excluded peril, the company is responsible for return of premiums and interest on the premiums or the cash value of the policy, whichever is greater.

Incontestable Clause Life insurance policies contain clauses that make the policies incontestable after a period of time. An example of such a clause reads:

> *Incontestability* The Company will not contest this policy after it has been in force during the lifetime of the Insured for one year from the date of issue.

The incontestable clause has great value for the insured. After a stated period of time, the company loses the right to challenge the validity of a contract, unless fraud has been perpetrated by one of the parties to the contract. The incontestable clause is in keeping with other provisions found in the life insurance contract. An aviation or similar restriction is not a contest of validity; it is a limitation on the death peril. The misstatement of age provision is not a contest of validity; it equitably adjusts benefits. The clause establishes a time limit on a challenge by the life company based on any alleged misrepresentations contained in the application for insurance.

For instance, if an insured listed his occupation as "construction executive" on the application when in fact he was a "sandhog"—someone specializing in digging tunnels—that misrepresentation, if it is to be contested, must be challenged within the contestable period. If it is not contested then, the contract is valid. General contract law does not usually impose such a short contestable period. The life company may challenge the validity of the contract at any time on the basis of fraud or that "no real contract" exists. An example would be one twin brother in good health taking a physical for the other, in poor health, in order to obtain insurance. No valid contract exists in that case.

Assignment As a valid piece of property, a life insurance policy may be assigned. It may be assigned to anyone, even those without a valid insurable interest in the life of the insured. The assignment clause spells out the procedural steps necessary to notify the life company of the assignment. These steps are necessary for the assignee (party obtaining the assignment) to make sure the assignee receives the proceeds in the event the insured dies after the assignment.

Beneficiary Designation This is a procedural clause outlining how beneficiaries to a policy will be determined and how they may be changed. There are usually two classes of beneficiaries: *primary* and *contingent* (secondary or other). If the primary beneficiary has died, the clause outlines how contingent beneficiaries may share in the proceeds. Beneficiary selection is first determined in the application for the life insurance. The beneficiary designation clause then establishes how a beneficiary may be changed. If a beneficiary is "irrevocable," there can be no change in the designation unless the irrevocable beneficiary has died or agrees to a change.

Settlement Options Settlement options are unique to American life insurance policies. Most insureds tend to think in terms of settlement in the form of a lump sum. There are other options available that the owner may pre-select or that the beneficiary may select after the insured's death.

General categories of settlement options typically available include:

1. Proceeds only
2. Options based on life contingencies
3. Other options

Proceeds Only Options. The first type of option leaves the proceeds on deposit with the company to accumulate interest, subject to a right of withdrawal of both proceeds and interest. This is called an *interest accumulation option.* Such deposits earn a guaranteed, though minimal, interest rate. In practice, most companies pay a higher rate of interest than the guaranteed amount. If a producer is helping a beneficiary to decide how to take the proceeds, the producer should find out from the insurer what the current interest rate is or what the rate paid the previous year had been. Some companies will never pay more than the minimum.

An option similar to the interest accumulation option is the *interest income option.* With selection of this option, the interest earned is sent to the beneficiary rather than being added to the principal.

A third option, *income for an elected period,* is to take the proceeds over a specified period. The table of settlement options shows typical time periods and the amount to be paid per $1,000 of benefits left under this option.

A similar, and fourth option, is to elect the size of the periodic payment rather than the length of the payment period. Under this *elected income* option, the size of periodic payments and the amount left under the option determine how long payments will be made.

The four options are all based on payments to the beneficiary for proceeds left with the insurer. There are four additional common options that are based on life contingencies.

Proceeds Based on Life Contingencies. The first of these options is the *life income option.* A table in the policy shows how much a beneficiary would receive each month for as long as the beneficiary lives. In some cases, the age of the beneficiary is "adjusted" based on the beneficiary's sex or on the year the benefits begin. But, when the beneficiary dies, income ceases. If $100,000 were left under this option and the beneficiary received only one payment before death, no portion of the remaining $100,000 would be payable to anyone. To overcome this possibility, a *life income with a guaranteed period option* is available. The shorter the guarantee period, the greater the monthly payment. Another variation is the *life income option with a guaranteed total amount.* Under this option, payments will continue for the life of the beneficiary. Should the beneficiary die before the total of the amount left under the option is paid out, payments will continue to another beneficiary until that amount is paid. Finally, there is a *joint and survivor option.* With this option, payments continue as long as one of the two beneficiaries involved survives. In some companies, payments to the survivor after the death of one party are reduced. In some companies, a guaranteed period can be added.

Other Settlement Options. While it may not be stated in the policy, life insurers usually are willing to consider any other type of option that will suit the beneficiary's needs—even some which are not spelled out in the settlement options section. Some life companies allow flexibility in shifting or splitting funds among options. The settlement option section of a life insurance policy can help the producer and the owner of the policy make sure that the financial planning that took place prior to death is actually carried out after death.

All life insurers have "spendthrift" provisions available. Basically, these allow the owner of a policy to predetermine the settlement option for a beneficiary. The beneficiary then has little or no chance to change the options. It is called a spendthrift arrangement because it prevents a beneficiary from exchanging a life income for a lump sum. The theory is that the beneficiary is less likely to squander periodic payments than an entire lump sum.

Checkpoints

1. Explain why the policy and issue dates are important in life insurance.
2. List and explain the nonforfeiture options in a life insurance policy.
3. Explain how the election of the automatic premium loan circumvents the reinstatement provision in a life insurance policy.
4. List and explain three settlement options based on:
   a. Life contingencies.
   b. Only the amount of proceeds left under an option.

Major Life Insurance Endorsements

The life insurance policy is designed to pay the face amount at the death of the insured. Of the five major endorsements (or riders, or options, as they are sometimes called) only one, accidental death benefit, relates to death. The other four riders either provide a supplemental health insurance benefit or protect the insured from future uninsurability.

Waiver of Premium The waiver of premium endorsement is a valuable addition to any life insurance policy. Subject to exclusions that are more numerous than in the life insurance policy, the company promises to waive future premiums if the insured becomes totally and permanently disabled. Subject to the definition of "total and permanent disability," the premiums may be waived for the balance of the insured's life.

The definitions and exclusions found in the waiver of premium endorsement are more complex because disability is harder to define and easier to fake than death. Generally all companies will require a "waiting period" of three to six months before any premiums are waived. Premiums due during the waiting period will be retroactively waived if disability continues beyond the period. The insured will be required to show continuing disability unless total and permanent disability has been determined.

Definition of Total and Permanent Disability. The definition of total and permanent disability is important to the insured and varies from insurer to insurer. One liberal definition holds that the insured is disabled if the insured is not able to work at the occupation held *prior* to disability. In this case, a traveling salesman who cannot travel because of a disability would have premiums waived even if a new desk job were found that paid as much or more money.

The most common definition of disability, however, holds that the insured is disabled if the insured is unable to work at any job for which the insured is reasonably fit by education and training. Under this definition, the salesperson's premiums would not be waived if a new job were found.

Other Aspects of Waiver of Premium. The exclusions should be checked as some life insurance companies have more restrictions on the coverage than others. For most life companies, the rider is incontestable after one or two years from issuance of the endorsement. The rider does have an upper age limit on eligibility. Usually the insured must become disabled prior to age sixty-five or seventy.

Value of Waiver of Premium. If possible, every life insurance policy should have the waiver of premium endorsement added to it. It would make no sense to have a life insurance policy become less valuable to an insured because premiums could not be paid due to a disability. The premium is inexpensive, running between 1 and 3 percent of the life insurance premium.

Accidental Death Benefit The accidental death benefit endorsement increases the face amount of the policy payable if the insured dies accidentally. Again, the definitions of what constitutes "accidental" death must be read and understood. There will be some accidental causes that are not covered, and these exclusions should be examined also.

The accidental death benefit, or "double indemnity," rider costs more than the waiver of premium rider. The accidental death benefit also terminates at age sixty-five or seventy.

Meaning of "Accidental" Death. To fit the usual definition of accidental death, death must occur within a specified time period following an accidental bodily injury—thirty, sixty, or ninety days. An accidental bodily injury may be caused by "accidental means" or "accidental results." Assume an insured takes a ladder and climbs onto the roof of the house to fix a shingle. While climbing the ladder, the insured starts "showing off" for the kids. He slips and breaks his neck. Death was an accidental result of clowning. The clowning was not an *accidental means,* and a rider that demands "accidental means" as part of its definition of accidental death would not pay. If the policy merely required *accidental results,* the rider would pay.

Value of Accidental Death. At certain ages, the probability of death by accident is significantly greater than at other ages. For most people under age thirty-five, accidents are the major cause of death. For higher ages, accidents decline as a cause of death. It may make sense for younger persons to add this rider to their life insurance policies, particularly if they are underinsured. But there is a tendency among insureds to feel that they have more life insurance because of the endorsement. A person with a $100,000 whole life policy and a $100,000 accidental death rider may feel he or she has a $200,000 policy.

A careful explanation of the benefit is necessary. The feeling of security with double indemnity can be compounded by some life companies that increase the amount of the accidental death benefit for specific types of accidents. For instance, the face amount could triple if accidental death occurs "while a passenger in a common carrier." This rider does *not* convert a $100,000 life policy into a $300,000 policy. That amount would be paid *only* if accidental death occurred while riding in a bus, airplane, or other common carrier.

Some life insurers use the accidental death benefit as a gimmick to make their sales presentations sound better. There can be value in the accidental death benefit, but it should not be oversold. The life insurance policy to which the rider is attached is the most important part of the package. The human life value or the insured's needs do not change if the insured dies in a bus accident rather than by natural causes. Some producers suggest that the premium dollars spent on accidental death insurance might be more wisely used on additional life insurance.

Guaranteed Purchase Option A guaranteed purchase option (GPO) protects the insured's ability to purchase life insurance in the future. The option states that no matter what the insured's health or occupation, at certain dates in the future, he or she may buy additional life insurance at standard rates. Some life companies even coordinate their guaranteed purchase options with the waiver of premium and would waive future premiums on the GPO purchased policy if the insured were disabled at the time. Such liberal provisions are rare, however.

When a GPO Can Be Exercised. There are usually six or seven specific ages stated in the rider when the insured may purchase more life insurance under the option. They would be typically at ages twenty-four, twenty-seven, thirty, thirty-three, thirty-seven, and forty. There may be specific events in an insured's life that would allow an age to be "advanced." For instance, an insured at age thirty-one may exercise the age thirty-three option if he or she marries in that year or if a child is born or adopted.

Value of the Option. For most young people, the GPO offers an attractive way to guarantee future insurability. The premium for the benefit would be in the $20 to $30 per year range and offers a great opportunity for a producer to make a sales call as each option date comes up. GPO is worth considering from the insured's and the producer's standpoint.

Disability Income Riders The disability income riders are not as prevalent today as during the 1930s. They are still available and offer the insured a monthly disability income benefit of between $5 and $20 for each $1,000 of life insurance, with $10 being the most common monthly benefit. In many respects, the provisions of the rider are similar to the waiver of premium. In fact, if both the waiver and the disability income riders are in a policy, the definition of disability, waiting period, exclusions, and age termination provisions will be the same.

The rider may fit some needs of the insured. It does not provide a large monthly income for a disabled person ($50 to $200 a month for a $100,000 life policy) but, depending on the insured's disability income protection, it could be a gap filler or cushion against inflation. Usually, however, the insured needs more life insurance and the premiums for the rider would be better spent on additional life insurance.

Cost-of-Living Rider Some insurers make the cost-of-living benefit discussed earlier available as an addition to the basic policy. As a rider, it operates in the manner described earlier.

"SOCIAL SECURITY"

The term *social security* has come to mean, in part, the benefits available under life and health insurance administered by the federal Social Security Administration. The details of the total social security package of federal legislation is beyond the scope of this course, but the basics are essential if life insurance is to be a product in a producer's marketing plan.

Essential Elements of Social Security

What some call social security is actually Old Age, Survivor's, Disability and Health Insurance, or OASDHI. While most people in the United States are covered by OASDHI, they may not realize that the FICA (Federal Insurance Contributions Act) taxes withheld from pay include separate charges for the four coverages under the act.

Old Age Benefits The bulk of the FICA tax and the employer's matching contribution is for retirement benefits. Workers covered under the old age provisions receive benefits at retirement based on the age of the retired person, the amount of their primary insurance amount, and the worker's status at retirement.[3] The amount of monthly retirement benefits is designed to be a floor of income—sufficient for sustaining life on the subsistence level. No one should rely on social security alone. Other plans should be made for a retirement income in excess of the subsistence level.

Retirement benefits are based on retirement at age sixty-five. Benefits are decreased for earlier retirement but do not increase for later retirement. Payments are automatically increased by law to reflect increases in the cost of living periodically. Benefits may be reduced or taxed if the retired person receives income in excess of some small amount.

Survivor's Benefits These benefits are payable to a covered worker's dependents at or after the worker's death. The social security figures used during the discussion of the human life value and needs approaches were survivor's benefits. The benefits are not limited to a surviving spouse and children. Others—such as dependent parents and former spouses—may also be eligible.

Disability Benefits Disability benefits are payable to an eligible worker who remains disabled for more than six months. There are certain federal requirements for eligibility and continuation of these benefits that can be found in a social security manual. Suffice it to say that there are disability benefits under the Social Security Act.

Health Insurance Health insurance coverage under social security contains some welfare provisions (Medicaid) and some insurance benefits (Medicare). These coverages are intended to provide health insurance for retired workers and the medically indigent (those who cannot afford health care).

Social Security and Life Insurance

When social security legislation was originally passed in the 1930s, there were many who prophesied doom for the life insurance business. In fact, social security has reduced both the ability to pay for and the need for private life insurance. Not only have tax rates increased, but the amount of income subject to the FICA tax has also increased beyond any reasonable level the public can afford.

Producers interested in life insurance sales cannot ignore the impact of social security. They should become familiar with benefit levels and eligibility requirements to assist prospects in determining the right amount of life insurance to purchase. The earlier example used to demonstrate the human life value approach showed the impact of social security on life insurance needs. Life field representatives can help the producer decide what parts of social security to learn in detail and how to estimate benefits.

LIFE VERSUS PROPERTY-LIABILITY INSURANCE

Gordon K. Rose, CLU, ChFC, while Vice President of The American College, said:

> The essential difference between the life and property-liability businesses is that in life insurance you have a relatively uncomplicated, easy to understand product with intricate application. In property-liability insurance, you have complicated products applied to relatively uncomplicated situations.

There is more than a grain of truth in that statement. Producers spend their entire working lives learning property and liability forms, coverages, and rates. The process never ends. When a feeling of comfort develops, new forms and rating methods or entire new product lines are introduced. In life insurance, the details of three policy types (term, permanent, and pure endowment) are all that is necessary to understand life insurance policies. A broad view of both fields of insurance includes a look at differences in product, price, product life cycle, underwriting, compensation, and selling.

Product Differences

Essentially, there are three types of property-liability contracts: limited specified perils policies, broader specified perils policies, and "all-risks" policies. The classic example of a limited specified perils policy is the standard fire policy. If the standard fire policy were written without other modifying provisions, the object (property) would be insured only for the perils of "fire, lightning, and loss by removal." The insured must read a highly legal form to discover coverage for three perils. For an additional premium, the insured can have broad form perils added. For "all-risks" coverage the insured must read a list of exclusions rather than concentrate on a list of perils.

In a sample life insurance policy, the perils are more easily understood:

> *Life Insurance Benefit*
>
> Life Insurance Company will pay the life insurance proceeds to the beneficiary promptly upon receiving proof of the Insured's death, if premiums have been paid in accordance with the Premiums section....

While policy wording may vary slightly from company to company, the simplicity is striking: "We will pay your beneficiary when you die, subject to a few exclusions during the first few years of the policy." *Term* life insurance policies (policies with coverage for a specific time period) would restrict the payment to the term of the policy—like a property or liability contract. A *pure endowment* policy (one that pays only if the insured survives a stated period of time) says, "We will pay you if you survive the term." An *endowment insurance* contract (pays at death or survival of a specific period of time) would add, "... but if you die during the period, we will pay your beneficiary."

Price Differences

Both life and property-liability segments of the insurance business base their "prices" on historical loss data. Historical data eventually becomes part of the insurance pricing system. Statistics are used to determine present premiums to pay for future losses.

The nature of the insured exposure accounts for rate development differences. The property-liability insurance contract covers total and partial losses. Property-liability rates take multiple losses into account within the policy period and over the life of the account. Consequently, property-liability policies are of short duration, typically six months to three years, and rates may be changed at the renewal anniversary date.

Life insurance, on the other hand, without any endorsements or riders, does not have to address partial or multiple losses. Further, because the contract is stated in fixed dollars, the premium is stable for the life of the contract. But by far the most significant difference is that with a permanent life insurance policy (as opposed to term or pure endowments) the probability of the insured event is one. Death will occur. It is a matter of *when* death occurs.

A property-liability policy does not anticipate a claim on each and every policy. A permanent life policy does. Consequently, the life company must either establish reserve accounts for permanent policies that anticipate an ultimate payment or charge the cash value of the policy a "pure death cost" fee. The insured literally builds equity in a permanent life policy. Even if the insured decides to drop the policy, the nonforfeiture values will be used if the policy has developed them by that time.

Product Life Cycle Differences

Property-liability policies are of relatively short duration. If an insured becomes "riskier" (by storing gasoline in the basement, a history of driving while intoxicated, and so on), the property-liability company can cancel or nonrenew, subject to state laws. In the life insurance company, after the contestable period, even an outright lie on the application cannot lead to cancellation.

For instance, assume that an insured stated on auto and life insurance applications that he was in good health. It is eventually discovered that in fact the insured had had a series of massive heart attacks and was told by a physician not to drive. The auto insurer may be able to cancel the policy or choose not to renew the policy when the truth is discovered. A life company, on the other hand, can do nothing except wait to pay, if the contestable period passes. For a life policy in effect long enough, even nonpayment of premiums may not eliminate the risk because of nonforfeiture provisions. The life insurer may still have obligations under the policy if the beneficiary or the insured selected a settlement option that would require the company to pay out the proceeds over time, perhaps based on the beneficiary's life contingency.

Life companies must look at each policy as a potential long-term relationship with the insured and the beneficiary. Property-liability companies can look at each policy as essentially short-term.

Underwriting Differences

For many property-liability insurers, producers are the first-line underwriters. Most independent insurance agencies have profit sharing (or contingency) arrangements with their companies. If underwriting results are good, the agency shares in the profits. Therefore, it is in the agency's interest to try to select average or above average insureds to help generate profit sharing commissions. Further, it is literally impossible for an underwriter in a home or branch office to know the nature of every neighborhood and the long-range changes taking place there. With average property-liability premium size relatively small in some accounts, underwriters cannot perform great amounts of investigative underwriting. Underwriters must rely on the information provided by the producer. Further, because the insurer has cancellation options, even if a producer writes a less than acceptable insured, the insurer can cancel, subject to state cancellation restrictions.

A life insurer, on the other hand, has very limited cancellation privileges (and then only during the first few years of the policy). Therefore, most underwriting is done in the home or branch office. With a longer period to spread acquisition expenses, life insurers can go to the expense of in-depth customized investigative reports and multiple physical examinations. Since the sales staff of life insurers is principally paid based on new production, life insurers rely less on them for information relative to the insured. Life producers *do* provide valuable underwriting information. But life insurers rely less heavily on information from producers than property-liability insurers do. Finally, the life producer has relatively less impact on the underwriting decision on a borderline application than the property-liability producer has. Of course, at certain times, a high volume life producer will get extra consideration on an applicant.

Compensation Differences

Commissions for property-liability producers are lower and more uniform across the nation than are life insurance commissions. A 20 percent commission is a rarity in most property-liability lines today. Nonetheless, commissions are paid each year at renewal. (Renewal commissions may be a significantly lower percentage of the premium than commissions on new business for exclusive or direct writing producers, but it will be paid annually for as long as the business remains on the books.)

The life producer may receive a large commission on the initial sale (limited to about 55 percent of the first year's premium for life companies operating in New York) and additional "overrides" for expenses and the like. For the next nine years, however, the typical contract would call for a drastically reduced commission—between 5 and 15 percent. After the first ten years, the producer will receive only a "persistency" commission of about 2 percent per year.

Selling Differences

Selling may be the most significant area of difference between life and property-liability insurance.

Life insurance is primarily a sales business. Producers are rewarded (rightfully) for making the sale. Property-liability insurance is more of a service business. Producers are compensated for providing a continuing service as well as for selling. Commission over and above cost of service is reward for sales and persistency. A property-liability producer who has developed a good book of business can make a good income by servicing existing accounts and replacing lost accounts. Life producers must sell new business continuously to maintain income.

A subtle but real difference in selling insurance occurs in the producer's overall attitude towards prospects. A quality life producer basically recognizes each and every individual as a prospect for life insurance. Even the aged and those with detrimental medical histories can be worked with. The life producer must convince the prospect to buy, collect the necessary information, in some cases arrange for a medical exam, and then send everything to the home office for ultimate acceptance or rejection. But property-liability producers, no matter what marketing system is involved, must produce business that generates a profit for their insurers. If producers are to stay in business, they must carefully select insureds.

No matter what the actual selling differences are, life producers can learn sales techniques from property-liability producers and vice versa. Bill Uhl, a property-liability agent by training, adapted a property-liability selling technique to life insurance to obtain annual premiums *in advance* for life sales. When talking to a commercial account about life insurance he asks, "Do you want to pay this three years in advance, like your other business with me, or would annual be better?" Immediately, the client does not think about monthly life insurance premiums. And it is surprising how many three-year prepaid life premiums Bill Uhl collects using this technique.

A life technique can similarly be applied to property-liability sales. Statistics from agency (sales) departments of life companies show that a policy will persist, stay on the books longer, and that the producer has a better chance to deliver a life policy, if the premium is collected at the time of application. Property-liability insurance producers could go a long way to reduce their accounts receivable (a problem for the independent agent or broker more than for producers in other distribution systems) if they attempt to collect the annual premium in advance.

Differences Summarized

There are significant differences between life and property-liability producers. Most of the differences are based on the inherent differences in the nature of the insured obligation. Yet there is much that can be learned and applied from one area of insurance selling to another. The alert producer will use techniques that work, no matter what the source. But the differences are not so great that the property-liability producer should ignore the potential value of the agency's prospect list for life insurance. Most insureds would like to have all of their insurance in one office and through one agent. The property-liability producer is in a far more attractive position to fulfill that wish, because of access to detailed agency files on insureds, than the life producer is. Capitalizing on that fact could generate increased income for the property-liability producer and provide better service to clients.

Checkpoints

1. List and explain the major coverages in OASDHI.
2. Describe the coverage under these life insurance endorsements:
    a. Waiver of premium
    b. Accidental death benefit
    c. Guaranteed purchase option
    d. Disability income rider

3. Describe the major differences between the life and the property-liability insurance business in the following categories:
   a. Product
   b. Price
   c. Product life cycle
   d. Underwriting
   e. Compensation for producers

SUMMARY

The sale of life insurance by a property-liability producer has definite advantages for the producer and his or her agency. The inherent differences between life and property-liability insurance account for much of the reluctance on the part of some producers to sell life insurance. But life insurance sales should be considered by producers in developing their marketing plans.

Life insurance rate construction was discussed. The nature of the life and health insurance risks was outlined. Two methods of determining life insurance needs were presented—the human life value and needs approaches. Each approach offers a logical, analytical tool with which to determine an amount of required life insurance.

Term, permanent, and pure endowment insurance policies were analyzed. These are the three types of life insurance policies that, singly or in combination, make up the life insurance policies sold today. Understanding the aims of all three leads to an understanding of how combinations of them can help an insured with his or her financial planning.

Major provisions and endorsements for life contracts were discussed. Finally, the major coverages of Old Age, Survivor's, Disability and Health Insurance (OASDHI or social security) were summarized.

Life insurance sales in a property-liability agency can make sense and fit a producer's marketing plan.

Chapter Notes

1. J. David Cummins, Dan M. McGill, Howard E. Winklevoss, and Robert A. Zelten, *Consumer Attitudes Toward Auto and Homeowners Insurance* (Philadelphia: The Wharton School, Department of Insurance, University of Pennsylvania, 1974), p. 42.
2. Discussions of Cost-of-Living, Variable, Universal and Adjustable Life Insurance are adapted from "Types of Life Insurance Policies," *Personal Risk Management and Insurance,* Volume I, Third Edition, Wood, Lilly, Malecki, and Rosenbloom (Malvern, PA: American Institute for Property and Liability Underwriters, 1984).
3. The primary insurance amount is in turn based on the "average monthly wage." Status is determined by the "number of quarters covered." See current Social Security Administration brochures for details.

Index

A

B

C

D

E

F

G

H

I

J

L

M

N

O

P

Q

R

S

T

U

V

W

Y